EcoArchitecture

This edition first published in 2011
© 2011 John Wiley & Sons, Ltd

Registered office
John Wiley & Sons Ltd, The Atrium, Southern Gate, Chichester, West Sussex, PO19 8SQ, United Kingdom

For details of our global editorial offices, for customer services and for information about how to apply for permission to reuse the copyright material in this book please see our website at www.wiley.com.

The right of the author to be identified as the author of this work has been asserted in accordance with the Copyright, Designs and Patents Act 1988.

All rights reserved. No part of this publication may be reproduced, stored in a retrieval system, or transmitted, in any form or by any means, electronic, mechanical, photocopying, recording or otherwise, except as permitted by the UK Copyright, Designs and Patents Act 1988, without the prior permission of the publisher.

Wiley also publishes its books in a variety of electronic formats. Some content that appears in print may not be available in electronic books.

Designations used by companies to distinguish their products are often claimed as trademarks. All brand names and product names used in this book are trade names, service marks, trademarks or registered trademarks of their respective owners. The publisher is not associated with any product or vendor mentioned in this book. This publication is designed to provide accurate and authoritative information in regard to the subject matter covered. It is sold on the understanding that the publisher is not engaged in rendering professional services. If professional advice or other expert assistance is required, the services of a competent professional should be sought.

Executive Commissioning Editor: Helen Castle
Project Editor: Miriam Swift
Assistant Editor: Calver Lezama

ISBN 978-0-470-72140-7

Cover design, page design and layouts by T. R. Hamzah & Yeang Sdn. Bhd. in association with Eskaywoo Communication Design
Printed in Italy by Printer Trento Srl

EcoArchitecture
the work of
KEN YEANG

By Sara Hart

Edited by David Littlefield

WILEY

A John Wiley and Sons, Ltd, Publication

Ken Yeang is at the forefront of thinking about the ecological imperative from an architectural perspective and as an avant-garde designer of the Bioclimatic Skyscraper and a realist he is one of the very few willing to operate in the gap between necessity, compunction and hope.

Charles Jencks

Roof-Roof House

T. R. Hamzah & Yeang's Office at Taman Sri Ukay

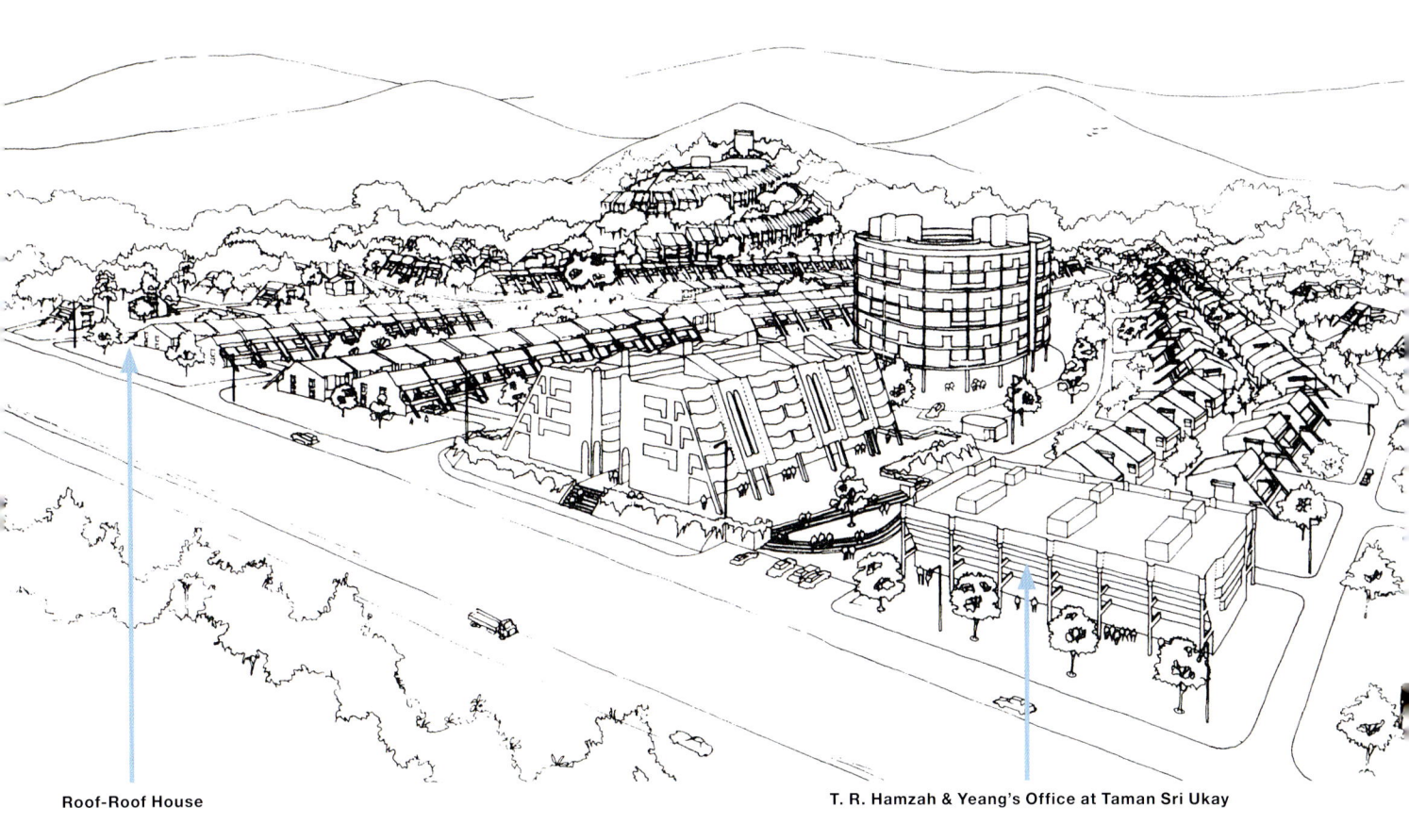

▲ **Taman Sri Ukay Housing and Shophouses, Kuala Lumpur, 1978-81.** In this scheme for an up-market housing development, a range of building types is brought together – terrace, semi-detached and detached housing – as well as apartments and shophouses. The house design is an abstraction of the Malay vernacular house with the stilts of the traditional houses reinterpreted as sloping beams along the building façade. T. R. Hamzah & Yeang's offices are highlighted in the three-storey shophouse building in the foreground and the Roof-Roof House is visible at the far left of the development. Drawing by Ken Yeang.

Contents

Preface 8
Lord Norman Foster

Introduction 10
John Frazer

EcoArchitecture 12
Sara Hart

Bioclimatic Design
Roof-Roof House 26
Menara Boustead 38
IBM Plaza 46
Menara Mesiniaga 56

EcoMasterplanning
Soma Masterplan 70
Huanan New City 84
Plaza of Nations 92

Transitional Projects
National Library Building 104
Mewah Oils Headquarters 114
MAAG Tower 124

Vertical Urbanism
BATC Tower 136
Nagoya Expo 2005 Tower 146
Tokyo-Nara Tower 156

Technical Innovation
Standard Chartered Bank Kiosk 166
UMNO Tower 172
West Kowloon Waterfront 182

Vertical EcoInfrastructure
EDITT Tower 192
Solaris 200
Spire Edge 210
L Tower 218
DiGi Technical Operations Centre 226
Zorlu Ecocity 232
Gyeong-Gi Complex 240

Essay 258
Ken Yeang

End Statement 264

Books and Publications 266
by Ken Yeang

Acknowledgements 268

Climate and Vegetation Maps 270

Picture Credits 272

Preface

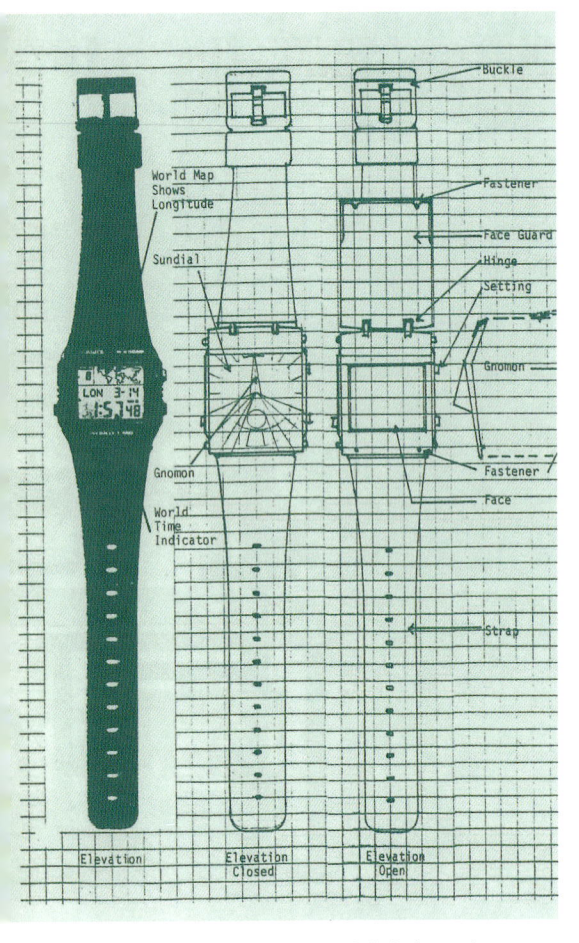

▲▼ This Yeang-designed digital watch, auctioned in 1997, incorporates a sundial. It is emblematic of the architect's approach – a blend of the high-tech and traditional, analogue responses.

Ken Yeang has developed a distinctive architectural vocabulary that extends beyond questions of style to confront issues of sustainability and how we can build in harmony with the natural world.

I recall that in 1997 he designed a watch for a charity auction at Christie's that could tell the time at any latitude. Hinged over its digital face was a silver cover that incorporated a sundial for use, he said, when the world runs out of batteries. This watch, in many ways, I think, provides the basic diagram for Yeang's architectural explorations. He has a commitment to new technology and the modern world, but is equally convinced that the simplest and most intuitive solutions can often be found by utilising natural resources. Among his many achievements as an architect has been to show how the tall building can be reconceived as an environmentally sensitive mechanism. At the core of his approach is his reversal of the established model of the high-rise in tropical climates. In contrast with the hermetically sealed, air-conditioned tower, his high-rise buildings comprise vertical assemblages of spaces that are naturally lit and ventilated, linked to terraces and interspersed with lush vegetation – even though they may be 30 storeys above ground.

We share, in this sense, a vision of urban life that is reinforced by Nature, not at odds with it, and where the buildings we create are environmentally responsive. These are themes that all architects must embrace if we are to find sustainable ways of building in the future.

Lord Norman Foster of Thames Bank
London

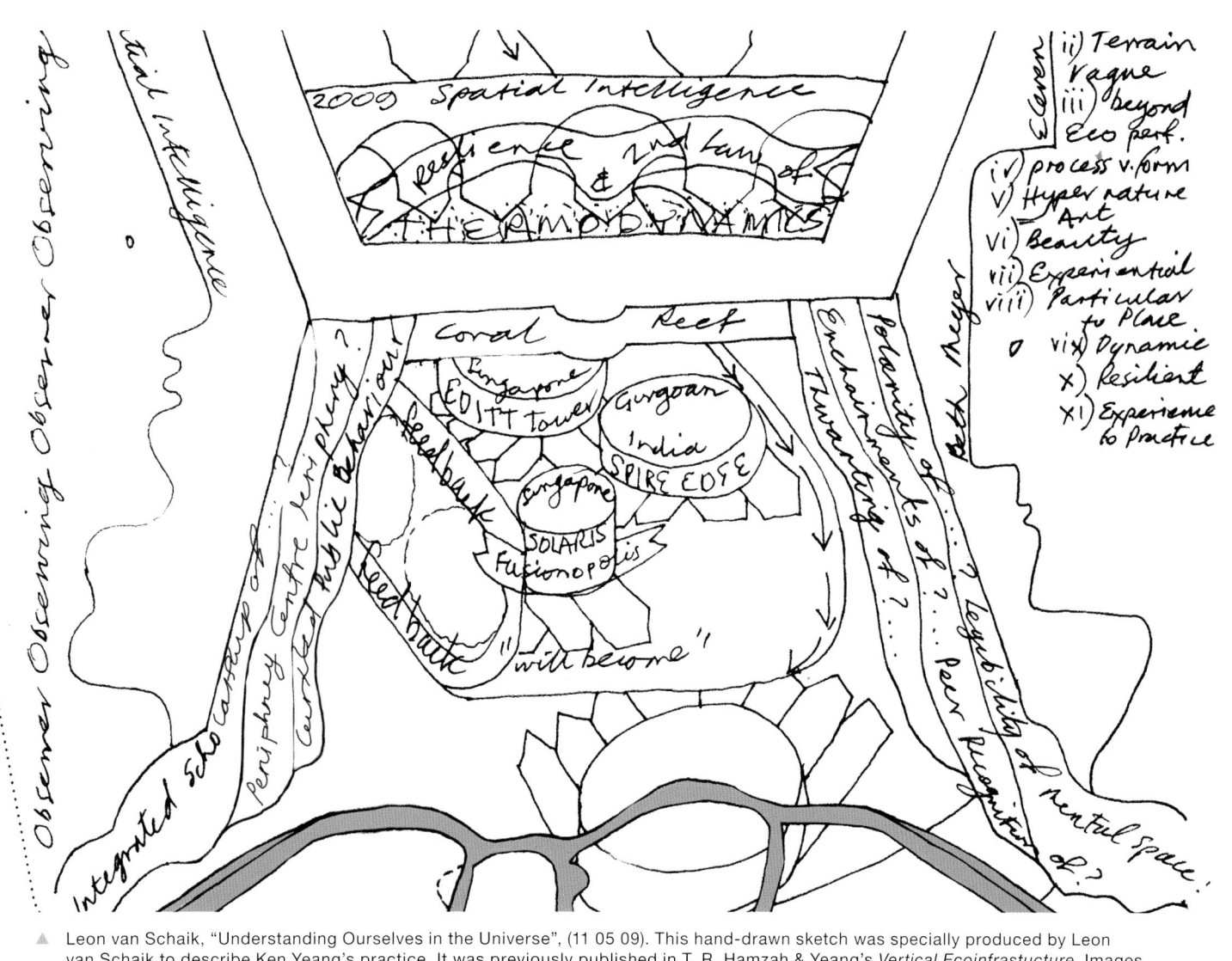

▲ Leon van Schaik, "Understanding Ourselves in the Universe", (11 05 09). This hand-drawn sketch was specially produced by Leon van Schaik to describe Ken Yeang's practice. It was previously published in T. R. Hamzah & Yeang's *Vertical Ecoinfrastucture*, Images Publishing, 2009.

Preface 9

Introduction

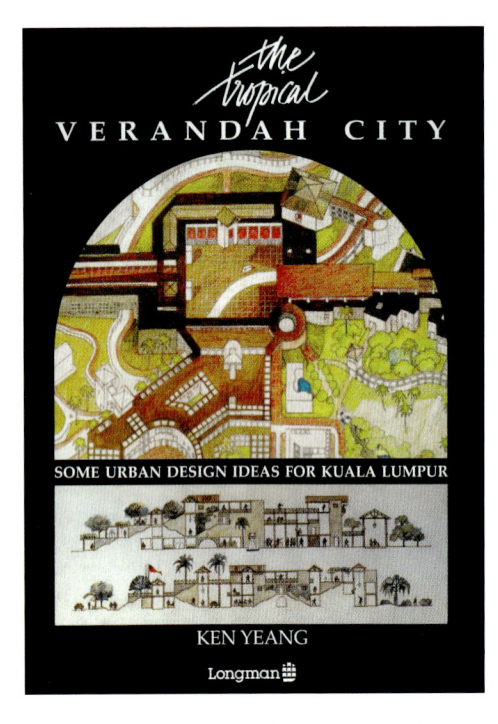

In 1970 a young Ken Yeang posed a remarkable question: What might be the characteristics of an ecologically responsible architecture? That the question does not seem so extraordinary now is in part a tribute to the success of Yeang and others in bringing environmental issues to the forefront of the architectural agenda. Yeang asked the question in the context of a growing concern for the environment, energy and sustainability. At the time he was studying architecture at the Architectural Association in London, where there was a tradition of radical questioning and where international Modernism had never been uncritically accepted. But never before had this simple direct question about the nature of an ecologically responsible architecture been considered. Yeang realised that to answer this question he would have to come up with not just a philosophical or scientific answer, but a whole new design methodology as well.

To develop a methodology, Yeang enrolled in a doctoral programme at Cambridge University in 1971 in the Department of Architecture. I was his supervisor. Yeang worked in the context of the Technical Research Division of the Faculty, which I had just founded with Alexander Pike. This division was later to merge with the Land Use and Built Form Studies group to become the Martin Centre – after Professor Sir Leslie Martin who headed the department when Yeang embarked on his studies. Cambridge University now boasts sustainability and energy studies as its main research focus in architecture. However, the situation was very different in 1971 and Yeang initially had an uphill struggle to get his ideas accepted beyond the circle of his immediate supervisors. And yet in the Cambridge environment Yeang's ideas rapidly expanded, influenced now not only by Buckminster Fuller but also by Eugene Odum's work on ecosystems, Alfred North Whitehead's work on the philosophy of the organism, Ian McHarg's ideas of ecological land-use planning techniques, and Ludwig von Bertellanfy's systems theory. Within a year, some of Yeang's fertile thinking was beginning to impact on a sleepy architectural profession when I introduced some of his ideas in a keynote speech at the 1972 Conference of the Royal Institute of British Architecture. Appropriately, the conference took "Designing for Survival" as its theme that year, echoing a growing public awareness of the major contribution of construction to environmental problems.

The theoretical framework that Yeang developed at this time underpinned his subsequent architectural practice and became the basis of several later books. Immediate publication of his thesis was delayed due to the death of his examiner, the biologist CH Waddington. It was a tribute to Yeang and the seriousness with which his ideas were finally being received that Cambridge asked such a distinguished figure as Waddington to examine the thesis, and that Waddington accepted. New examiners were appointed and finally the Yeang's dissertation, submitted in 1974, under the title "A Theoretical Framework for the Incorporation of Ecological Considerations in the Design and Planning of the Built Environment", was accepted. He received his PhD in 1981. The dissertation was published as *Designing with Nature: The Ecological Basis for Architectural Design* in 1995.

In the meantime Yeang had returned to his native Malaysia to form an architectural practice with Tengku Robert Hamzah. Yeang was now faced with the problem of how to turn his new theoretical methodology into built form and work with clients and developers who did not necessarily share his commitment to environmental idealism. Yeang was keen to give a local context to his thinking and he began researching local vernacular and indigenous architecture;

▲ **Book cover for Ken Yeang, *The Tropical Verandah City: Some Urban Design Ideas for Kuala Lumpur*, Longman, 1986.** In Yeang's first book, he developed a set of urban design ideas for Kuala Lumpur. His "verandah city" concept recognised the vital role that the traditional verandahways of the city play in providing pedestrians with shelter from the sun and the rain. In Yeang's design the verandahway is elevated into a streetscape organising device, aspiring to endow Malaysia's capital city with a cohesive regional urban image and national identity.

indeed, he wrote three books on the subject (see page 266). What was needed now was not just a new theoretical methodology, but a whole new vocabulary of building forms. Yeang's emerging building types were driven by three forces. The first was climatic, where designing to optimise the ambient conditions in line with his new methodology inevitably led to new building forms.

Secondly, he was concerned with how architecture responded to the needs of the local way of life, in addition to climatic considerations. Finally, the third driver acknowledged the aspirations of countries in the tropical zones to join the developed world, requiring a shift from traditional low-rise structures to a modern high-rise strategy. So while a study of the veranda lifestyle associated with traditional vernacular and indigenous buildings might be an inspiration, they could not be copied or developed.

Yeang's response was the development of the concept of the bioclimatic skyscraper as a more environmentally appropriate model, which consumes less energy and provides a better and more humane environment for its users while establishing a unique cultural identity related to the location. The architectural design principles that emerged include a number of dominant themes and concepts: the integration of vegetation and vertical gardens; the use of skycourts; and the influence of solar geometry to achieve self-shading structures. This led to his subsequent theoretical and technical work on ecological design and the publication of a number of books (page 266) which challenged the very notion of an international style through the proposal of ecologically responsible world architecture.

These publications set out his ideas for a climate-generated architecture and they radically changed preconceptions of appropriate high-rise building forms for the tropics. Having developed a tropical model of the bioclimatic skyscraper, Yeang then generalised his approach and developed related forms for the subtropics and temperate zones. Yeang's design practice has always been to maintain a strong research and development ethos, despite tight commercial pressures, funded entirely from real projects when the budget and enlightened clients allowed. In every project Yeang has found the energy and resources to experiment with the application of at least one part of his vision. Now as a partner in the international firm Llewelyn Davies Yeang in London, he has the opportunity to apply his thinking to a range of climatic and cultural environments.

Yeang's work is recognised and celebrated with a number of major awards and significant publications. For instance, in *T.R. Hamzah and Yeang* in the Master Architect series (Images, 1999), Leon van Schaik demonstrates that in Yeang's vision, ecological design need not be a retreating battle for sustainability, but can contribute positively to an ecologically responsible future through energy production. The debate Yeang helped to start in 1970 is still going strong. In 2008 the Goethe Institute in New York announced a series of conversations and lectures on "What is Green Architecture?"; the institute stated "This conversation is more timely than ever given the rising consciousness in the US about environmental issues in architecture and urban planning". What have architects been doing for the last 40 years?

John Frazer
Brisbane

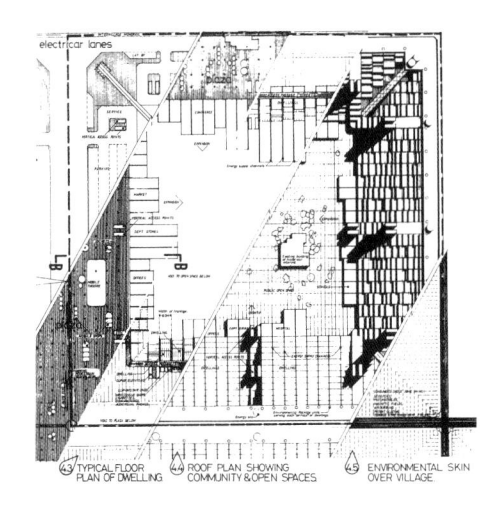

▲ **Cutaway plan for "Global Village" project, late '60s.** This competition entry for the Shinkenchiku Residential design competition organised by Japan Architect was undertaken by Yeang while he was still at the AA. The global village concept might be influenced by Marshall McLuhan's notion of the earth being contracted into a single village or community with the onset of electric technology, but the graphics and the architecture are heavily inspired by the work of the Japanese Metabolists and Archigram.

▲ **Ken Yeang and Tengku Robert Hamzah in the 1970s.** When Yeang returned to Kuala Lumpur after his studies at Cambridge in 1976, he set up office with Tengku Robert Hamzah, a prince in the Malay Royal family who had preceded him in at the AA in London and completed his studies at the AA Tropical School. Before the partnership, he was a principal project architect at Pakatan Akitek in the early '70s. Yeang and Tengku Hamzah remain in partnership in Kuala Lumpur to this day.

EcoArchitecture

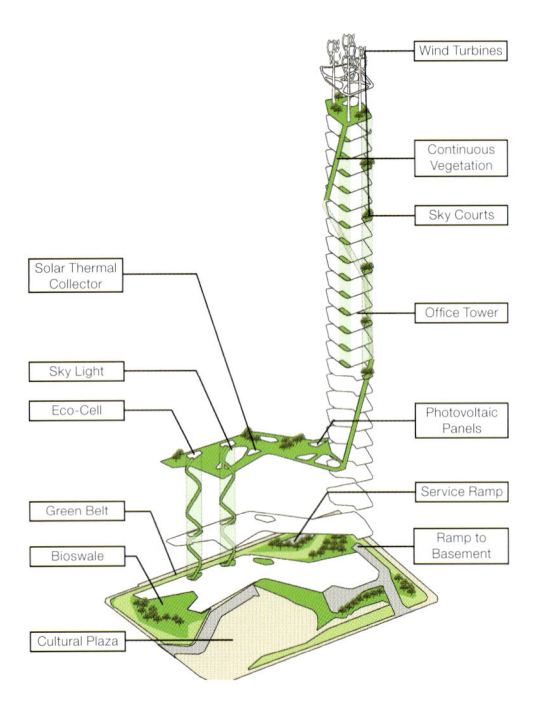

Axometric diagram for Chong Qing Tower, China. A demonstration of the project's vertical eco-infrastructure concept.

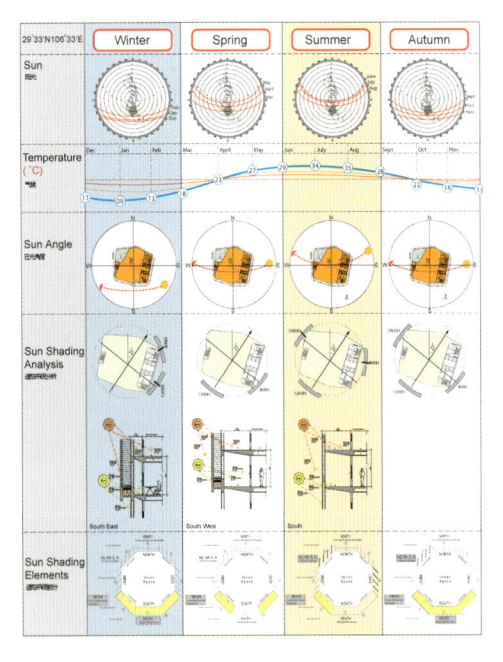

Bioclimatic analysis for the Chongqing Tower, China. Underpinning Yeang's approach to architecture is a programme by which the interplay of climate, latitude, topography and other natural conditions leads to distinctive building forms.

Ken Yeang is perhaps the world's only architect who can legitimately claim the mantle of ecologist-architect by virtue of education, research and practice. One of the first architects to undertake a PhD on the subject of ecological design in the early 1970s at Cambridge, he proceeded to undertake his own independent research into climatically sensitive vernacular structures in the tropics from his office in Kuala Lumpur in the 1980s; by the mid-90s, through his work on the bioclimatic he had come to international attention as the advocate of the green skyscraper and through the 2000s this reputation was consolidated as he became the architect of choice for ecological masterplans and projects around the world[1]. Yeang's passion for ecology can be traced back over three and half decades to the teachings of Scottish landscape architect and planner Ian McHarg, whose seminal 1969 book *Design with Nature*[2] introduced the concept of ecological land-use planning. In 1973 Yeang briefly attended McHarg's course at the University of Pennsylvania, an experience which changed his world view of architecture. Upon returning to his research studies at Cambridge University, he embarked on intensive studies in environmental biology, which became the foundation for his doctoral dissertation: "Understanding ecology changed my perception of the world and humbled my own role within it, where humans are simply one species among thousands in the biosphere each functioning as part of the ecological nexus."

This ecology-based focus drove all his work, placing Yeang ahead of other "green" architects in the effort to respond to environmental crises, global warming, resource depletion, greenhouse gases and so on which, now finally out of necessity, are being addressed at a global level. Since Yeang began to explore the links between architecture and ecology in the early 1970s, it has taken the best part of three decades for the wider construction industry to move beyond scepticism and try to develop policies to slow and even reverse environmental damage. The pressure to conserve natural resources and curb greenhouse emissions (just one part of Yeang's wider mission) now presses down heavily on industry. Certification systems – the Building Research Establishment Environmental Assessment Method (BREEAM) in the UK, Leadership in Energy

▲ **The Guthrie Pavilion, Malaysia.** Completed in 1998, this building, says academic Leon van Schaik, adopts the aesthetics of iconic aircraft construction from the 1930s. "A strong substrate of heroic Modernism" underlies Yeang's work, says van Schaik.

and Environmental Design (LEED) in the US, Green Star in Australia, Haute Qualité Environnementale in France and Green Mark in Singapore – have proliferated to create standards for "green" design and construction. Certification is largely voluntary, although pressure to conform has motivated the architecture profession to embrace these assessment regimes. A new era of environmental advocacy is full of promise and fraught with distractions, and Yeang finds himself having to react by separating myth from reality. The term "green architecture" is painted with such a broad brush today that almost any gesture aimed at sustainability, even a symbolic one, constitutes green design. The current term to describe these skin-deep gestures is "greenwashing" – the shallow attempt to recast standard practice in a green light, or to retrofit an energy saving technology as a lever with which to rebrand a project as "ecological". In the United States, this style over substance has become so prevalent that there is a Greenwashing Index[3] which identifies companies whose claims do not hold up under scrutiny. To Yeang, ecological design concerns much more than just low-energy buildings or the reduction of carbon emissions and water use; and he finds it especially painful that a lifetime of establishing a coherent theory of ecomimetic architecture can become confused with the practice of adding high-tech gadgetry to an otherwise standard structure. To Yeang, ecoarchitecture cannot be reduced to a list of techniques; it is a "totally new way of thinking".

As an early pioneer and radical innovator in the ecology of sustainability, Yeang has sought to research, experiment, document and build a foundation for authenticity in sustainable development. His theories, techniques and ideas have evolved from empirical scientific enquiry and are admittedly dense, complex and often nuanced. The notion that there is a universal formula for sustainability is antithetical to the way nature's ecosystems actually perform. Yeang realised early on that developing a theory of ecological design would yield processes and methodologies which could be codified and adapted locally and circumstantially. Yeang sees current green design, still very much in its infancy, as lacking a comprehensive and formal theoretical framework. His practice of ecological design began with his first project, the Roof-Roof

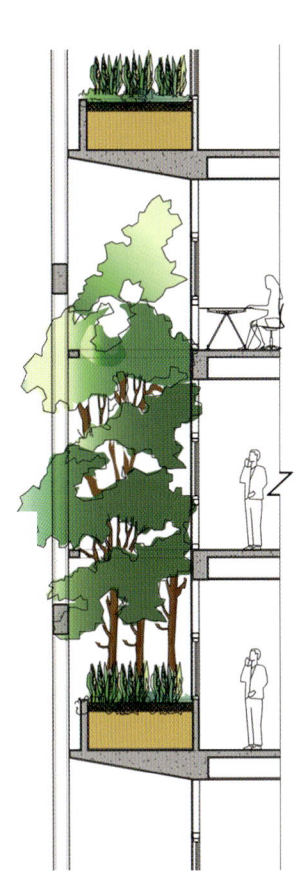

▲ **Skyrise greenery section.** Typical of Yeang's continuing explorations into the potential of vegetated façades.

▲ **Reliance Tower, Mumbai, India.** Yeang's concept of "vertical ecoinfrastructure" brings together all strands within his thinking: vertical living, bioclimatic responses, technical innovation, habitat creation, reducing the carbon footprint and greening buildings.

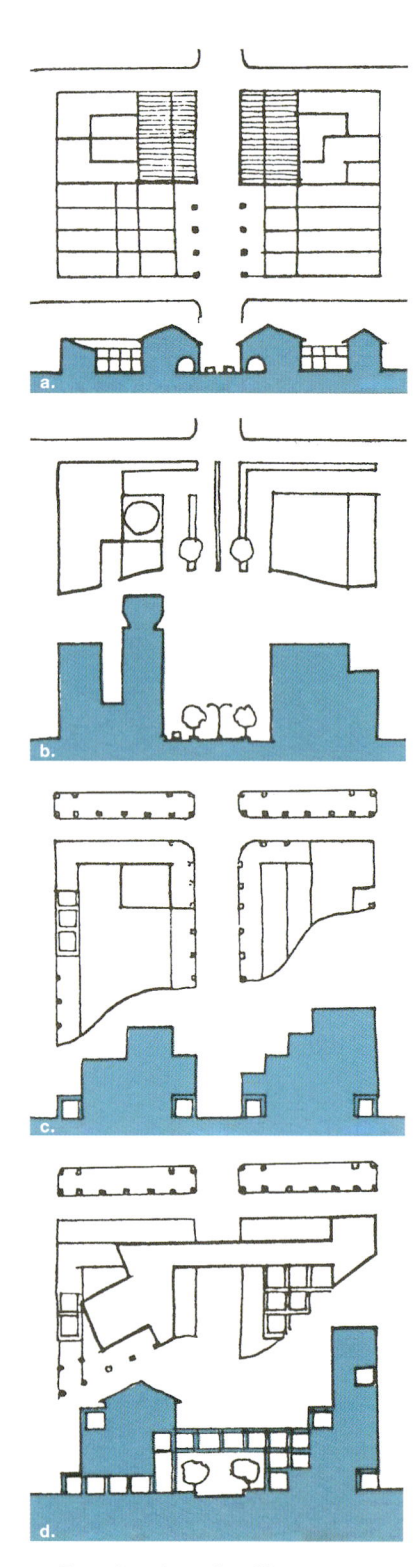

▲ **Four drawings that illustrate the reintroduction of the verandahway streetscape into the urban fabric, 1986.** This set of drawings from Yeang's *The Tropical Verandah City* illustrate: (a) the way that the existing, traditional verandahways provide important semipublic and private transitional zones for the shophouses in the city; (b) the threatened destruction of the verandahways by modern developments; (c) how the verandahways might be reintroduced into the city; and (d) that verandahways should not inhibit innovative variations.

House in Malaysia, which he designed for himself in the mid-1980s. Because it was his own house, he was able to experiment freely, creating a test-bed for bioclimatic design which would prove the efficacy of green principles to conventional clients; the result was a passive-mode/low-energy building which responds to local climatic factors through form, orientation and experimental architectural devices. "It was an appropriate starting point then and remains an obvious initial strategy for green design today," he says.

Yeang has a well choreographed career, using a mix of built projects, publications, teaching and speaking opportunities, exhibitions and, in 2005, a directorship of UK firm Llewelyn Davies to put his work and ideas in front of a global audience. By the early 1990s, as a 40-something architect with an emerging portfolio in Kuala Lumpur, Yeang could easily have settled down to a relatively comfortable life with a thriving practice. But Yeang has always understood the importance of leveraging opportunities; as well as developing his own distinct aesthetic and approach to design, he is also commercially astute. He has exhibited his work everywhere from London and Berlin to Tokyo and Washington DC and where his architectural principles could not be fully explored through design and built work, Yeang developed them through writing. Before completing his doctorate, Yeang was writing academic papers on the use of biological analogies for design. These included "Bionics: The Use of Biological Analogies in Design", in *AAQ* (*Architectural Association Quarterly*), No 4, 1974, and two articles in *Architectural Design,* "Bases for Ecosystem Design", as early as 1972, and "The Energetics of the Built Environment" two years later.

Yeang has continued to advance a textual and visual "eco-architectonic" language through a series of publishing projects which seek to reconcile his ecological theories with established architectural principles. *Ecodesign: A Manual for Ecological Design* (2006) is a primer that integrates a decade's worth of research. "The basic premise for ecodesign is that our health, both as human beings and as one of the millions of species in nature, depends upon the air that we breathe and the water that we drink, as well as on the uncontaminated quality of the soil from which our food is produced. In the coming decades the survival of humanity will depend on the quality of the natural environment and, crucially, on our ability to continue to carry out all our human activities – without further impairment and pollution of the natural environment. Simply stated, our health as human beings depends on the continued health of our natural environment," he wrote.

It is important to avoid the trap, however, of mistaking Yeang for a high-rise designer. True, many of his projects resolve themselves as towers, and Yeang can claim serious credit for redefining the skyscraper as an ecologically sensitive building type (as opposed to an energy-hungry symbol of power and machismo). But Yeang's portfolio of built works does include a number of thoughtful low and medium-rise buildings, including a delightful little banking kiosk, while masterplans and their links with pre-existing landscapes are beginning to form a particular oeuvre within Yeang's work. *EcoMasterplanning* (2009) sets forth Yeang's approach to ecological masterplanning based on the concept of "eco-infrastructure" which links biotic (living organisms) and abiotic (soils, nurtrients, etc) elements. Ecoinfrastructure expands conventional ideas about architecture's relationship to the land, delivering vegetated, biomimetic habitats via "ecobridges", "ecoundercrofts", "ecocells" and green "living" walls, corridors and fingers which reach out into the landscape, dive deep beneath it and ramp upwards into the skies.

ECOLOGY VS ENVIRONMENTALISM

Yeang is well aware of the misconceptions about what constitutes ecological design and he has always been wary of the impulse to engineer our way out of the crises confronting industrialised nations. In his Cambridge dissertation, "A Theoretical Framework for the Incorporation of Ecological Considerations in the Design and Planning of the Built Environment", Yeang wrote frankly about the dangers of mistaking low-energy devices for environmentalism:

It is easy to be misled or seduced by technology and to think that if we assemble enough eco-gadgetry in the form of solar collectors, photovoltaic cells, biological recycling systems, building-automation systems and double-skin façades in one single building that this can automatically be considered ecological architecture. Although these technologies are commendable applications of low-energy systems, they are merely useful components leading towards ecological architecture; they represent some of the means of achieving an ecological end product. Ecological design is not just about low-energy systems; to be fully effective, these technologies need to be thoroughly integrated into the building fabric; they will also be influenced by the physical and climatic conditions of the site. The nature of the problem is therefore site specific. There will never be a standard "one size fits all" solution.

That was in 1981, and he was saying very much the same thing a quarter of a century later in *Ecodesign*: "Many designers wrongly believe that if they stuff a building with enough ecogadgets such as solar collectors, wind generators, photovoltaics and biodigestors then they will instantly have an ecological design. Of course, nothing could be further from the truth. While we should not deny the experimental usefulness of these technological systems and devices, which may eventually lead us to the ideal technological product or infrastructure or plan, they are certainly not the be-all and end-all in ecodesign. Many of these are just empty attempts at an ecological architecture. There is a sanctimonious mythology around what is basically a collection of admirable engineering innovations."

He goes on in a similar vein of evangelism. But he has to. So great is the momentum behind tick-box certification systems, greenwash, wannabes and eco-gadgetry that Yeang feels he has to shout loudly to be heard – especially if he wants to make clear that his is not a fashionable architecture made more efficient by clever mechanical and electrical engineering. This, he says, is the ecoarchitecture of low expectations. Yeang does not deny that new construction practices will have a positive impact on the way buildings are designed, assembled and integrated but he is determined not to let the environmental agenda become one that is limited to political, populist fads. In contrast, Yeang the ecologist-architect sees the history of the built environment as a series of callous assaults on the planet's delicate biosystems. "The objective of ecodesign is a benign and seamless biointegration with the environment," he says.

The word "benign" is an interesting one, as it suggests that building projects should not just minimise their impact on the biosphere. Building projects should, he believes, lead to positive outcomes (as against minimal impacts). They should be so integral with the biosphere that, if the biosphere was sentient, it would barely register their presence. This obviously requires a wholly different view of context than considering just topography, density, proximity, aesthetics and cultural/political/economic parameters – it forces a discipline which includes matters such as microclimate, biodiversity, diet and social organisation. Yeang the ecologist analyses context in terms of the impact human intervention will have on existing biosystems.

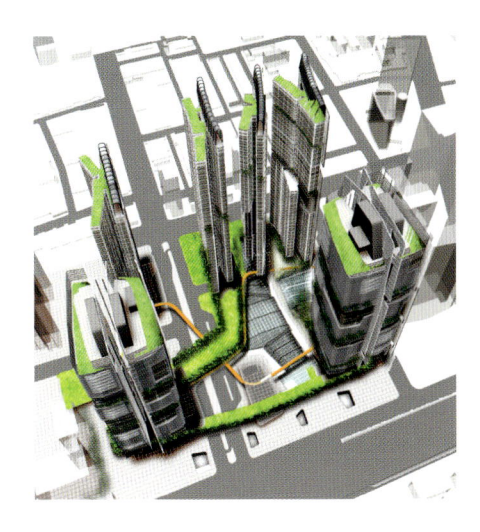

▲ **Winning competition entry for the Beijing World Science and Trade Center, China.** The dominant ecological feature of the design is a linear green park which extends from the western corner of the site, at street level, and connects to all parts of the built form via landscaped ramps and bridges.

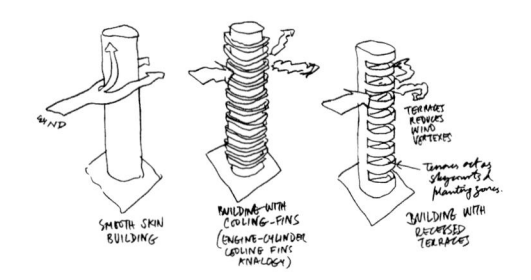

▲ Sketches in which Yeang explored the action of prevailing winds, and the role balconies and specially located fins can play in natural cooling and ventilation strategies.

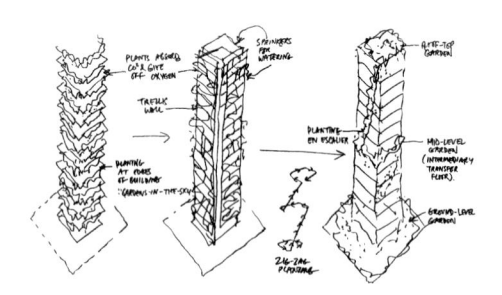

▲ Hand drawings through which Yeang began to develop the idea of organising vegetation around and within a tower. These early sketches, dating from the early 1990s, signal Yeang's development of bold diagonal slices through building façades, in which come to be located skycourts and vegetated ramps.

Emitters

Paints
- formaldehyde
- xylene/tolune
- benzene
- alcohols

People
- acetone
- ethyl alcohol
- methyl alcohol
- ethyl acetate

Chairs
- formaldehyde

Photocopiers
- xylene/toluene
- benzene
- trichloroethylene
- ammonia

Chipboards
- formaldehyde
- xylene/toluene
- benzene
- alcohols

Correction Fluids
- acetone

Computer Screens
- xylene/toluene

Absorbers

Bamboo Palm
- formaldehyde
- trichloroethylene
- benzene

Peace Lily
- formaldehyde
- trichloroethylene
- benzene
- alcohols
- acetone

English Ivy
- formaldehyde
- various others

▲ Matrix illustrating the relationship between building-integrated vegetation and indoor air quality.

But his real achievement, arguably, is not that he has been able to formulate a coherent ecological approach to architecture; what makes his work so compelling is that he has managed to give it a real world application. And that is something which requires not just academic rigour, but a focused and very practical mindset.

FROM THEORY TO BUILDING

Yeang's career could easily be interpreted as a methodical and uninterrupted journey: beginning as a precocious student at London's Architectural Association (AA) in the early 1970s; developing in the more rarified, and perhaps idealistic, academic atmosphere of Cambridge; finding expression in his Roof-Roof House in the mid-1980s; and emerging from a period of energetic experimentation in the 1990s as a fully rounded ecoarchitect capable of combining commercial and sustainable agendas into a single, astonishing and inventive language. That wouldn't quite be true, however, no matter how appealing such a simple narrative may be. What is true is that Yeang benefited from a fortunate background and some very clever early decisions, but none of it has been easy – it's been exhausting, in fact. Yeang grew up in a Modernist house in Malaysia (completed in 1954 by the Dutch architect Iversen van Sitteren), and his exposure to the business and processes of architecture was part of the family DNA. Both his parents dabbled in real estate – though his father was a medical doctor – and two of his uncles had studied at the AA and the Regent Street Polytechnic (now the University of Westminster). As an AA student, Yeang found himself in top flight company – he was tutored by, among others, Martin Pawley, Peter Cook, Elia Zenghelis, Charles Jencks, Bernard Tschumi and Colin Fournier while Piers Gough, Roger Zogolovitch, Janet Street Porter, Simon Fisher were fellow students. Yeang is a natural questioner (and note-taker), and the AA gave him the wherewithal to experiment, giving him permission, at an early age, to ask fundamental questions and to tackle questions from an entirely new angle. The move to Cambridge was just as important: "It was for me a change from a liberal experimental environment to a serious academic one, where new propositions are immediately suspect unless substantiated by theoretical and empirical verification. This had a great impact on the rest of my work, and subsequently I felt that any postulations and ideas had to be well substantiated."

At Cambridge, Yeang began as a post graduate researcher on the "Autonomous House Project" (an exploration of the work of Buckminster Fuller) under the tutelage of Alexander Pike, a pioneer in sustainable building technologies. The programme called for designing a dwelling unconnected to urban infrastructure and utilities. Yeang, however, judged the project lacked a firm theoretical foundation so he left to pursue an independent research doctorate concentrating on ecological design and planning, under the supervision of John Frazer and John Meunier. Yeang refers to his dissertation as the real starting point of a lifelong pursuit. JWL Beament of Cambridge's Department of Applied Biology further influenced Yeang's research in environmental biology, which led to his becoming a member of the British Ecological Society.

In 1974, Yeang returned to Malaysia to start a practice. Teaming up with fellow AA student Tengku Dato Robert Hamzah, a prince from the Malay Royal family. The pair formed T. R. Hamzah & Yeang in 1975 but the young architects hardly found clients queuing up for passive-mode/low-energy green architecture. What did work in the practice's favour, however, was Yeang's natural entrepreneurial flair. He has, on a number of occasions, introduced developers to owners of specific building plots, securing for himself the design work once the client has become convinced of its commercial viability. This is a practice Yeang has continued to the present, and he remains at ease talking the language of business. Furthermore, he never expects clients to indulge him. Yeang has never benefited from the continued patronage of a client who sees it as their role to underwrite forward thinking architectural brilliance; rather, Yeang has remained acutely aware that everything must be explained, rationalised, purposeful and paid for. His success in securing the number of ecologically sensitive projects that he has is more to do with his ability to make his design commercially attractive, and deliver it efficiently. Indeed, Yeang says that clients only really began to make a point of requesting green architecture as late as 2005. Securing for himself a reputation for being able to deliver truly green buildings, now that political opinion has come around to the idea, has been nothing less than a long, hard slog involving much unbuilt work, innumerable competition entries, exhibitions and writing projects. But the fact that the world is more receptive to the ideas that Yeang was pursuing three decades ago has not necessarily made life any easier – there is now competition from firms Yeang describes as "wannabees", architects who offer seemingly credible sustainable solutions which, very often, is merely standard architecture whose energy performance has been boosted by more efficient engineering. "My contention is that you should design buildings as living artificial ecosystems. The problem is that clients can't tell the difference between the authentic solution and what the others offer," he laments.

Part of Yeang's solution was to seek a bigger platform, which he found by acquiring a stake in UK firm Llewelyn Davies as director of design in 2005. Yeang had an earlier involvement with the firm, as they had jointly bid for some World Bank work in the late 1970s. But thirty years later (during which Llewelyn Davies had moved from a second to a fourth generation firm) both parties came to realise that each could offer the other significant advantages. For Llewelyn Davies, Yeang represented an architectural figurehead, signature design and unarguable ecological expertise and innovation; for Yeang, the firm offered "a base in the industrialized world". Yeang became a senior shareholder in the company, while maintaining his own business in Malaysia. Following the move, the firm rebranded as Llewelyn Davies Yeang.

ECOINFRASTRUCTURE AND AESTHETICS

Yeang's best-known (but not the only) contribution to green design has been his reinvention of the skyscraper. The irony is that, as Yeang readily admits, the very tall building is arguably the least environmentally sustainable building type civilisation has yet devised – it is energy- and resource-hungry to build, maintain and demolish. However, skyscrapers do have much going for them, especially in terms of density, and they can be efficient urban structures when placed on or near transportation hubs, so Yeang (knowing how to strike a balance between idealism and practice) determined to transform these buildings into something more ecologically acceptable. His phrase is "well-tempered skyscrapers" (after Rayner Benham), designed to be as humane and pleasurable to inhabit as possible, built at the right locations and as green as possible, with a more healthy integration of inanimate and organic matter underpinning the tower's performance and design. "In rethinking the typology of tall buildings, it seemed obvious that they have been designed and built as simply stacks of repetitive homogeneous concrete trays essentially piled one on top of the other for engineering expediency. I started to look at skyscraper design as 'vertical urbanism' and took existing ideas and principles of urban design (conventionally applied horizontally) and reapplied

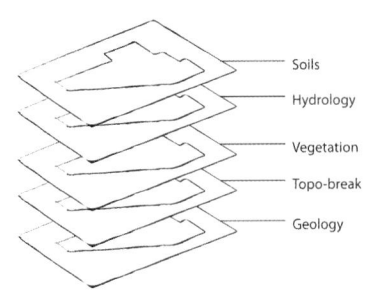

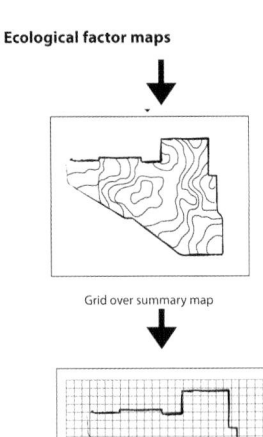

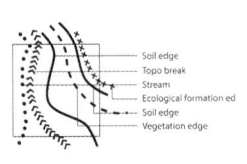

Ecological factor maps
(Soils, Hydrology, Vegetation, Topo-break, Geology)

Grid over summary map

Blow up of square
(Soil edge, Topo break, Stream, Ecological formation ed, Soil edge, Vegetation edge)

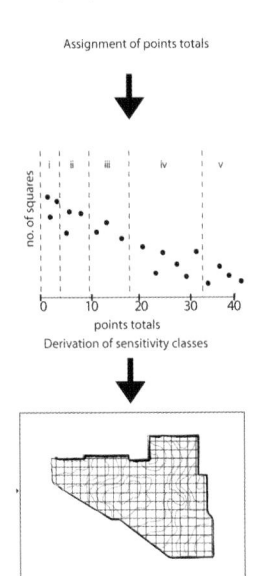

Assignment of points totals

Derivation of sensitivity classes

Composite ecological sensitivity map

Diagram describing the ecological sieve mapping technique for landuse planning. "Understanding ecology changed my perception of the world and humbled my own role within it, where humans are simply one species among thousands," says Yeang.

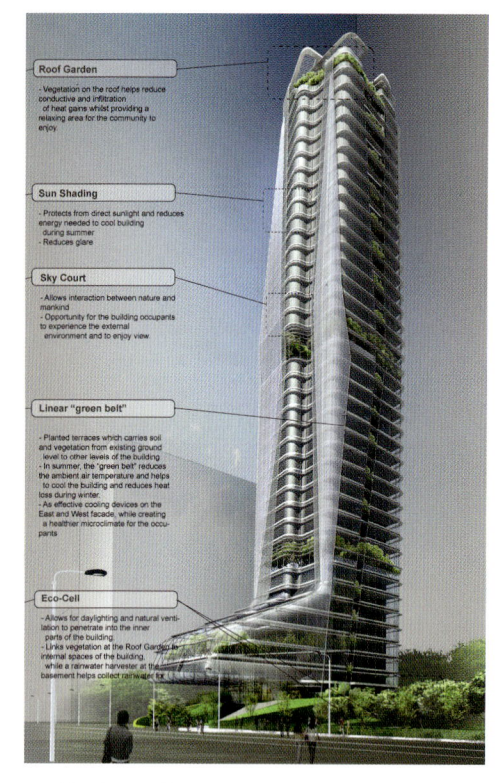

Ecological features, BIDV Tower, Ho Chi Minh City, Vietnam. Rising within the tower, a vertical boulevard infuses each floor with greenery before descending to merge back with the urban street grid.

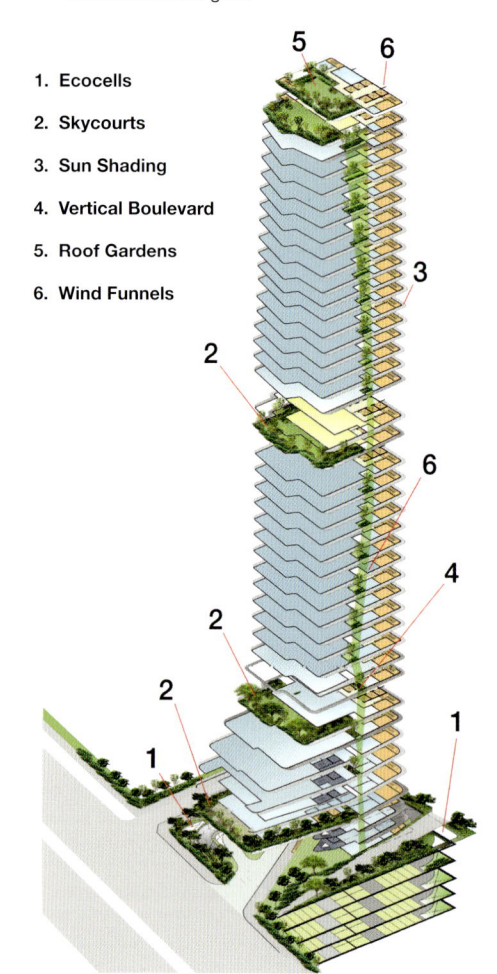

1. Ecocells
2. Skycourts
3. Sun Shading
4. Vertical Boulevard
5. Roof Gardens
6. Wind Funnels

these vertically. All of a sudden I found myself with a reservoir of design opportunities, and I realised that this would be my approach to skyscraper design," he recalls. This enquiry into the nature of "vertical landscaping" and "placemaking in the sky" eventually resolved itself in the books *The Skyscraper Bioclimatically Considered* (1996) and *Reinventing the Skyscraper: A Vertical Theory of Urban Design* (2002).

It is important to understand that this work (with which Yeang is most often associated) relies on a more fundamental, deeper body of research concerning the nature of ecology and architecture. It is an ever-developing subject, coming to embrace over the years certification systems, biodiversity, social behaviour and even vertical farming. Yeang's view of green architecture is not restricted to low-energy design and sustainably-sourced construction materials. By the early 2000s Yeang had begun to consider green design as designing "ecoinfrastructures", a term which came to be considered as embracing four distinct "armatures", or dimensions, within an overall, coherent system. This colour-coded system, set out in Figure 1, groups ecological considerations into clear categories, covering natural habitats, engineering, water management and human culture (embracing everything from laws and customs to diet and social organisation).

GREEN

Ecological EcoInfrastructure: *Nature's Utilities, Biodiversity Balancing, Ecological Connectivity, Etc...*

GREY

Engineering EcoInfrastructure: *Renewable Energy Systems, Eco-Technology, Carbon Neutral Systems, Etc...*

BLUE

Water EcoInfrastructure: *Sustainable Drainage, "Closing the Loop", Rainwater Harvesting, Water Efficienct Fixtures, Etc...*

RED

Human EcoInfrastructure: *Enclosures, Hardscapes, Use of Materials, Products, Lifestyle and Regulatory Systems.*

▲ Fig. 1. The Four Strands of EcoInfrastructures

Ever the list-maker, Yeang underpins this four-part system with a further four definitions of what green design should aspire to be. Readers will note that these definitions steer clear of being overly prescriptive in terms of technologies and performance standards; they outline something more akin to an attitude, a sensibility about the role and responsibility of the architect.

1. Green design should be considered as bio-integration – physical, systemic and temporal. Yeang sees the work of architects as similar to that of surgeons applying an artificial prosthesis to an organic host, ie the human body. By analogy, Yeang sees the built environment as a collection of prostheses requiring biointegration with the host organism, ie the ecosystems present within the biosphere.

2. Green design involves the conservation of non-renewable and the care of renewable resources to ensure that they remain sustainably available for future generations. This includes designing environments that are less dependent, or not at all dependent, on non-renewable energy resources.

3. Green design is ecomimetic, that is imitating the properties of ecosystems. Yeang's third strategy is to encourage designers to imitate the properties, processes, structure, features and functions of nature leading to the idea of the human built environment as an ecocyborg. "Our built environment must imitate ecosystems in all respects, such as its ability to recycle, to extract energy from the sun through photosynthesis, to remain energy efficient and to maintain a holistic balance of biotic and abiotic constituents, and so forth," says Yeang.

4. Green design as monitoring and reacting to ecological interactions over the life span of built systems. This strategy includes the study of human impact and environmental devastation as well as natural disasters. It assumes a sense of ecological stewardship and an aim for environmental stability.

This set of design strategies is very Yeang. The contents of his ideas, grounded in a lifetime of research and practice, are difficult to contradict, but their expression is idiosyncratic. Yeang is an incredibly precise and methodical thinker, and he instinctively sets out anything but the most simple thoughts as bullet points. Yeang will tell you, for example, that there are five types of architect (the stylist, the discourse-based, the building-type specialist, the innovator and the expert deliverer). He will tell you the five things the complete architect should do (research, write, design, build and teach). And he will give you the five reasons why an architect's life is, almost by definition, a stressful and difficult one (cash flow, the focus on delivery, the multi-tasking, the need for "fire-fighting" and rapid responses to the unforeseen, and client management). There is a precision about Yeang's thinking that appears to push instinct to one side, leaving little room for the irrational. But he is a man of some passion, and his designs are too expressive to be the product of purely rational thought. Apart from his crusade to green design and effect a more benign way of inhabiting the Earth, Yeang is concerned with placemaking, with creating responsible structures which are, simultaneously, spaces in which people can live their lives pleasurably. "Ken's buildings demonstrate a commitment to the future of the planet, but also to a rethinking of our social and cultural engagement with it," says Leon van Schaik, Professor of Architecture at the Royal Melbourne Institute of Technology and a colleague of Yeang's at the AA. "The Library in Singapore is determined to create a

▲▼ **Shenzhen Baoan Central District residential development, China.**
In his work on ecomasterplanning, Yeang emphasises interconnectivity. Here, sky-bridges and eco-bridges provide green routes throughout the development on a vertical as well as horizontal axis.

▲ **Shenzhen Baoan masterplan,** emphasising the extensive landscaping and car-free zones. Low level car parks are naturally ventilated and illuminated.

new role for the library in the city, as a new public realm. The outside spaces are as important as those inside. Clients who embrace this work are signalling an optimism about the future."

Yeang says that his work is both an enquiry into an ecomimetic architecture and a search for an eco-aesthetic. Ecodesign, he says, is situational; is an eco-aesthetic situational also? Yeang has certainly been influenced by Kenneth Frampton's ideas of critical regionalism, whereby architecture arises naturally out of a singular place and time (nostalgia and sentimentalism notwithstanding). Climate, topography, latitude, ecology and prevailing weather conditions will force, surely, a particular design approach which will inevitably guide the aesthetics of a building down a particular regional path. More than that, however, Yeang is determined to celebrate the ecological credentials of his buildings – he wants them to look green. His buildings do not demurely cover themselves up, appearing as one thing but behaving like quite another. If his buildings are different, then they ought to look different, Yeang believes, those differences, no matter how organic or technological or ambitious or "green and hairy" collectively begin to shape an aesthetic of their own. Yeang is famously reluctant to cite sources or precedents, preferring instead to let the architectural programme and an objective pragmatism conjure up an aesthetic of their own. Van Schaik, who compares Yeang's Guthrie Pavilion country club to the swooping lines of iconic 1930s' aircraft like the Tupolev Maxim Gorky, believes that "a strong substrate of heroic Modernism" lies buried deep within Yeang's psyche, formed from his time at the AA. There is also "a tropically induced lyricism", he adds. One could probably further add a dash of Archigram, of High-Tech, of Apollo launch-pad, of Russian Constructivism. Yeang's is a 21st century architecture whose roots lie wherever he can find nourishment, knowingly or unknowingly – providing, of course, it is ecologically useful.

In the projects which follow in this book, one becomes aware of the refinements Yeang has made over the years to resolve basic but critical issues concerning land use, human comfort, accessibility, transportation, performance, ecological behaviour and marketability. These advances have even led to the generation of new vocabulary – bioclimatic design, vertical urbanism, ecoinfrastructure and so on. These terms, and others, are used to group projects together to help illustrate how Yeang uses projects to develop ideas for use later on, creating a series of overlapping works which often look backwards towards more tentative phases of development while suggesting ways in which new ideas can be developed further. It is an intense process of incremental advancement with few "Eureka!" moments. It is interesting, then, that Yeang brings together a set of works under the collective title "Transitional Projects" which include the Singapore National Library. These projects may indeed be thought of as transitional when considered between notions of "then" and "now". But as Yeang continues to grow in terms of ambition, scale and sophistication, that perception of transition will surely shift. If Yeang's work teaches us anything, it is that Nature, and our response to it, is always on the move.

Sara Hart
Edited by David Littlefield

◀ ▲ Yeang's childhood home, Cantonment Road, Penang

NOTES

1 Ken Yeang undertook a doctoral programme at Wolfson College, Cambridge University,1971-4. Yeang's PhD Dissertation, "A Theoretical Framework for the Incorporation of Ecological Considerations in the Design and Planning of the Built Environment", 1981, was subsequently published as *Designing with Nature* (McGraw-Hill, 1995). For a full list of Yeang's publications, see page 266.

2 Ian L. McHarg, *Design with Nature* (New York: Natural History Press, 1969. Published in paperback by Wiley in *Sustainable Design*, 1995).

3 The Greenwashing Index (greenwashingindex.com) is promoted by EnviroMedia Social Marketing in partnership with the University of Oregon School of Journalism and Communication.

All uncredited quotes from Ken Yeang in the text were provided by the architect in 2009 in the course of the writing and editing of this book.

EcoArchitecture Chronology

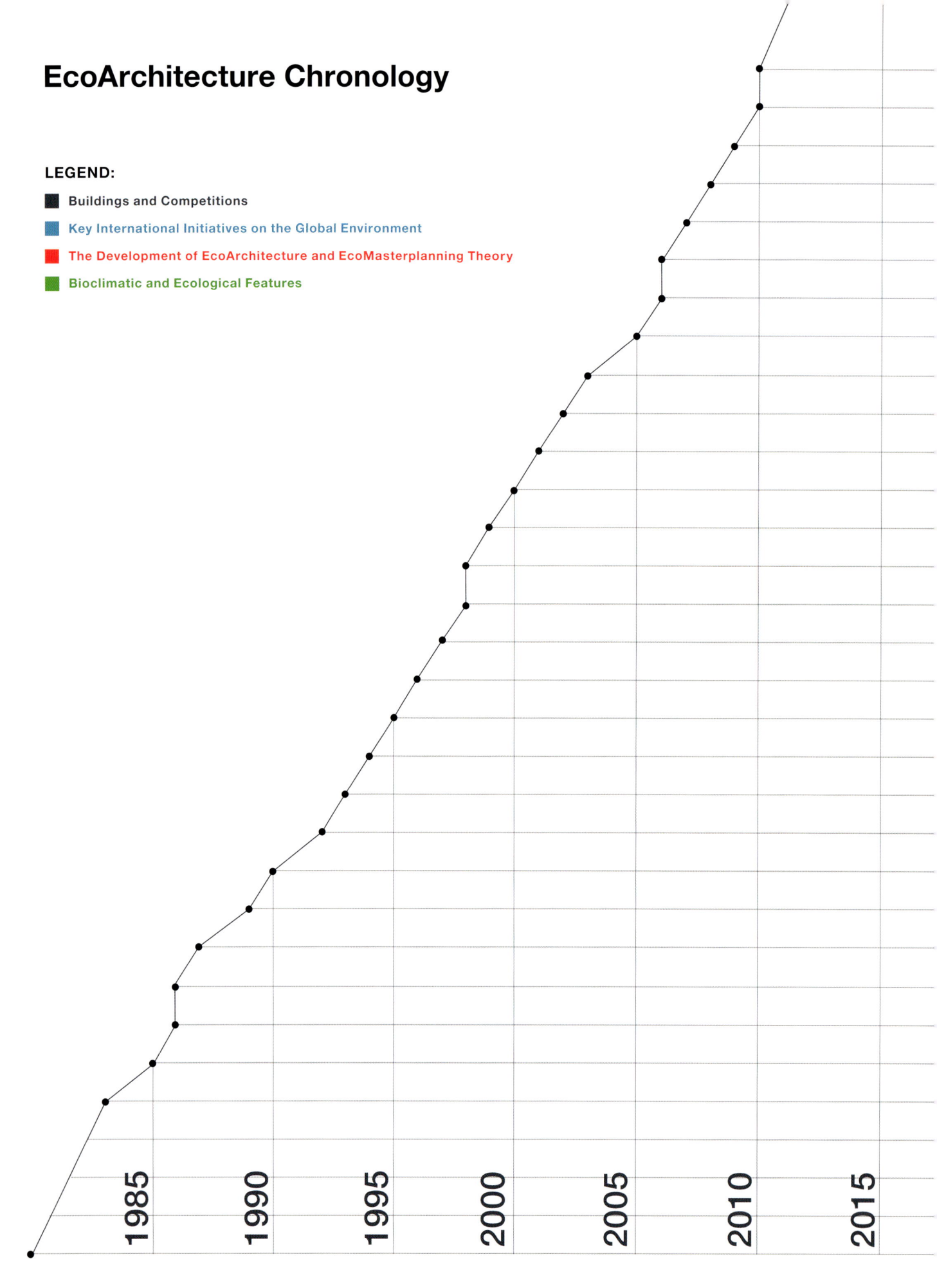

LEGEND:
- Buildings and Competitions
- Key International Initiatives on the Global Environment
- The Development of EcoArchitecture and EcoMasterplanning Theory
- Bioclimatic and Ecological Features

1985　1990　1995　2000　2005　2010　2015

22　ECOARCHITECTURE | THE WORK OF KEN YEANG

2010 Solaris, Singapore; Digi Data Centre, Kuala Lumpur, Malaysia; 1.5km vertical landscaped ramp, Naturally ventilated atrium,
Roof gardens, Ecocell, Light shaft, Green Mark Platinum Rating, Continuous green walls, Vertical eco-infrastructure, GBI Gold Rating

2010 Gyeong-Gi Provincial Government Office, Korea; Ken Yeang & Lillian Woo, *Dictionary of Eco Design*
Orientation on E/W axis, Biodiversity targets, Ecological connectivity, Rainwater harvesting

2009 Jabi Lake Gardens, Nigeria; KBZF & ATA Towers, Abu Dhabi; Leon van Schaik, *Vertical EcoInfrastructure*
Ken Yeang, *Eco Masterplanning*; Malaysia Green Building Index Introduced; Ecological connectivity, Green walls, Skycourts / gardens

2008 ZORLU, Turkey; Plaza of Nations, Vancouver, Canada; RIVA Ecomasterplan, Turkey; Spire Edge, Manesar, India
Ecological connectivity, Eco-bridges, Eco cells, Rainwater harvesting, Retention ponds, Skycourts, Roof gardens, Sun shading

2007 GNOME Research Building, Hong Kong; Premier City, Almaty, Kazakhstan;
Ken Yeang, *Eco Skyscrapers*

2006 The Residence TTDI Phase 6DI; Kuala Lumpur, Malaysia; Chong Qing Tower, China; Eco Bay, Abu Dhabi
Mixed-mode non-air conditioned retail complex, CFD analysis, Wind scoops, Internal airwells, Solar shading

2006 Kucukcekmece Ecomasterplan, Istanbul, Turkey; Ken Yeang, *Eco Design: A Manual for Ecological Design*
Ecomimisis, Eco-bridges, Wetland habitat

2005 Singapore Green Mark Introduced

2003 National Library of Singapore; Kyoto Protocol comes into force
Solar shading, Naturally ventilated atrium, Light shelves, Thermal buffers, Skycourts, Green Mark Platinum Rating

2002 Ken Yeang, *Reinventing the Skyscraper*
World Summit on Sustainable Development

2001 Kowloon City Waterfront, Hong Kong; Ivor Richards, *Groundscapers and Subscrapers of Hamzah & Yeang;*
Ivor Richards, *T R Hamzah & Yeang: Ecology of the Sky*; LEED Certification Introduced

2000 Elephant & Castle Tower, London
Orientation, Response to prevailing winds, Natural ventilation, Solar shading, Passive heating

1999 Bishopsgate Tower, London; Robert Powell, *Rethinking the Skyscraper;*
Ken Yeang, *The Green Skyscraper*; Leon van Schaik, *T R Hamzah & Yeang*

1998 Editt Tower, Singapore
CFD analysis, Wind wing walls, Green ramp, Natural daylight, Deep set windows, Natural ventilation

1998 Menara UMNO, Penang, Malaysia
Sky courts, Sky gardens, Continuous green ramp, Ecological connectivity, Wind wing walls

1997 Ken Yeang, *The Skyscraper Bioclimatically Considered: A Design Primer;* Kyoto Protocol to the UN Convention on Climate Change
Orientation, Continuous landscaped ramp, Park in the sky, Solar shading, Eco bridges

1996 Central Plaza, Kuala Lumpur, Malaysia
Deep balconies, Stepped planter boxes, Naturally ventilated stair cores & toilets

1995 Ken Yeang, *Designing with Nature*

1994 Casa del Sol (Metrolux Tower) Kuala Lumpur, Malaysia; Alan Balfour, *Ken Yeang: Bioclimatic Skyscrapers*
Stepped planters, Skycourts, Natural ventilation to lift lobby cores, Cross ventilation

1993 MBF Tower Penang, Malaysia
Naturally ventilation atrium, Stepped planter boxes, Natural ventilation, Sky gardens

1992 Menara Mesiniaga, Sengalor, Malaysia; Earth Summit, Rio Declaration, Agenda 21; Orientation/sunpath, Spiralling sky courts,
Recessed terraces, Sunshading louvres, Roof top pool, Naturally ventilated stair wells and lift cores, Solar panels (intended)

1990 BREEAM Introduced

1989 Robert Powell, *Ken Yeang: Rethinking the Environmental Filter*

1987 Ken Yeang, *Tropical Urban Regionalism*; World Commission on Environment & Development (Bruntland Report)

1986 Plaza Atrium, Kuala Lumpur, Malaysia Ken Yeang, *The Tropical Veranda City*
Orientation, Trickle irrigation, Landscaped balconies, Double-skin wall, Service core location, Large wind-scoop, Recessed windows

1986 Menara Boustead, Kuala Lumpur, Malaysia
Landscaped balconies, Orientation, External atrium

1985 IBM Plaza, Kuala Lumpur, Malaysia
Orientation, Sunpath, Shading by higher floors, Vertical Land scaping

1984 Roof-Roof House, Ampang, Malaysia
Orientation, Double layer roof/shading, Evaporative cooling, Passive cooling, 'Venturi' effect

1980 World Conservation Strategy

Diagram by Robert Powell

CHAPTER 1   Bioclimatic Design

This first set of projects covers Yeang's early bioclimatic work. When he started out in professional practice, after teaming up with fellow Architectural Association student Tengku Hamzah, Yeang quickly began to develop the ecological principles discovered at Cambridge University. This involved a search for an architecture that responds so well to its environment that building form is derived from climate – an idea that arose from the debate into "critical regionalism", largely associated with critic Kenneth Frampton, which sought to replace the skin-deep application of local symbol with an architecture that was truly derived from its locality. The concern in the 1980s was that Modernism and Post-Modernism had all but done away with a sense of place and that architects needed to reconsider the role of context, both physical and cultural. For Yeang, an architecture of place was to be reached via a close study of climate and (later) ecology – an architecture which, responding to conditions such as prevailing winds, temperatures, humidity, sun paths and angles, the needs of wildlife and vegetation, would almost inevitably become distinctive and different from a similar building type situated in another climatic zone. Yeang describes this as "optimising the ambient energies of the locality with a resultant configuration and performance that is passive mode". It is, he says, basically about "design and climate". The result is buildings that shade themselves appropriately; ones that guide the wind; ones that cool and insulate themselves. They become, when set in the tropical climate of Malaysia, characterised by deep louvres, double-roofs, large fins, sliding partitions, lush planting and pools of water exploited for their evaporative cooling effects. It is an enquiry that would eventually result in Yeang's notion of the "bioclimatic skyscraper". As well as reducing the energy load and programmatically cutting CO_2 emissions, the forms of these buildings are so rooted in their locale that they simply would not work if transplanted to, say, Europe or North America. Yeang's buildings become, then, a contemporary version of "tropical architecture".

Yeang is not, in fact, comfortable with the term "tropical architecture". The idea of a single tropical architecture is fundamentally, he believes, a Western notion which seeks to wrap the buildings of an entire global region into one of pitched roofs, verandas, stilts and ceiling fans. "My contention is that by building environmentally and climatically, you get an architecture which responds to the locality. But if I were to ask you what Western architecture is, it would be impossible to answer, the forms are so varied and the styles so diverse. There is not a single Western architecture and there is not one tropical architecture." Yeang regards bioclimatic design as a subset of ecodesign, enabling a building to be a passively performing, low-energy structure, designed to respond to the local climate, while establishing a regional identity. But the architecture of place is not a style guide. Yeang believes that a bioclimatic, low-energy design can gain a cultural identity in any one of, or combination of, five ways: it can replicate, reinterpret or abstract local culture and iconography; it can exploit notions of a genus loci, or a contemporary lifestyle; and it can provide a neutral backdrop for the lives of people. "Which strategy is used depends on the location and the building programme. But remember, it is people who create a culture," says Yeang.

When considered bioclimatically, the design of a building will be a particular response to the locale's climate and natural resources. This, in turn, will guide the appropriate orientation and configuration, as well as informing the façade design (the solid-to-glass ratio in particular). The use of natural ventilation, the use of vegetation for shading, cooling and biodiversity enhancements, the application of appropriate colours and materials, as well as other interdependent functions, will further influence the final aesthetic and sense of place. The results can be intriguing, surprising even. But never cliched.

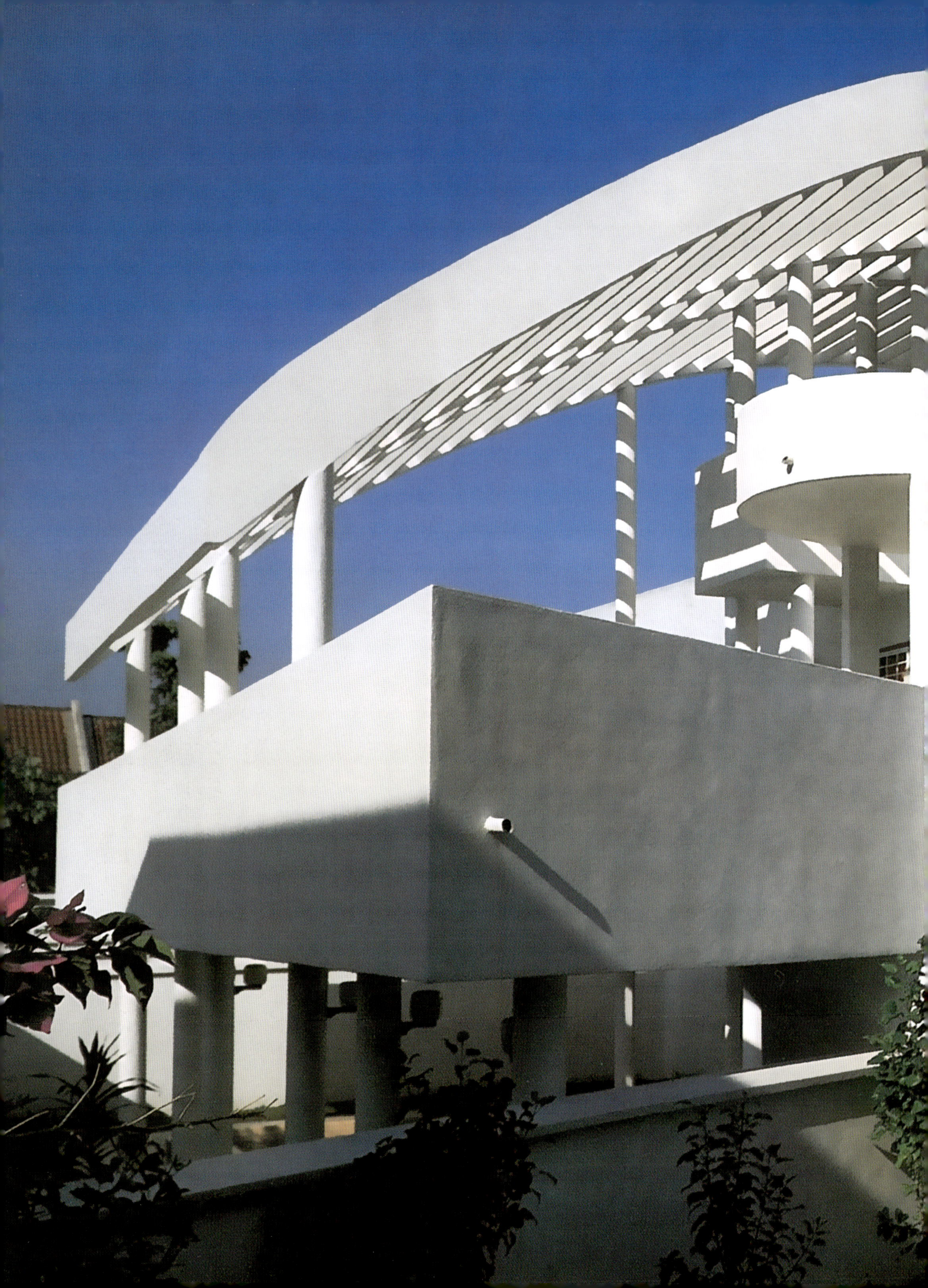

Roof-Roof House

Roof-Roof House

TYPE	:	Bioclimatic Design
LOCATION	:	Ampang, Malaysia
CLIMATE ZONE	:	Tropical
VEGETATION ZONE	:	Rainforest

AREAS:

SITE AREA	:	646 m²
NO. OF STOREYS	:	2 (with roof terrace)
STATUS	:	Built
DATE OF COMPLETION	:	1985

▲ Exterior of the Roof-Roof House

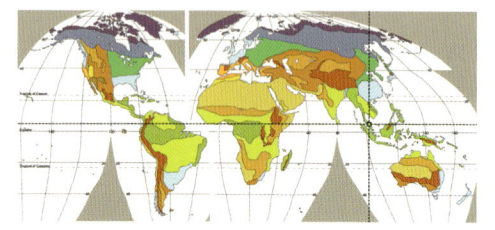

CLIMATE REGION

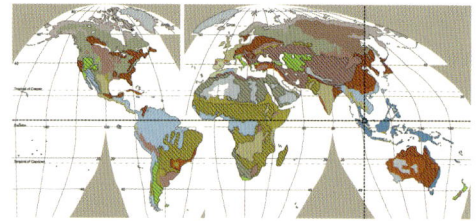

VEGETATION ZONE

Conceptual

Yeang was his own client for this house, completed a decade after leaving Cambridge University and starting a practice in Malaysia. Roof-Roof House is a seminal project for Yeang in which he explores a number of experimental bioclimatic tactics such as "wind walls" and the use of a swimming pool for its evaporative cooling qualities. The novel idea of the double roof has since been reused in a number of other Yeang projects, such as the Limkokwing University College in the Malaysian township of Cyberjaya.

Yeang still owns (and still likes "immensely") this small building, which was built as a permanent residence, but acknowledges that it did not receive much public recognition at the time of its completion. He attributes this to its novel built form which was regarded as unconventional for a house and was not easily understood in 1985. "There were too many experiments in a single project," admits Yeang, who used the house as a test-bed and demonstration project. "People thought I was a design maverick. They didn't understand the concepts then... although these are evidently understood now." The building was, however, featured in a 1985 exhibition at Tokyo's Ginza Pocket Park - Yeang's first venture outside Malaysia. This project sparked off more than three decades of bioclimatic experimentation and theoretical development for Yeang.

The Roof-Roof House is a full-scale, live-work prototype, designed and built to give form to Yeang's earliest theories regarding bioclimatic design. Conceptually speaking, Yeang defines Roof-Roof House and other bioclimatical buildings as "enclosure systems that operate as environmental filters within the landscape". Emphasis is placed on the systemic effort to use climatic factors opportunistically in order to shape the building's configuration and spatial organisation. The mood at the AA when Yeang was there in the late '60s and early '70s was one of experimentation. Though this has proved formative throughout his career, it is particularly apparent in the formal qualities of the house. In the Roof-Roof House, Yeang drew heavily on the work of three influential architects: Le Corbusier's approach to plan making and aesthetics (this is most

Drawing by Beverly (4 years)

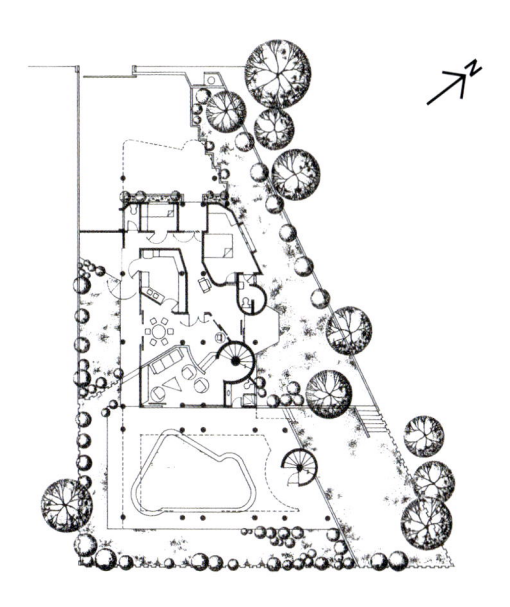

Ground Floor

Second Floor

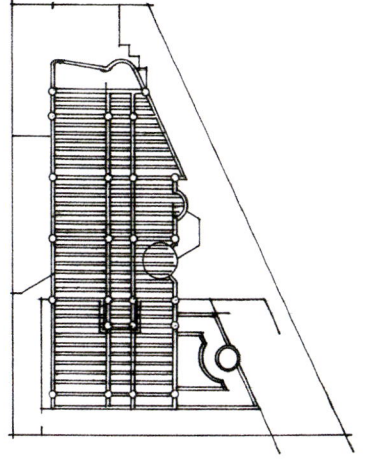

Roof Plan

apparent in the use of white and formal elements that draw on Le Corbusier's tropical architecture at Chandigardh in India, particularly the curved stairs and reinforced-concrete hooded windows); Charles Correa's use of trellised canopies (Correa actually visited the house upon completion); and Victor and Aladar Olgyay's technical solutions to energy conservation and shading devices.

The house is in the district of Ampang, a suburb of Kuala Lumpur, a 15-minute drive from the city centre. Located near a dilapidated rubber plantation, it is on a 30-acre residential development; along the same road is a row of 3-storey shophouses, also designed by Yeang, where his office is located. Yeang is also the architect of this development and, like the IBM Plaza project (see pages 146-55), the development came about through Yeang's own initiative; he acted as the go-between for the landowner (Malayan Credit) and the developer. The Roof-Roof House is a four-bedroom house, with further accommodation for a maid. The downstairs living area consists of a kitchen and living room with an adjacent space for dining, which is slightly lower in level. The living area leads through to the swimming room. The house is constructed of reinforced concrete with masonry plastered walls; full-height, sliding, glazed walls face the courtyard on the ground floor. The choice of white for the exterior is influenced by both Le Corbusier and climatic considerations. White external surfaces perform best in tropical climatic zones, as Yeang points out: "Studies have shown in Los Angeles by the Lawrence Berkerley Laboratories that whitening roofs in a locality lowers the heat island effect on the built environment."

On the western edge of the Malaysian peninsula, Ampang has warm, humid, sunny days and cool nights all year round with occasional evening rainfall. Yeang exploited design devices including sunpath and wind flow orientation, building mass and shading (tactics which contribute to what he calls "passive mode design") as a response to these climatic conditions. Furthermore, the building includes moveable sliding grilles, adjustable blinds, glazed screens and solid panels to control the amount of air and light that penetrates

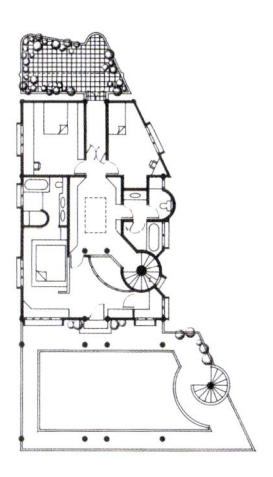

SHADOW OF HOUSE – APRIL TO AUGUST

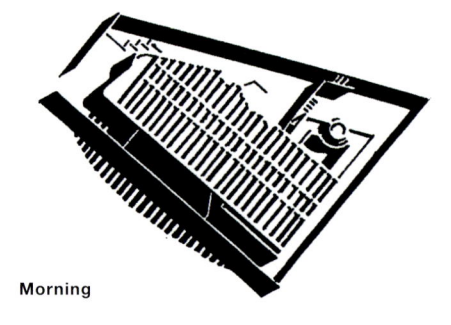

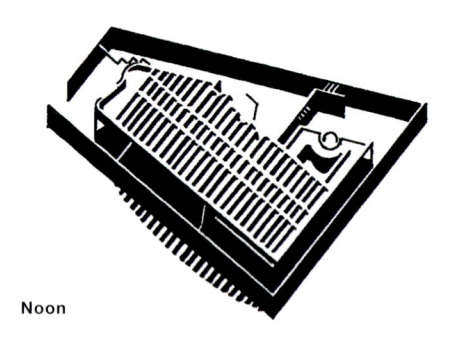

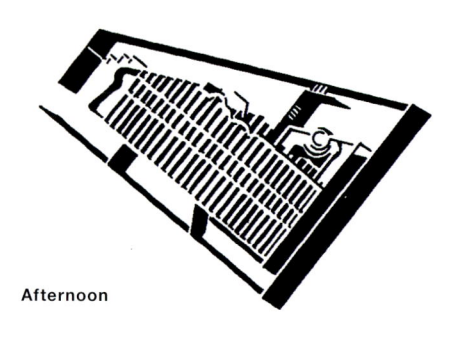

Morning

Noon

Afternoon

SHADOW OF HOUSE – MARCH AND SEPTEMBER

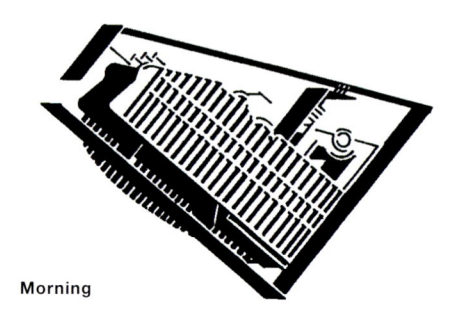

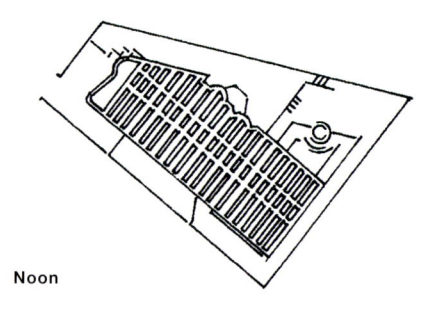

Morning

Noon

the interior. Acting like a valve, the enclosure filters out undesired climatic elements, such as solar radiation, while admitting those that are conducive to comfortable living, such as ventilation. The result is a climatically derived aesthetic which Yeang terms tropical functionalism.

Appropriate solar orientation on the small and restricted site was the first challenge. The building footprint has a north–south orientation to take advantage of local climatic conditions, while protecting the major spaces from the tropical sun. The ground-floor living spaces face east to capture the prevailing winds. The repetitive name of this reinforced-concrete structure comes from the fact that it deploys a pair of roofs. A standard flat roof, offering an elevated garden, completes the enclosure; above, a trellis resembling an open umbrella and functioning as a pair of "louvred sunglasses" arches across the building and continues over the pool terrace. The slats on this three-dimensional trellis are angled to reduce the noonday solar gain, while allowing the morning sun to wash the east façade. This filtering device in other contexts could extend to the building walls. The house's swimming pool doubles up as an evaporative-cooling device, placed on the predominantly windward side of the house (in the west courtyard) – at the same time complying with traditional Feng Shui practice. Further, the use of splayed garden-walls deflects wind into the interior, while providing internal, ground-floor spaces with their own private courtyards.

"Effective low energy design has to start by responding to the climate of the place, as the penalty for not doing so results in a built form that is in conflict with the sensibilities of climate and tends to require higher energy to maintain," says Yeang. "The significance of this project was the discovery that the bioclimatic design approach provided an expedient and fundamental starting basis for ecodesign – a passive-mode framework upon which I could integrate other aspects of green design."

▲ View of the overarching "second roof" or louvred trellis that is the key feature of the house.

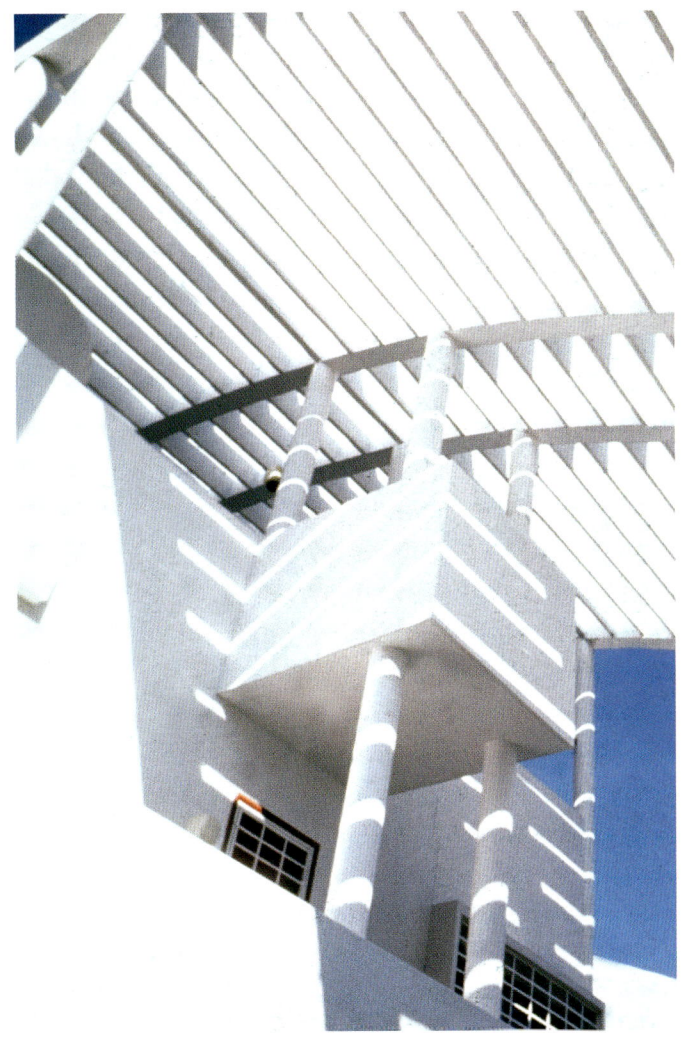

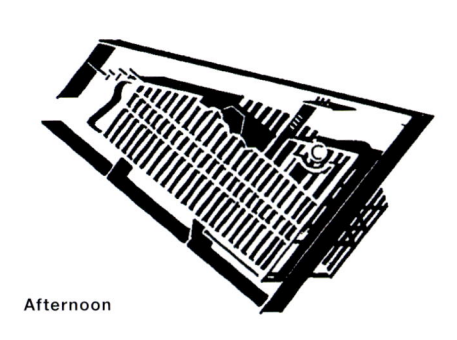

Afternoon

SHADOW OF HOUSE – OCTOBER TO FEBRUARY

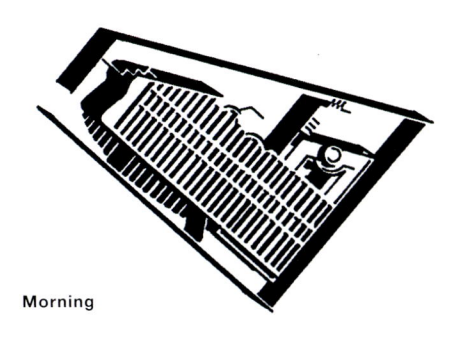

Morning

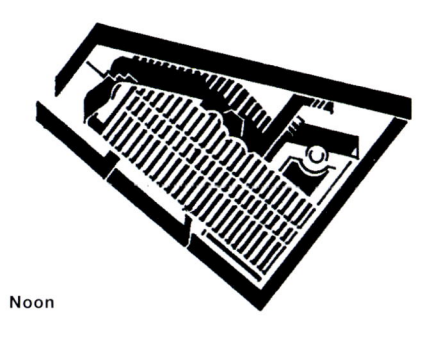

Noon

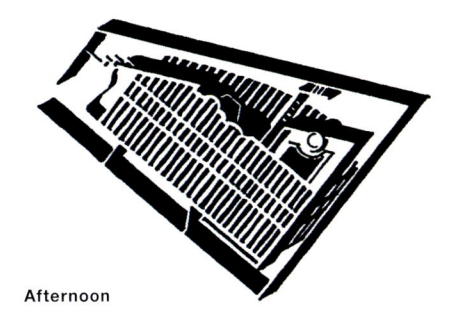

Afternoon

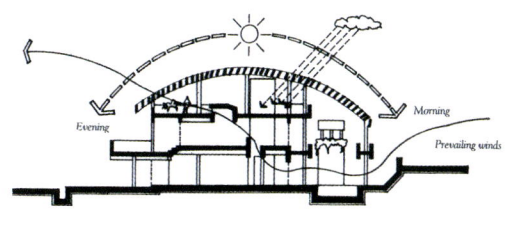

▲ Louvred trellis from below

Cross Ventilation

Bioclimatic Design | Roof-Roof House 31

▲ The swimming pool is oriented to the south so prevailing winds blow over it.

▲ Pool deck

▲ Interior hallway

▲ Living room

Bioclimatic Design | **Roof-Roof House** 33

▲ Roof-Roof House night view

▲ The louvred roof trellis

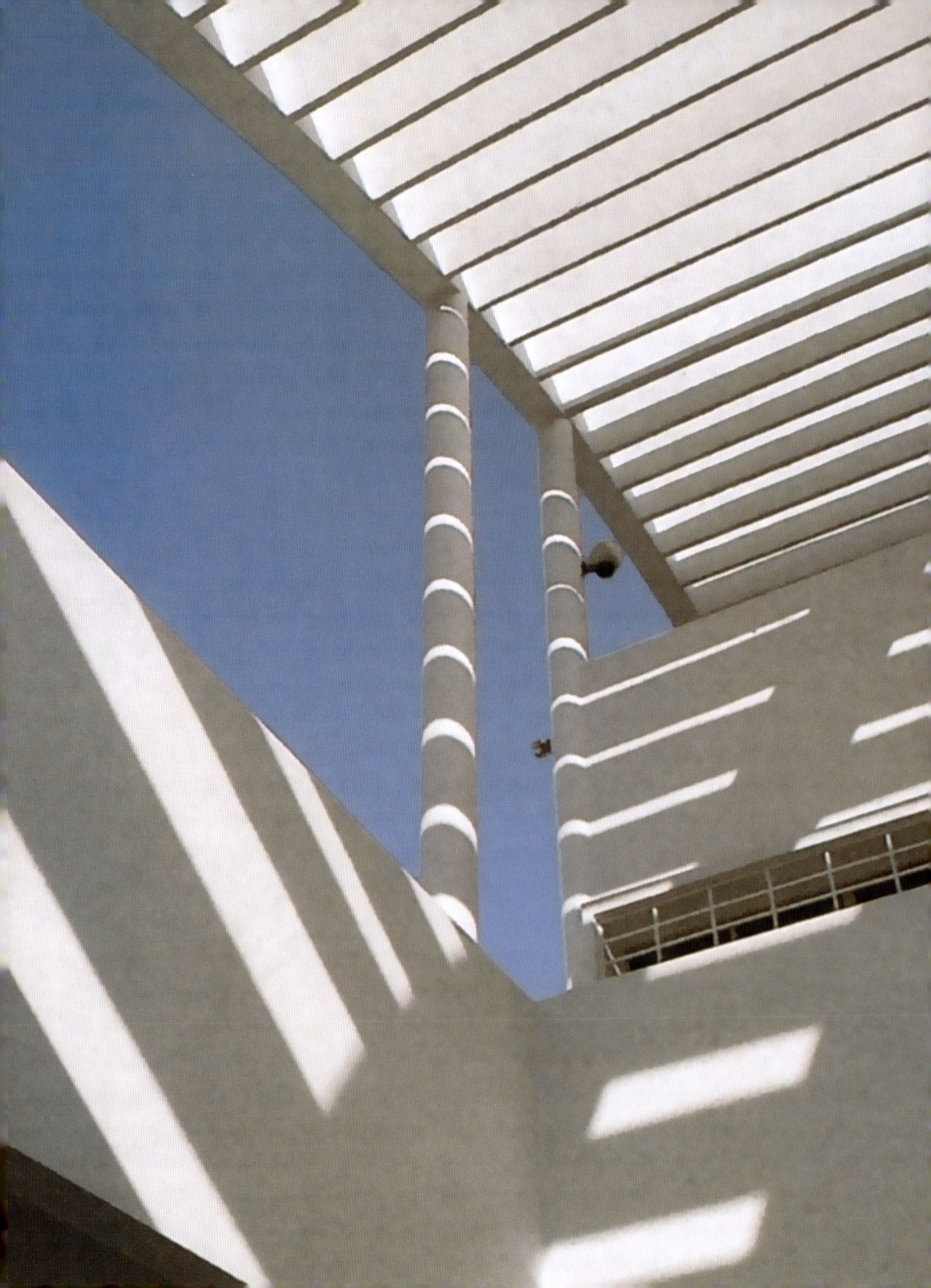

▲ Details of the louvred trellis

◀ View of louvred trellis from the pool deck

Bioclimatic Design | **Roof-Roof House** 37

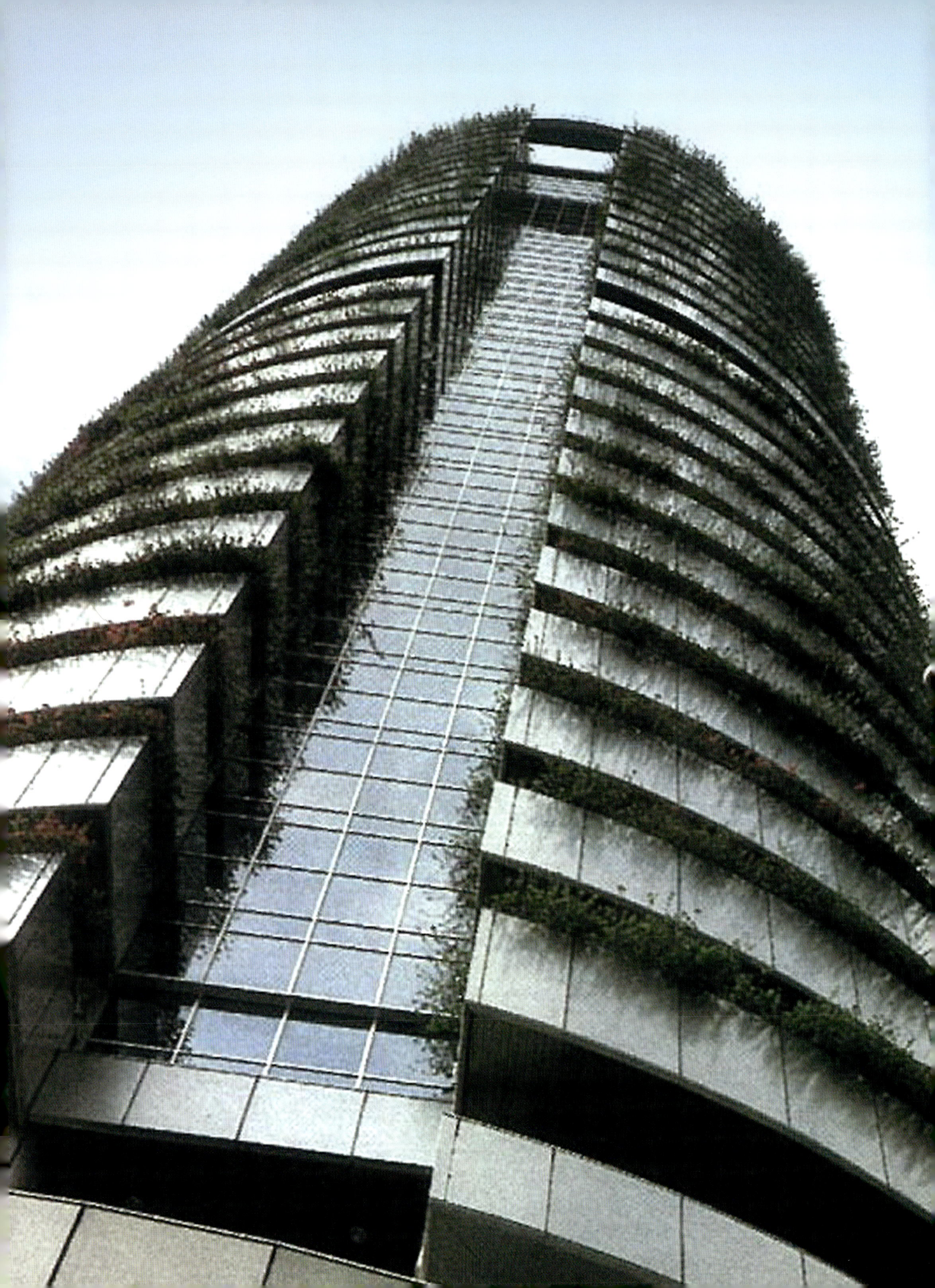

Menara Boustead

Menara Boustead

TYPE	:	Bioclimatic Design
LOCATION	:	Kuala Lumpur, Malaysia
CLIMATE ZONE	:	Tropical
VEGETATION ZONE	:	Rainforest

AREAS:

GFA	:	29,840 m²
SITE AREA	:	4,300 m²
PLOT RATIO	:	1:7
NO. OF STOREYS	:	31
STATUS	:	Built
DATE OF COMPLETION	:	1986

▲ View looking up at the tower with planting in place

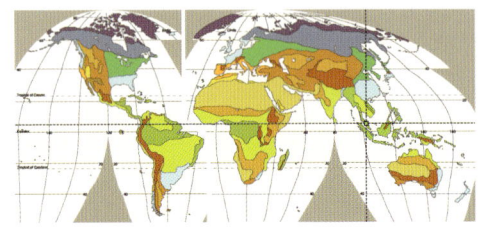

CLIMATE REGION

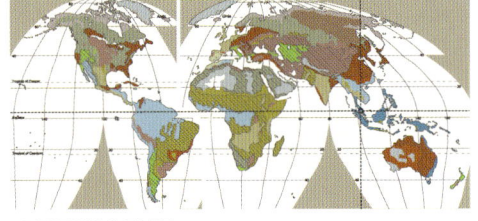

VEGETATION ZONE

Conceptual

This commission allowed Yeang to apply his bioclimatic theory to a tall building for the first time. Designed for Boustead Holdings – a publicly listed company with interests in agriculture, engineering, shipping and insurance – the client required a distinctive yet first-class headquarters designed and built on a tight schedule on a city-centre site. Bioclimatic design runs counter to conventional skyscraper design, in which the architect creates a prismatic object without regard to the sun's path across the sky; what Yeang achieved with this building was to create a structure which responds to the local climate and the equatorial sun path. This is representative of Yeang's early experimental bioclimatic towers (after Plaza Atrium, 1985) and was one of several "Tropical Skyscrapers" he exhibited in 1992 at the Tokyo Designer's Space, in the Axis Building. Yeang's mentor, Kisho Kurokawa, delivered the opening address. Introduced by Charles Jencks while still a student at Cambridge, Kurokawa told Yeang that the best thing he could do as a young architect was to write a book; even if it remained unpublished, he told the young Yeang, marshalling the material for a book would help consolidate, deepen and test one's thoughts. This advice eventually manifested itself as *The Skyscraper Bioclimatically Considered* (Wiley-Academy, 1996), a title Yeang appropriated from Louis Sullivan's seminal essay "The Skyscraper, Aesthetically Considered".

At the Menara Boustead building ("menara" being Malay for "tower") Yeang placed the main elevator, wash rooms and escape core at the periphery of the floor plate (instead of locating it at the centre of the building) offering a column-free floor with a 29-metre clear span. Also, configuring the building this way provides solar buffers, shading the east and west façades (which receive direct sun), while facing the north and south façades, which receive little or no direct sunlight in the tropics, with clear glass. Yeang also points out that placing circulation cores on the periphery of buildings allows occupants to remind themselves of where they are as they move around the structure – if elevator lobbies are glazed, occupants become more familiar with their geographical location. "Architecture must relate to place. To relate to place the architecture must help the users appreciate where they are; architecture must

Exterior view of Menara Boustead

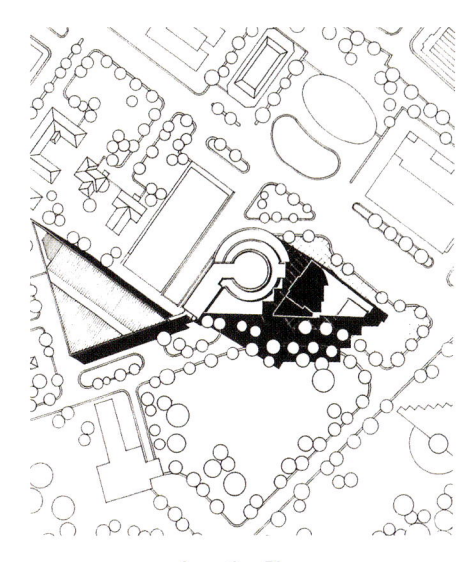

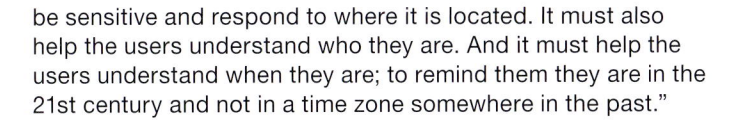

Location Plan

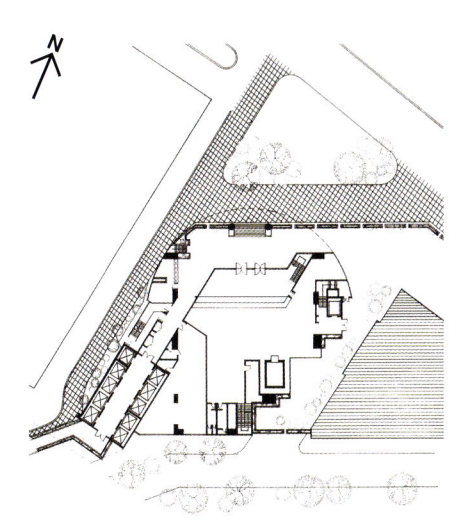

Ground Floor

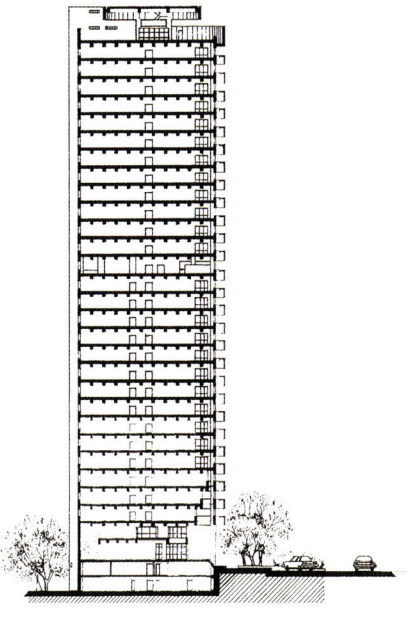

be sensitive and respond to where it is located. It must also help the users understand who they are. And it must help the users understand when they are; to remind them they are in the 21st century and not in a time zone somewhere in the past."

The structure is a composite of reinforced concrete and steel. Other early ideas for the "bioclimatic skyscraper" were also incorporated into the design: a double-skin, rain-check, external wall of masonry and recycled aluminium cladding; provision of natural ventilation opportunities to the elevator lobbies to eliminate the need for fire-protection pressurisation ducts; natural ventilation to the main stair, escape stair and toilets; and garden terraces ("skycourts") with edge planting at strategic locations within the typical floor plate. Excess plumbing, waste pipes and ducts were also provided within the skycourts to enable the future addition of toilets and pantries. "The aesthetic is a simple techno-looking cylinder but visually expressing the bioclimatic features with profusely vegetated small skycourts on the exterior," says Yeang. "The vegetation gave the built form a hairy and fuzzy indeterminateness. It is an evocative image of what an ecoarchitecture could look like."

The Menara Boustead's interiors were renovated and upgraded by Yeang in 2009.

Section

▼▲ Exterior views of Menara Boustead

▲ View looking up at the tower from entrance

PASSIVE SOLAR CONCEPT DIAGRAMS

1. UNPROTECTED CURTAIN WALL

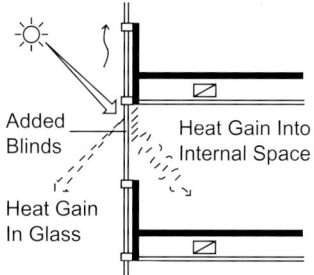

Unprotected Glazing

- Added Blinds
- Heat Gain Into Internal Space
- Heat Gain In Glass

2. DEEP RECESSES AND BALCONIES

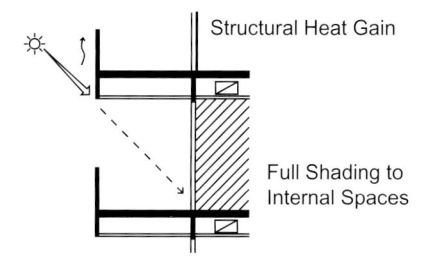

Recessed Glazing and Balconies

- Structural Heat Gain
- Full Shading to Internal Spaces

3. RECESSED WINDOWS

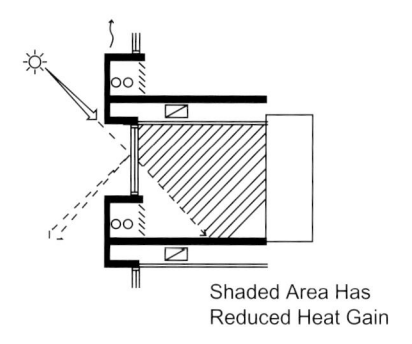

Recessed Windows

Shaded Area Has Reduced Heat Gain

4. HORIZONTAL FINS

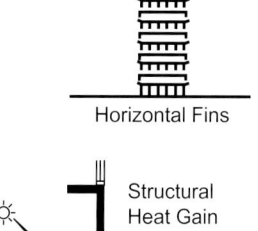

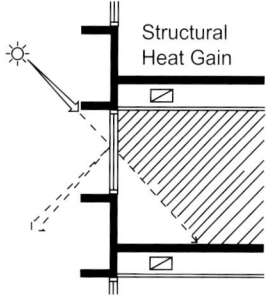

Horizontal Fins

Structural Heat Gain

5. VERTICAL FINS

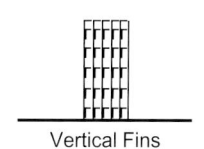

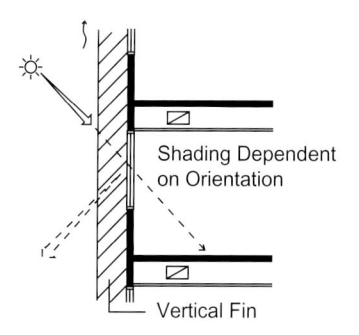

Vertical Fins

- Shading Dependent on Orientation
- Vertical Fin

6. DEEP RECESSES COMBINED WITH BALCONY TERRACES, PLANTERS, HEAT-SINK CLADDING

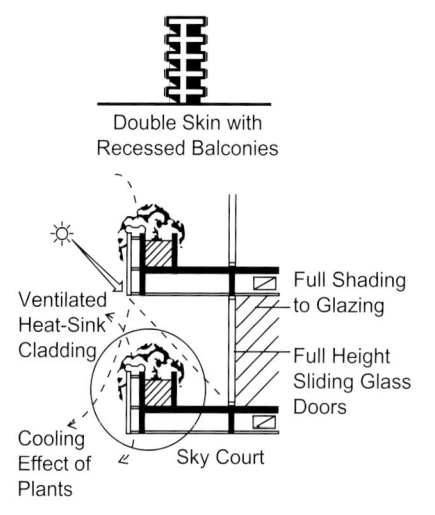

Double Skin with Recessed Balconies

- Ventilated Heat-Sink Cladding
- Cooling Effect of Plants
- Full Shading to Glazing
- Full Height Sliding Glass Doors
- Sky Court

Bioclimatic Design | Menara Boustead

▲ Cafe interior view

▶ Street level view of tower

◀ Menara Boustead lift lobby

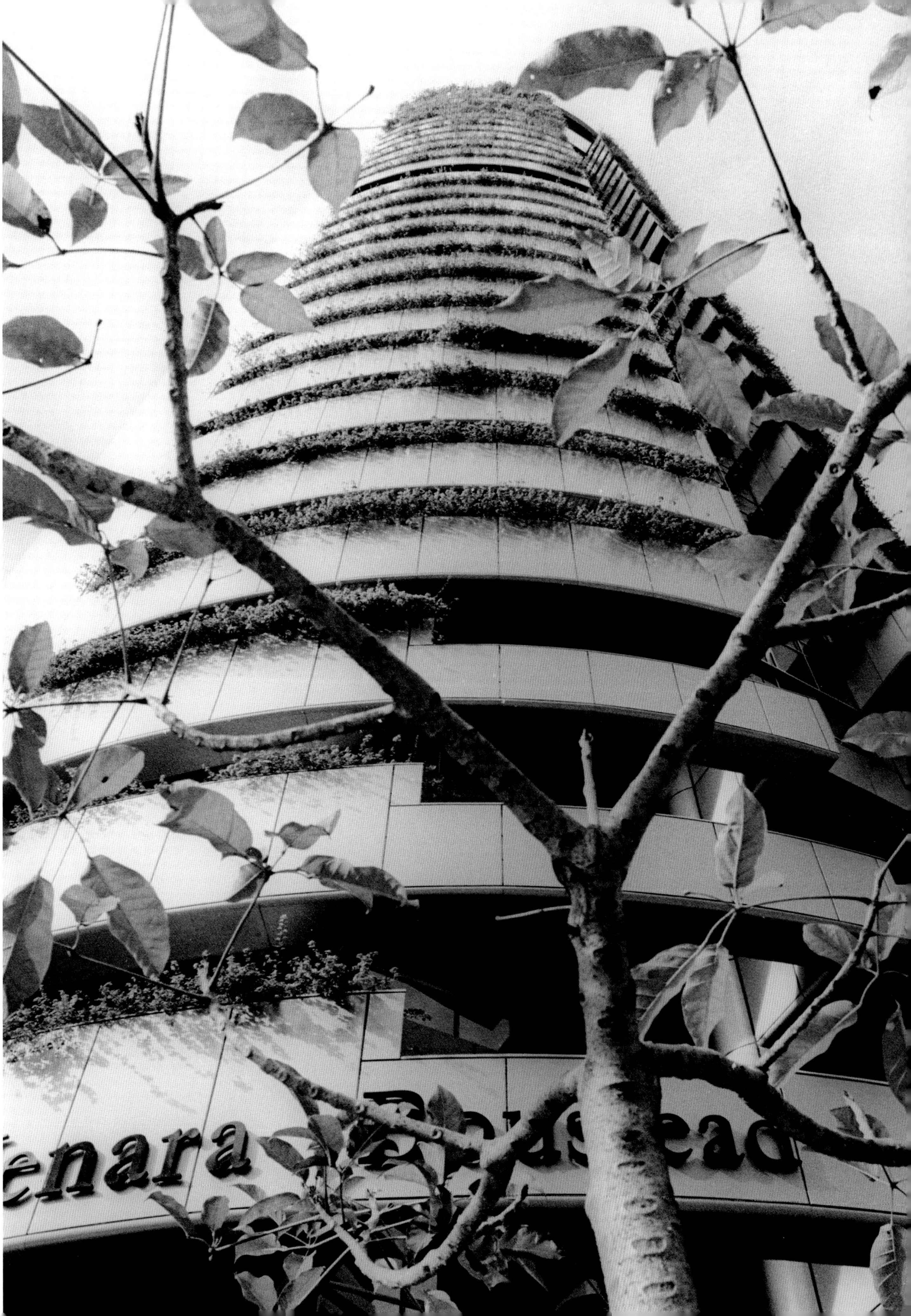

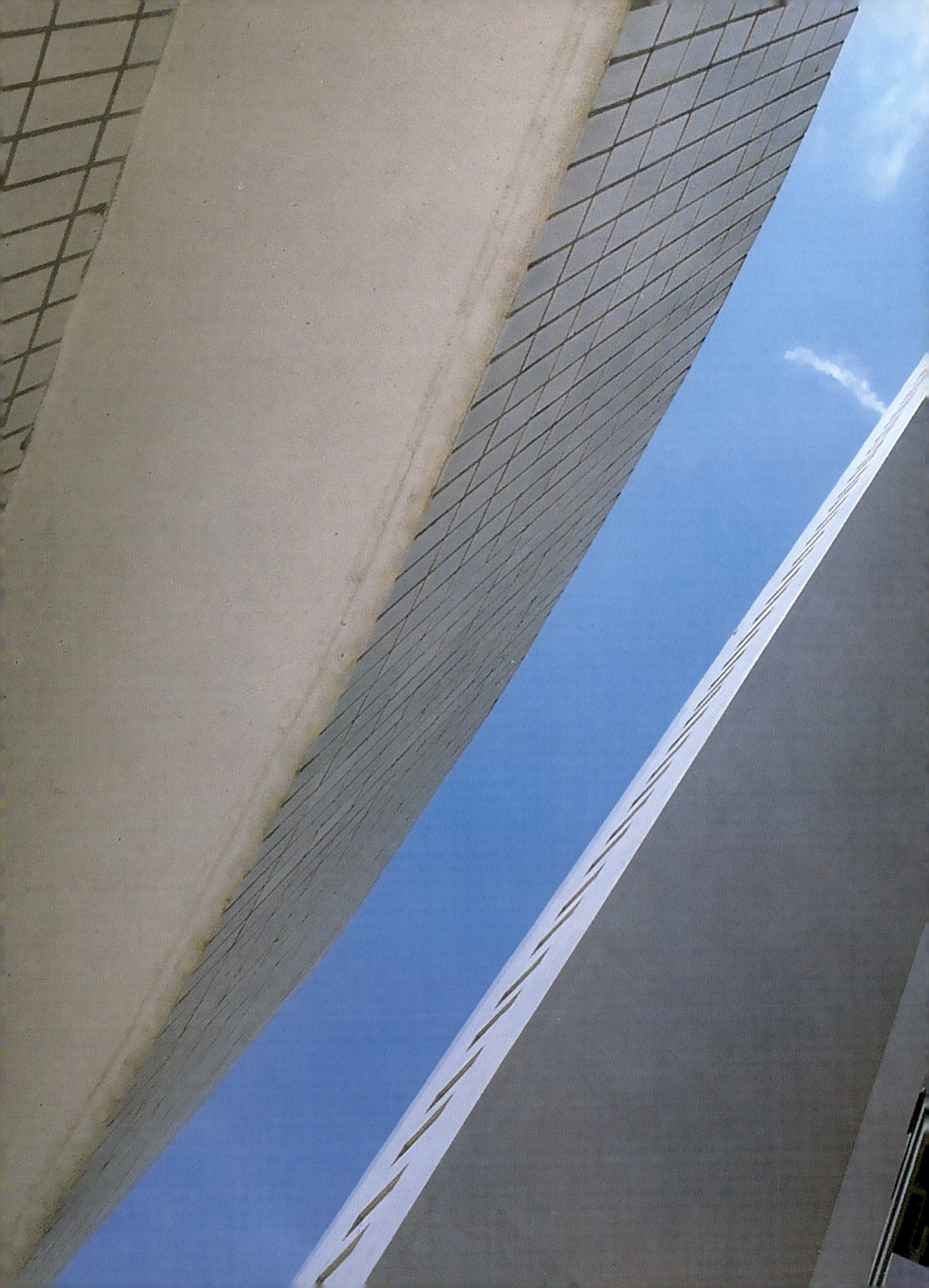

IBM Plaza

IBM Plaza

TYPE	:	Bioclimatic Design
LOCATION	:	Kuala Lumpur, Malaysia
CLIMATE ZONE	:	Tropical
VEGETATION ZONE	:	Rainforest

AREAS:

GFA	:	26,000 m²
SITE AREA	:	6,500 m²
PLOT RATIO	:	1:4
NO. OF STOREYS	:	24
STATUS	:	Built
DATE OF COMPLETION	:	1985

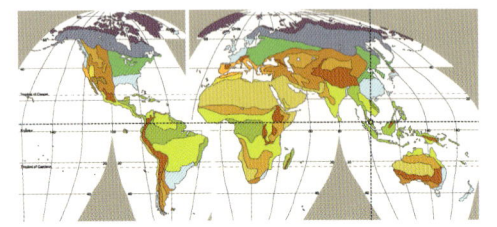

CLIMATE REGION

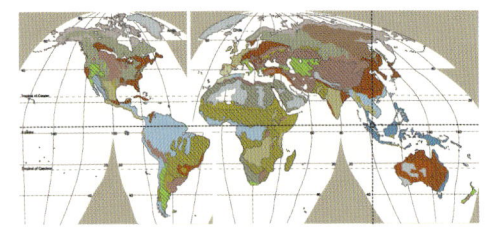

VEGETATION ZONE

Conceptual

▲ Exterior view of IBM Plaza

Soon after receiving the commission for the Menara Boustead Tower (pages 38-45), Yeang began work on the design of the 24-storey IBM Plaza building, located at the western edge of Kuala Lumpur. The commission was the result of what Yeang calls "proactive marketing"; it was Yeang himself who catalysed the project by introducing IBM as a tenant to the landowners, who eventually signed a pre-construction long-lease agreement with the computing company. This project is, then, a rather good illustration of the ways in which Yeang operates – he is as practical as he is theoretical, and a strength for innovation links the two.

Yeang argued as early as 1983 that an ecologically-sensitive building must contain linked landscaping that extends from the ground plane to the top of (and within) the entire building. This was Yeang's first exploration of the idea of a continuous green façade. Here, the planting across the façades of the building, unlike at Menara Boustead, became linked. Yeang used a system of stepped planter-boxes with vertical trellises between the planters, which he later developed into a continuous linear park in the Solaris building (pages 200-9). The design was another Yeang prototype for a passive-mode/low-energy and critically regionalist bioclimatic skyscraper. The positioning of the elevator and stair cores is typical of his early bioclimatic skyscrapers – located at the hot sides of the floor plate, they act as buffers on the hot east and west elevations. Elevator lobbies, toilets and fire stairs are naturally ventilated. Here, the ground floor lobby is also naturally ventilated as a transitional space between the outside and the environmentally controlled upper floors of the tower, eliminating the use of air conditioning at ground level. The sun-shading is provided by precast-concrete components.

IBM PLAZA PLANS

IBM Plaza is a fully realised example of Yeang's principles of the bioclimatic skyscraper, with features that reflect the principles of proper orientation, appropriate built form configuration, use of sun-shading and natural ventilation. In common with the Boustead tower, the building expresses its key bioclimatic features on the exterior.

The pitch of the north–south oriented tower's roof is reminiscent of the region's residential vernacular forms. Traditional landscaping techniques and indigenous plants were introduced via a vertical system of boxes, which rise diagonally up the face of the tower. Midway, the planters traverse horizontally to the adjacent façade, then resume their diagonal rise to the roof terraces. This external planting has become critical to Yeang, who argues that buildings should aim to preserve the ecology, and increase the biodiversity, of the site on which they sit – otherwise cities will continue to expand as "abiotic heat traps", that is, synthetic, lifeless environments which alter the natural environment and climate. Edward O Wilson's theories of "biophilia", which examine how people are instinctively drawn to (and sympathetic with) other living systems, further underlie Yeang's determination to make buildings "ecomimetic". This is substantiated by the evidence-based work of Robert Ulrich, who has demonstrated that hospital patients recover faster if they are provided with external views filled with natural vegetation. The addition of planting to a building's exterior is a multi-layered exercise, in fact; quite apart from biophilic and biodiversity benefits, vegetation is an oxygen-producing sun-screen and rain-collection device which helps integrate the host building into its unique climatic, environmental and ecological zone. Apart from its bioclimatic purpose, this spiralling planting movement announces a departure from the conventional vertical slab associated with tall buildings, although the IBM building remains clearly a commercial venture. Yeang's experiments with planting developed much further in the 1990s and 2000s. "Nevertheless," comments Yeang, "the significance of this experimental endeavour was not then understood by other architects and the public."

The tower adopts a boxy aesthetic with blue and white horizontal bands reminiscent of the IBM brand identity. An office tower is linked by a curvilinear bridge to a two-storey restaurant and food court located on a pedestrian plaza adjacent to surrounding shops. Yeang has since established a long association with IBM via regional franchise owner Mesiniaga Bhd., which has become a life-long client of Yeang's. In addition to a number of interior renovations, Yeang designed the Mesiniaga building in Subang Jaya (1992) and the Mutiara Mesiniaga tower in Penang (in 2003). Yeang also designed a house and apartment for Ismail Sulaiman, the CEO of Mesiniaga and a house for his son Fathil Ismail in 2004.

Today IBM Plaza is no longer occupied by IBM. It is currently occupied by the software company VADS. Yeang is presently upgrading the building's exterior and interior, as well as expanding its accommodation and maintaining the overall planting strategy.

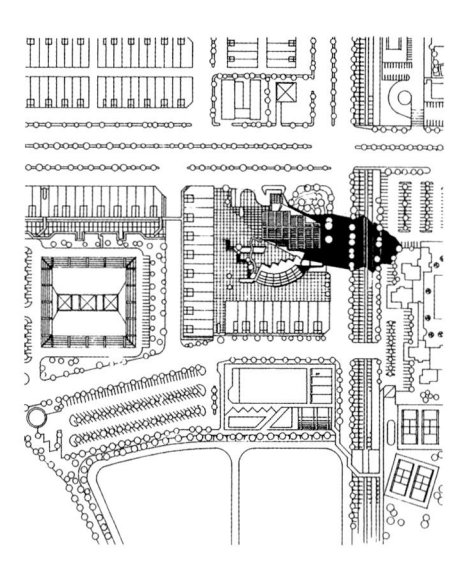

Site Plan

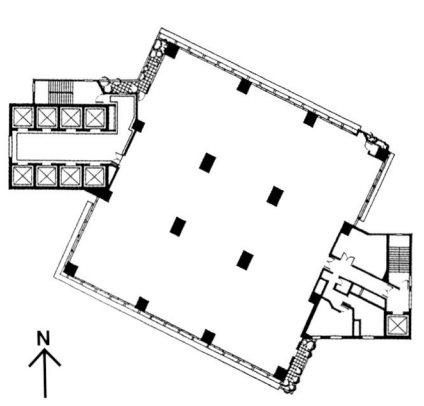

Tower Floor Plan

Axonometric of Landscape Concept

SITE PLAN CONCEPTS

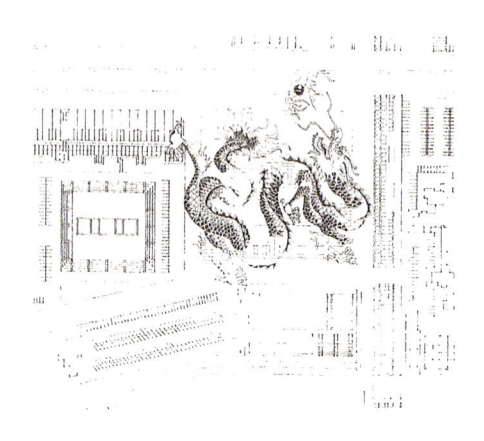

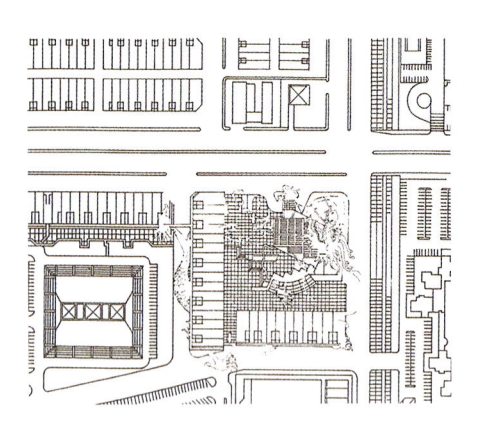

▲ The ground floor of the IBM Plaza provides shade for pedestrians and links to the surrounding low-rise commercial context.

▲ Food court

50 ECOARCHITECTURE | THE WORK OF KEN YEANG

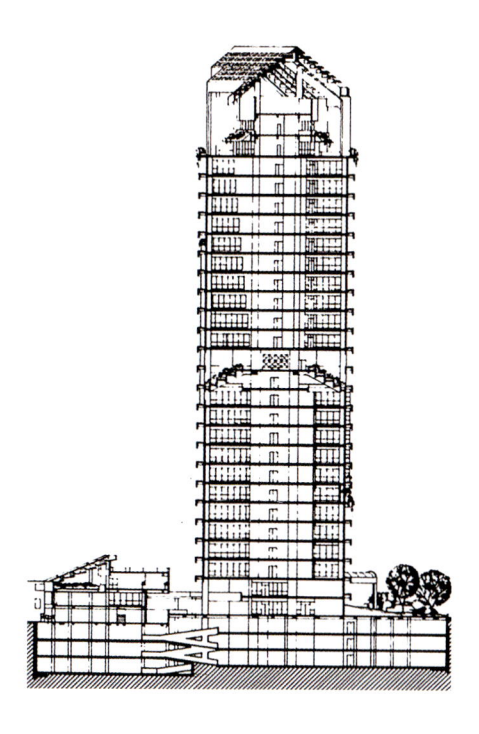

▲ Roof garden planting and balconies

Section

▲ Street view

Bioclimatic Design | **IBM Plaza** 51

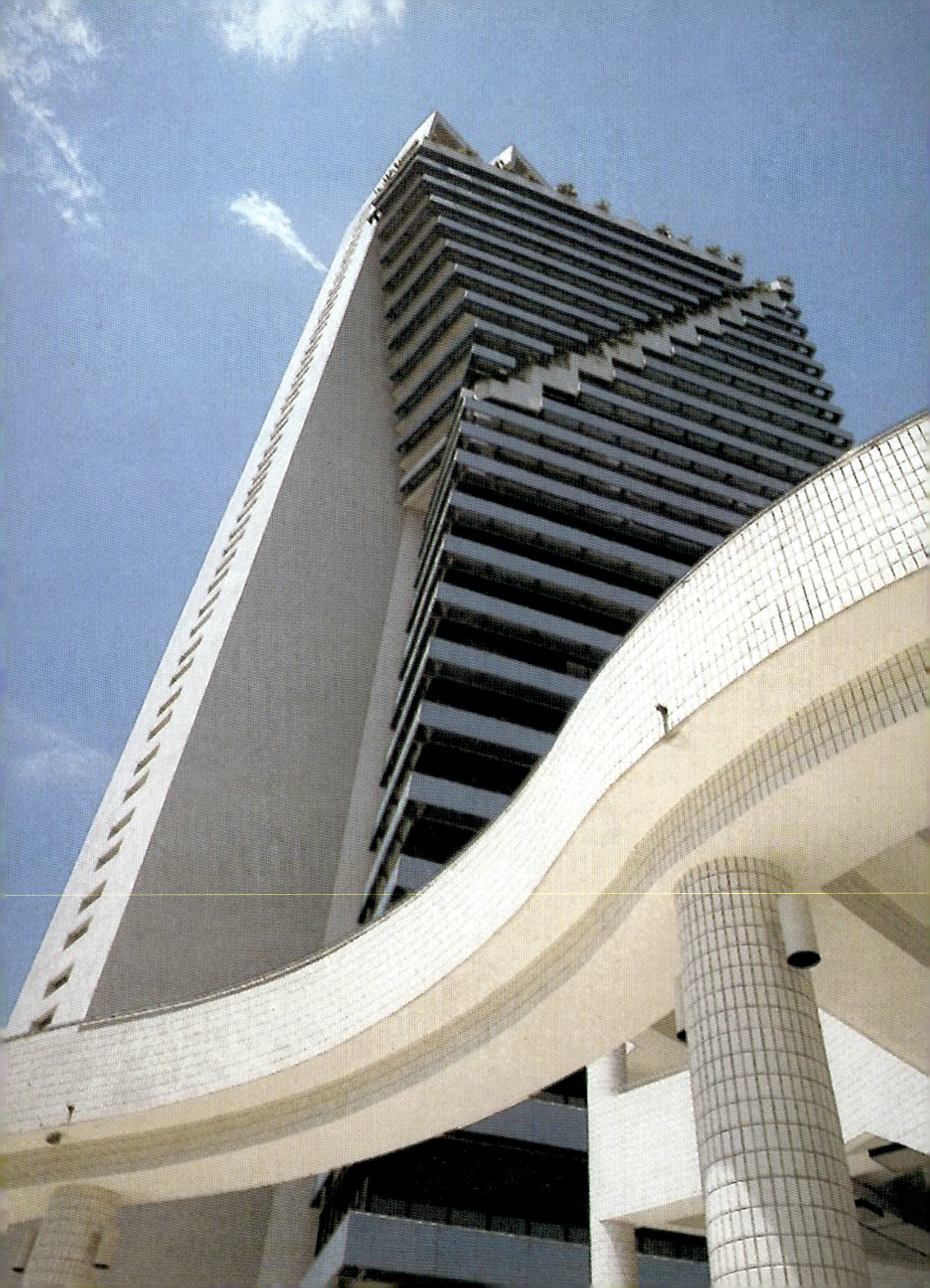

◂ Sunshade detail from below

◂ View of tower from ground level plaza

▲ T. R. Hamzah & Yeang's 2010 design for tower retrofit and annex block

▲ The annex block's vertical greenery

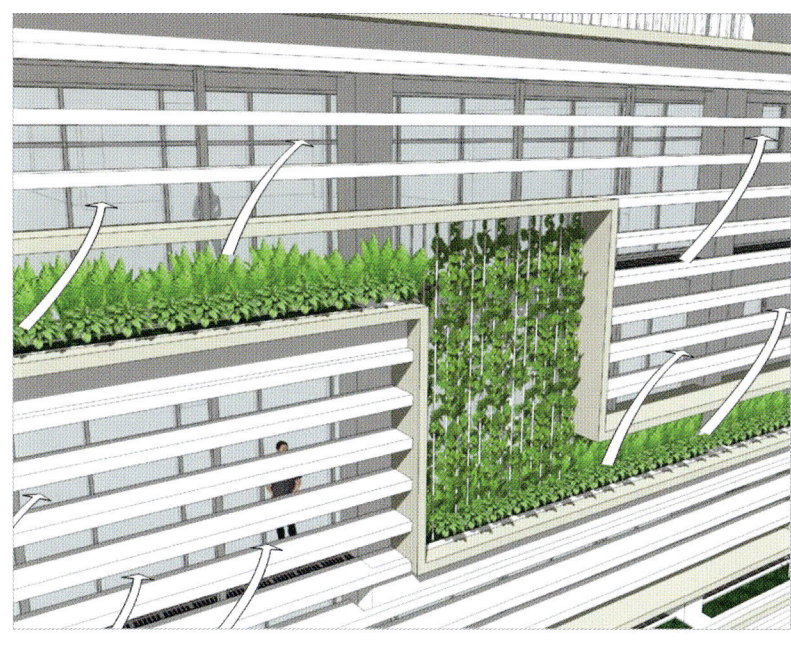

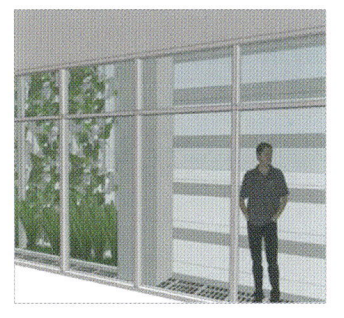

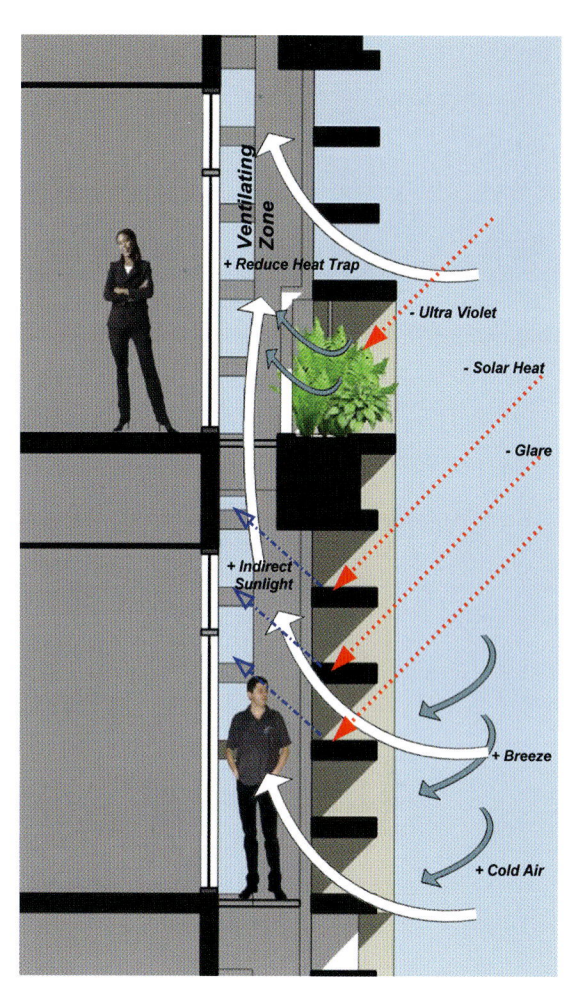

▲ Façade ventilation study

Bioclimatic Design | **IBM Plaza** 55

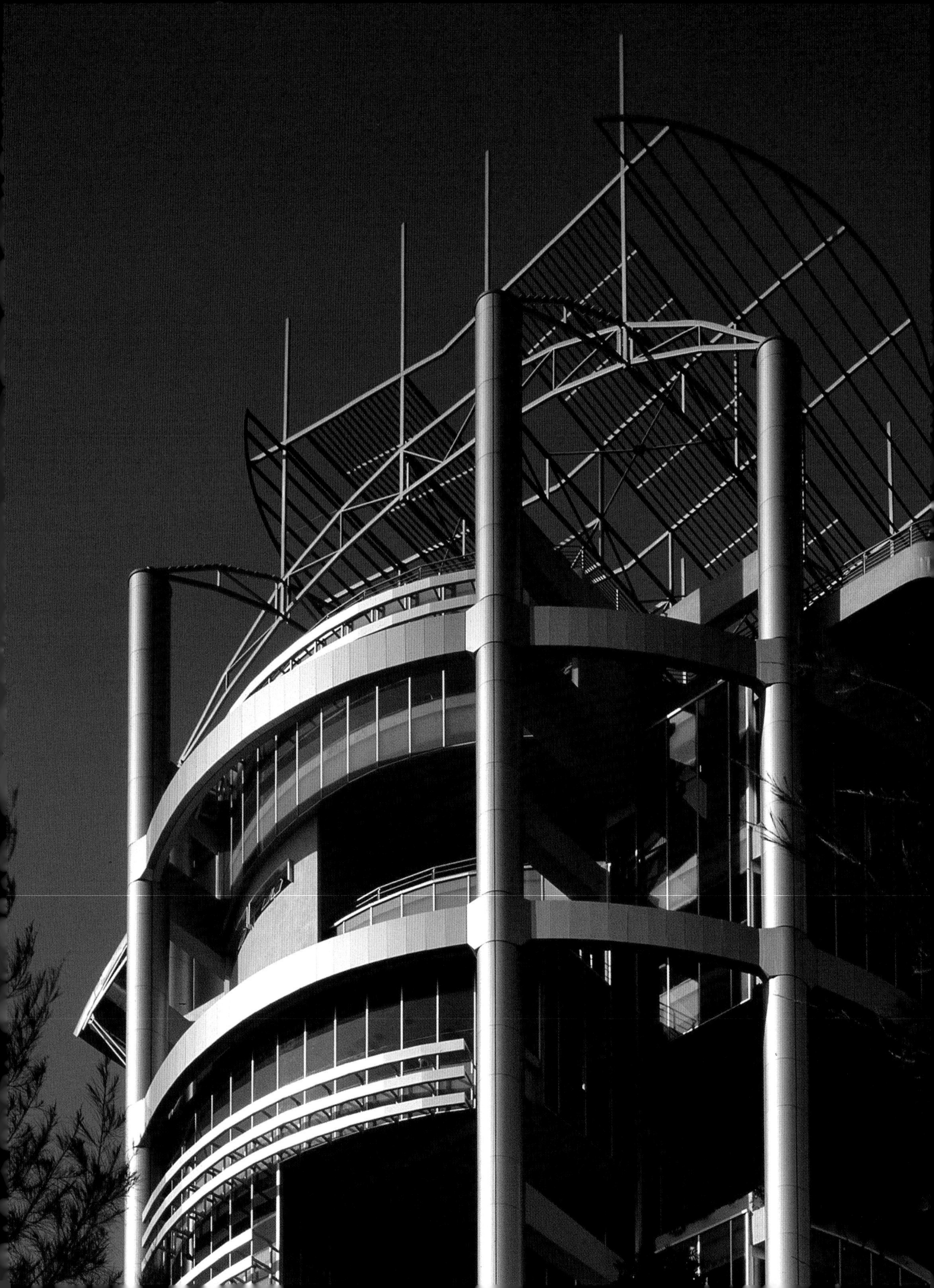

Menara Mesiniaga

Menara Mesiniaga

TYPE	:	Bioclimatic Design
LOCATION	:	Selangor, Malaysia
CLIMATE ZONE	:	Tropical
VEGETATION ZONE	:	Rainforest

AREAS:

GFA	:	10,340 m²
NFA	:	6,741 m²
SITE AREA	:	1,760 m²
PLOT RATIO	:	1:6
NO. OF STOREYS	:	15
STATUS	:	Built
DATE OF COMPLETION	:	1992

▲ Entrance lobby interior

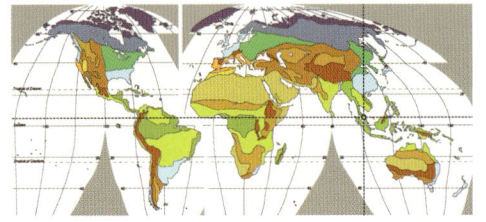

CLIMATE REGION

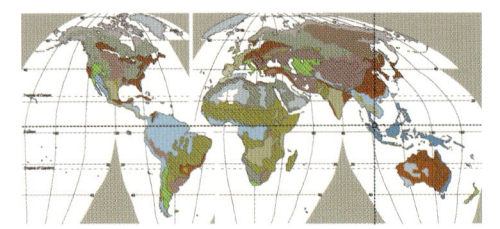

VEGETATION ZONE

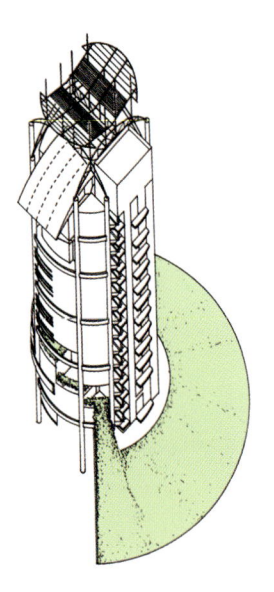

Conceptual

Menara Mesiniaga, completed seven years after his Roof-Roof House, was a further benchmark project for Yeang. It also set out a new direction for Yeang in helping him explore a techno-green aesthetic. The building brings together in a single coherent form a series of experiments and ideas from the architect's preceding bioclimatic skyscraper projects, such as: multi-storey wind-catcher boxes (pioneered in the Plaza Atrium); solar-buffer placement of the elevator cores, multiple skycourts and solar-path-responsive sunshading (Menara Boustead); and continuous stepped-planters (IBM Plaza). All that Yeang had learnt from these projects was finally assembled and reinterpreted in this tower, which is located in Subang Jaya, a suburb that is a 40-minute drive outside Kuala Lumpur city centre. It is also worth noting that the commission was a further example of Yeang's proactive marketing approach; it was Yeang who introduced the land to the building's owner.

This design for the 15-storey IBM headquarters was, in fact, the second scheme Yeang presented to the client. The first proposal contained an internal ventilating atrium and air-well (later used in the design for the MAAG Tower), but the client rejected this configuration. At the design stage, Yeang carried out a comparative Overall Thermal Transmission Value (OTTV) analysis that evaluated the thermal performance of alternative elevator core locations (central, north and east). OTTV is an energy index calculated using a formula that takes into consideration the insulation value of each façade. The results demonstrated that locating the core on the eastern flank of the building offered the best OTTV value. It was this exercise that further confirmed in Yeang's mind that low-energy design should begin with passive-mode bioclimatic strategies that become embedded in the project's built form.

The term "mesiniaga" was coined by the company's CEO, Ismail Sulaiman, combining Malay words which link with franchise IBM ("International Business Machines"); "mesin" means machine; "niaga" means business. "Menara" is the Malay for tower. The cylindrical building comprises a series of recessed atria that step from a ground floor characterised by turfed-mounded sides. The building offers two forms of sunshading – external louvres and a dramatic, arching, trellised canopy which extends over the uppermost floor. This solar canopy includes the facility to retrofit photovoltaic panels, reducing the building's dependency on fossil fuels in the future. An employee swimming pool and gymnasium are located at the top of the building; an auditorium is placed at second floor level. The building became, for Yeang, "virtually a built catalogue of bio-climatic techniques".

This project is also especially important for Yeang because it brought his ideas to international attention – chiefly because it won the Aga Khan Award for Architecture in 1995. Menara Mesiniaga won a number of other awards, but the Aga Khan prize was significant because the tendency had been to reward projects with conservation and/or conventional Modernist characteristics. The Aga Khan jury, however, found this corporate showcase to be a successful and promising approach to the design of multi-storeyed structures in a tropical climate. The building was also published internationally, receiving reviews in the *Architectural Review* and *Architectural Record*. Yeang also included a model of the project in the 1992 "Tropical Skyscrapers" exhibition in Tokyo, curated by Japanese architect Hidenori Seguchi. The tower has become a local landmark, and the value of surrounding property has increased because of it.

The client later commissioned Yeang to design a smaller building, based on similar principles, in Penang. The brief was stretching: "We wanted the Mesiniaga Penang building to reflect a sense of the corporate high-tech image in line wirth the business that Mesiniaga is in, and in keeping with the image of the HQ facilities in Subang Jaya," said Mr Mohd Puzi Ahmad, the client. This smaller cousin of Menara Mesiniaga is a further example of how commercial and ecological imperatives can be made to converge: design features include double-volume skycourts, roof terraces and other low-energy tactics deployed in earlier Yeang schemes.

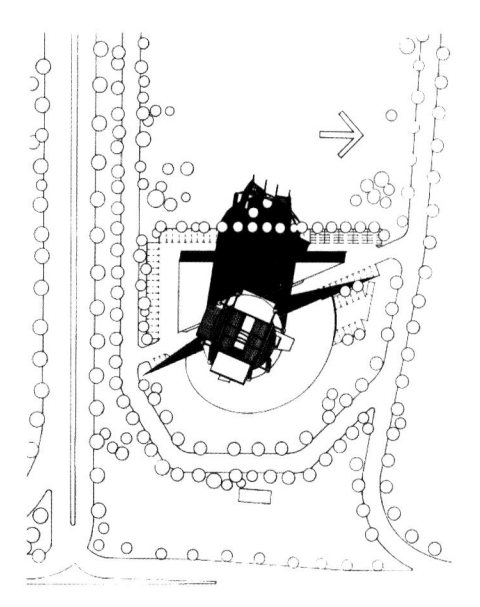

Site Plan

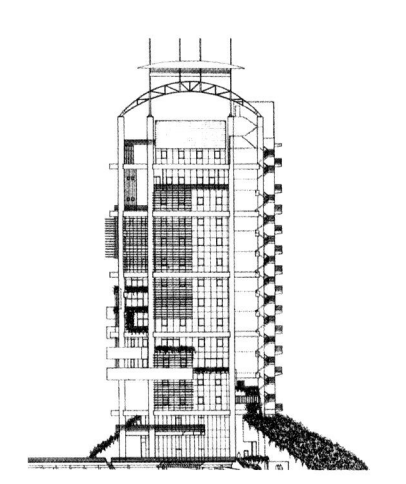

South Elevation

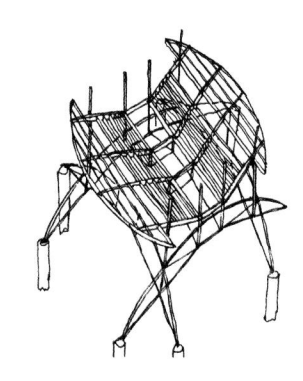

Roof Canopy

SUMMARY OF PLANS

Ground Floor

Mezzanine

Level 1

Level 2

Level 3

Level 4

Level 5

Level 6

Level 7

Level 8

Level 9

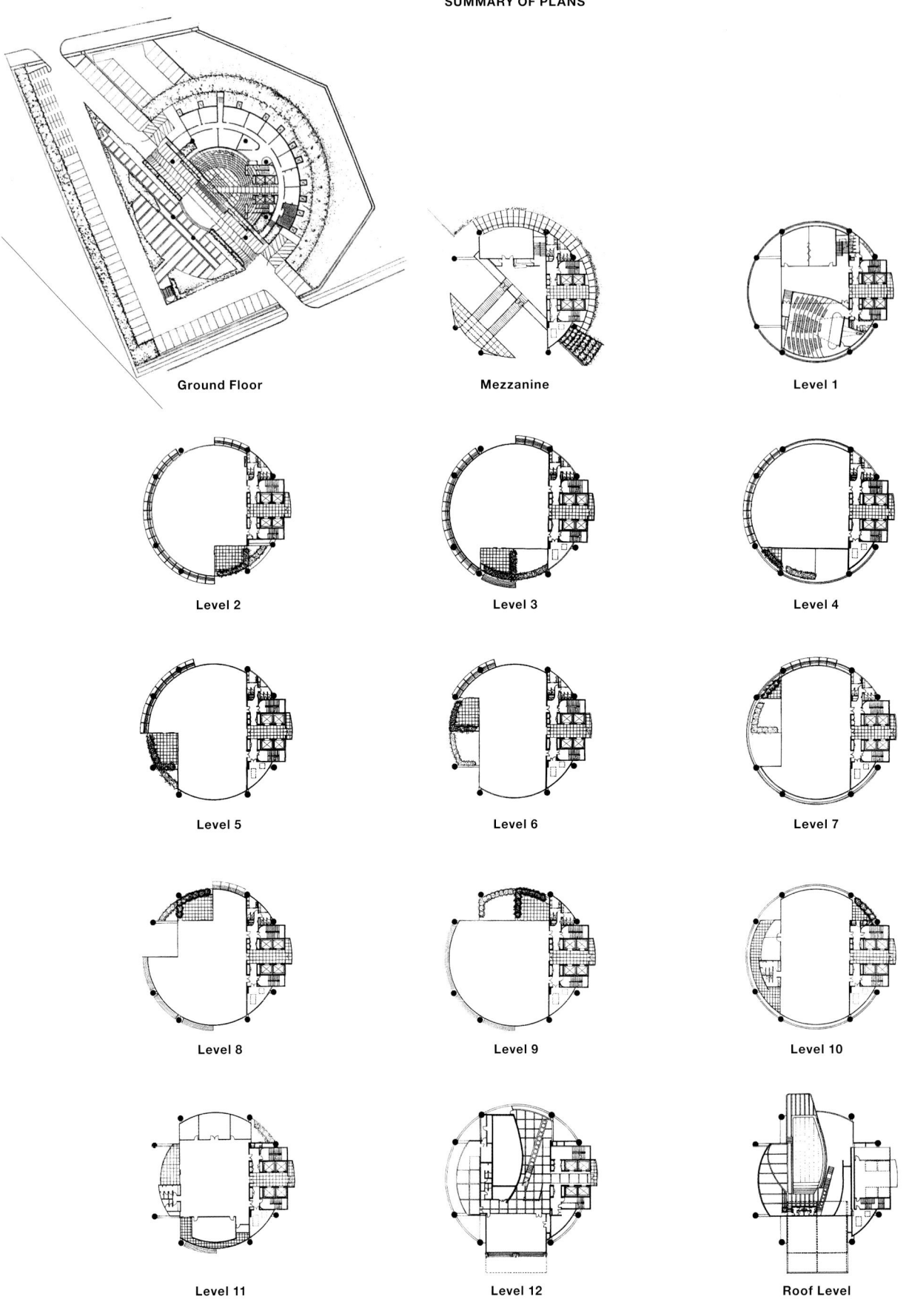

Level 10

Level 11

Level 12

Roof Level

▶ Ground level view of shading devices

PASSIVE SOLAR STRATEGY

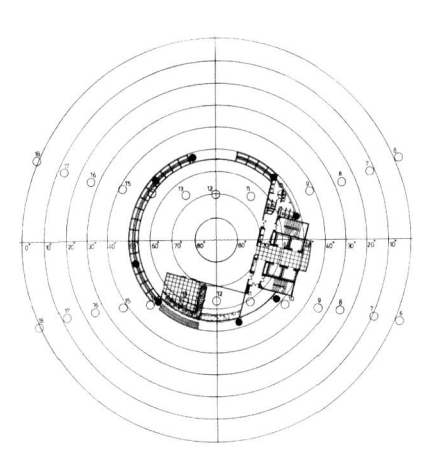

Sun Path Diagram

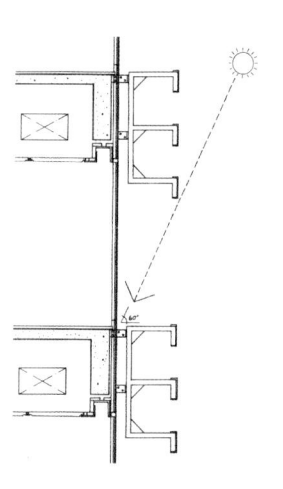

Sunshade Detail

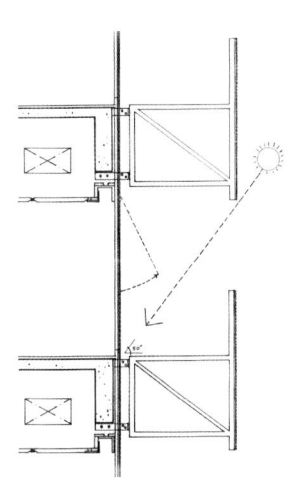

Sunshade Detail

CONTINUOUS LANDSCAPE CONCEPT

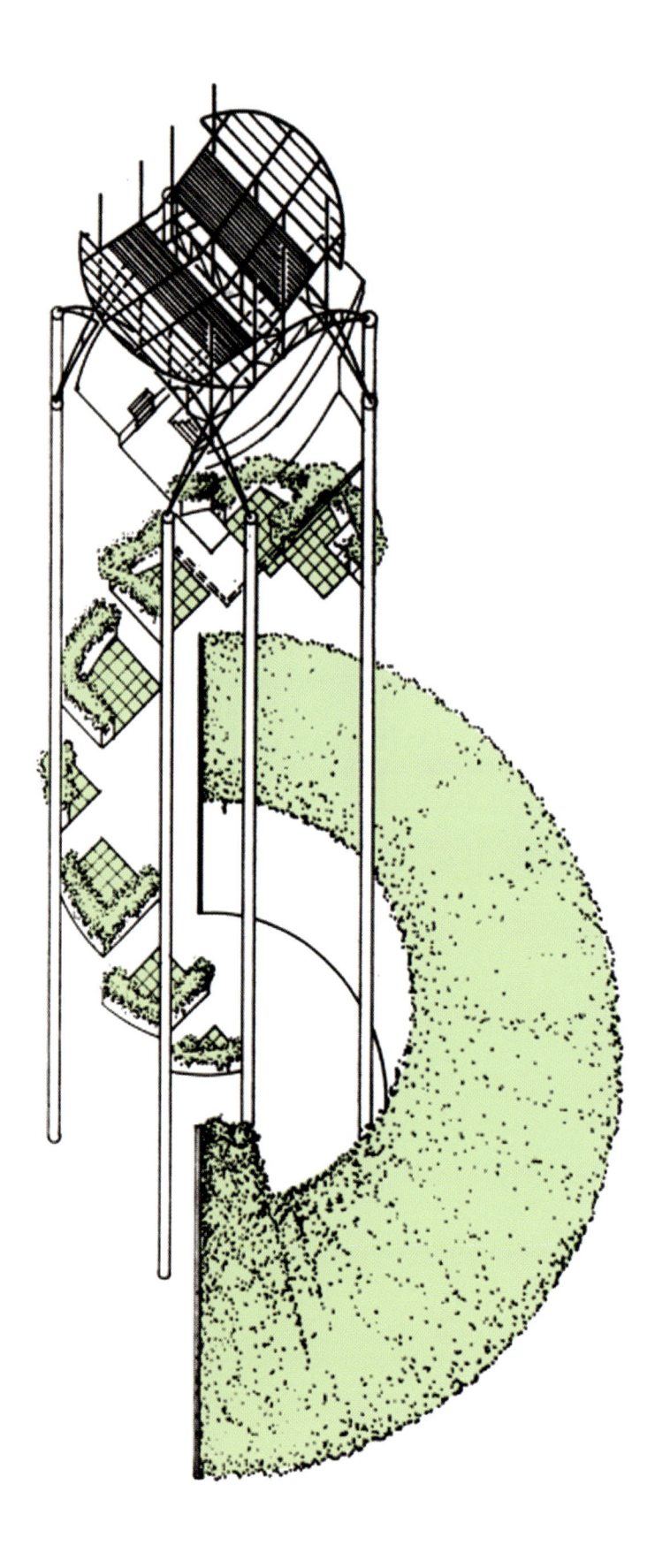

SKETCH PERSPECTIVE

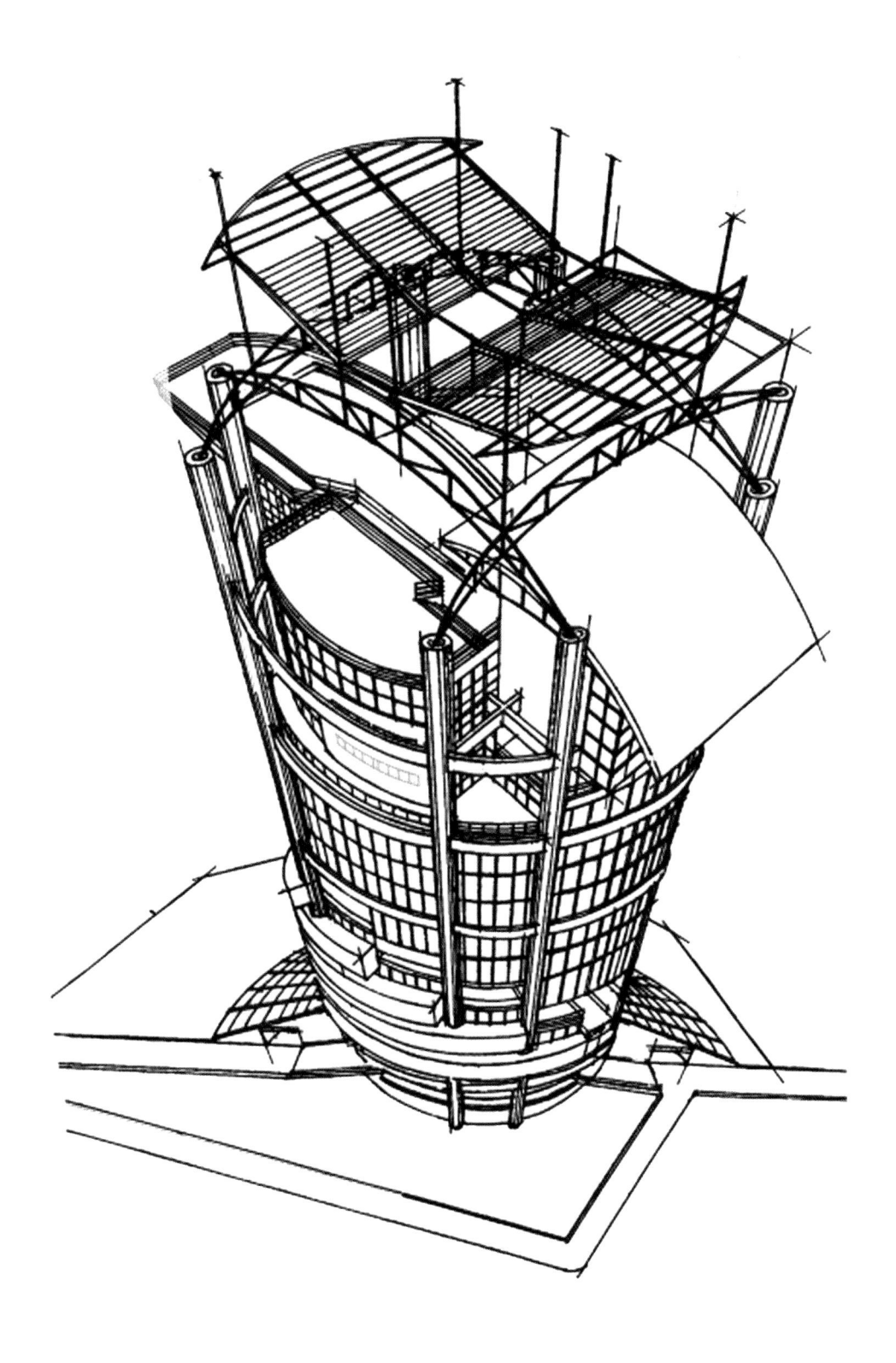

▲ The Menara Mesiniaga on the skyline ▶ Roof canopy from below

64 ECOARCHITECTURE | THE WORK OF KEN YEANG

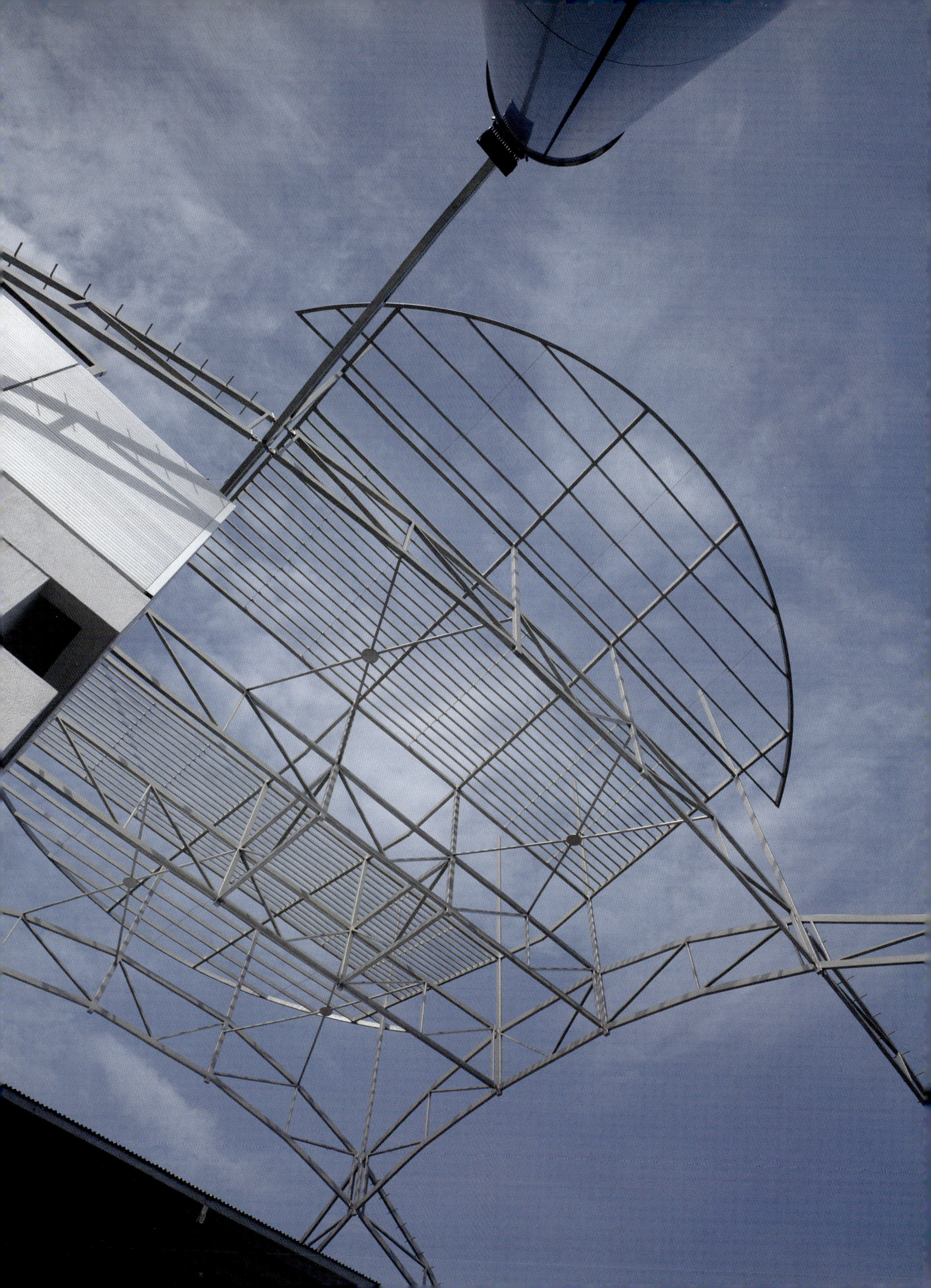

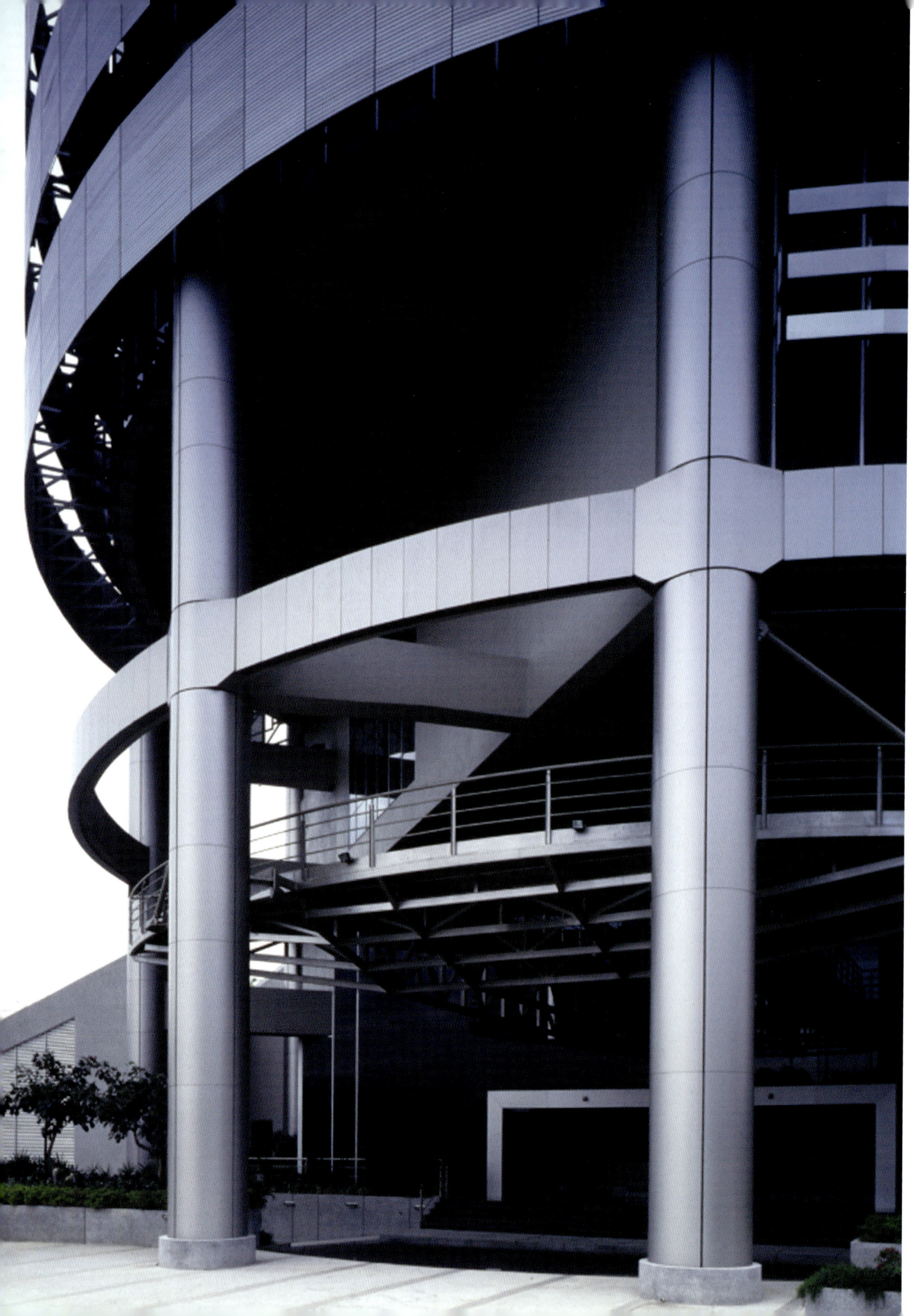

▲ The expressed structure of the entrance canopy

▲ Skycourt accessible from adjacent offices

▲ Rooftop swimming pool
◀ Entrance to the Menara Mesiniaga

CHAPTER 2 EcoMasterplanning as Biointegration

After his early work developing the principles of bioclimatic buildings, Yeang began exploring how an environmentally responsive approach could be applied to masterplans and landscapes. Greatly influenced by the ecological land-use planning approach of the Scottish landscape architect Ian McHarg (one of Yeang's early mentors), Yeang developed a method based on the integration of what he calls "the four armatures for masterplanning". These colour-coded strategies comprise:

• green (nature's processes such as photosynthesis, decomposition and food chains);

• grey (ecotechnologies, hard infrastructure and clean engineering);

• blue (water management and sustainable drainage); and

• red (human systems, the uses to which spaces are put, and regulatory systems).

Yeang has sought to integrate all four armatures throughout his masterplanning activities, for which he has developed his own nomenclature such as "ecological corridors", "green walls", "ecobridges and ecoundercrofts", "ecocells" and "skycourts". It is an architecture of inter-connectivity, one which seeks create physical links between all elements within a masterplan with the intention of making it act, like a natural ecosystem, as a coherent whole. This approach differs from more conventional approaches in that the ecomasterplanning agenda seeks to retain the integrity of ecological connectivity and habitat functions, preserving (and enhancing where possible) biodiversity, and habitat resilience and survival. An important feature of the masterplanning process, which at the time of writing was moving into the realm of biodiversity targets, is that the designs put a premium on both horizontal and vertical connectivity. That means designing not just in plan, but in section. Yeang's approach, when all four armatures are in balance, combines social utility with drainage, shading with biodiversity, landscaping with animals' need for migration. He contrives to stretch pre-existing flora across a development site, and will compensate for development in one zone by enhancing the "green armature" in another. These masterplans are conceived as attempts to achieve an overall ecological balance, that of a rain forest, from basement to rooftop.

The first masterplans in which Yeang developed these principles were designed for Huanan and Kowloon. Here, he employed landscaped bridges, for ecological connectivity, and ecocells – a void which brings light, air, water and vegetation down to basement level, at which point water is stored and recycled. These devices were further developed in the Soma Masterplan. In terms of process, Yeang conducts a site and programme analysis in order to determine which of his four armatures provides the best starting point – rather than work across all four of his colour-coded strategies simultaneously, he selects the one which best matches site need and then wraps the others around it. Yeang first identifies the characteristics of the four infrastructures, then pursues strategies that will merge them. With the Soma masterplan (pages 70-83) in Bangalore, Yeang allowed the concept of a green infrastructure to drive the process; in contrast, the Huanan masterplan (pages 84-91) began with the "grey" infrastructure of access roads and a utilities network – an approach he repeated with the Zorlu project (pages 232-9). Extreme climates require different strategies. With the Plaza of Nations scheme (pages 92-101) in Vancouver, the green infrastructure resides in small enclosures, creating winter gardens, to protect it from the cold and the climatic swings of a temperate climate. Here, Yeang uses eco-bridges to connect the towers at their upper levels, extending vegetation high into the air.

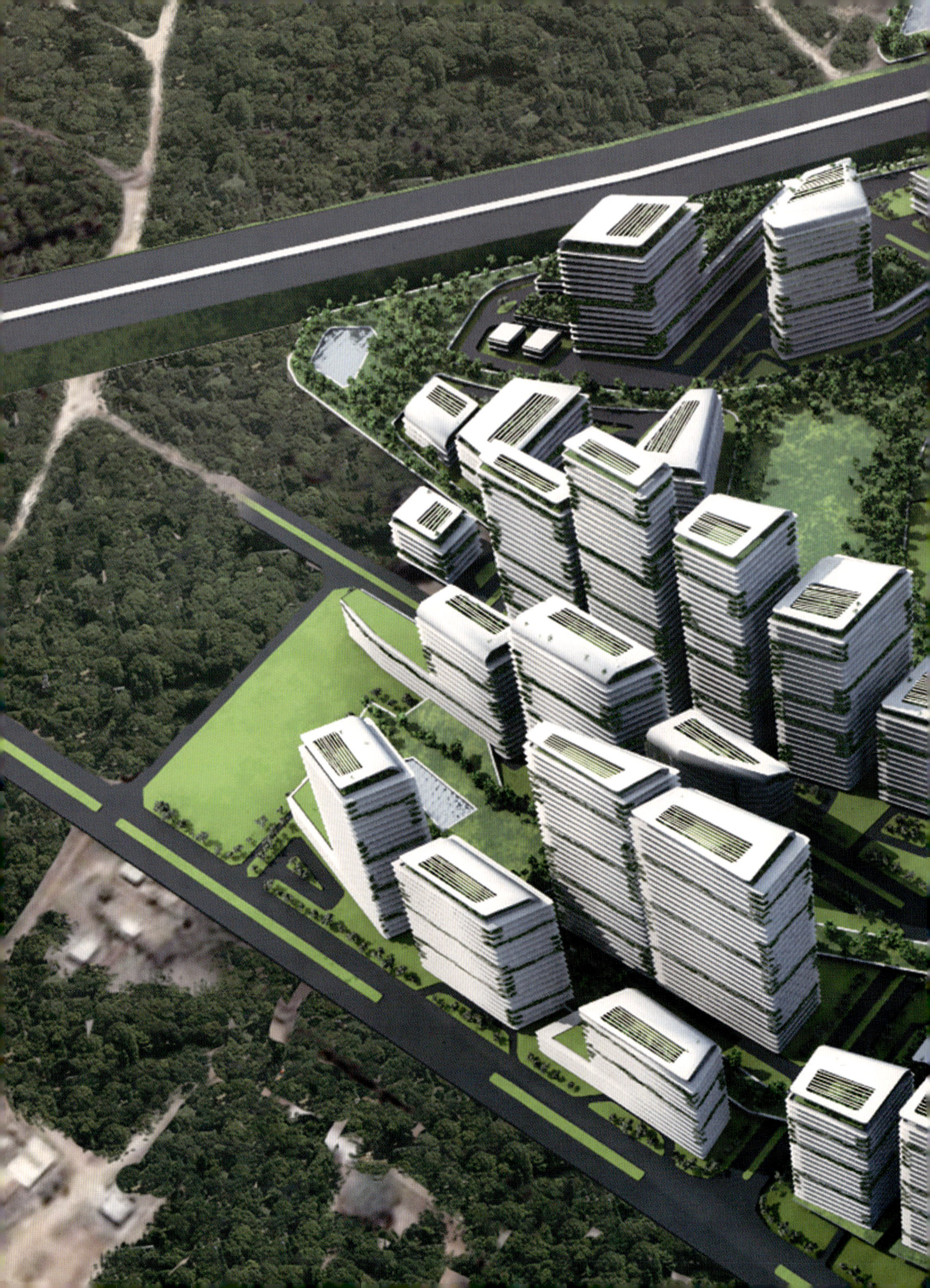

Soma Masterplan

Soma Masterplan

TYPE	:	Eco Masterplan
LOCATION	:	Bangalore, India
CLIMATE ZONE	:	Tropical
VEGETATION ZONE	:	Rainforest

AREAS:

GFA	:	2,000,000 m²
SITE AREA	:	867,500 m²
PLOT RATIO	:	1:2.3
STATUS	:	Under Construction
DATE	:	2008

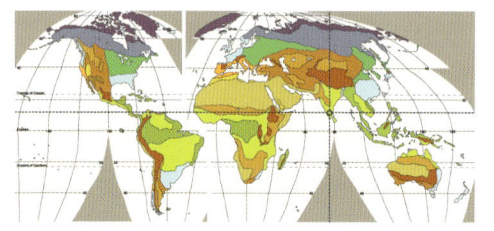

CLIMATE REGION

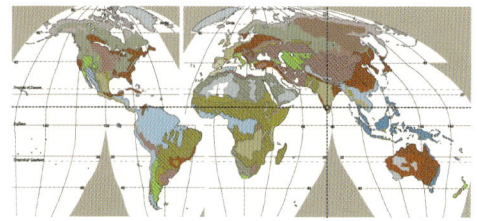

VEGETATION ZONE

Conceptual

▲ Computer model, night view

This masterplan for a middle-class suburb outside Bangalore commissioned by a private development company based in Ahmedabad represents a pivotal advancement of Yeang's theories-into-practice process. It signifies a benchmark in the development of a search for a green aesthetic in masterplanning which began with Yeang's earlier Huanan masterplan in Guangzhou in China (pages 84-91) and which was later refined in the Zorlu scheme for Istanbul, Turkey (pages 232-9). The project also introduces green ecoinfrastructure as the driving configuration for the masterplan.

The design takes advantage of the site's "green hinterland" and stretches fingers, or ecological corridors, from this neighbouring zone right across the development site "like chewing gum", says Yeang. "These ideas were advanced here into a full-blown landscaped, urbanism-masterplanning approach driven by the green ecoinfrastructure. It pursues notions of an ecological nexus that links natural and artificial ecosystems. The platform that emerges has its own ecological aesthetic that defines it as a style for ecomasterplanning," he says. In the same way as Yeang had often asked what a green building should or could look like, here he asks the same question of a green masterplan.

The site, covering nearly 87 acres, abuts an existent forest reserve. Yeang began by setting out a long green corridor along the forest edge which is then drawn across the masterplan to establish a framework of green ecoinfrastructure. As explained elsewhere in this book, Yeang describes ecomasterplanning as that which incorporates four strands of thinking and areas of attention, which Yeang colour-codes as green, grey, blue and red. Green strategies concern what he calls "nature's utilities", such as photosynthesis and food chains; Grey encompasses man-made infrastructure; Blue describes water management and sustainable drainage; and Red covers human systems such as culture, diet, rules and regulations. Although the four strands need to be considered together in order to arrive at a coherent and meaningful ecomasterplan, Yeang admits, however, that it is often difficult to take all four elements as a starting point. What the designer must do, he says, is ask which colour best catalyses the others for the site in question, which colour is the most appropriate jumping off point for the brief and the site. Here, it was green.

Here, the green ecoinfrastructure of continuous corridors of vegetation provides a framework for all other infrastructure systems. A blue water management system feeds a number retention ponds distributed across the site that enables the land's aquifers to be recharged; the grey ecoinfrastructiure manifests itself as access roads and transportation systems that encourage the reduced use of private vehicles (as well as other ecoengineering utilities and systems); while the red ecoinfrastructure drove the organisation of the communities, spaces, "hardscapes" and structures. Interestingly, Yeang also deployed the principles of Vaastu Shastra – the Indian system of "geomancy" which directs direction, movement and space through a study of earth, air, fire and water –

▲ Ecological bridge

Zoning

Grey EcoInfrastructure: Traffic & Road Hierarchy

Green EcoInfrastructure

▲ Computer model, tower greenery

as a further "tentatively metaphysical" way of balancing the organic and inorganic throughout the masterplan.

The masterplan provides for a development of a variety of functions and building types, including a daycare centre, a retirement home, schools, a sports centre and a health clinic. Fifty per cent of the programme is devoted to residential construction, responding to the demand for housing from the burgeoning middle class in Bangalore as the city rapidly expands in size. It includes luxury villas and low- and high-rise apartments and townhouses. Public outdoor spaces vary in size and character; high-rise and larger buildings occupy larger, more open plots than smaller units. Apart from roads, water and sewage plants, the development includes an electricity sub-station and a telecommunications tower. Eighteen per cent of the plan is reserved for green open spaces, which weave through the site across bridges and within tunnels to maximise connectivity and prevent flora and fauna being marooned on green islands. Bioswales and retention ponds return storm water runoff back into the local aquifer. The masterplan specifies the use of sustainable and recycled materials for building construction, and maximum openings for light and natural ventilation.

The principles established in the Soma masterplan influenced Yeang's thinking on the ecoskyscraper as a vertical landscape – best expressed, perhaps, in the design for the Spire Edge Tower in Manesar (pages 210-7). For this project, Yeang took Soma's horizontal ecoinfrastructure and tilted it vertically. The ideas explored in the Soma masterplan are developed in Yeang's book *Ecomasterplanning* (published by John Wiley & Sons, 2009).

SITE SECTIONS

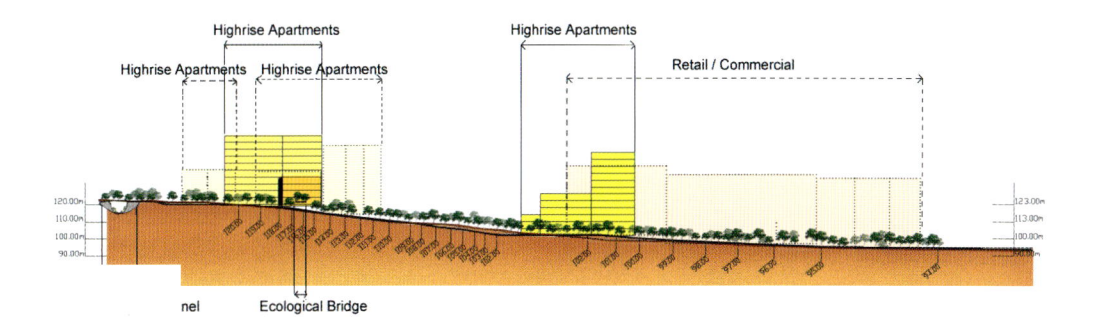

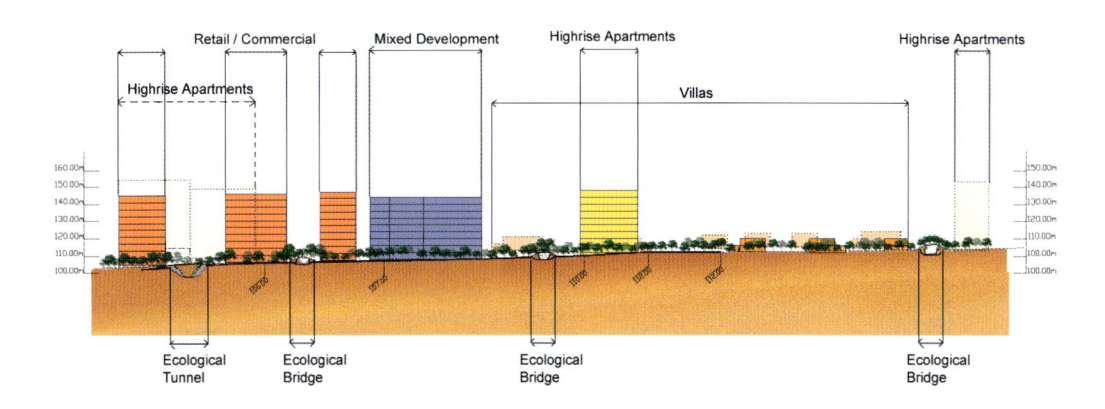

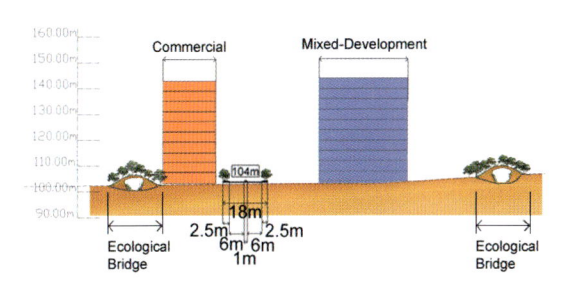

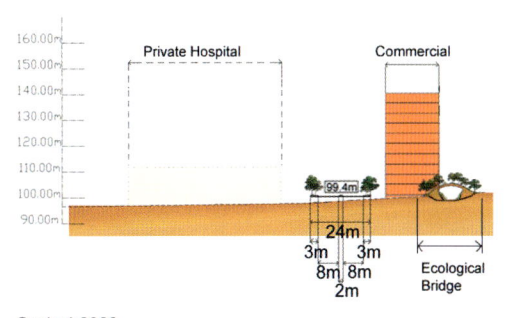

Scale 1:2000

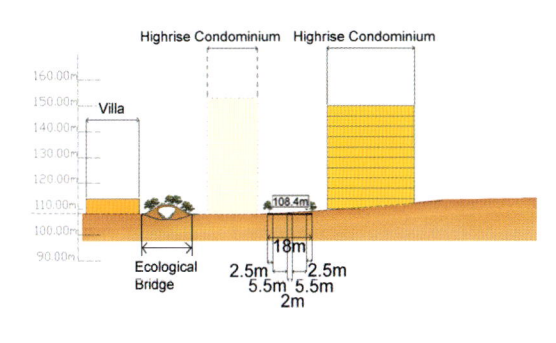

Water Reticulation System

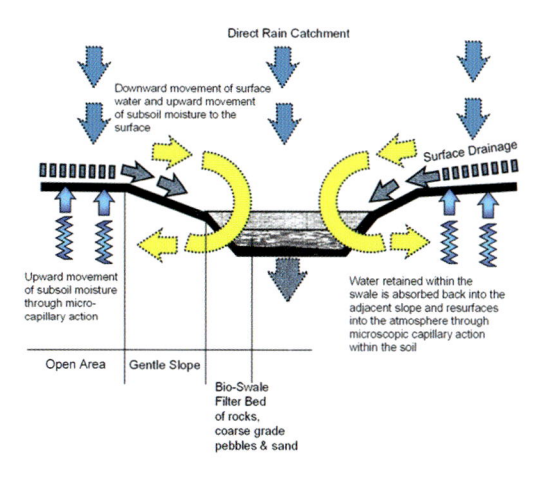

Bioswale Drainage Diagram

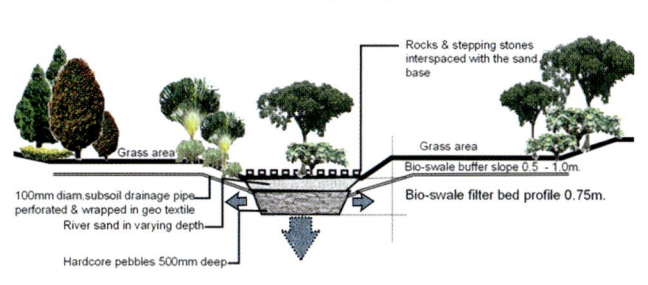

EcoMasterplanning | **Soma Masterplan** 75

▲ Masterplan

76 ECOARCHITECTURE | THE WORK OF KEN YEANG

LAND USE ZONING

Landuse	Nos	%	Acre	Hectares	GFA (sqm)
Residential		50%	41.17	16.66	446,366
Luxury villas	53				
Low rise luxury apartments	526				
High rise apartments	444				
Row house	200				
Service apartment	193				
Commercial / Retail	4	14.5%	12	4.83	103,357
Green open space		18%	14.8	6	
Civic amenities	4	4%	3.3	1.33	7,455
Infrastructure		13%	10.7	10.7	
		100%	82.33	33.31	557,198

Legend
- Residential
- Retail/commercial
- Mixed
- Civic amenities
- Services
- Propose Future Expansion for Labour Housing

EcoMasterplanning | Soma Masterplan

Legend
- Ecological Corridors (Big Trees)
- Boulevard Trees
- Secondary Vegetation
- Ground Cover

▲ Ecological and vegetation concept

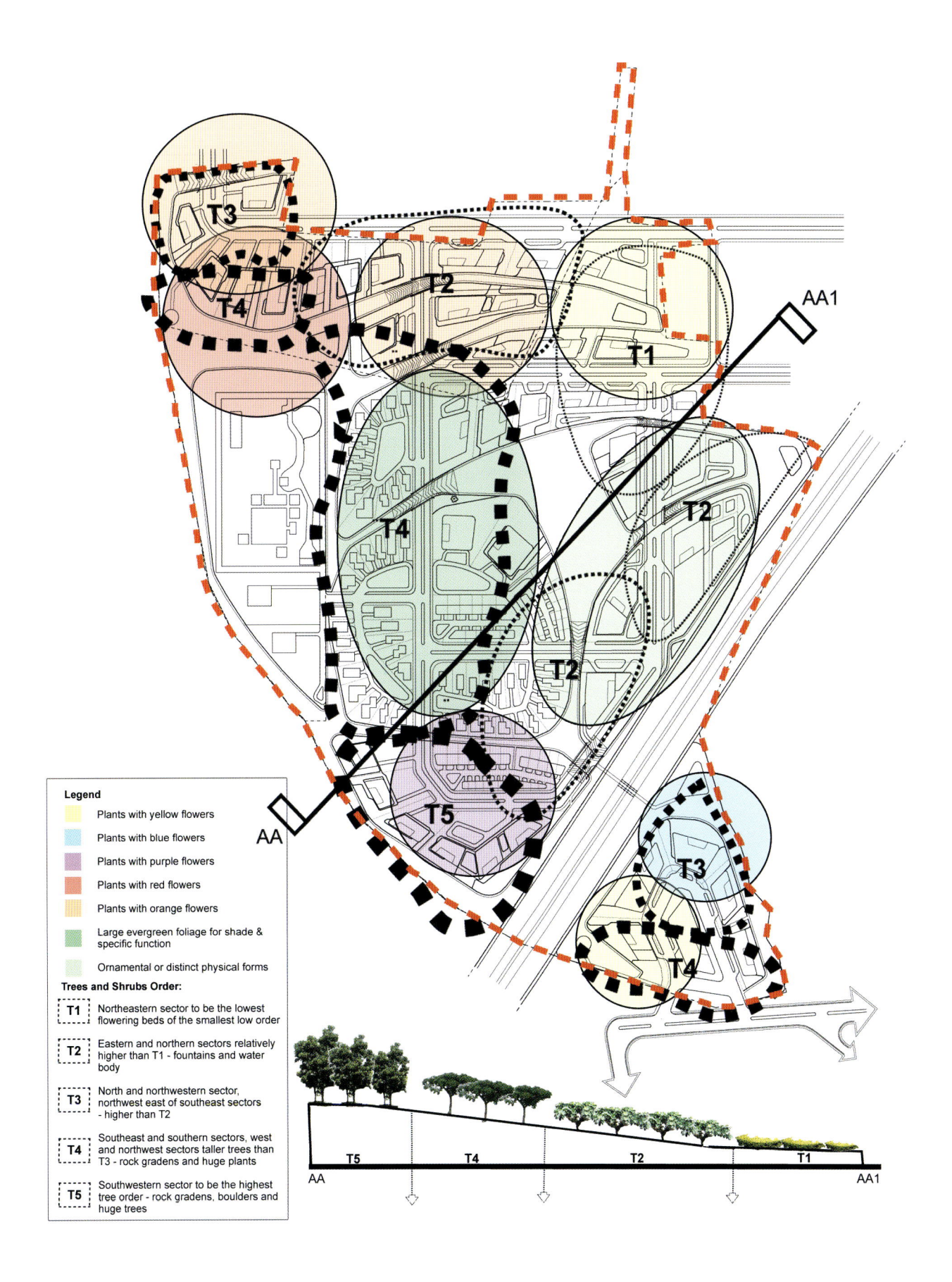

LANDSCAPE CONCEPT

Legend

- Plants with yellow flowers
- Plants with blue flowers
- Plants with purple flowers
- Plants with red flowers
- Plants with orange flowers
- Large evergreen foliage for shade & specific function
- Ornamental or distinct physical forms

Trees and Shrubs Order:

- **T1** Northeastern sector to be the lowest flowering beds of the smallest low order
- **T2** Eastern and northern sectors relatively higher than T1 - fountains and water body
- **T3** North and northwestern sector, northwest east of southeast sectors - higher than T2
- **T4** Southeast and southern sectors, west and northwest sectors taller trees than T3 - rock gradens and huge plants
- **T5** Southwestern sector to be the highest tree order - rock gradens, boulders and huge trees

EcoMasterplanning | Soma Masterplan 79

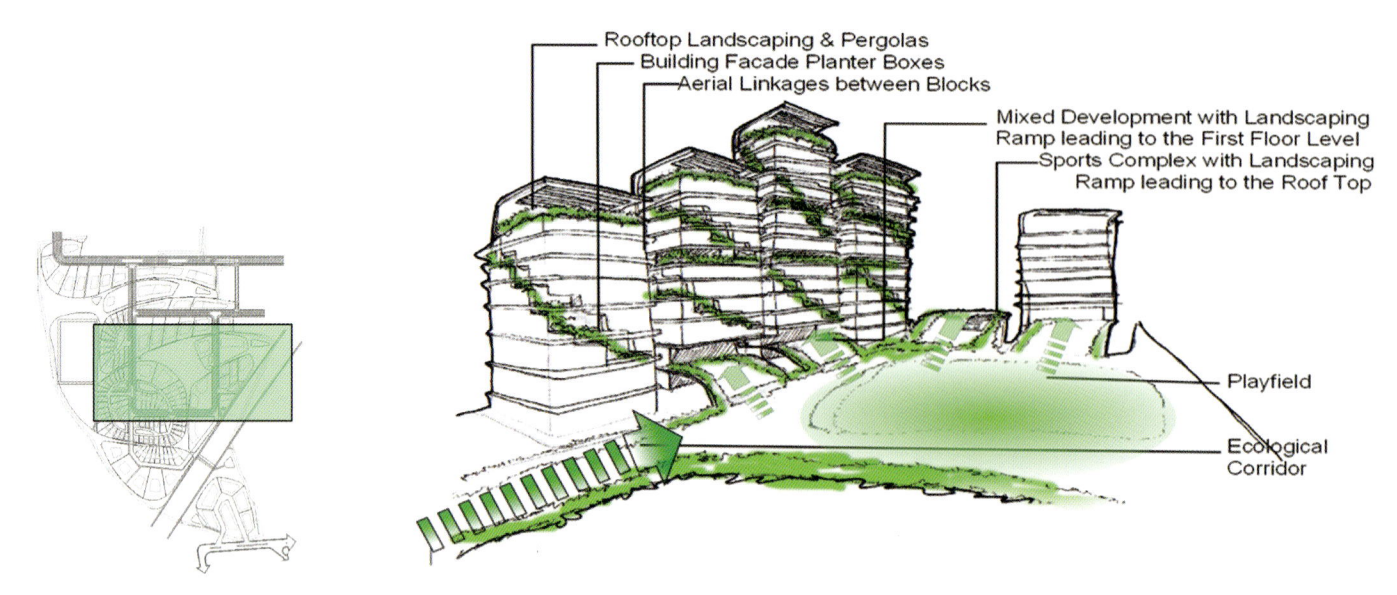

Reference Plan

Sketch Showing the Correlation Between Open Spaces and Buildings

Labels:
- Rooftop Landscaping & Pergolas
- Building Facade Planter Boxes
- Aerial Linkages between Blocks
- Mixed Development with Landscaping Ramp leading to the First Floor Level
- Sports Complex with Landscaping Ramp leading to the Roof Top
- Playfield
- Ecological Corridor

Neighbourhood Cluster Detail

Labels:
- Forest Planting
- Children's Playground
- Contributory Planting From Adjacent Buildings
- Rooftop & Aerial Linkages
- Temple Building
- Bio swale Wetland & Retention Pond
- Sports Club Gymkhana
- Primary School
- Polyclinic, Daycare Centre Post Office
- Senior Home
- Ecological Corridor Planting & Eco Bridge
- Space linkages from small children's playground to larger open space
- Central Multi use Open Space incorporated as part of the Ecological Corridor

80 ECOARCHITECTURE | THE WORK OF KEN YEANG

Reference Plan

Components of the Ecological Corridor – Ecobridges, Ecotunnels and Bioswales

Planting medium on the ecological bridge is about 1 meter deep for shrubs and small trees with non-extensive rooting

Use of earth berms to create surface undulations and space definitions

Planting on slopes for erosion control and soil replenishment

Use of bio-swales for surface water management and replenishment of subsoil

- Watering tank from grey water from apartment
- Clubhouse
- Contributory planting from adjacent apartment
- Walkways & Playarea
- Forest Planting
- Bio swale
- Bio swale & wetland
- Eco bridge & planting
- Rooftop planting & pergolas
- Ornamental pond

Neighbourhood Cluster Detail

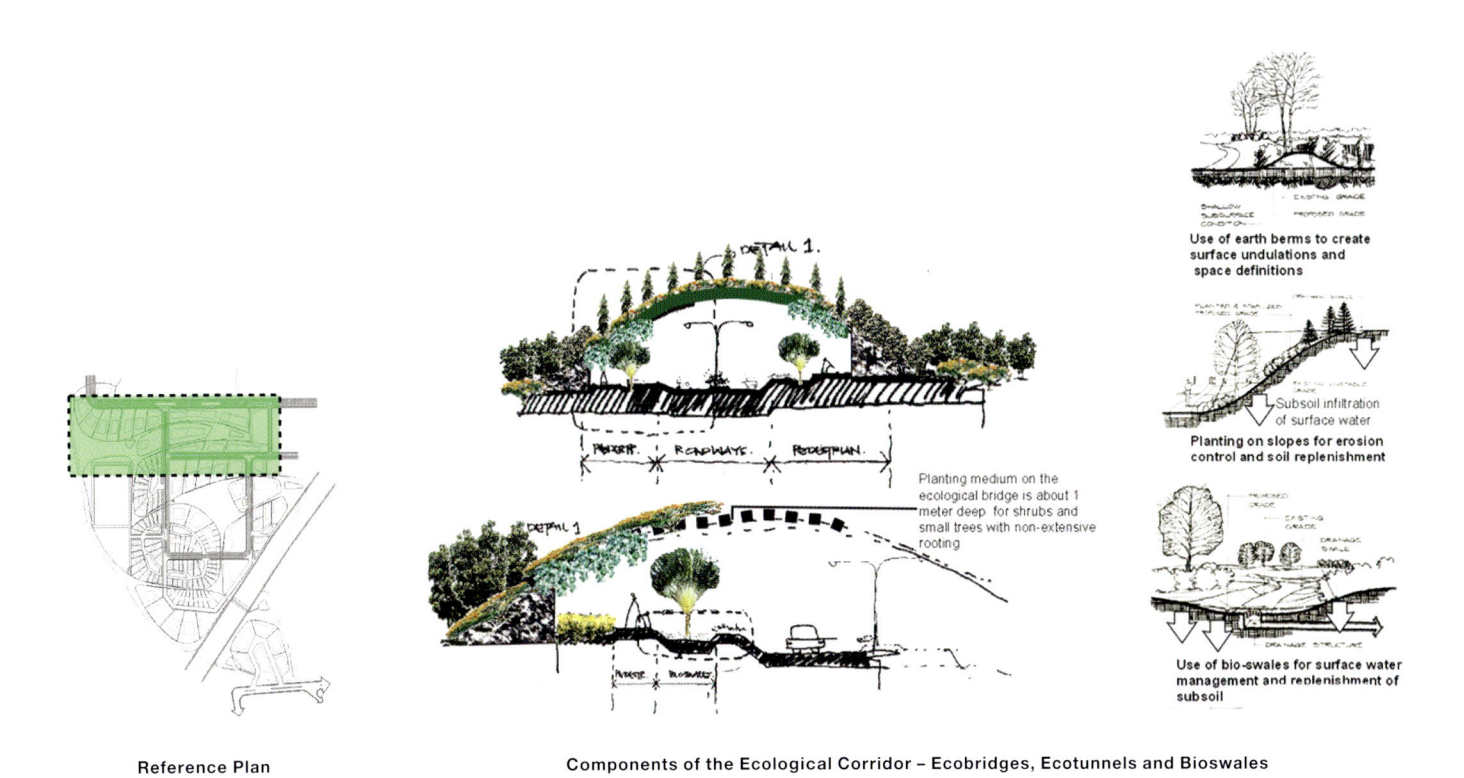

EcoMasterplanning | Soma Masterplan 81

▲ Computer model, aerial view

CONSTRUCTED WETLAND FOR WATER PURIFICATION

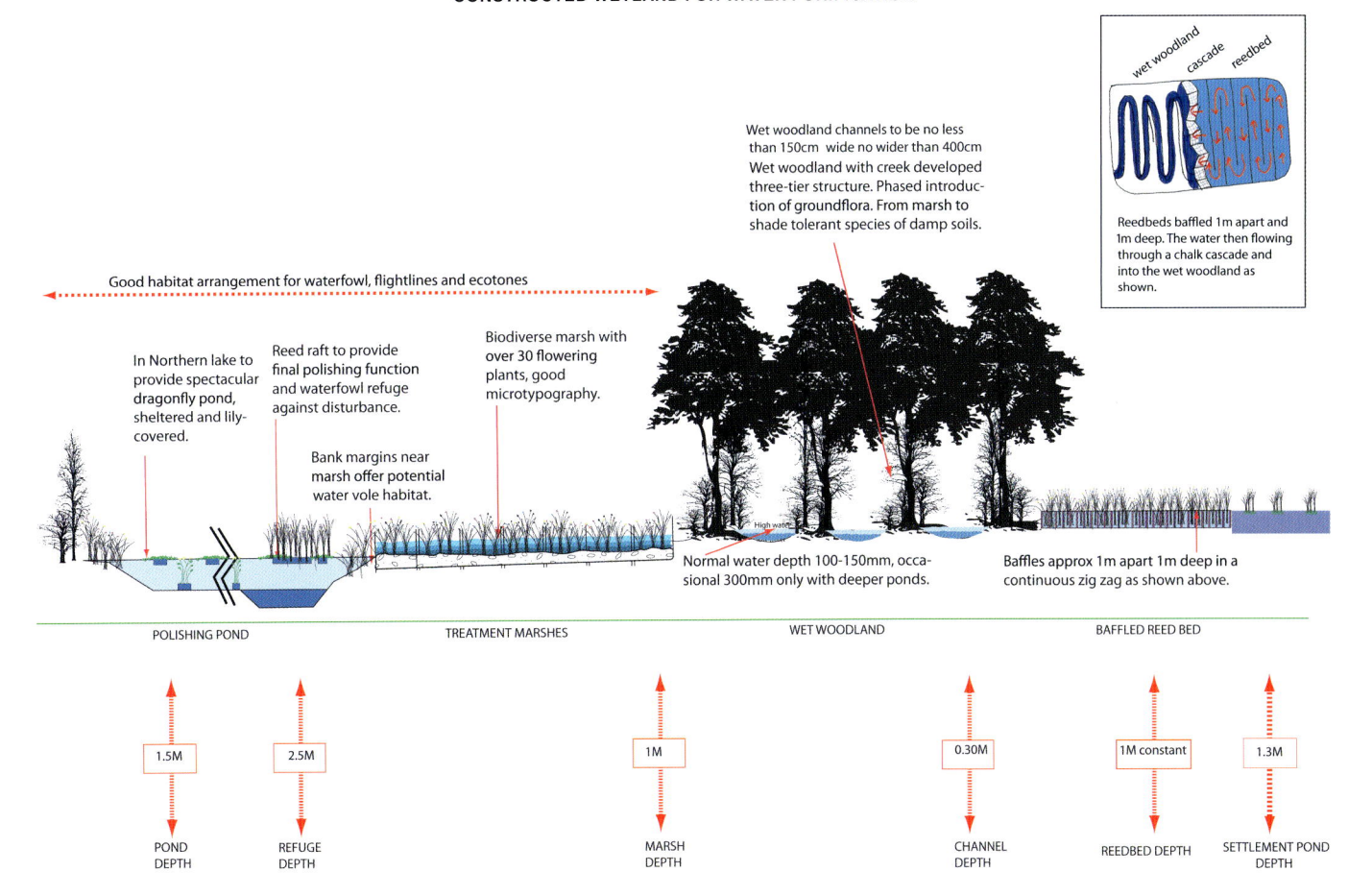

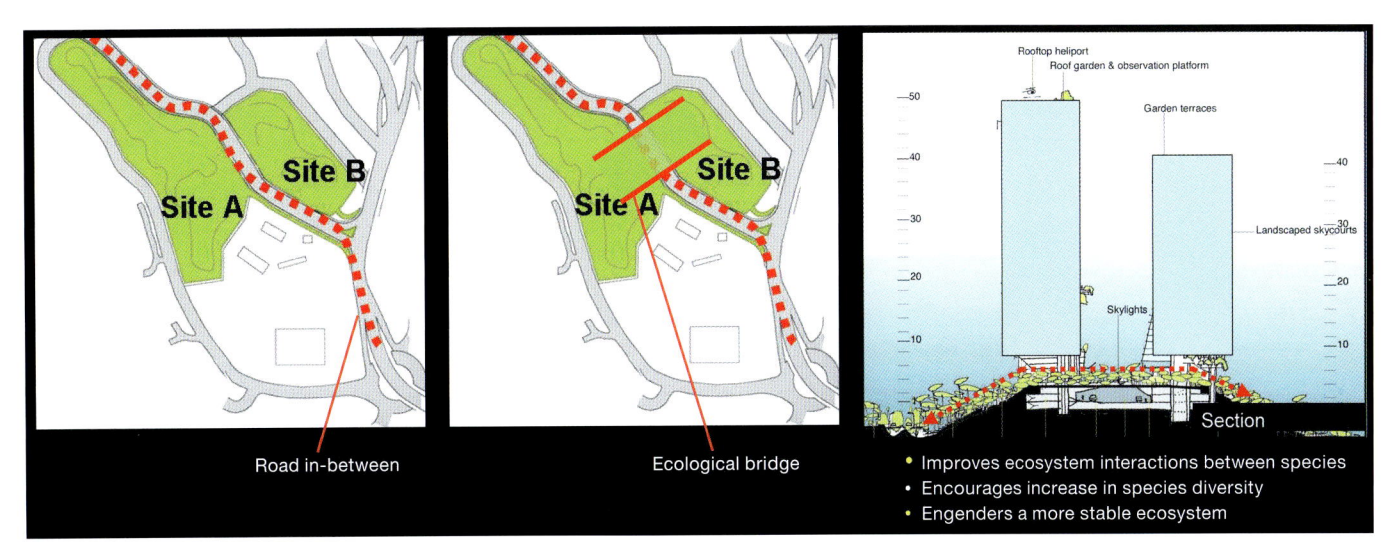

Reedbeds baffled 1m apart and 1m deep. The water then flowing through a chalk cascade and into the wet woodland as shown.

Good habitat arrangement for waterfowl, flightlines and ecotones

In Northern lake to provide spectacular dragonfly pond, sheltered and lily-covered.

Reed raft to provide final polishing function and waterfowl refuge against disturbance.

Bank margins near marsh offer potential water vole habitat.

Biodiverse marsh with over 30 flowering plants, good microtypography.

Wet woodland channels to be no less than 150cm wide no wider than 400cm. Wet woodland with creek developed three-tier structure. Phased introduction of groundflora. From marsh to shade tolerant species of damp soils.

Normal water depth 100-150mm, occasional 300mm only with deeper ponds.

Baffles approx 1m apart 1m deep in a continuous zig zag as shown above.

POLISHING POND | **TREATMENT MARSHES** | **WET WOODLAND** | **BAFFLED REED BED**

1.5M	2.5M	1M	0.30M	1M constant	1.3M
POND DEPTH	REFUGE DEPTH	MARSH DEPTH	CHANNEL DEPTH	REEDBED DEPTH	SETTLEMENT POND DEPTH

Road in-between

Ecological bridge

- Improves ecosystem interactions between species
- Encourages increase in species diversity
- Engenders a more stable ecosystem

▲ Ecological bridge concept diagram

EcoMasterplanning | Soma Masterplan

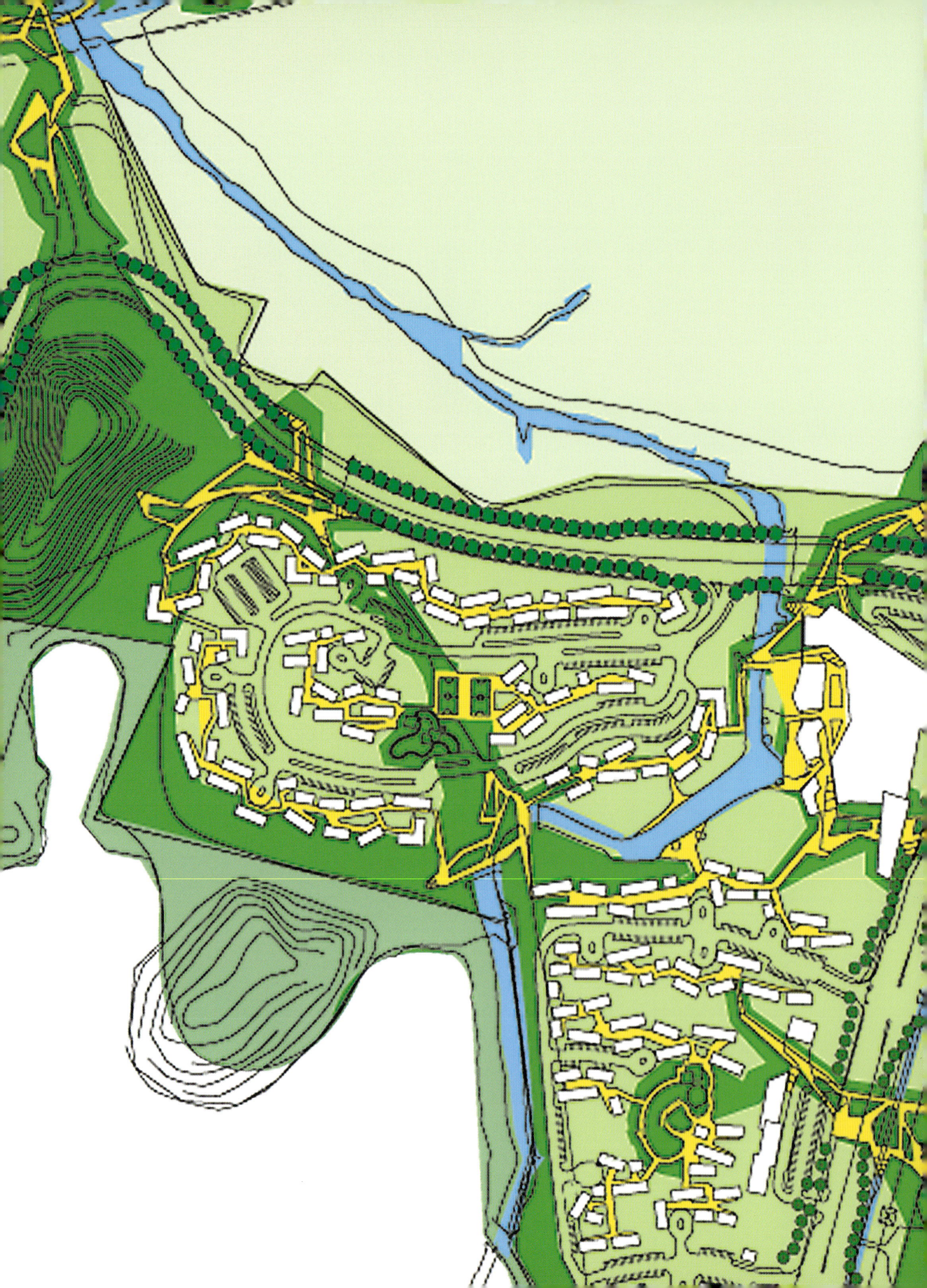

Huanan New City

Huanan New City

TYPE	:	Eco Masterplan
LOCATION	:	Guangzhou, China
CLIMATE ZONE	:	Subtropical
VEGETATION ZONE	:	Temperate Rainforest

AREAS:

GFA	:	4,000,000 m²
SITE AREA	:	2,900,000 m²
PLOT RATIO	:	1:1.4
STATUS	:	Concept Design
DATE	:	1999

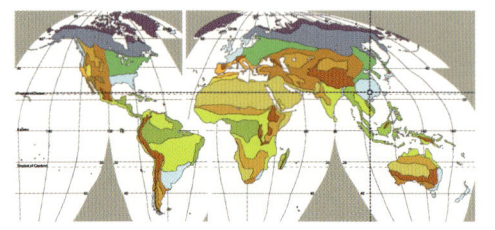

CLIMATE REGION

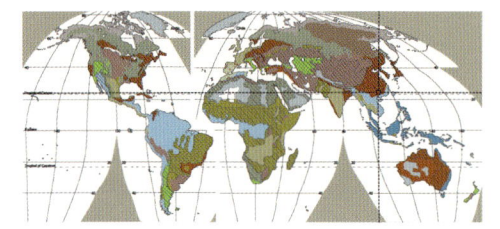

VEGETATION ZONE

Conceptual

▲ Aerial view of model, emphasising contours

This masterplan for a small township in southern China enabled Yeang to show what an iconic, green masterplan could look like. Yeang designed the scheme as a demonstration of the principle that human development can be integrated within nature, allowing it to remain interconnected and whole rather than blighted and diminished. This is significant, especially in China – as a nation with a poor record on ecology, the country is now conscious of the need to develop more sustainably. It was with this project that Yeang developed the idea of linked elements of vegetation which weave across the development zone, preserving the ecology, biodiversity and micro-climates of the site. "For the first time we used eco-bridges and undercrofts to extend the natural world into and throughout the site. In nature, everything is linked – it is only human beings who fragment nature, fragment the landscape. With this project we link the site with its hinterland, demonstrating that you can maintain the ecological nexus of the habitat while also developing the site," says Yeang. What is distinctive within the design is Yeang's use of wide landscaped ecobridges and eco-undercrofts (also used in an earlier scheme for the University of Amsterdam) as devices to maintain large scale ecological connectivity.

This masterplan is a competition-winning scheme for a new residential settlement at Huanan New City, located on 500 acres on the northern banks of the Pearl River near Guangzhou. It contains a full range of public and commercial facilities, transportation links and public, open spaces. The waterfront complex, when complete, will include a marina supported by retail and recreational venues. The site, adjacent to an elevated highway, is laid out as a patchwork quilt, with particular areas left undisturbed while ecobridges traverse the site as green "saddle stitches". These landscaped bridges act as a device to connect the green spaces and hills on the site, "maintaining an integrated ecological whole which performs as a single connected habitat," says

▲ Aerial view of masterplan

Yeang. "This is an approach to masterplanning not done elsewhere – based on the principle of urban design based on maintaining the ecological nexus as a key planning criterion."

This masterplanning approach is classic Yeang. The ecomasterplanning begins with a series of ecological landuse mappings to ascertain the parts of the site which permit building – a planning technique which he learnt from McHarg. Overlaid, these studies created a composite map that enabled Yeang to lay out access roads and a utilities network, over which (in turn) the ecological ecoinfrastructure is set. This approach was again adopted in Yeang's Zorlu masterplan for Istanbul, but it is, in fact, the reverse of the process by which the Soma masterplan was handled (pages 70-83); with Soma, a flat site, Yeang began by laying out the green infrastructure. At Huanan, the site contains a number of small but identifiable knolls which have remained untouched, preserved as natural features within the masterplan. Communities are laid out to minimise the use of private cars and encourage walking, cycling and the use of public transportation. These communities are threaded together by pedestrian paths, independent of the main tree-lined boulevards. Each neighbourhood is designed to be self-sufficient with its own commercial, recreational and educational facilities.

The buildings largely comprise high-rise apartments and two-storey row houses. The high-rise units, oriented north–south, cluster around courtyards to aid natural ventilation, while folding and louvred shutters will allow tenants to control the amount of solar infiltration. Further shading is provided by courtyard overhangs. The low-rise "court-houses", arranged in rows around the knolls, contain raised terraces (large enough to support future expansion of the house) which overlook ground-floor courtyards. This is a seminal project for Yeang, who believes it is as close to an ideal ecomasterplan as he could achieve.

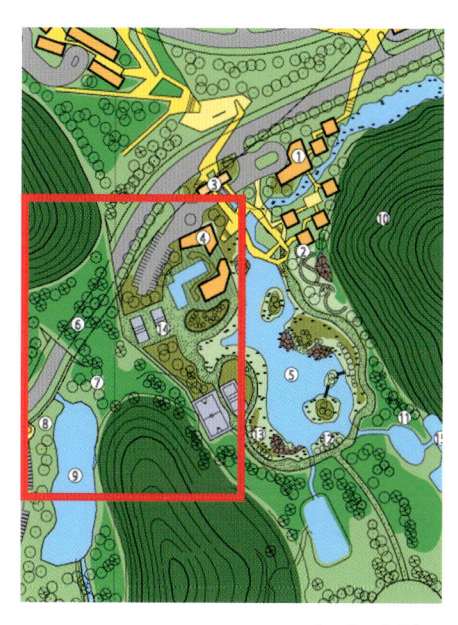

▲ Ecobridge

EcoMasterplanning | Huanan New City 87

▲ Landscape masterplan and ecological linkages

88　ECOARCHITECTURE　|　THE WORK OF KEN YEANG

Small Scale Landscape Linkages to the River Edge
小型绿化地带与人行道

Pedestrian Walkways
人行道

Tree-lined Avenue
树林排之林荫大道

Existing Hillocks Vegetation to be Conserved
保护山丘的植物

N 0 50 250 500 metres

EcoMasterplanning | Huanan New City 89

▲ Aerial view from across the river

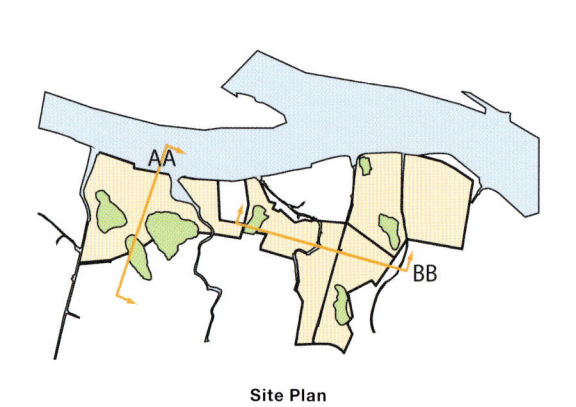

Site Plan

boundary line | natural hillock | apartment units | open & recreational space | apartment units

+30 m
+20 m
+10 m
+0 m
-10 m
-20 m

90 ECOARCHITECTURE | THE WORK OF KEN YEANG

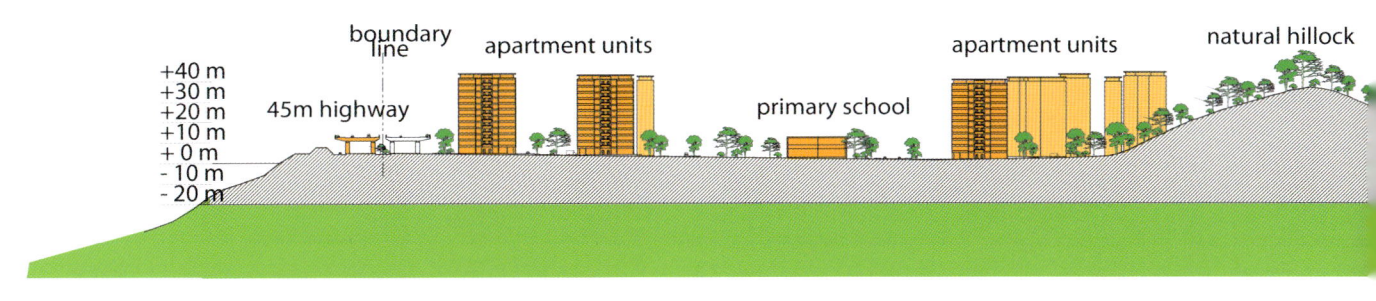

▲ Section A-A

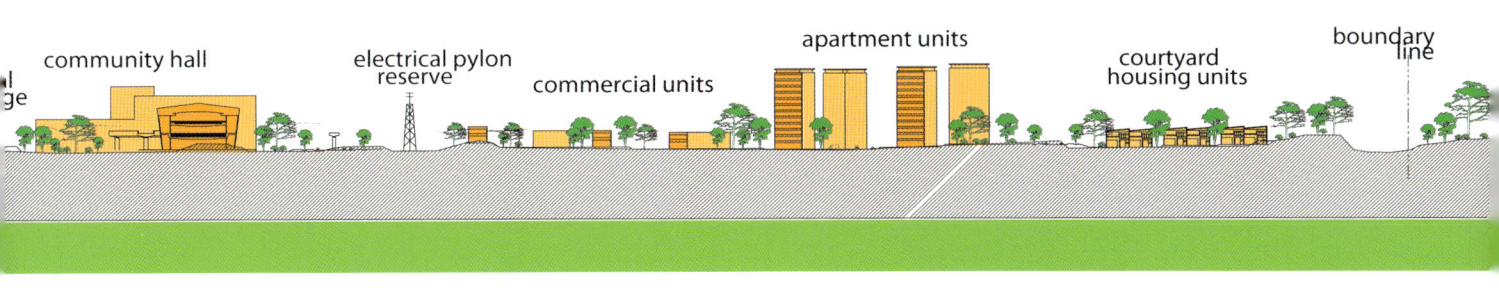

▲ Section B-B

EcoMasterplanning | Huanan New City

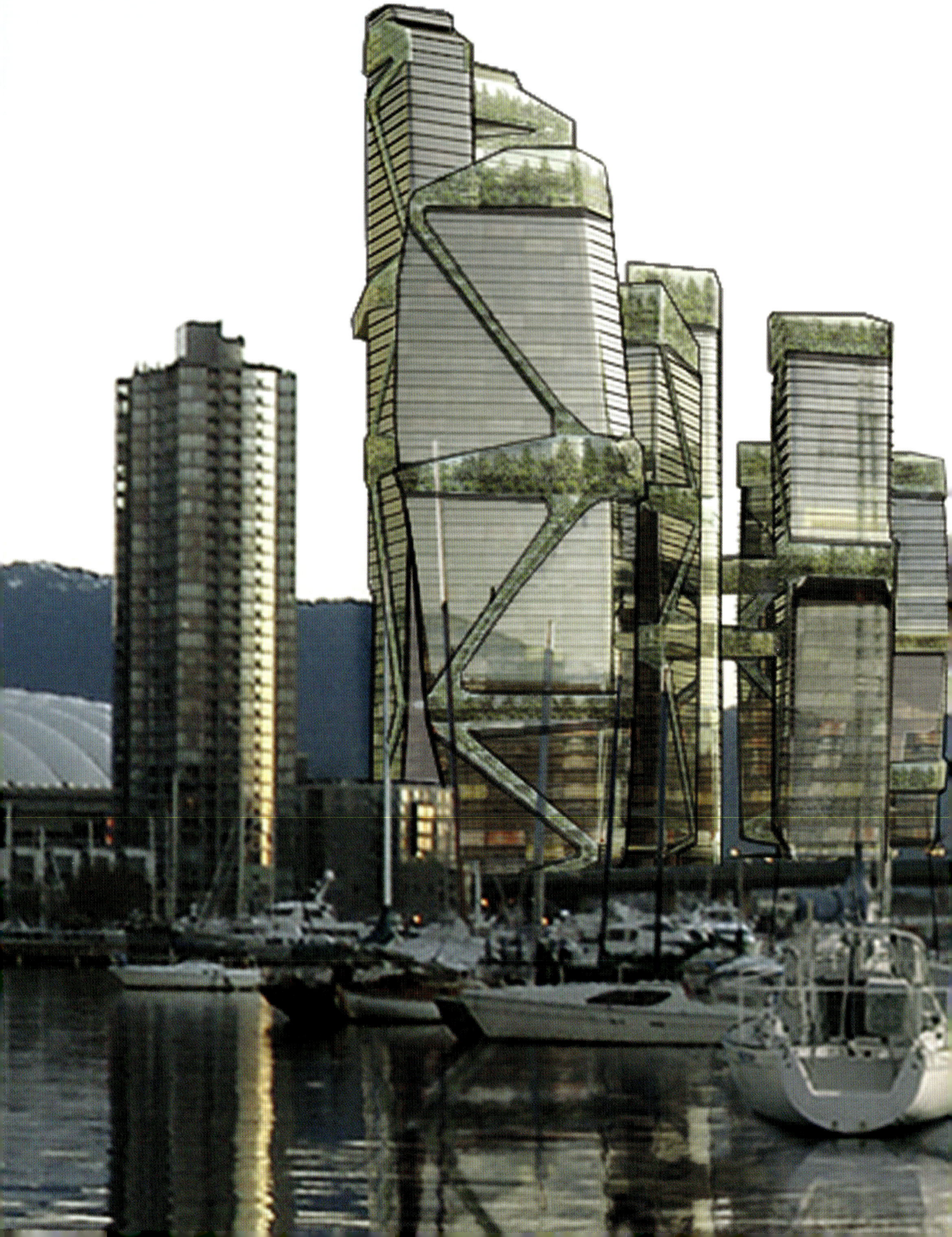

Plaza of Nations

Plaza of Nations

TYPE	:	Eco Masterplan
LOCATION	:	Vancouver, Canada
CLIMATE ZONE	:	Temperate
VEGETATION ZONE	:	Temperate Rainforest

AREAS:

GFA	:	300,000 m²
SITE AREA	:	27,000 m²
PLOT RATIO	:	1:11
NO. OF STOREYS	:	60
STATUS	:	Concept Design
DATE	:	2007

▲ Development (on far right) within the wider False Creek context of Vancouver

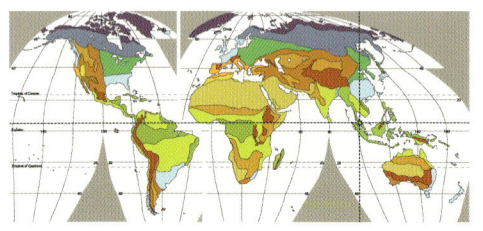

CLIMATE REGION

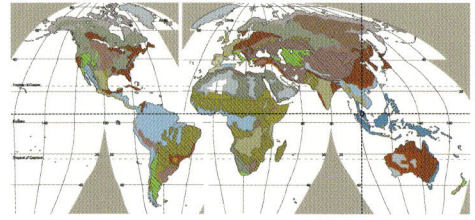

VEGETATION ZONE

Conceptual

The Plaza of Nations complex is one of Yeang's key developments designed for a cold climate; he has also designed for Beijing and London (the Great Ormond Street Children's Hospital Extension), but this scheme for Vancouver is probably the most ambitious demonstration of how Yeang's design principles can be applied outside the tropics.

The project comprises six tower blocks which sit atop a park-covered retail podium. The greenery of the park steps through 90 degrees and then winds up the façades of the towers, and across high level connecting bridges and skycourts, finally arriving at roof level. "My contention is that you should design buildings as artificial ecosystems, as ecomimetic systems," says Yeang. The high-profile planting within this project is a development of the green-bridge concept pioneered in the landscaped bridges of the Huanan masterplan (pages 84-91), and it prefigures the atrium planting of the later Gyeong-Gi Complex . The continuous planting does, in fact, rise in diagonal stretches, giving the towers a green ziggurat pattern. Here, though, the planting is enclosed within the building, which entirely wraps the vegetation during colder periods to convert these green enclosures into winter gardens; glass screens are partially opened during intermediate seasons (spring and autumn) and are fully opened during summer months. The recessed planting, however, is balanced by the protruding, mid-level skycourts. These green, ecological walls lower the ambient temperature within the buildings during hotter seasons, reducing the heat load; they are irrigated by grey water recycling.

Further ecological design features include: passive air circulation, facilitated by taking advantage of the "stack effect" within the seven towers; the installation of micro wind turbines; solar shading; and a strategy of planting only indigenous plant species. "Ecologically, the design possesses a number of unique biodiversity features that will make it the greenest development in the city," says Yeang. "The design is a new urban high-rise typology – one that is iconically and explicitly green. Its integration of built form with gardens, ramps and bridges in the sky will showcase a new exemplary form for future eco-skyscrapers."

The overall design of the project was driven by a desire for low-energy design and the need to establish a sense of place within a newly rejuvenated area of Vancouver. Situated on a dramatic waterfront location, along the city's False Creek shoreline, the site previously accommodated the park for the 1986 Expo. The development offers a softer, greener alternative to much of the building that characterises recent redevelopment in the city, where post-industrial space has been replaced with closely spaced, near identical tower blocks and hard landscaping. Vancouver's rapidly expanding population has placed increased pressure on housing provision, but local authorities are determined to retain the city's reputation as a desirable place to live – placing an emphasis on inner-city construction rather than suburban sprawl.

The development also includes a number of measures to control and reduce the speed of motor vehicles in the immediate area to improve conditions for residents and other users of the buildings. This has involved a major consultation exercise and complex planning as the nearby Pacific Boulevard is a major thoroughfare. "Mobility should be at the heart of sustainable communities and can help create better places – places with a local distinctiveness and identity with reduced use of private transportation," says Yeang.

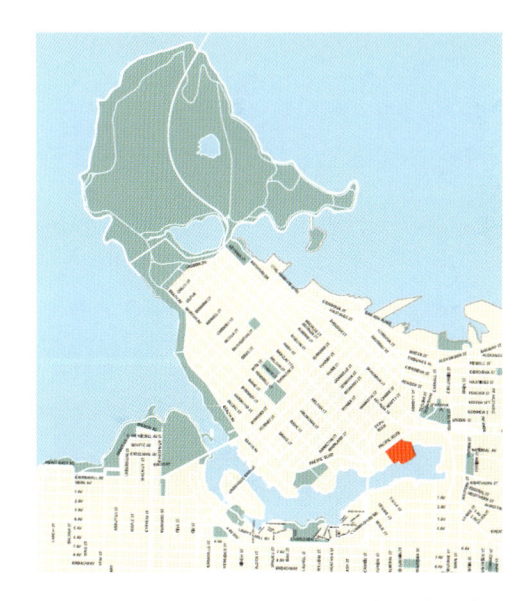

▲ Location plan

▲ Entrance to the Plaza at False Creek

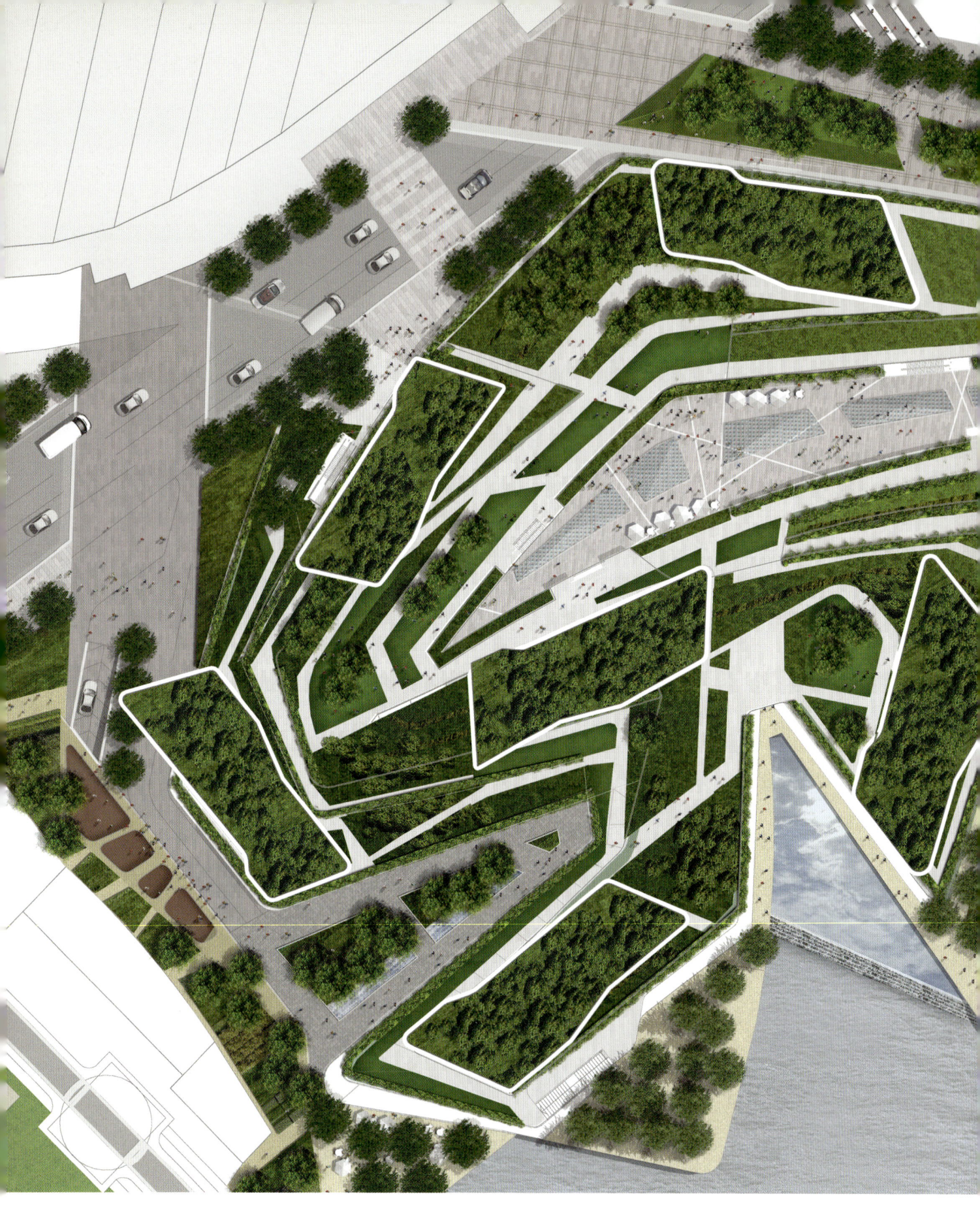

▲ Masterplan

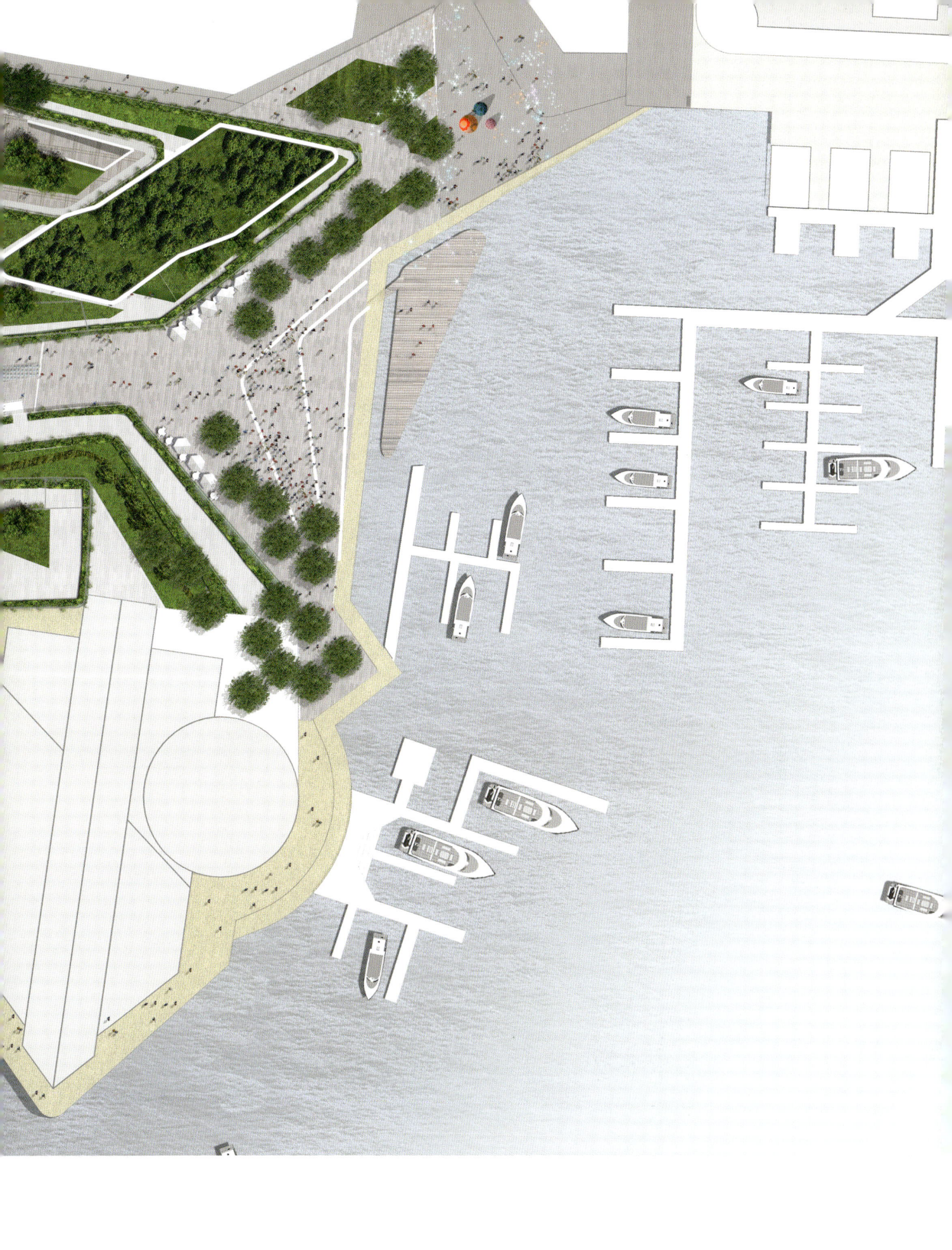

EcoMasterplanning | **Plaza of Nations**

Summary of Plans

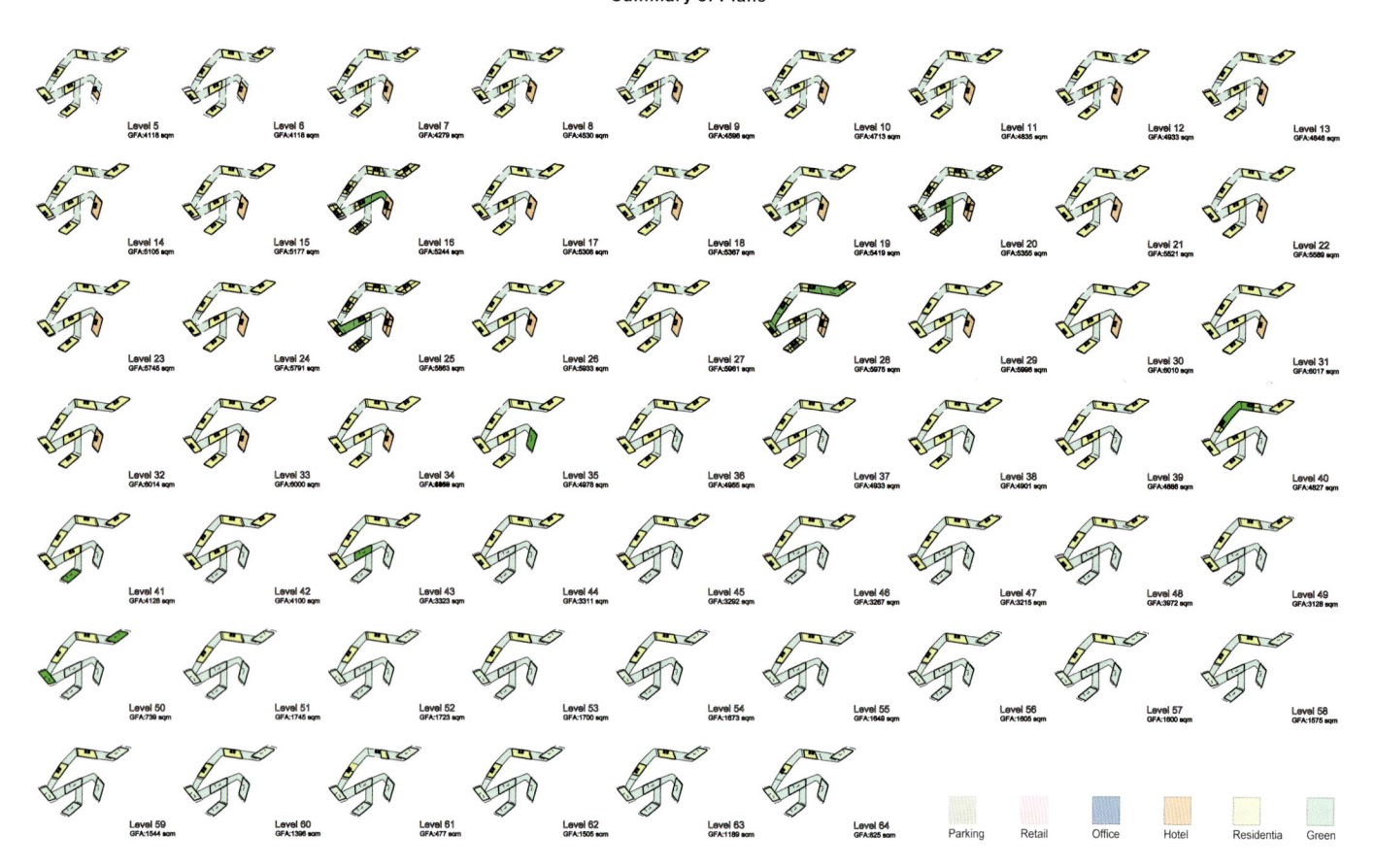

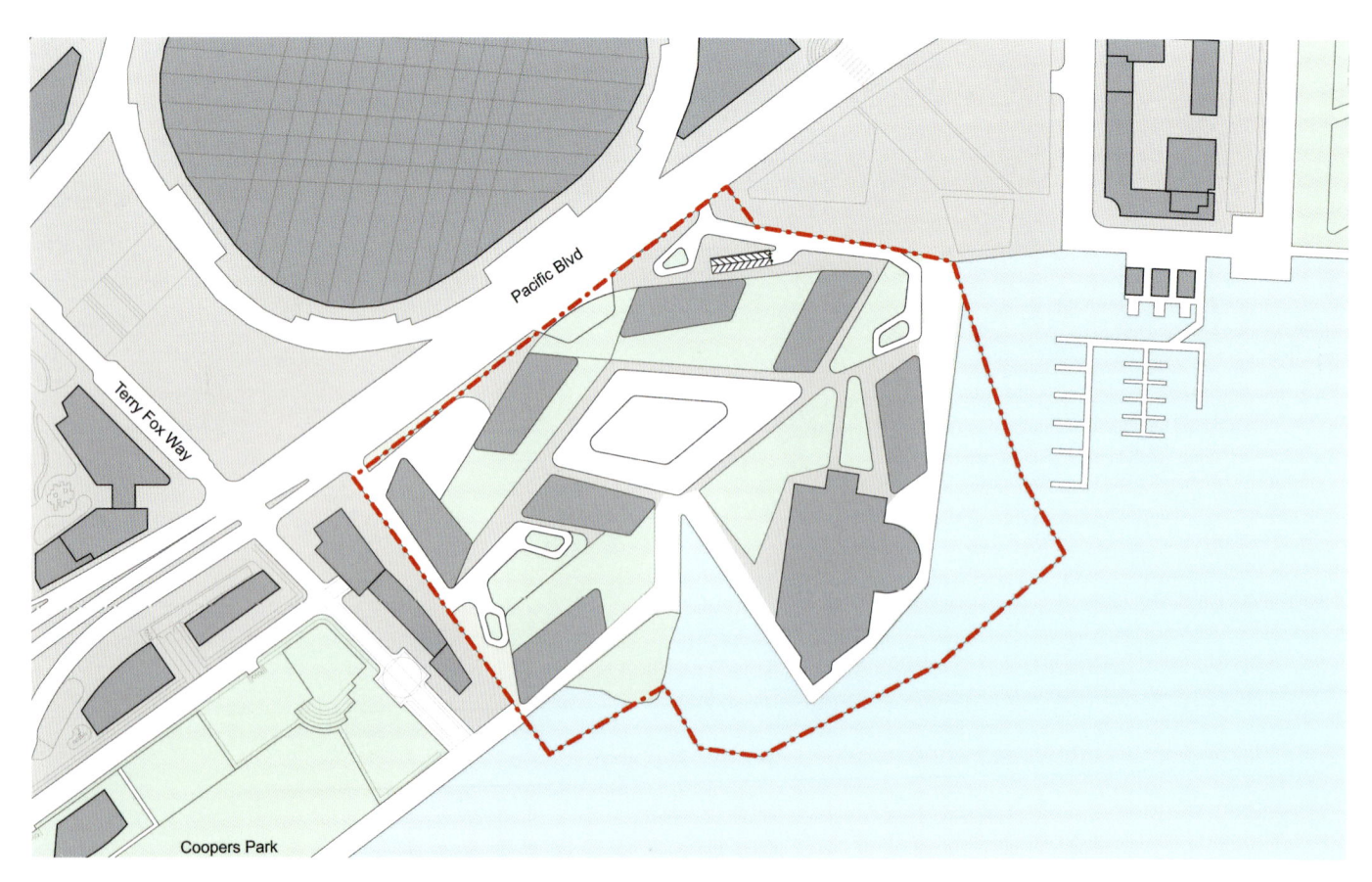

▲ Site plan

▲ Impression of the terraced nature of the scheme at ground level

▲ View from the False Creek seawall

EcoMasterplanning | **Plaza of Nations** 99

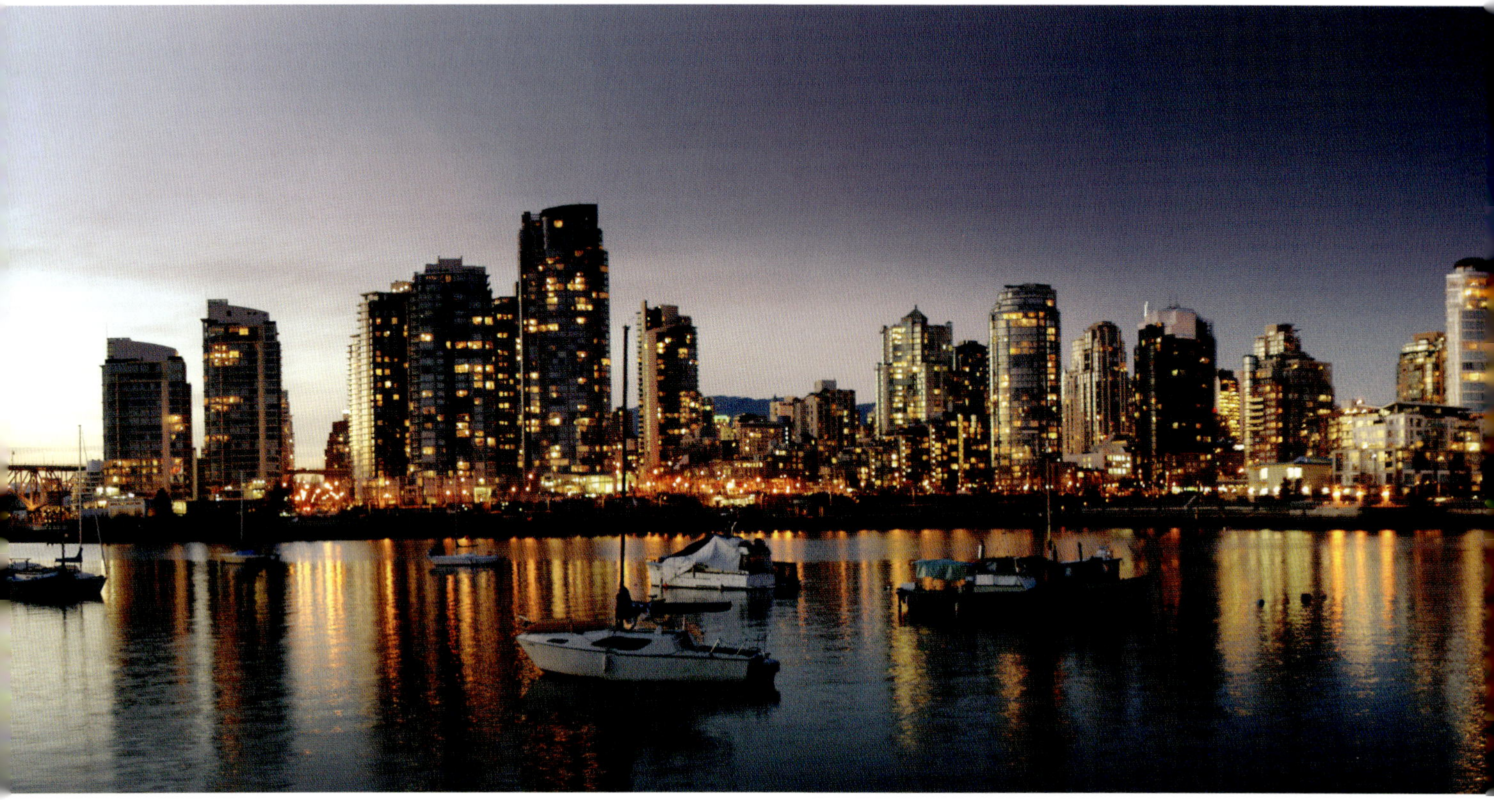

Montage view of False Creek (Plaza of Nations located at far right)

CHAPTER 3 Transitional Projects

Like any architect with a large body of work extending across a number of decades, Yeang's portfolio of built and unbuilt schemes plots a clear trajectory in which a distinctive language is developed and refined. Yeang can now, also, begin to identify particular projects as "transitional" ones – those that mark turning points or imaginative leaps which began to take him elsewhere. This transitional period, covering (roughly) the late 1990s to the middle of the following decade, was one in which Yeang completed the National Library of Singapore, drew up a series of ambitious masterplans, and published widely. Looking back, Yeang describes this as a "period of indeterminacy".

Yeang was also, he admits, exhausted. Apart from developing his theories on architecture and evolving them into a more fully ecological approach, Yeang had been overseeing complex construction works and dealing with the fallout from financial meltdown in Asian markets. The financial crisis of 1998, in which governments were pitted against international hedge-fund managers, caused many South-East Asian currencies to drop in value by significant margins. The Malaysian Ringgit lost 40 per cent of its value, making Yeang (on paper at least) 40 per cent poorer almost overnight. Although busy, much of Yeang's work was not commercial – his conceptual work far outweighed the number of built projects, and Yeang also filled his time entering design competitions, researching and speaking at conferences and international schools of architecture. He took time away from the office to attend the business course on "Leading a professional service firm" at Harvard Business School.

During this frantic, transitional period, Yeang managed to hone his ideas about the aesthetics of ecodesign, taking the subject far beyond the generally acknowledged definition of "sustainable design". He also began to become more certain about the economics of ecodesign, and the ethics of developing in an environmentally sensitive manner. Moving, perhaps, a little away from notions of "critical regionalism", Yeang grew more comfortable with the idea that green architecture is something which has to be paid for, which can accrue value and which, ultimately, depends on the commitment and moral backbone of the developer. "Cost control is absolutely crucial. We must design and deliver within the client's budget," says Yeang. "But there will always be a cost premium for ecodesign. We can, of course, present a business case for green buildings, but it is difficult to persuade critics and clients to go green and become sustainable if they are averse to it from the outset. We usually present ecodesign as an ethical issue that responsible citizens must address. Fortunately, we are now getting clients who are actively commissioning green architecture from us, rather than having to be convinced that this is what they should have."

At the same time, Yeang started to get to grips with certification systems – largely through his experience of designing the Singapore National Library under the terms of the country's Green Mark system. Yeang has an ambivalent attitude towards such systems; while they are useful in raising public awareness of the environmental credentials of one building over another, and in providing a framework within which architects can work, he says that systems like Green Mark, BREEAM and LEED cannot pretend to provide comprehensive cover: "We must be careful about reducing green design to simplistic indexes. Nature is very complex. Yes, there are indexes covering matters such as biodiversity, but even these are subject to debate. Even ecologists cannot agree on which species should be considered for conservation."

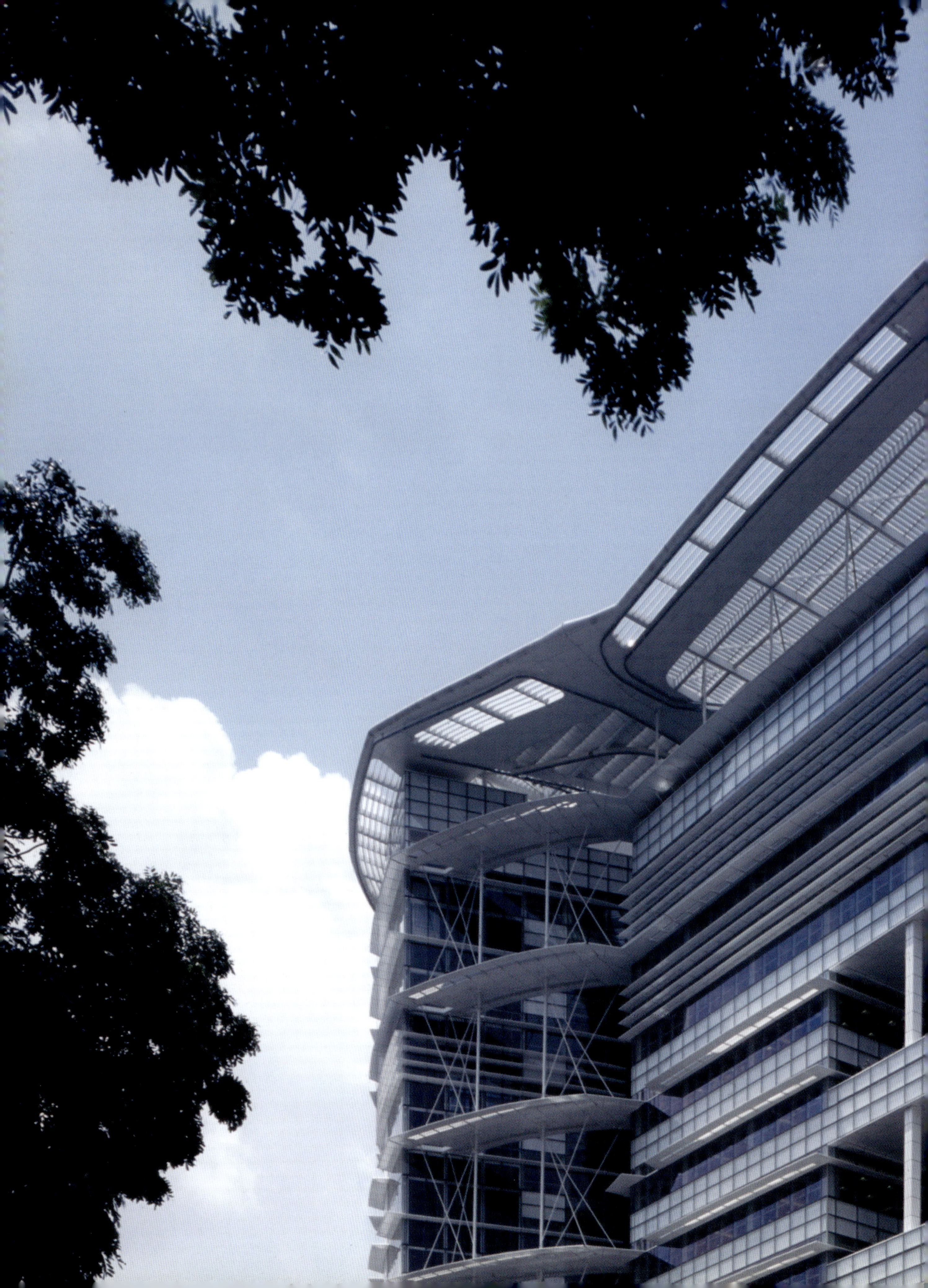

National Library Building

National Library Building

TYPE	:	Transitional Project
LOCATION	:	Singapore
CLIMATE ZONE	:	Tropical
VEGETATION ZONE	:	Rainforest

AREAS:

GFA	:	58,783 m²
NFA	:	44,087 m²
SITE AREA	:	11,304 m²
PLOT RATIO	:	1:5.2
NO. OF STOREYS	:	14
STATUS	:	Built
DATE OF COMPLETION	:	2005

▲ The National Library Building on Victoria Street

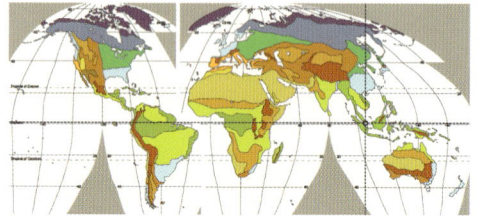

CLIMATE REGION

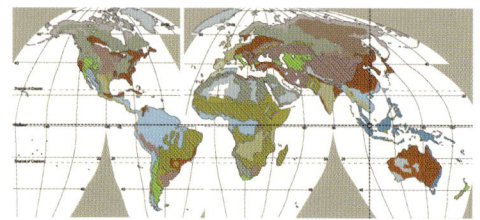

VEGETATION ZONE

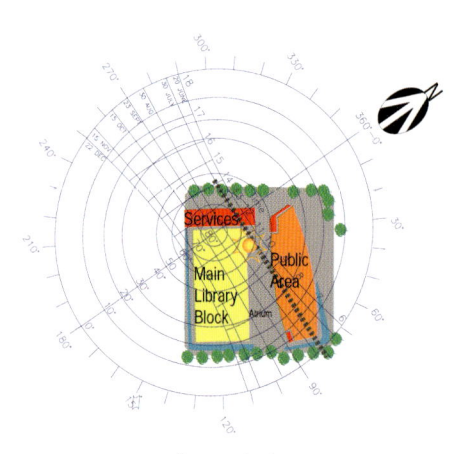

Conceptual

The Singapore National Library commission represents Yeang's first large-scale built project outside Malaysia. Won in competition against firms including Michael Graves, Moshe Safdie and Nikken Sekkei, the 120m high library also marks the beginning of a performance-based approach to architecture. It was with this project that Yeang really got to grips with certification procedures, in this case Singapore's "Green Mark" system (the equivalent of the UK's BREEAM and the US's LEED models) under which the building was awarded the highest rating – Platinum. At the time of completion Christopher Chia, chief executive of the National Library Board, predicted the building would be "one of Singapore's most endearing buildings for the coming decades".

The client brief from the National Library Board was demanding. As well as providing library services of the highest order, the building had to function as a national and cultural icon, and be modelled as a civic institution of international standing. The building, specified the brief, should have "a distinct character, reflecting Singapore's multicultural heritage and its aspirations to be a learning nation". The building is located on what was once a grassed-over space containing a number of buried construction piles; these piles needed to be extracted, requiring the total clearance of the land. At the outset Yeang mapped the vegetation within a 500m radius of the site; in his taxonomy of land types, Yeang categorised the development zone as "Mixed Artificial Land".

The library is composed of two distinct blocks that are separated by a day-lit, semi-enclosed and naturally ventilated internal "street"; the blocks are connected by bridges at the higher levels. The larger of the two elements, which contains the book collections and library services, sits over a large, open, naturally ventilated plaza; the thick concrete slab which forms the soffit of the plaza is of sufficient size to evaporatively cool the space below through its thermal mass. Beneath this plaza is a pair of partial "ecocells" – vegetated water-collection devices that Yeang first began exploring in his Kowloon Waterfront competition

106 ECOARCHITECTURE | THE WORK OF KEN YEANG

entry (pages 182-9). The smaller, curvilinear block contains facilities for noisier activities such as exhibitions, lectures and multi-media performances. The plaza and "street" at the ground plane have been designed to function as part of the public realm, replete with cafes and retail units.

One of the features of this project is that the building benefits from what Yeang calls Passive Mode, Mixed Mode and Full Mode features – that is, a variety of energy and environmental solutions that range from the manipulation of building form to the installation of conventional air conditioning. "There is nothing wrong with using electricity," says Yeang. "The bigger issue is how that electricity is generated." Passive Mode features include optimised day lighting, solar orientation and configuration; sun shading; natural ventilation; responsive façade design; and landscaping. The building's distinctive louvres, which perform solar shading and anti-glare roles, are up to 6m deep in places, and help define a uniquely tropical aesthetic for the library as well as serving as light shelves to deflect natural light into the inner parts of the library.

Most of the library work areas (which contain triple-height reading rooms) operate in Full Mode, deploying air conditioning and electric light. Mixed Mode, where passive controls are supplemented as necessary, typically operates in transition spaces such as lobbies and foyers. Computational Fluid Dynamics simulations, carried out by the Singapore National University's Total Building Performance Team, were used to predict acoustic performance, airflow and heat loading, demonstrating where passive design techniques would need a mechanical/electrical boost. Daylight penetration and energy consumption were also evaluated through computer simulations, while wind-tunnel tests provided the basis for façade design and specifications, as well as for the assessment of comfort conditions in the plazas and semi-enclosed skycourt spaces. Materials were specified according to their environmental impact over the life-cycle of the building and its associated systems. Studies were carried out on the embodied energy content of the building by engineers Battle McCarthy.

More than 6,300m^2 of this building are devoted to green space in the form of urban skycourts, consituting more than 60 per cent of the building's footprint. The north-east façade contains a pair of 40 metre-high skycourts planted with 3-metre-high trees. These skycourts are protected by wind-breakers that reduce the impact of the high wind speeds which can occur at higher levels of this 120m tall building – gusts can reach more than 35 metres per second. The windbreakers baffle the wind and break it into smaller, weaker eddies before it enters the skycourts. Post-occupancy evaluation has shown that over 90 per cent of library users and staff are satisfied with the building. Studies show that the environmental impact of the National Library is lower than that of a typical office building of similar size. The Energy Efficiency Index of the building is around 172 kWhrs/m^2/annum, compared with the index of a typical office building in Singapore which consumes around 250 kWhrs/m^2/annum. The building received several prizes, including an award from the World Association of Chinese Architects.

▲ Day-lit reading room

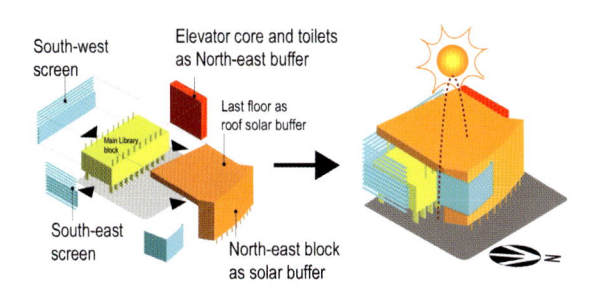

Composite of Buffer Zones

SUMMARY OF PLANS

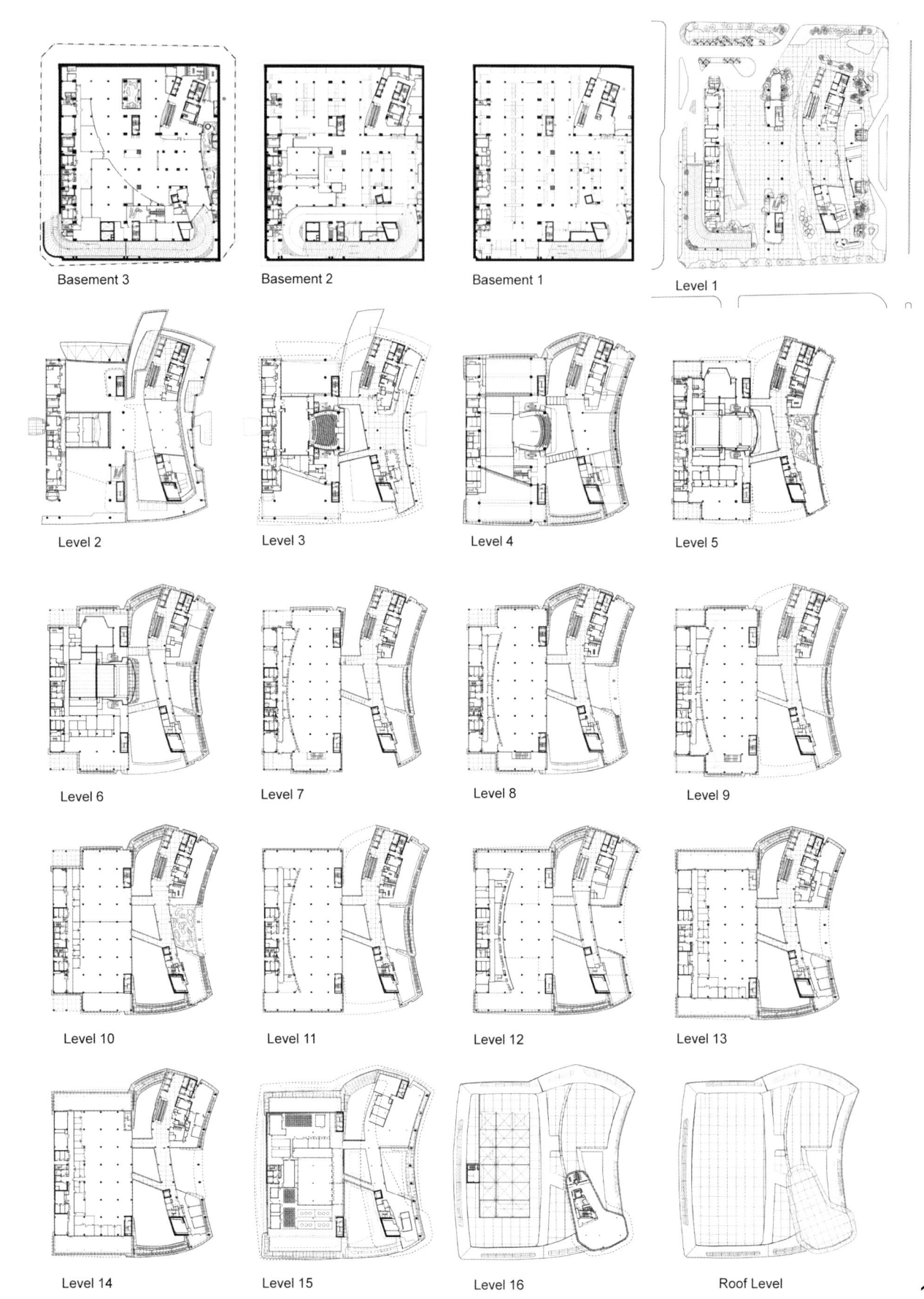

Basement 3

Basement 2

Basement 1

Level 1

Level 2

Level 3

Level 4

Level 5

Level 6

Level 7

Level 8

Level 9

Level 10

Level 11

Level 12

Level 13

Level 14

Level 15

Level 16

Roof Level

108 ECOARCHITECTURE | THE WORK OF KEN YEANG

▲ Atria create dramatic shows of light and shade

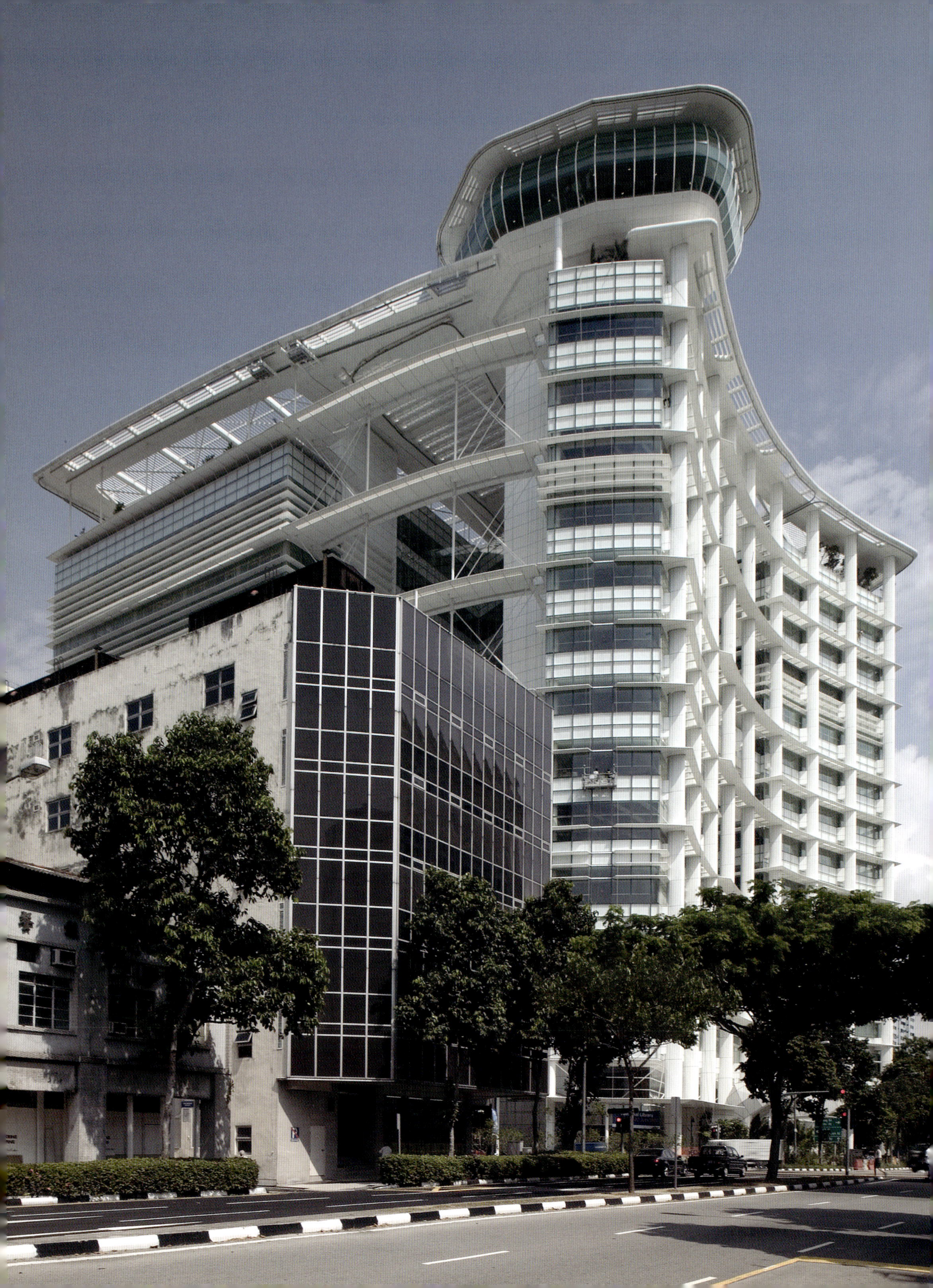

◀ View from North Bridge Road

▲ Skycourt

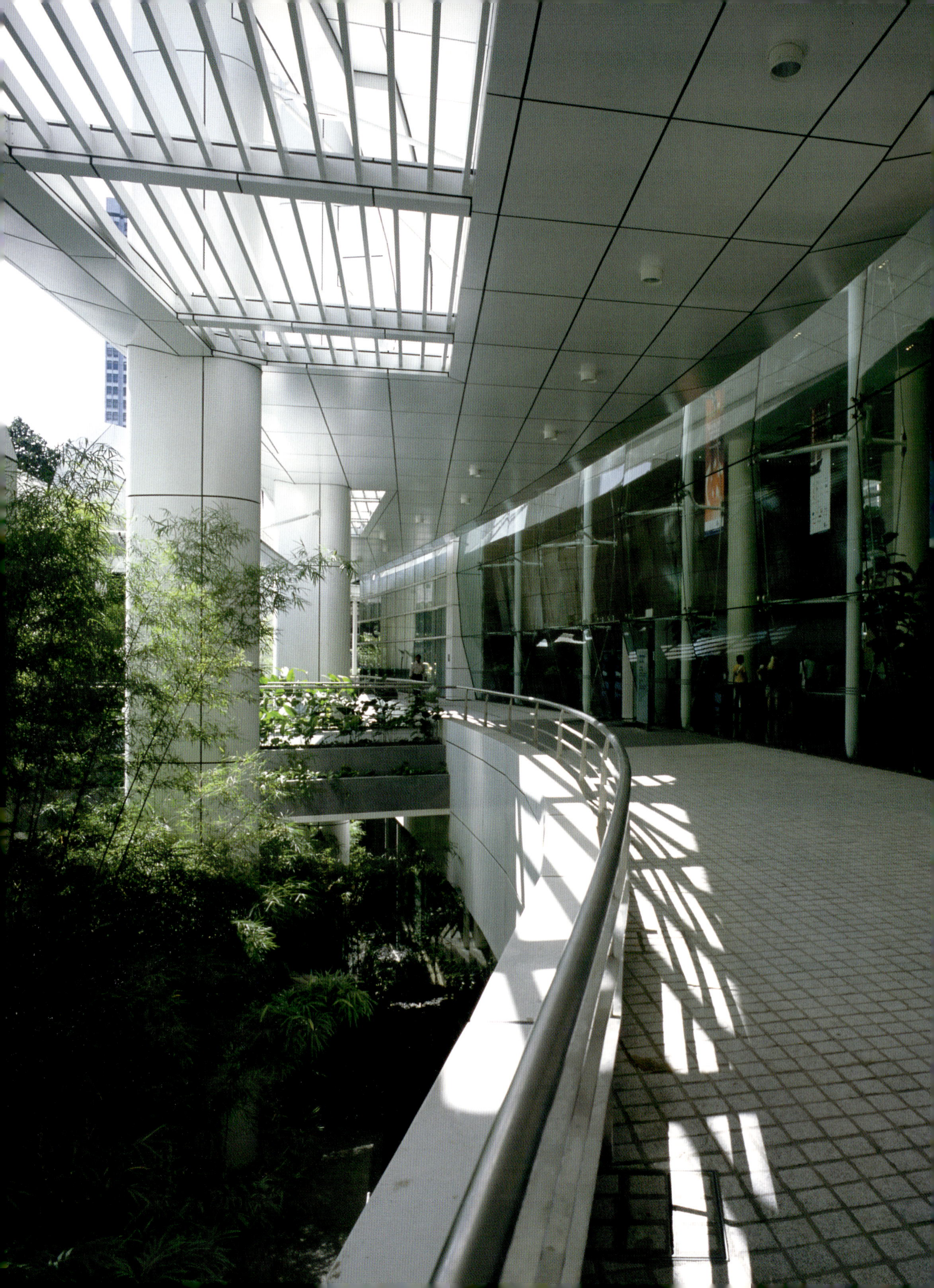

POST OCCUPANCY EVALUATION

750 users' response
Overall = 99.7 %
Satisfaction score

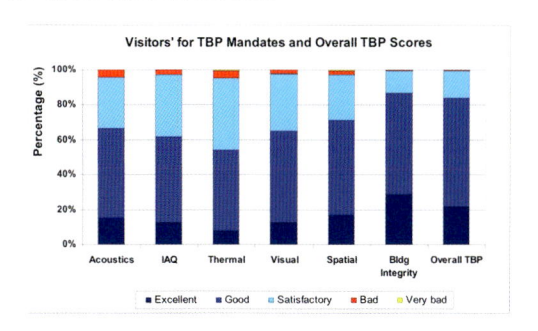

Visitors' for TBP Mandates and Overall TBP Scores

105 staff response
Overall = 87.5 %
Satisfaction score

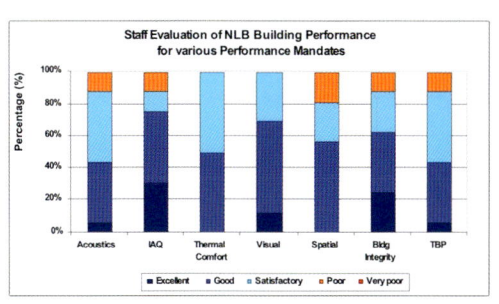

Staff Evaluation of NLB Building Performance for various Performance Mandates

◄ Ecocells bring light and air into basement reading rooms

▲ Street level view of atrium sunshade louvres

Transitional Projects | National Library Building

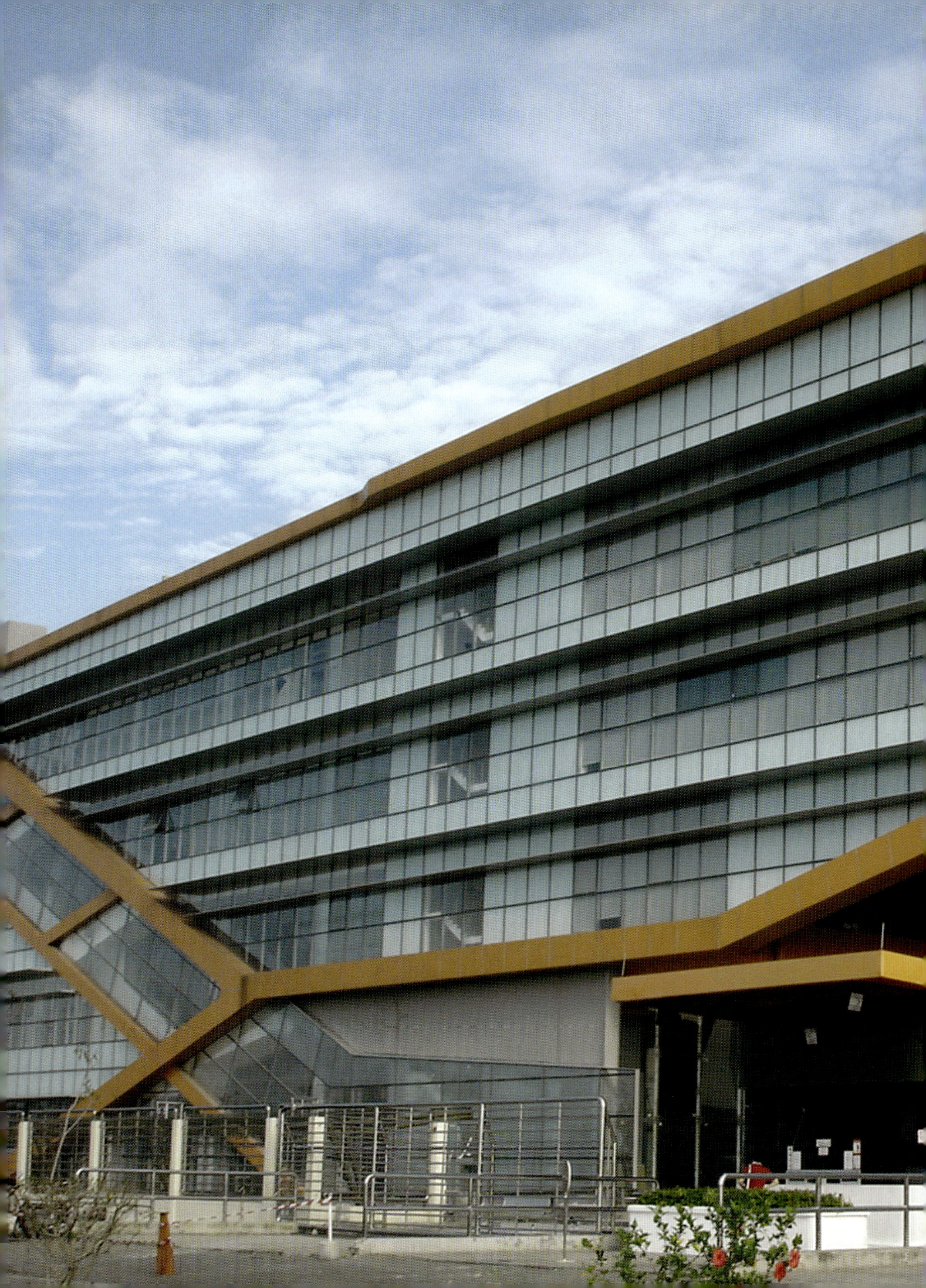

Mewah Oils Headquarters

Mewah Oils Headquarters

TYPE	:	Transitional Project
LOCATION	:	Selangor, Malaysia
CLIMATE ZONE	:	Tropical
VEGETATION ZONE	:	Rainforest

AREAS:

GFA	:	19,258 m²
SITE AREA	:	16,379 m²
NO. OF STOREYS	:	4
STATUS	:	Built
DATE OF COMPLETION	:	2005

▲ East façade

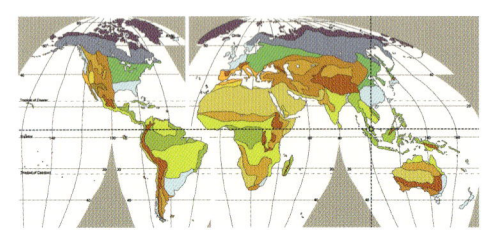

CLIMATE REGION

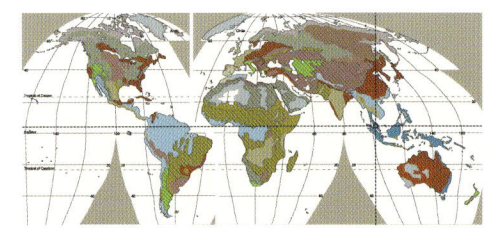

VEGETATION ZONE

Conceptual

This medium-sized, four-storey company headquarters was built for Mewah Oils, a Singaporian firm involved in the production of palm-oil products and speciality fats. It is located at Port Klang that is a 40-minute drive from Kuala Lumpur. Situated in an industrial area, it is built alongside a large industrial shed which accommodates processing and warehousing facilities. In terms of urban context, the site has no uplifting features and the client was keen to have a signature building capable of livening up the surrounding area. Being low-rise and ground-hugging makes it, by Yeang's definition, a groundscraper.

The significance of this project is that here the vegetation becomes internalised, in contrast to other tropical projects where the planting is largely located on the outside of buildings – within recesses or skycourts, or within inside/outside transitional spaces. Here, the internal planting has similarities with the system developed for the Plaza of Nations project in Vancouver, which encloses vegetation within winter gardens (pages 92-101).

The main feature of the building is a continuous landscaped ramp, which rises from the ground level to the roof. The ramp is thickly vegetated with tropical plants, maintained using recycled rainwater. A cascading water feature, running alongside the planting troughs, is designed to provide a "calming ambience" while performing as a cooling agent through evaporation. The vegetation (or "green ecoinfrastructure") is placed centrally within an inclined entrance lobby; it then steps gradually upwards via a densely foliaged inclined planter that extends all the way to a rooftop garden, accessed via a wide, straight flight of stairs.

"This inclined foliaged garden serves as an internal lung, scrubbing clean the air of the building's interiors as well as providing biophilic benefits for the building's users," says Yeang. Yeang earlier used plants to improve internal air quality in the design for a set of conference rooms for Austrade, the Australian Trade Commission, in Kuala Lumpur; English Lily was used as an integral part of the

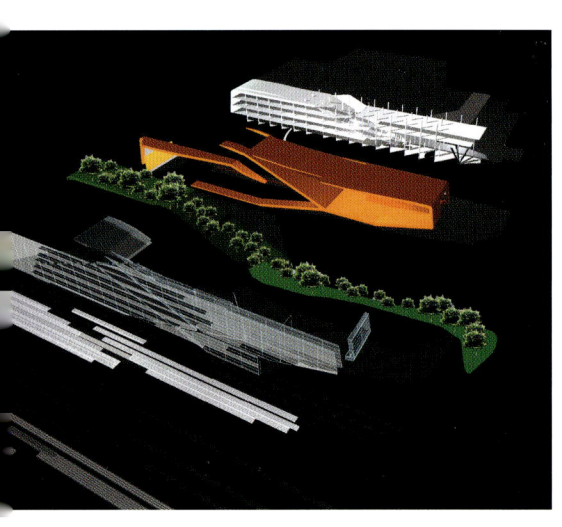

▲ The landscaped ramp and adjacent water feature

interior design to absorb air-borne Volatile Organic Compounds. This design was based on the work of NASA's Tom Wolverton who recommended the use of English Lily or bamboo (at 1 plant per m^2 of floor space) as being effective in absorbing these compounds. By internalising the greening, the building's ecoinfrastructure is not obvious from the outside, but its presence is expressed on the exterior by a striking, diagonal, orange-clad frame.

While the interior atrium is designed to be a naturally ventilated zone, it is possible to switch to a mixed-mode system in which air flow can be boosted mechanically. "Natural ventilation is effective where it contributes to lowering energy consumption. It is particularly important in tropical climates, and could also be applied during the mid-seasons in temperate climates – that is, spring and autumn," says Yeang. "Reduction of, or the elimination of, the use of fossil fuels and making buildings carbon neutral are, of course, important in ecodesign. However, they are only part of the equation. There are other factors to take into account."

The 34m high Mewah Oils HQ building is constructed of reinforced concrete, clad in aluminium and curtain-wall glazing. Conceptually, it is configured as large wrap, where the interior volumes are enveloped in a folded plane which divides to mark the presence of the ecoramp.

▲ The internal landscaped atrium

▲ Street view: the orange ribbon marks the presence of the internal, planted ramp

▼ Employee cafeteria from entrance lobby

▶ Structure of main cantilever

118 ECOARCHITECTURE | THE WORK OF KEN YEANG

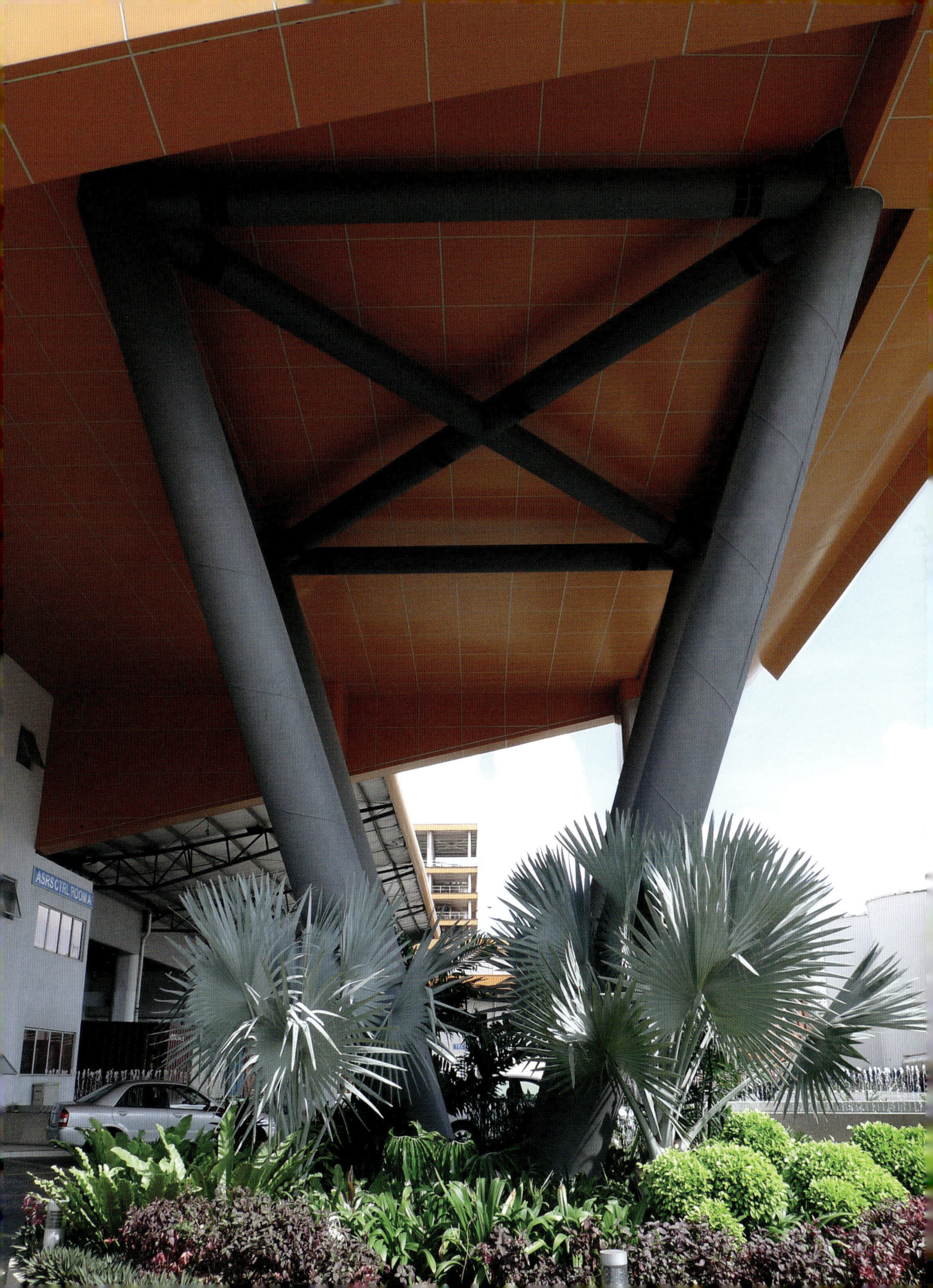
ASRS CTRL ROOM A

▲ South façade

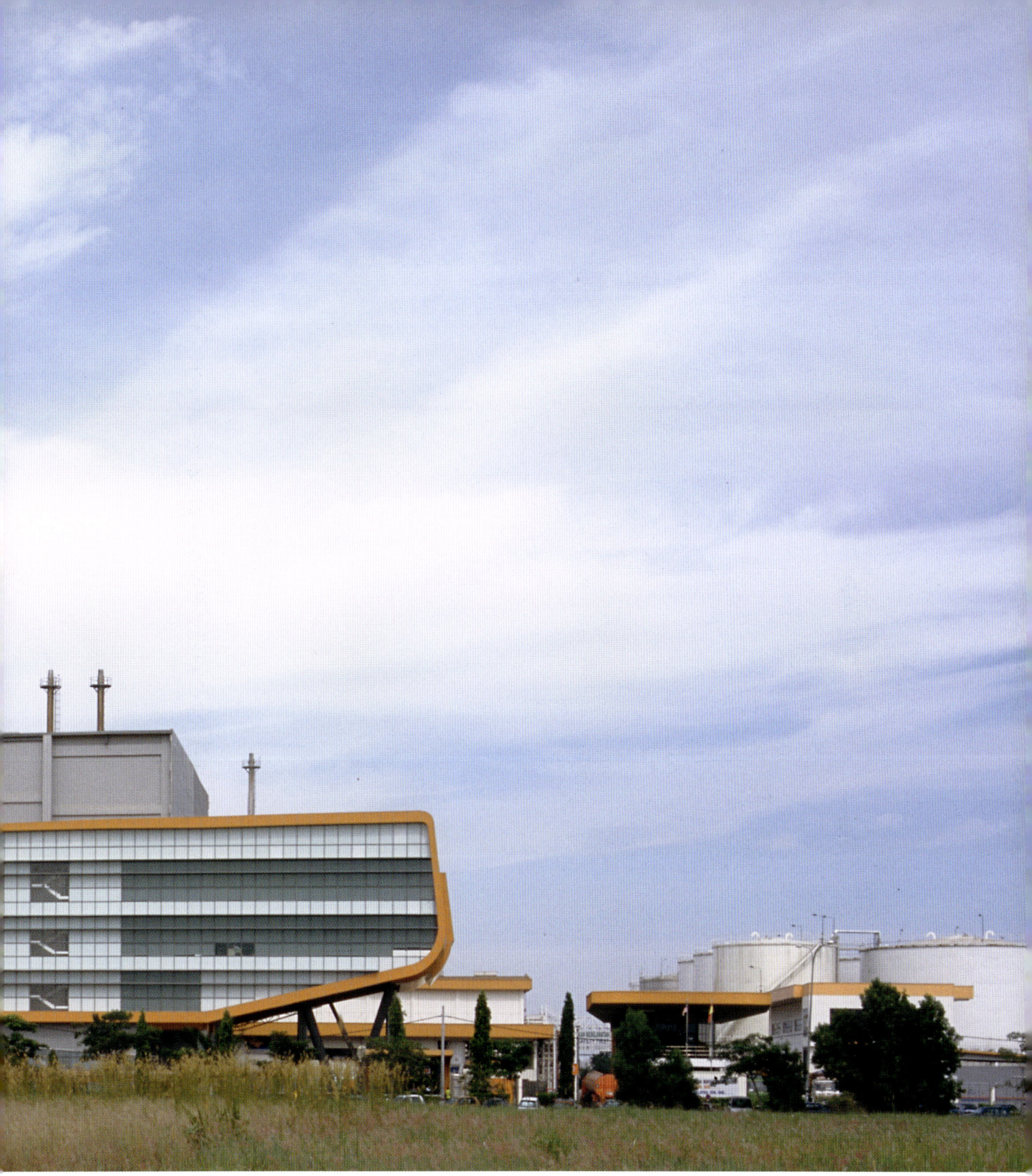

▲ View from south-west

Transitional Projects | **Mewah Oils Headquarters**

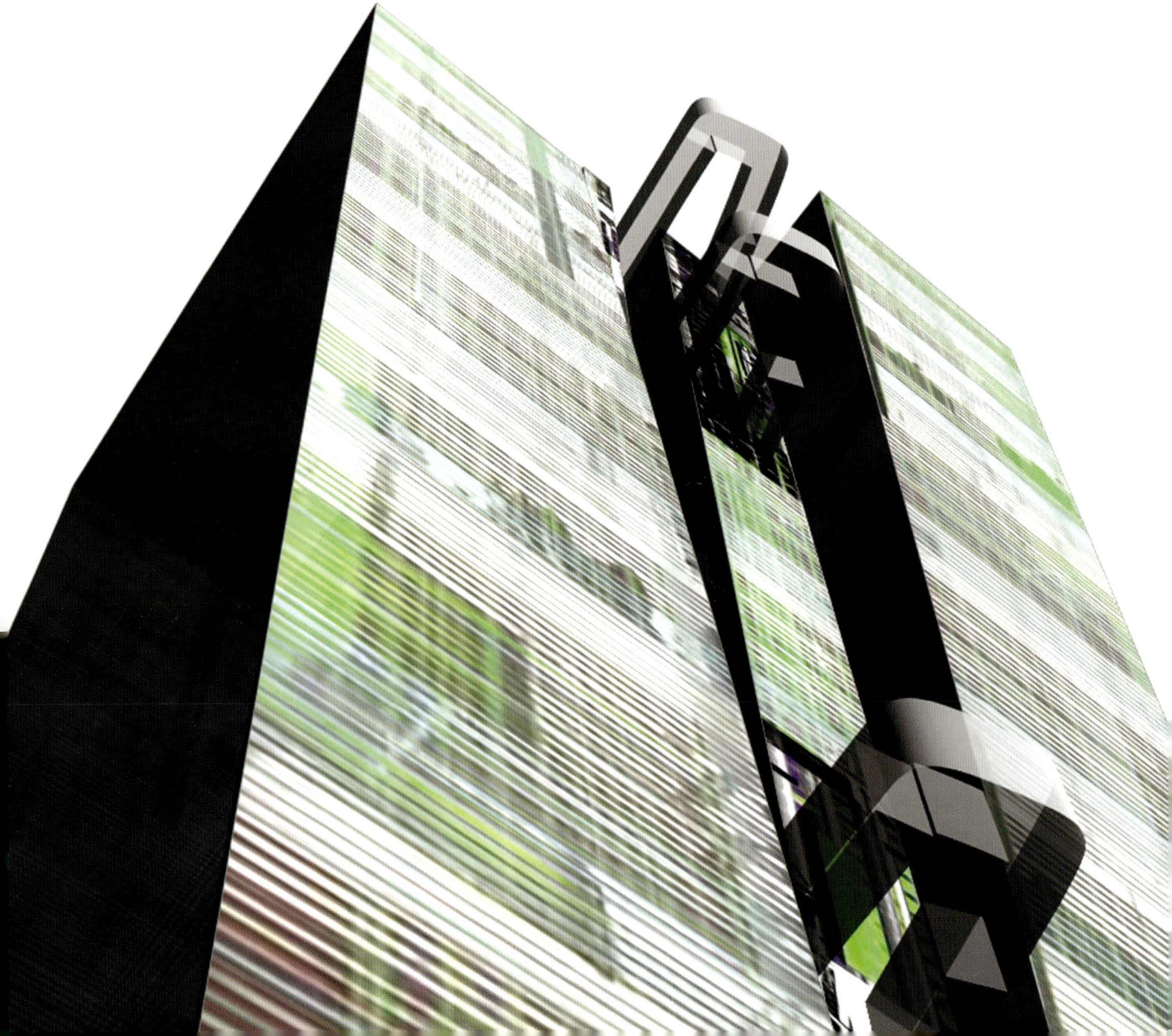

MAAG Tower

MAAG Tower

TYPE	:	Transitional Project
LOCATION	:	Zurich, Switzerland
CLIMATE ZONE	:	Temperate
VEGETATION ZONE	:	Alpine

AREAS:

GFA	:	47,788 m^2
NFA	:	35,841 m^2
SITE AREA	:	5,487 m^2
PLOT RATIO	:	1:9
NO. OF STOREYS	:	34
STATUS	:	Competition
DATE OF COMPLETION	:	2005

▲ Elevation view of model

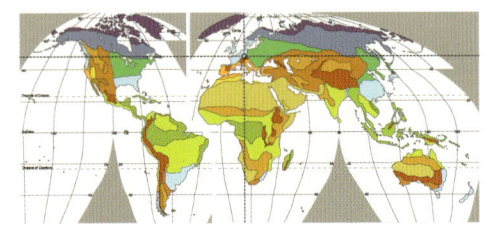

CLIMATE REGION

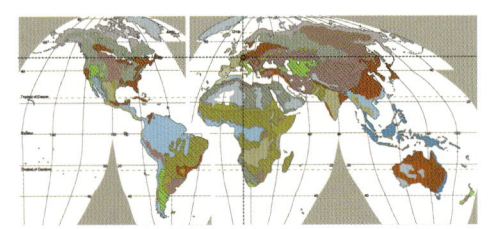

VEGETATION ZONE

Conceptual

This competition entry, for a tower on the edge of Zurich, included elements of almost every approach Yeang had developed until this point. He describes it as the architectural equivalent of the "hot rod" – just as the hot rod is a customised racing car loaded with every conceivable technology to move over a quarter of a mile as quickly as possible, this design contains every technique in the sustainable engineer's toolbox. Designed for a formerly industrial site – containing several vacated sheds, disused low-rise buildings and little or no vegetation – the tower was part of a strategy to increase biodiversity as well as rehabilitate the zone for human occupancy while seeking to reduce the dependency on fossil fuels and head towards carbon neutral design. "This was, for me, a transitional period," says Yeang. "I was anxious to find a definitive approach to green building design and here I turned to exploring how 'grey ecoinfrastructure' systems could be fully integrated into a tower's built form."

As envisaged, the tower contained expanded, slightly cantilevered, upper floors which wrap around a central elevator core – this represented a departure from Yeang's other towers (designed for tropical zones) which tended to place circulation cores on the east–west periphery. Further, floorplates were designed to contain a central air shaft void to provide natural ventilation to elevator lobbies and washroom facilities during the mid-seasons. This shaft was designed to contain vegetation chosen for its properties that clean the air before it enters the building's interior spaces. The void was also designed with extra capacity to enable the building to perform just as well if services (such as event spaces, conference rooms, AV equipment, kitchens, toilets and cafes) were installed post-completion.

BUILDING SYSTEMS

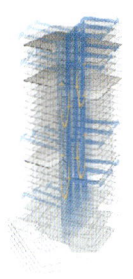

Ventilation System

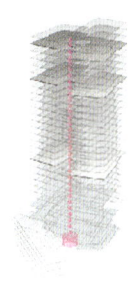

Recycling System

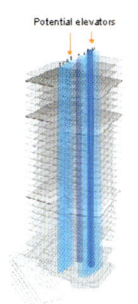

Primary Circulation System

Secondary Circulation System

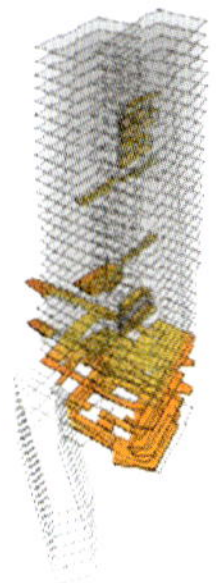

Tertiary Circulation System

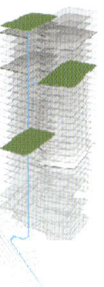

Water Recycling System

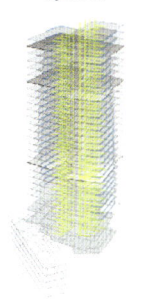

Daylighting System

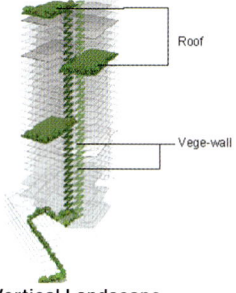

Vertical Landscape System

The façade design is characterised by recessed, diagonally shaped atria within which is located the "green ecoinfrastructure", protecting it during cold months. This biomass actually begins in a basement level "eco-cell", providing continuous landscaping from the basement to the top of the tower. A modified version of this system was deployed in the design for the Plaza of Nations towers, Vancouver (pages 92-101).

Finally, Yeang developed a novel system to enable the façades to respond to daylight conditions. A rank of transparent tubes was designed to project sunlight deep into the office spaces, while an outer, opaque layer telescopes over these tubes in order to control light penetration in summer months. Passive-mode strategies, then, still underlie the building's response to climatic conditions, particularly with regard to shading and solar absorption. Yeang also experimented with the introduction of fibre optics as a way of bringing natural light deep into the tower's interior.

"The aesthetic, with its emphasis on the grey ecoinfrastructure, is appropriately that of a high-technology green machine," says Yeang. "Ecological architecture deserves an ecological aesthetic. Much of my work is also about the search for this aesthetic."

▲ Computer montage of design proposal, showing void between towers

Transitional Projects | MAAG Tower | 127

Helipad

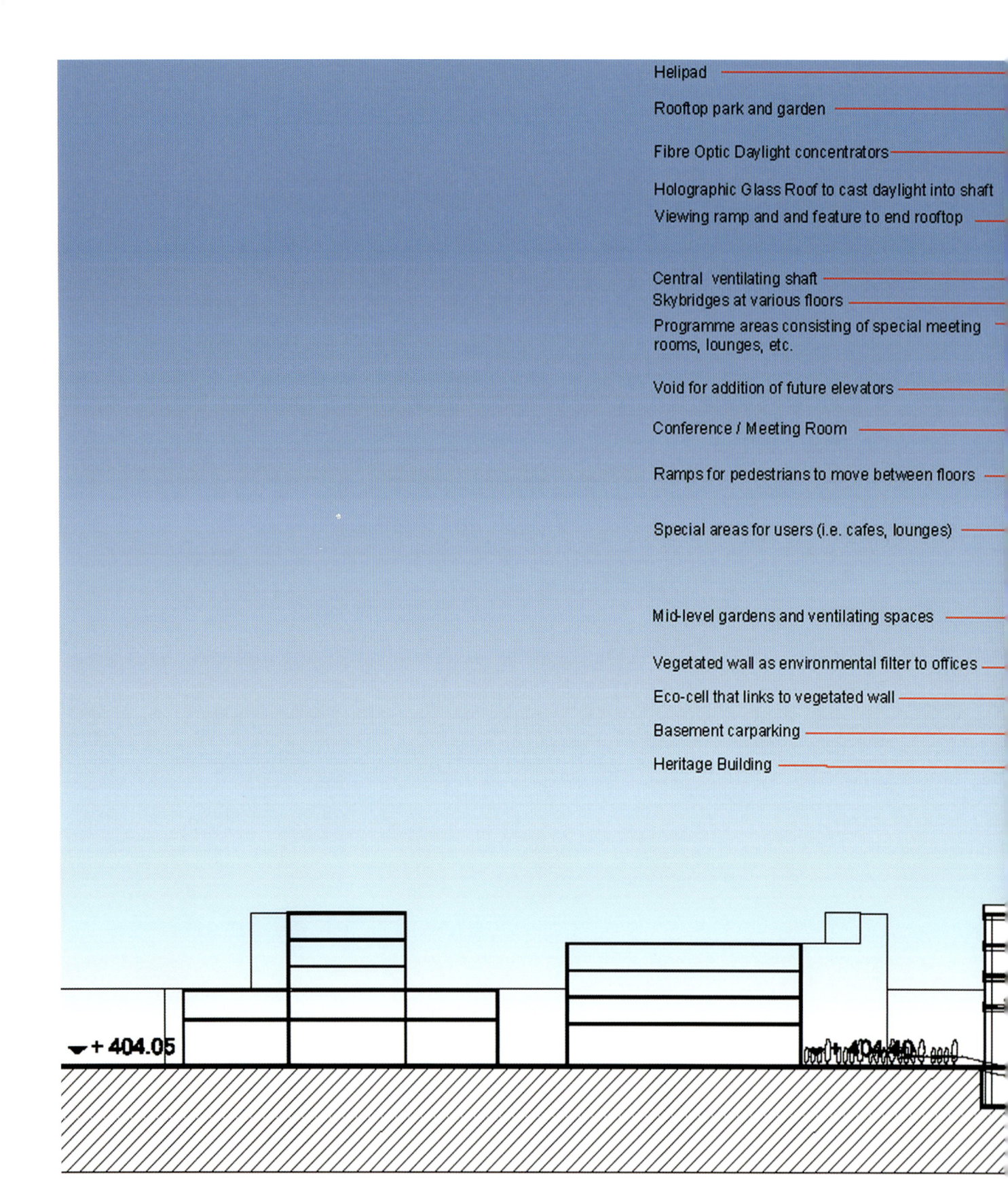

Rooftop park and garden

Fibre Optic Daylight concentrators

Holographic Glass Roof to cast daylight into shaft

Viewing ramp and and feature to end rooftop

Central ventilating shaft
Skybridges at various floors
Programme areas consisting of special meeting rooms, lounges, etc.

Void for addition of future elevators

Conference / Meeting Room

Ramps for pedestrians to move between floors

Special areas for users (i.e. cafes, lounges)

Mid-level gardens and ventilating spaces

Vegetated wall as environmental filter to offices

Eco-cell that links to vegetated wall

Basement carparking

Heritage Building

+ 404.05

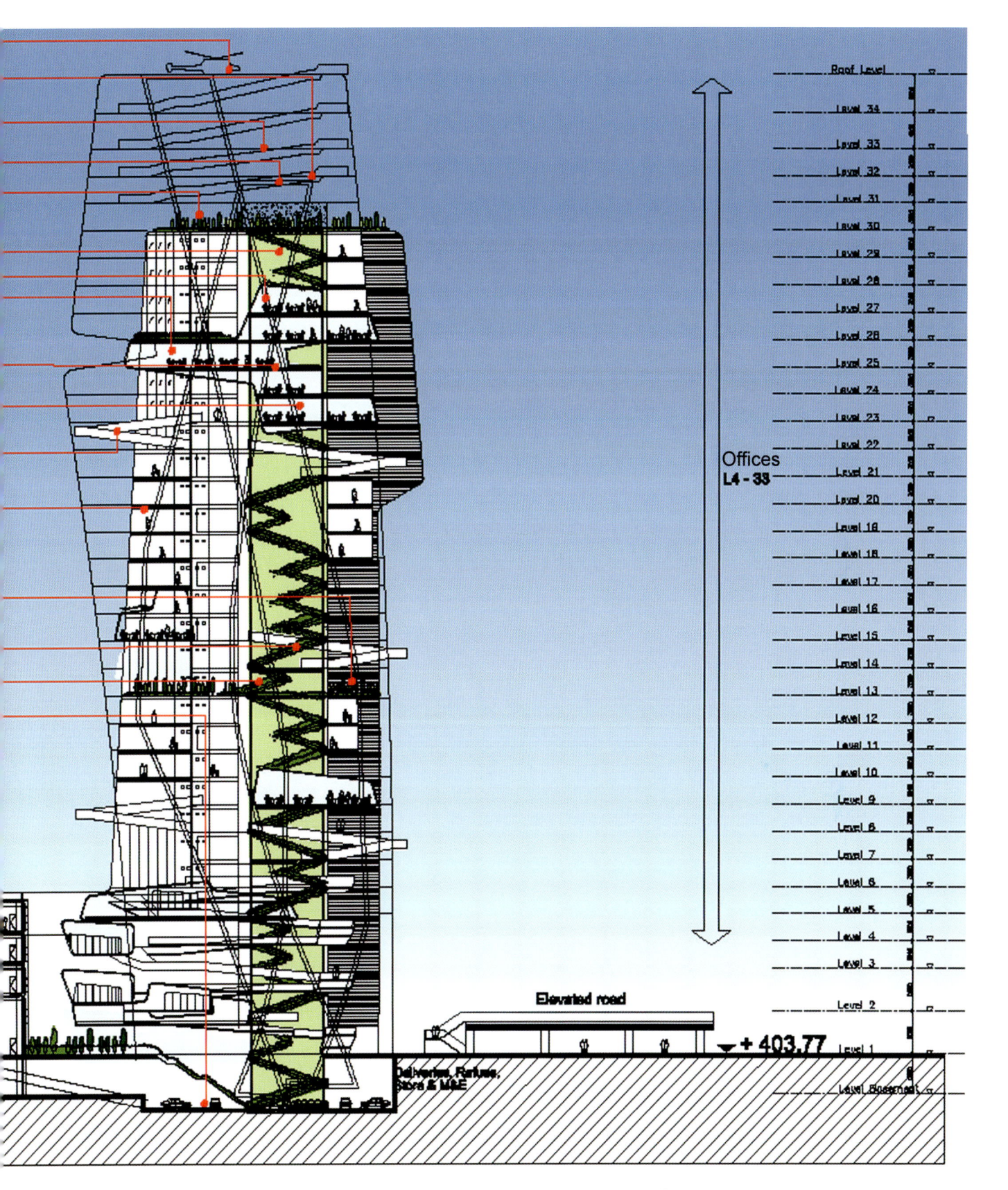

▲ Section, showing principal building features

▲ Photograph of model: elevation

▲ Photograph of model: street level view

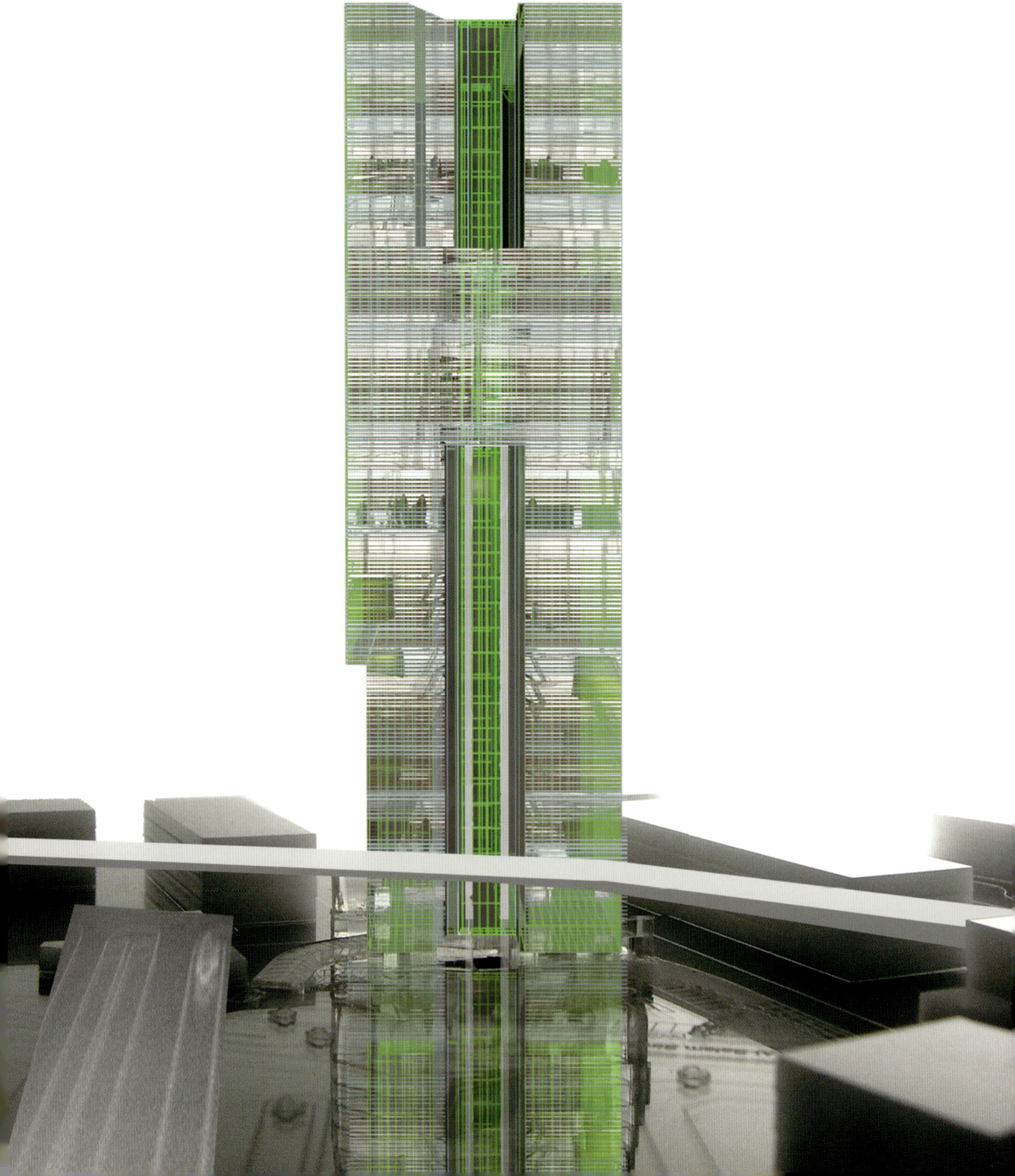

▷ Digital analysis of central air shaft void
◁ Computer montage of elevation

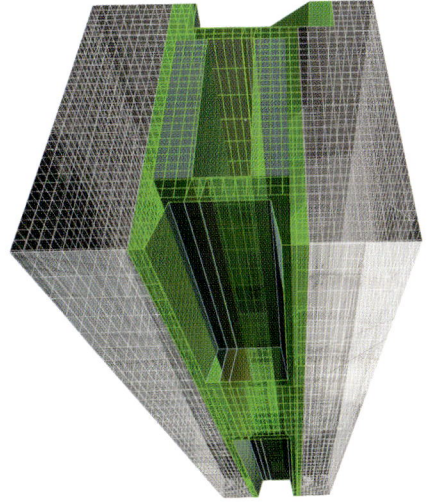

CHAPTER 4 Vertical Urbanism

By the early 1990s, Yeang had completed a number of tall buildings and designed many more which remained unbuilt. Although Yeang had accumulated a range of technical solutions to the problem of limiting the environmental impact of a skyscraper, and indeed making a tall building ecologically responsible, he began to consider how the "bioclimatic skyscraper" could become successful in terms of placemaking. "Why do tall buildings have to exist as a series of bland, homogeneous, concrete trays, one stacked on top of another? Why the vertical repetition?" he asks. Also, Yeang began to wonder why the architect of such stacks would very probably create a very different, more articulated ground-hugging building with complex cross-sections and spatial configurations. "There is no rationale for it," he concluded, "other than cost and an engineering phobia. Tall buildings could certainly be designed with similarly articulated, organically connected spaces and sections."

Yeang, whose portfolio of work includes more towers than any other building type, is the first to admit that tall buildings are not the most sustainable structures to construct and maintain. However, their benefit is that their footprint is small compared with the amount of accommodation they provide and, argues Yeang, providing they are designed to exacting ecological standards and are positioned close to (or above) transport nodes, skyscrapers have a valuable role to play. But they are, largely, spatially impoverished, causing Yeang to ask how towers could borrow from low to mid-rise buildings (or even horizontal masterplans) for placemaking strategies. If skyscrapers could be reimagined as embodying a "vertical urbanism", they become true cities in the sky. At least until a viable economic alternative to the tower presents itself.

The result, published in the book *Reinventing the Skyscraper - A Vertical Theory of Urban Design* (John Wiley & Sons, 2002), was to flip ideas for horizontal placemaking through 90 degrees, creating towers of with a multitude of spatial configurations, distinct zones, winter gardens and multi-level voids. The three concept towers outlined in this section are arguably the most powerful expressions of this thinking – and perhaps the Nagoya Expo Tower in particular, as this building was designed with the specific intention of saving woodland from development by piling the spaces for an international exposition high up in the air. Yeang proposed a vertical expo located within a tower that contained three-storey voids for international pavilions, and rapid transport links that wound up the façades like funicular railways. Similarly, the 500m tall Tokyo Nara building, described by Yeang as a "hyper-tower", was envisioned as a high-tech, ecologically balanced, habitable machine containing as many spatial conditions as a horizontal settlement. These ideas have become further refined by Yeang's proposal to include the facility for growing crops within façades, typically in hydroponic tubes. Not only would such a solution ensure that towers protect arable land from low-rise sprawl, but they actually supplement the food production of farmed land.

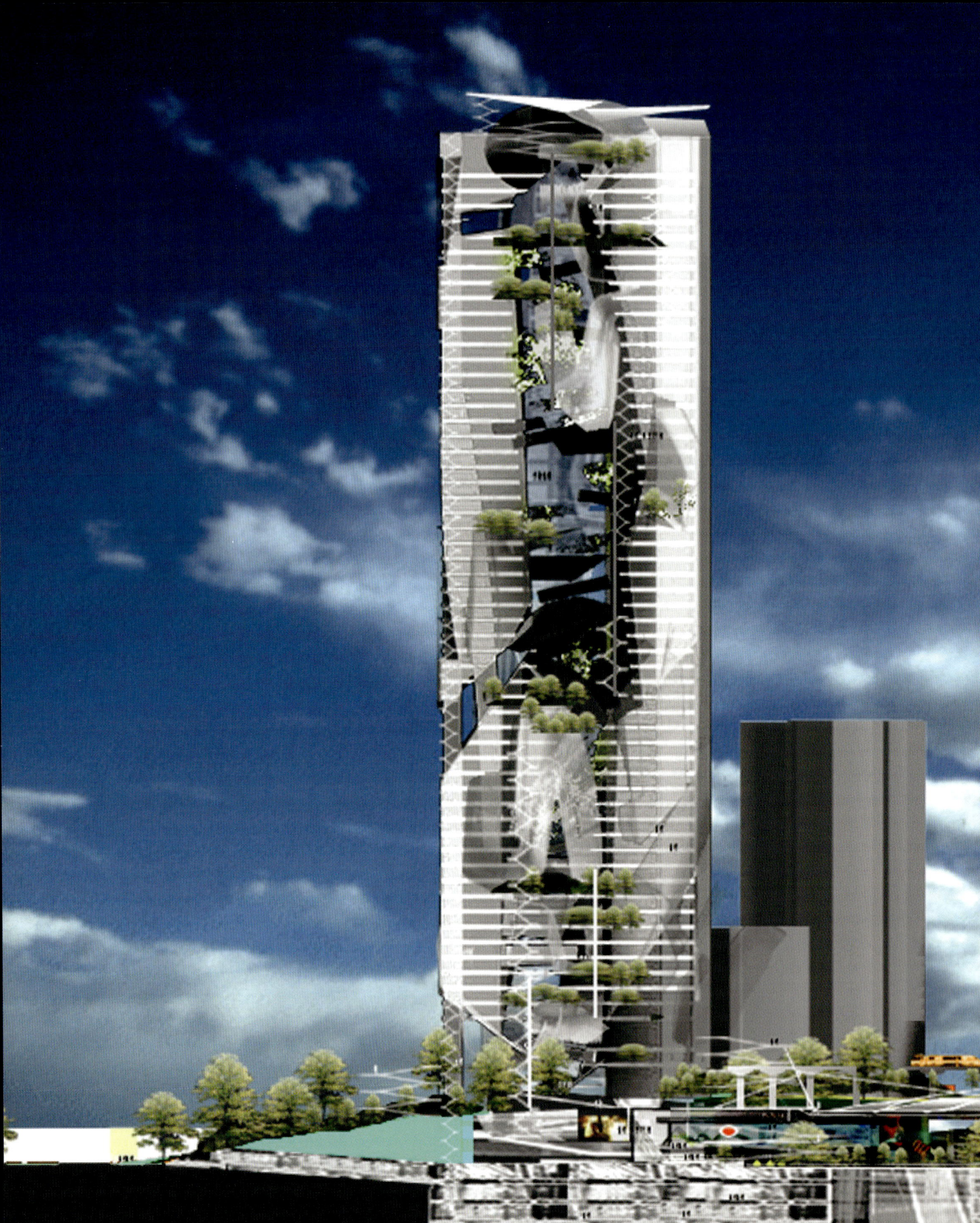

BATC Tower

BATC Tower

TYPE : Vertical Urbanism
LOCATION : Germany
CLIMATE ZONE : Temperate
VEGETATION ZONE : Forest

AREAS:

GFA	:	708,178 m²
NFA	:	530,669 m²
SITE AREA	:	167,286 m²
PLOT RATIO	:	1:4
NO. OF STOREYS	:	60
STATUS	:	Concept Design
DATE OF COMPLETION	:	1998

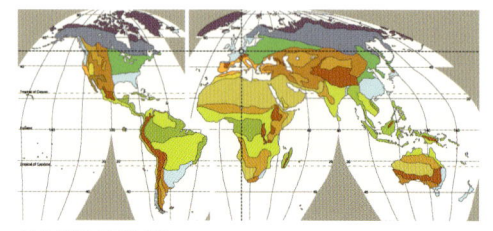

CLIMATE REGION

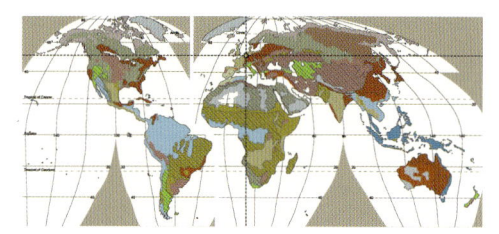

VEGETATION ZONE

Photograph of the tower cluster model

Conceptual

The BATC Tower was a competition entry for a large-scale urban development, organised by a mass-transit railway engineering company, for a location in a German city that cannot be specified. It articulates Yeang's ideas for urban design and vertical high-rise design – the ways in which conventional horizontal concepts for placemaking can be turned through 90 degrees to allow skyscrapers to replicate the life culture of the ground plane. This is a seminal project as it radically defines a new and more habitable approach to tall buildings as "vertical urban design". Yeang presented this approach in his book *Reinventing the Skyscraper: A Vertical Theory of Urban Design* published by John Wiley & Sons (2002) which has become something of a manifesto for high-rise design. The ideas in this project were further developed into his concept of "green vertical infrastructure", explored in the Edge Spire building.

Yeang found it odd that low-rise buildings are often configured as built forms with a wide range of open volumes and diverse inter-connectivity, but when buildings become very tall architects "inexplicably" manifest them as "homogeneous stacks of repetitive floorplates". The BATC Tower sought to demonstrate an alternative approach and create a 60-storey building which offered the diversity of urban life found in more ground-hugging forms. The project is a strong demonstration of Yeang's inventiveness.

"Essentially, I took conventional urban design principles and realigned them vertically, creating a new 'vertical urbanism' with a variety of parks and green spaces in the sky. This included mixed-use programmes and multiple circulation systems like those found on the ground plane – all designed to replicate pleasurable urban design concepts but locate them in the sky rather than on the ground," says Yeang. The building was designed to contain a mix of uses including a hotel, apartments, offices, an art gallery, children's nursery, retail units and cafes – linked via a range of "vertical movement

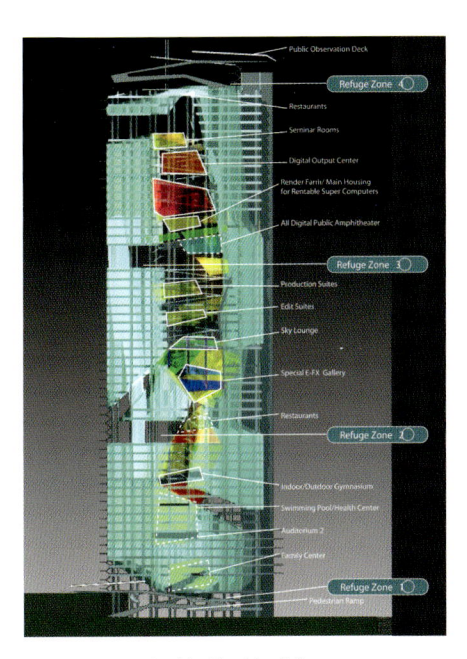

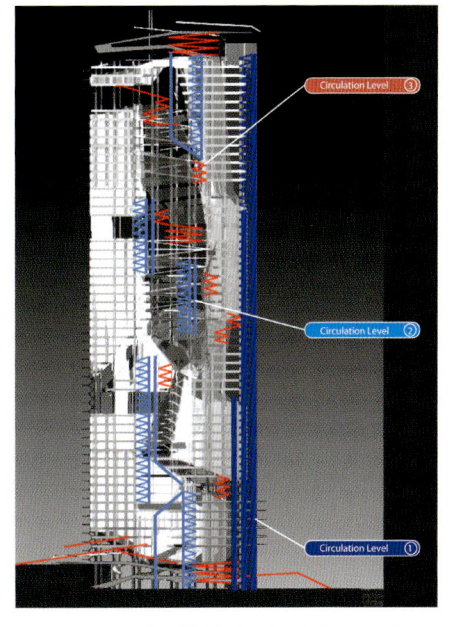

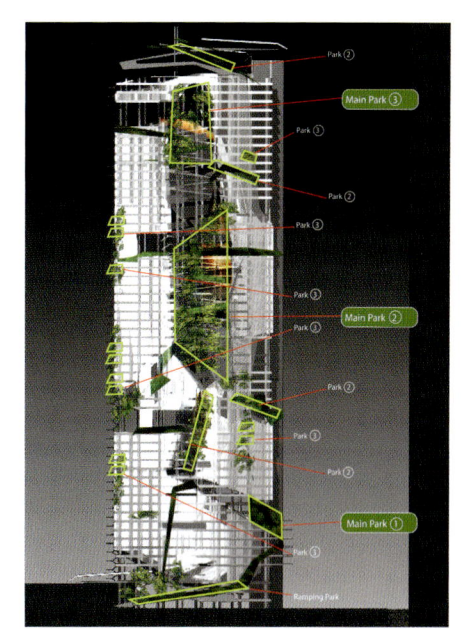

▲ Vertical building programme   ▲ Multiple circulation systems   ▲ Hierarchy of park systems

systems". Elevators move people quickly from one zone to another, while ramps and escalators enable people to move within zones. Landscaped terraces and sky courts are incorporated on all floors, providing occupants with access to greenery even at the highest levels.

The tower was also to form part of a wider, 47-acre, Yeang-designed masterplan. A light rail system was designed to traverse the site north–south, while an elevated, commercial podium creates a park on which towers would be positioned. The edges of the podium become softened and more rounded as they approach low-rise buildings ranged along one edge of the site. Vegetation from the park was designed to extend upwards into all the towers, creating a single, intensive, continuous, artificial urban ecosystem. This concept was later employed in the Zorlu (pages 232-9) and Plaza of Nations projects (pages 92-101). "My rationale for high-rise buildings is they are simply one way to accommodate urban growth without expanding over arable land or into the city's green belt. They are acceptable as built forms provided they are constructed near or over transportation interchanges," says Yeang. However, skyscrapers are among "the least ecological of all building types", cautions Yeang. "They normally consume around one third more energy and materials, taking into account construction and maintenance, than low-rise buildings. Not to be underestimated are the additional measures that must be incorporated to face wind and gravity forces. This is the reason why skyscrapers must be designed and built to be as green as we can make them."

The park contains ecobridges (see Huanan Masterplan pages 84-91) spanning east–west to retain the connectivity of the site's ecology as an integral habitat. Vehicular routes are broadly segregated from pedestrian zones.

▲ South elevation

Vertical Urbanism | BATC Tower 139

SUMMARY OF PLANS

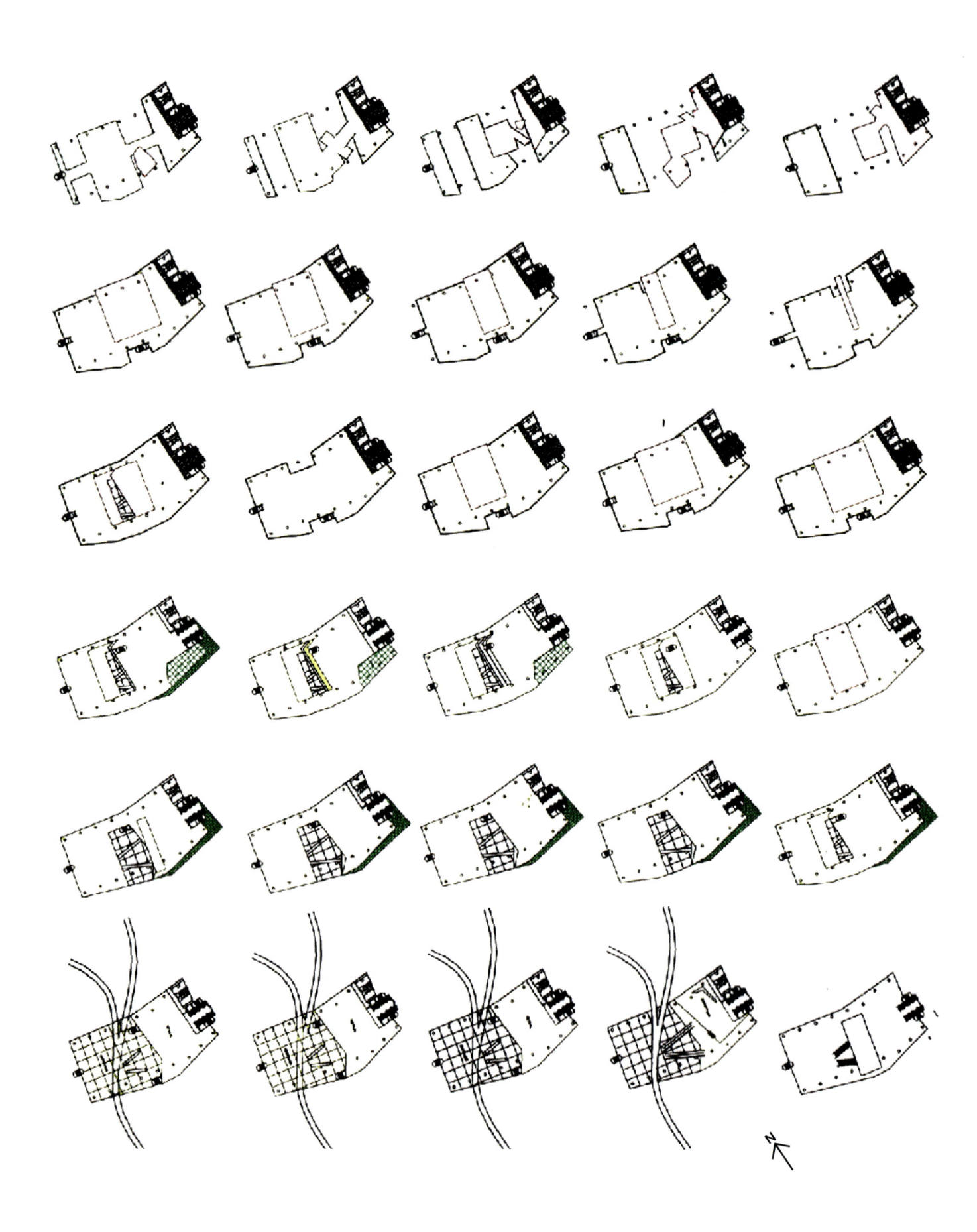

▲ Central public plaza and LRT station

▲ Model of the BATC Tower

AXONOMETRIC FLOOR PLANS DIAGRAM

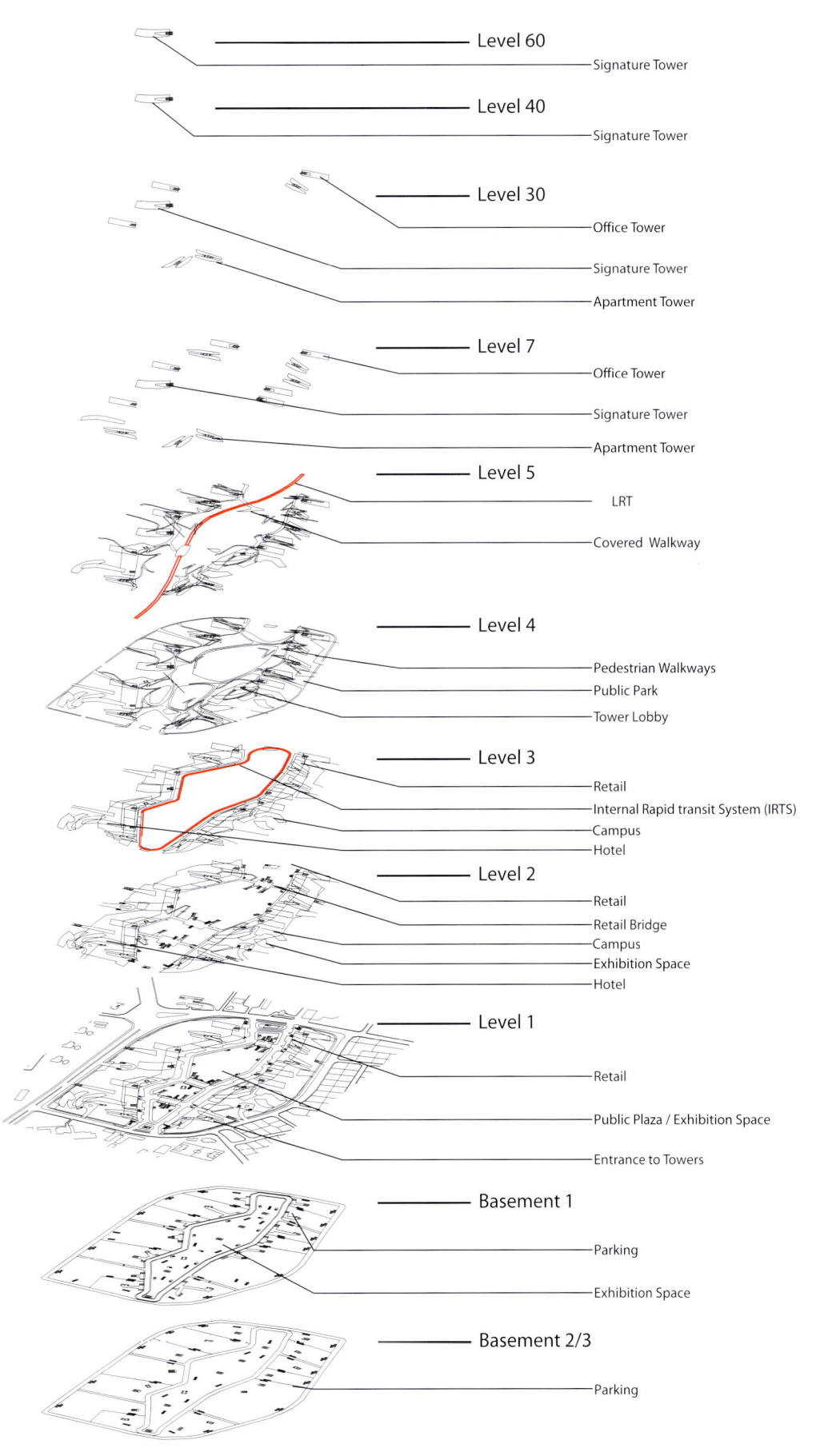

Level 60 — Signature Tower

Level 40 — Signature Tower

Level 30 — Office Tower
— Signature Tower
— Apartment Tower

Level 7 — Office Tower
— Signature Tower
— Apartment Tower

Level 5 — LRT
— Covered Walkway

Level 4 — Pedestrian Walkways
— Public Park
— Tower Lobby

Level 3 — Retail
— Internal Rapid transit System (IRTS)
— Campus
— Hotel

Level 2 — Retail
— Retail Bridge
— Campus
— Exhibition Space
— Hotel

Level 1 — Retail
— Public Plaza / Exhibition Space
— Entrance to Towers

Basement 1 — Parking
— Exhibition Space

Basement 2/3 — Parking

Vertical Urbanism | **BATC Tower** 143

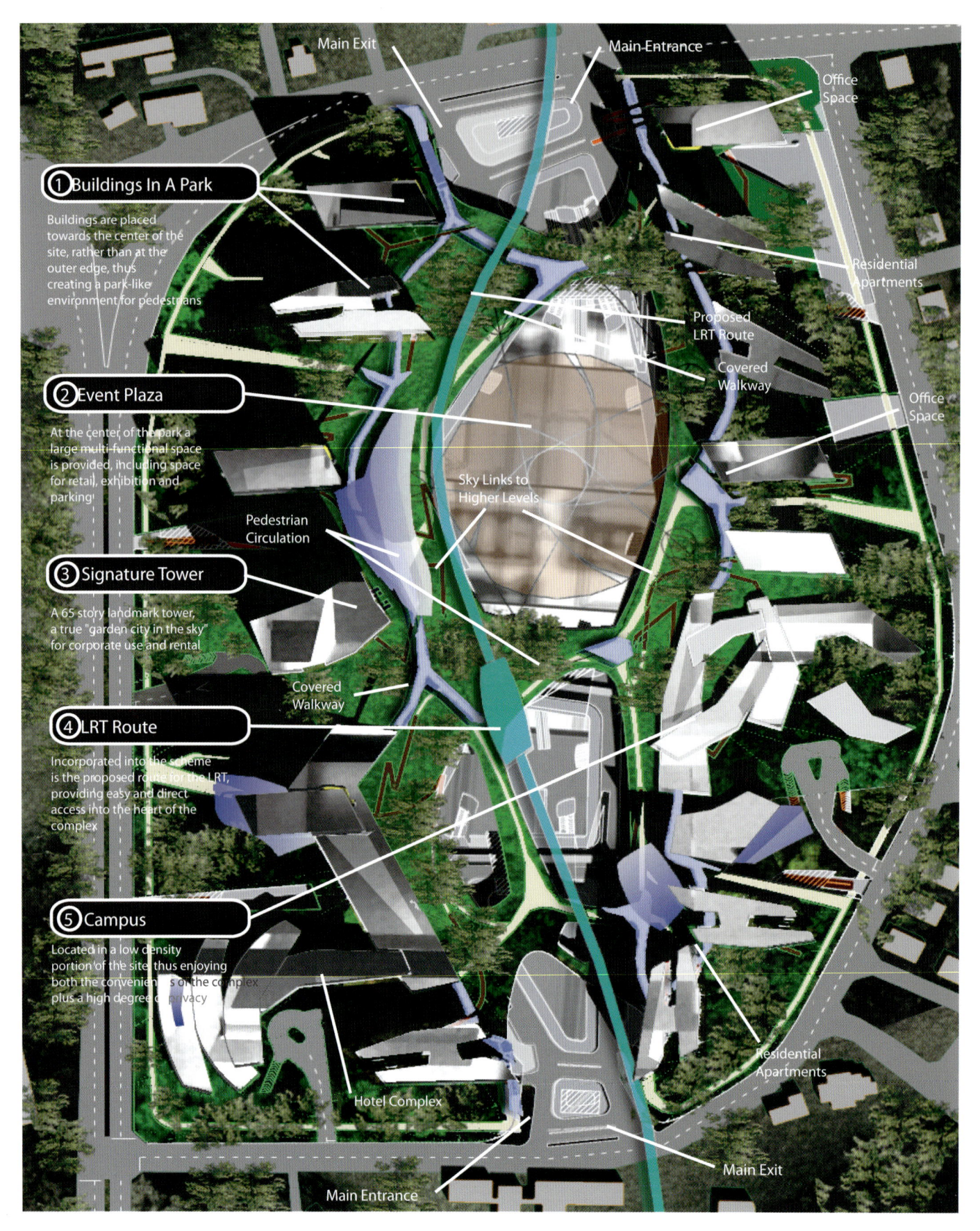

1. Buildings In A Park
Buildings are placed towards the center of the site, rather than at the outer edge, thus creating a park-like environment for pedestrians

2. Event Plaza
At the center of the park a large multi-functional space is provided, including space for retail, exhibition and parking

3. Signature Tower
A 65 story landmark tower, a true "garden city in the sky" for corporate use and rental

4. LRT Route
Incorporated into the scheme is the proposed route for the LRT, providing easy and direct access into the heart of the complex

5. Campus
Located in a low density portion of the site, thus enjoying both the conveniences of the complex plus a high degree of privacy

Labels on image: Main Exit, Main Entrance, Office Space, Residential Apartments, Proposed LRT Route, Covered Walkway, Office Space, Sky Links to Higher Levels, Pedestrian Circulation, Covered Walkway, Residential Apartments, Hotel Complex, Main Exit, Main Entrance

▲ Masterplan, showing key features, including rapid transit line

▶ Diagram highlighting key elements as they appear on the vertical axis

144 ECOARCHITECTURE | THE WORK OF KEN YEANG

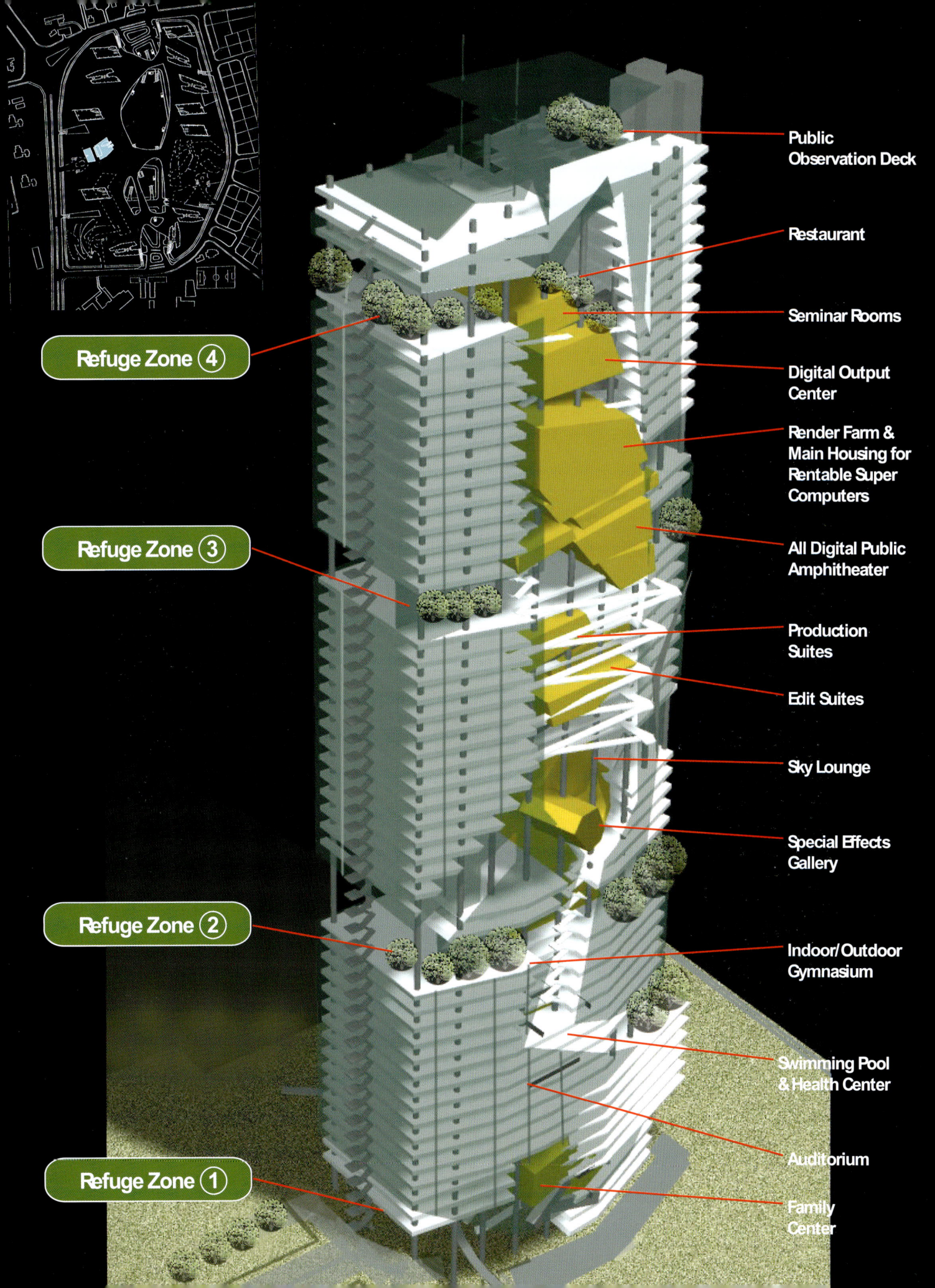

- Refuge Zone ④
- Refuge Zone ③
- Refuge Zone ②
- Refuge Zone ①

- Public Observation Deck
- Restaurant
- Seminar Rooms
- Digital Output Center
- Render Farm & Main Housing for Rentable Super Computers
- All Digital Public Amphitheater
- Production Suites
- Edit Suites
- Sky Lounge
- Special Effects Gallery
- Indoor/Outdoor Gymnasium
- Swimming Pool & Health Center
- Auditorium
- Family Center

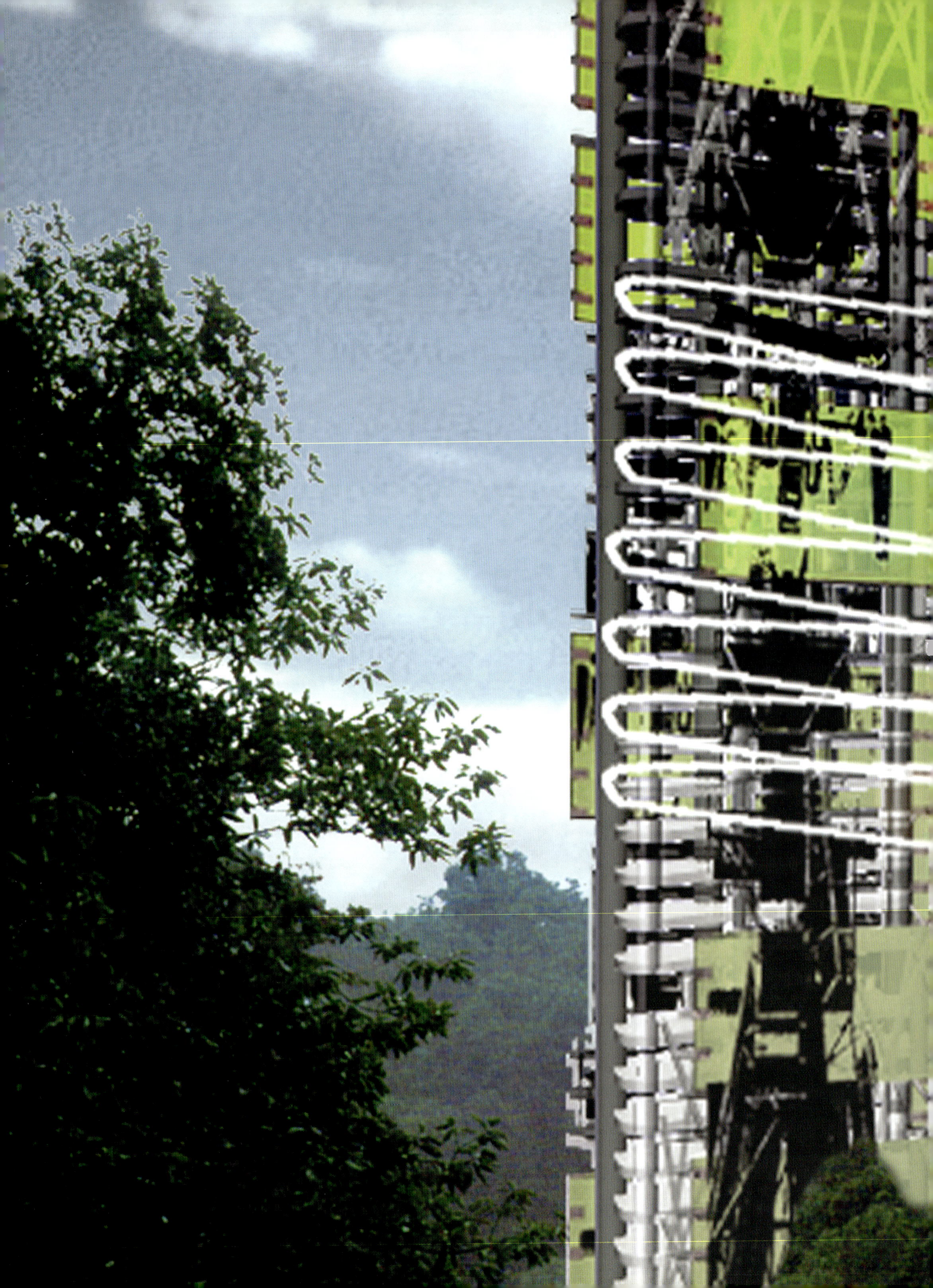

Nagoya Expo 2005 Tower

Nagoya EXPO 2005 Tower

TYPE	:	Vertical Urbanism
LOCATION	:	Nagoya, Japan
CLIMATE ZONE	:	Temperate
VEGETATION ZONE	:	Deciduous Forest

AREAS:

GFA	:	902,458 m²
NFA	:	631,316 m²
SITE AREA	:	607,035 m²
PLOT RATIO	:	1:5
NO. OF STOREYS	:	50
STATUS	:	Competition
DATE	:	2003

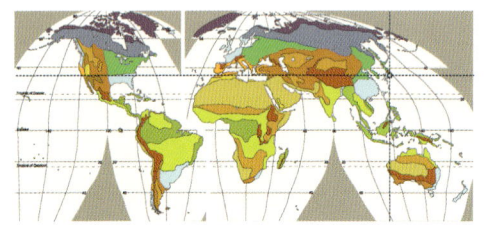

CLIMATE REGION

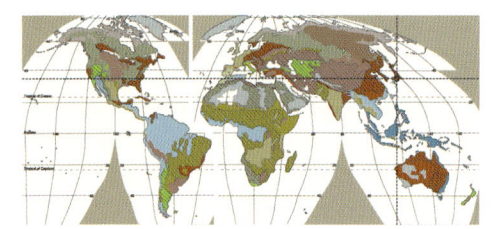

VEGETATION ZONE

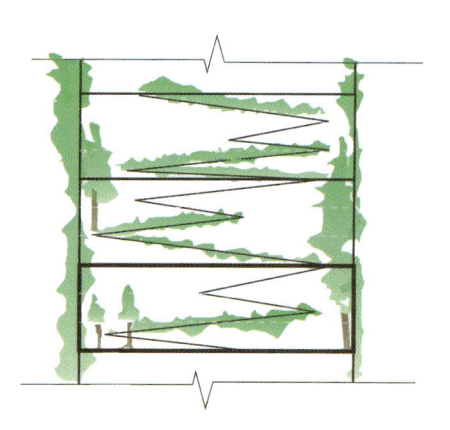

Conceptual

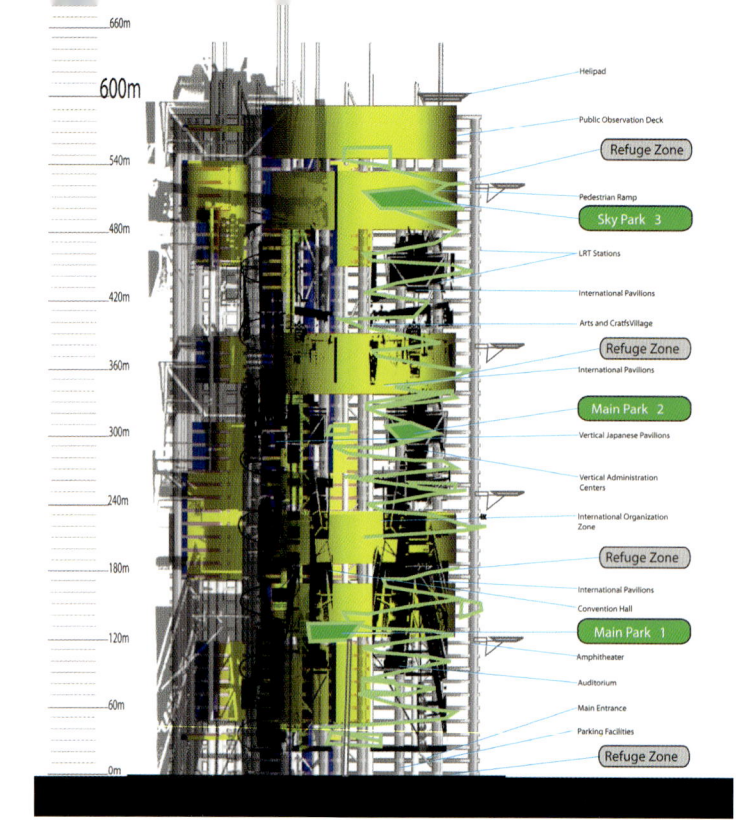

▲ Elevation with indication of building programme

Yeang's design for a vertical exposition facility was drawn from his ideas of "vertical urbanism" expressed in the BATC masterplan (pages 136-45). The proposal was in response to a "call for ideas" by the organisers of Expo 2005, located on a 150 hectare, green site near Nagoya, Japan. Encouraged by the organisers' theme of "Nature's Wisdom", Yeang proposed to arrange the international expo vertically, thereby reducing its physical impact and helping to preserve the fragile eco-system of the site. "The site was situated in an ecologically diverse and sensitive location, which was host to a number of rare species of flora and fauna including butterflies," says Yeang. "I felt that a horizontal expo would devastate the site's ecology and devastate its natural inhabitants and habitat."

Yeang's proposal, therefore, was to build upwards rather than outwards, creating a tower with a small footprint and setting out generous vertical spaces for participating nations to create pavilions in the sky. Floor slabs would be configured with large voids, allowing pavilions 12m in height to be erected (rising through three storeys). And just as he had already flipped ideas of placemaking through 90 degrees to create vertical landscapes, Yeang set about creating a "vertical pedestrian promenade" – the skyscraper equivalent of the horizontal axis that characterises the typical ground-hugging exposition.

The site contained a mature ecosystem (following a period of secondary ecological succession), and Yeang was concerned that 2.5 million visitors would trample everything underfoot, while the creation of expressways and other hard surfaces would carve the site into distinct

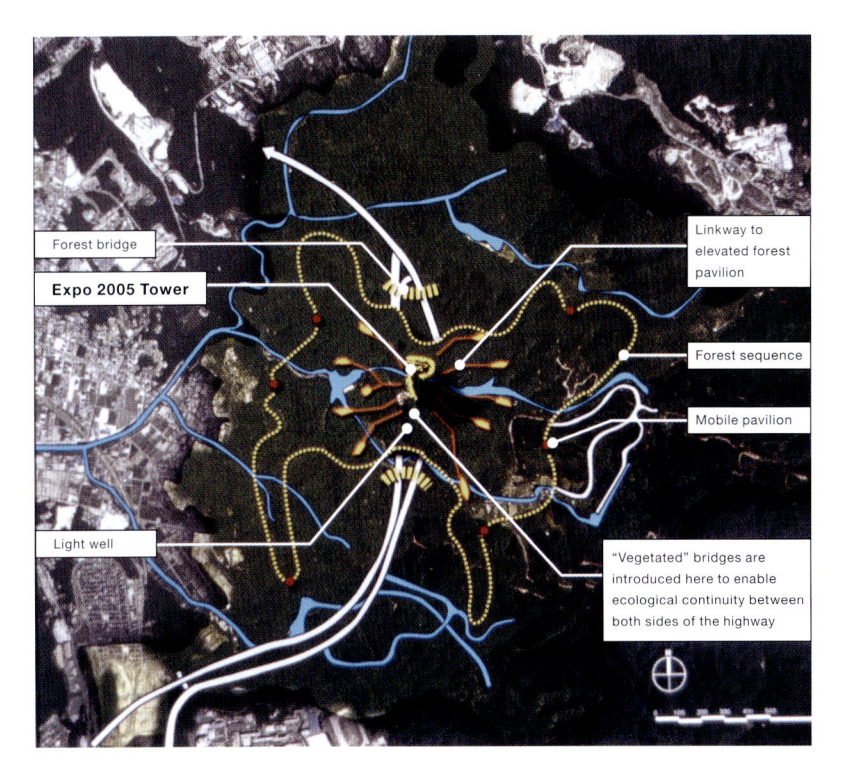

▲ Expo 2005 site

▲ Nagoya EXPO 2005 Tower: perspective view

pockets. Yeang further proposed a series of "forest bridges" both to lift visitors off the ground of the woodland and maintain green connections below, engendering a more stable ecosystem, reducing the fragmentation of land, retaining migration routes and ecological diversity.

The tower itself was imagined to rise 300m above the forest floor, served not only by a vertical pedestrian ramp and a system of elevators and escalators, but by a light rail system which wrapped the building in tracks configured as a double helix. Small stations would be located at regular intervals along the tower's façade, in much the same way as an elevator operates. At the close of the expo, Yeang imagined the tower being converted into "real estate in the sky". It was an approach that US architect Neil Denari called "a high-tech Archigram-style aesthetic".

As it turned out, history has proved rather different. Expo organisers still insist the site was "designed with the conservation of nature and the local environment as the top priority". Indeed, the expo website declares: "Finding answers for today's world must be done in the context of technology. Thus, the concept of eco-communities was developed." But a conventional landscape format was eventually selected for the event. Little now survives of the expo – the pavilions have been dismantled, leaving just a ferris wheel and a museum on site. After rebuilding works, the site reopened in 2006 as Aichi Expo Memorial Park (often called Morikoro Park), containing an ice rink and other municipal facilities. A large exhibition hall and sports centre was due to be completed in 2010.

SUMMARY OF PLANS

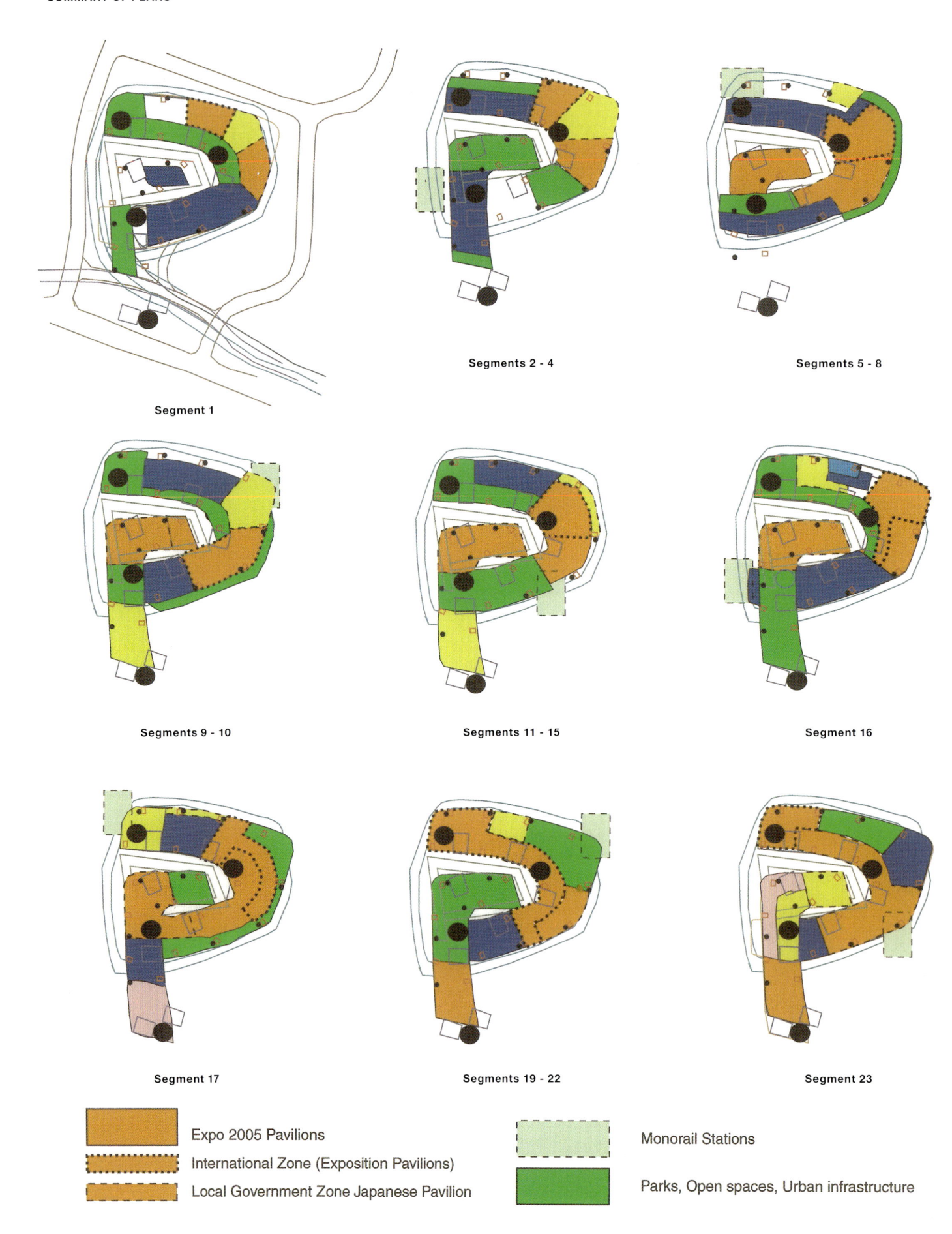

Segment 1

Segments 2 - 4

Segments 5 - 8

Segments 9 - 10

Segments 11 - 15

Segment 16

Segment 17

Segments 19 - 22

Segment 23

Expo 2005 Pavilions
International Zone (Exposition Pavilions)
Local Government Zone Japanese Pavilion

Monorail Stations

Parks, Open spaces, Urban infrastructure

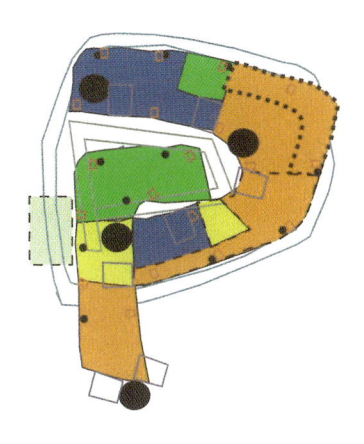

Segment 24

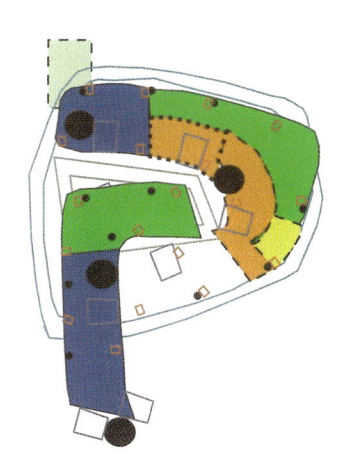

Segments 25 - 31

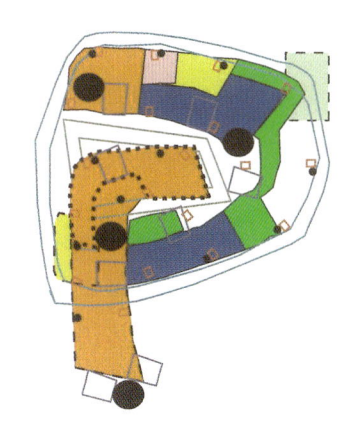

Segment 32

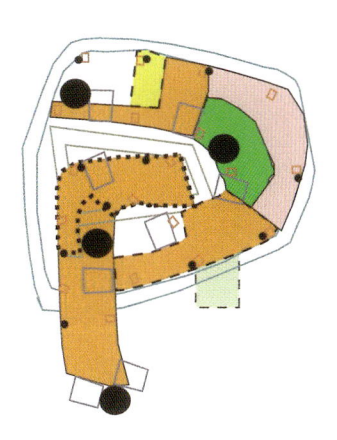

Segments 33 - 36

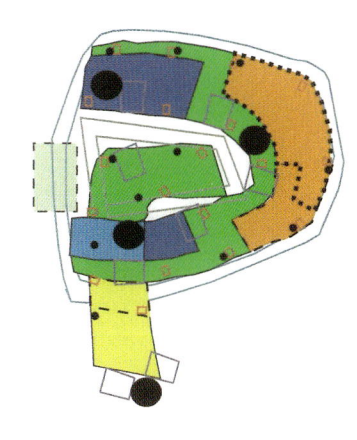

Segments 37 - 42

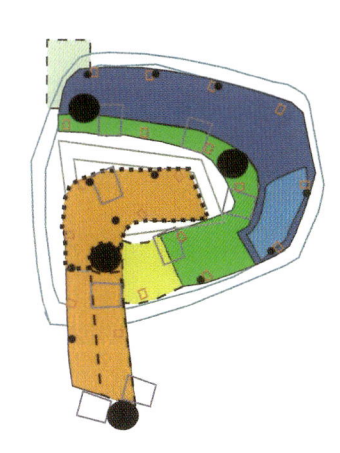

Segments 42 - 47

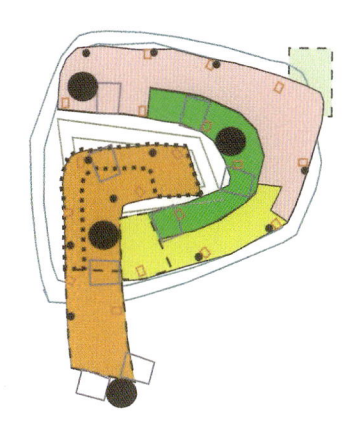

Segment 48

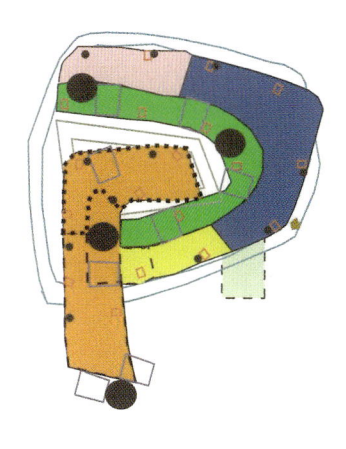

Segment 49

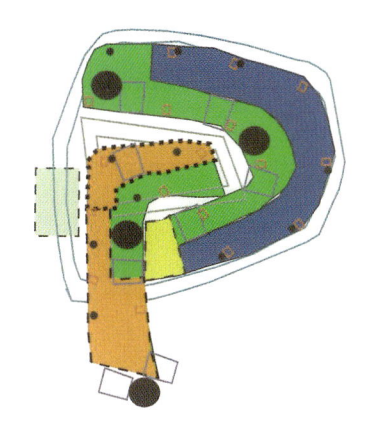

Segment 50

Hotels & Commercial,

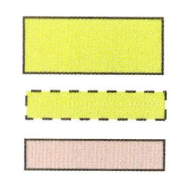

Light Industry

Offices and Administration

International Organisation Zones

Residential buildings

Vertical Urbanism | Nagoya Expo 2005 Tower

CIRCULATION CONCEPT

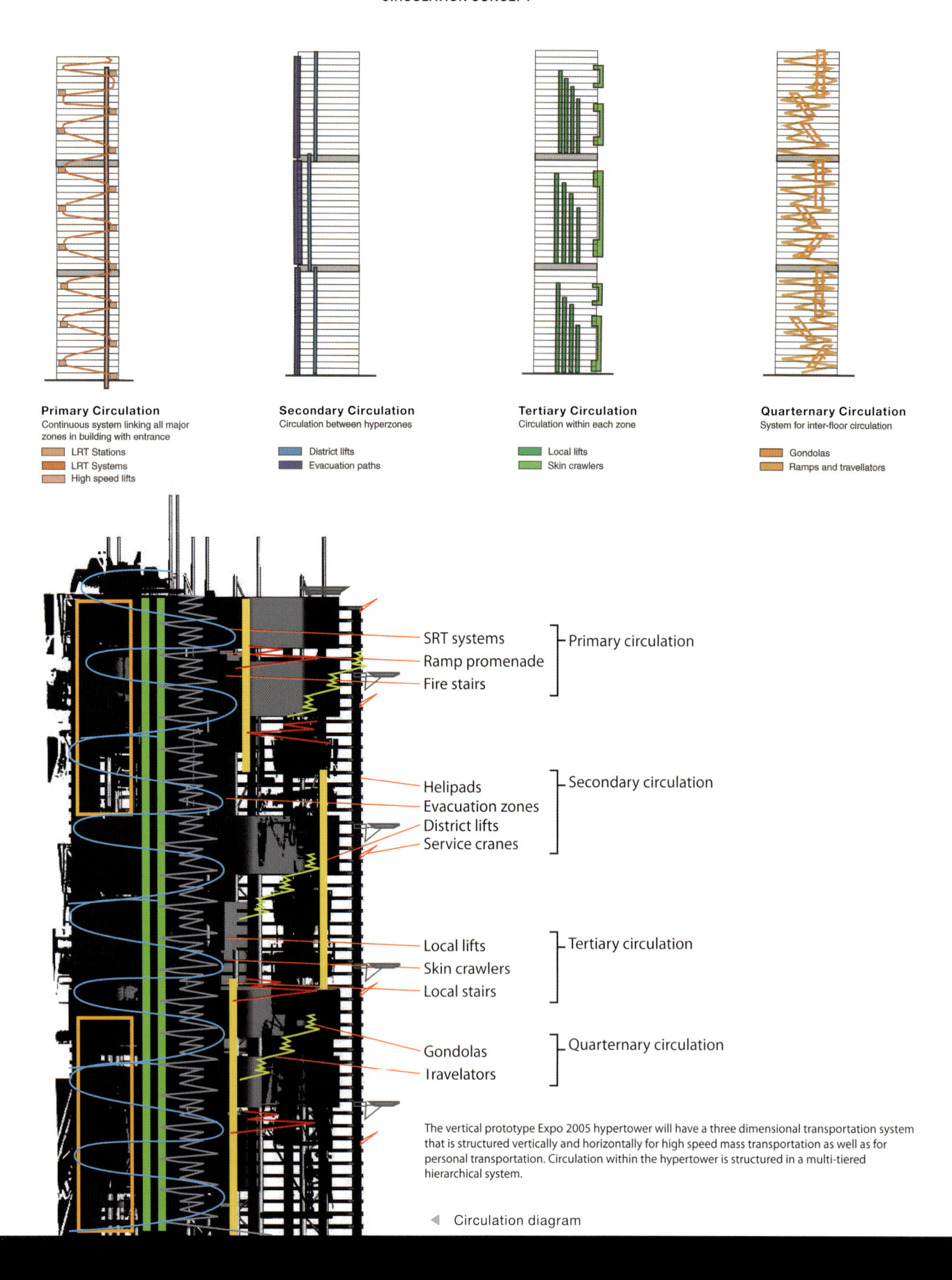

Primary Circulation
Continuous system linking all major zones in building with entrance
- LRT Stations
- LRT Systems
- High speed lifts

Secondary Circulation
Circulation between hyperzones
- District lifts
- Evacuation paths

Tertiary Circulation
Circulation within each zone
- Local lifts
- Skin crawlers

Quarternary Circulation
System for inter-floor circulation
- Gondolas
- Ramps and travellators

Primary circulation
- SRT systems
- Ramp promenade
- Fire stairs

Secondary circulation
- Helipads
- Evacuation zones
- District lifts
- Service cranes

Tertiary circulation
- Local lifts
- Skin crawlers
- Local stairs

Quarternary circulation
- Gondolas
- Travelators

The vertical prototype Expo 2005 hypertower will have a three dimensional transportation system that is structured vertically and horizontally for high speed mass transportation as well as for personal transportation. Circulation within the hypertower is structured in a multi-tiered hierarchical system.

◀ Circulation diagram

ZONING CONCEPT

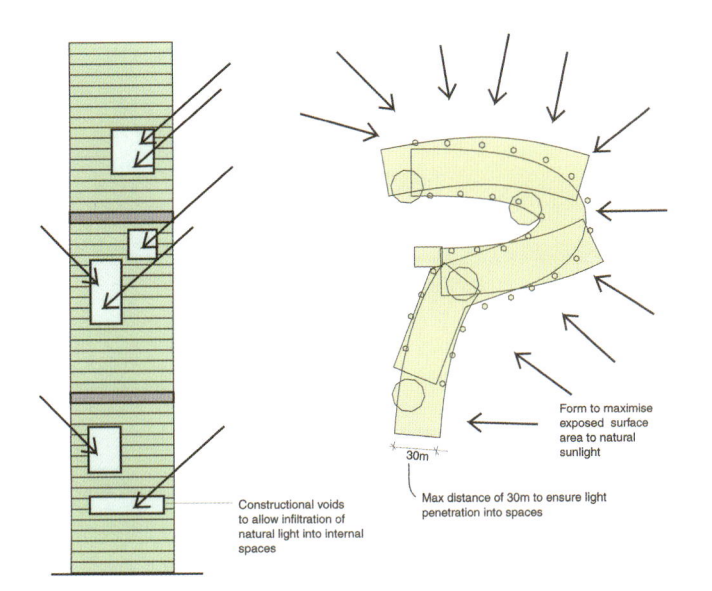

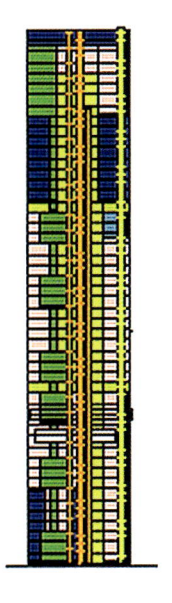

Site Study, with Vertical / Horizontal Comparison

Constructional voids to allow infiltration of natural light into internal spaces

Form to maximise exposed surface area to natural sunlight

30m

Max distance of 30m to ensure light penetration into spaces

Vertical Zoning

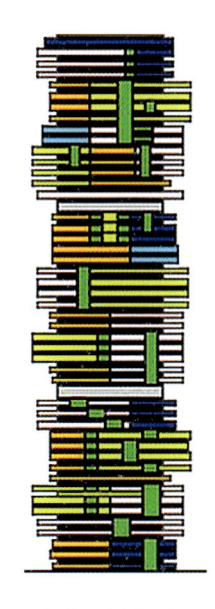

Horizontal Zoning

- 1-EXPO 2005 pavilions
- 2-Hotels and commercial
- 3-Office and administration
- 4-Light Industry
- 5-Residential buildings
- 6-Urban Infrastructure

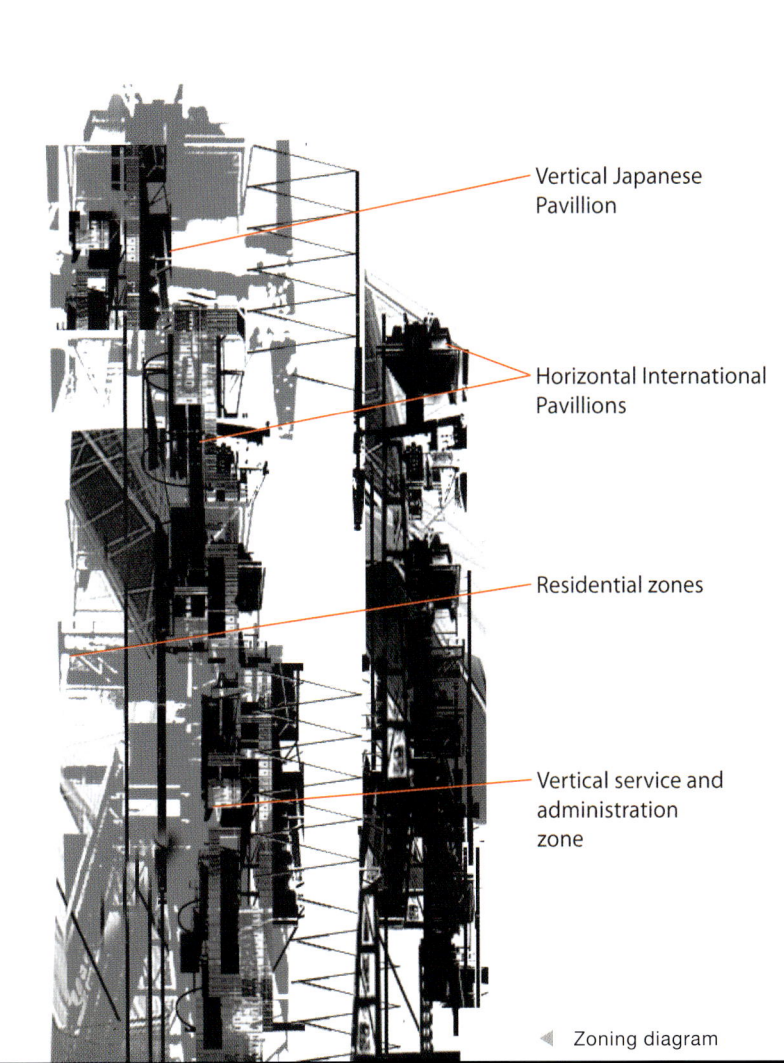

Vertical Japanese Pavillion

Horizontal International Pavillions

Residential zones

Vertical service and administration zone

◀ Zoning diagram

Vertical Urbanism | Nagoya Expo 2005 Tower

◄ Aerial view of model

SKYSCRAPER RAPID TRANSIT CONCEPT

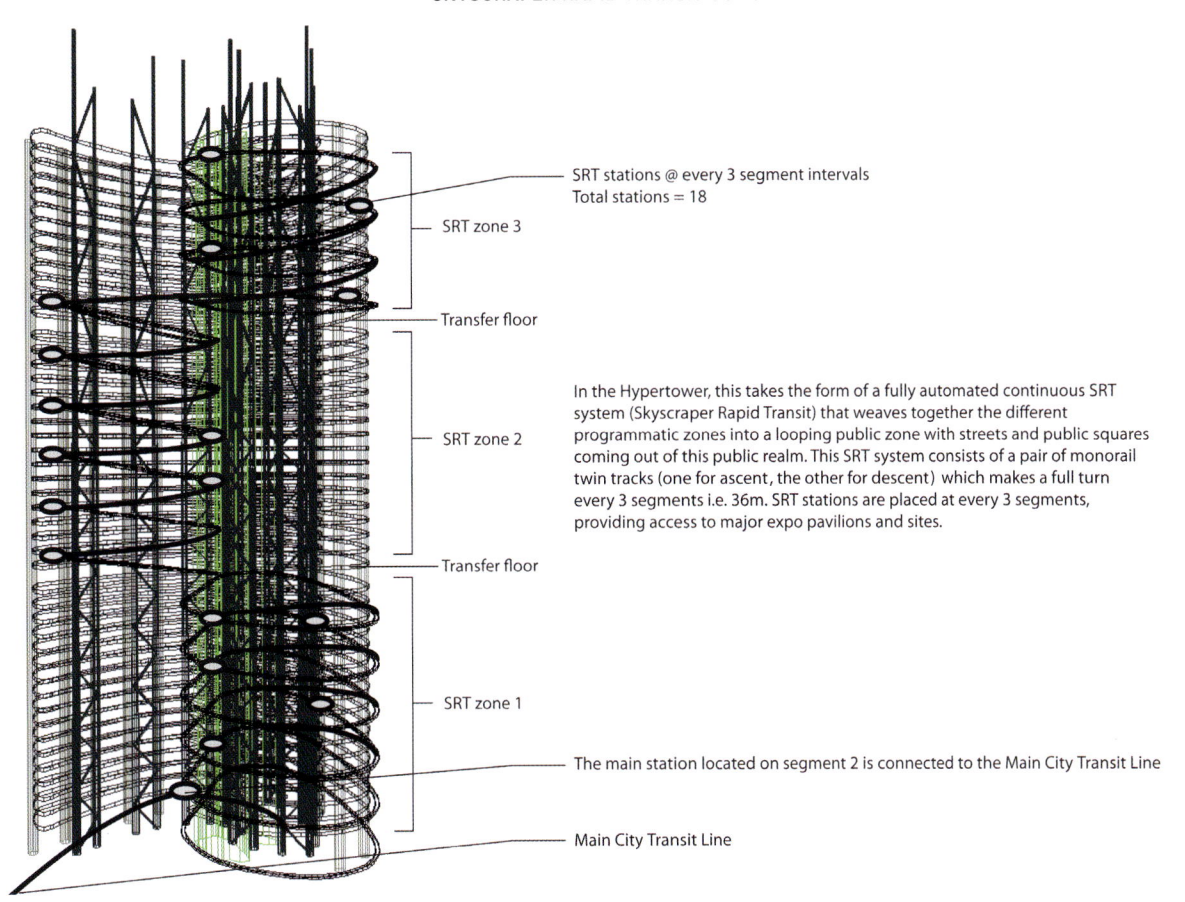

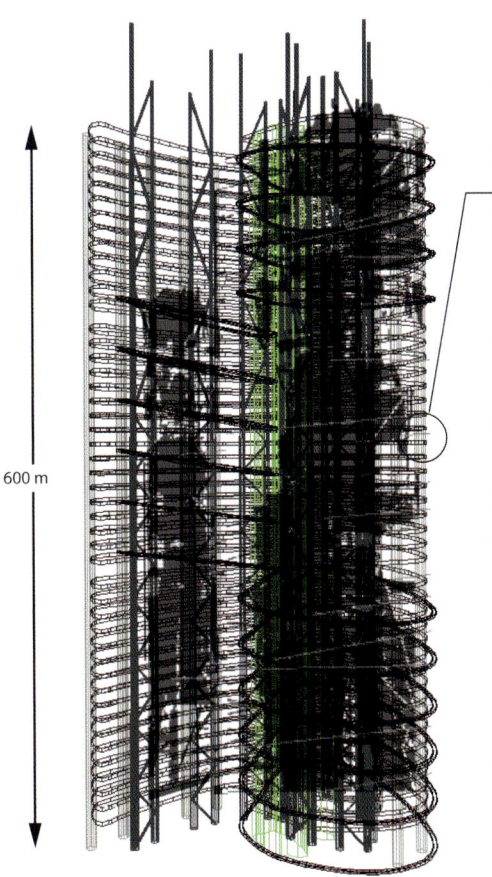

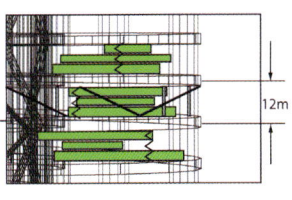

- SRT stations @ every 3 segment intervals
  Total stations = 18
- SRT zone 3
- Transfer floor
- SRT zone 2
- Transfer floor
- SRT zone 1
- The main station located on segment 2 is connected to the Main City Transit Line
- Main City Transit Line

In the Hypertower, this takes the form of a fully automated continuous SRT system (Skyscraper Rapid Transit) that weaves together the different programmatic zones into a looping public zone with streets and public squares coming out of this public realm. This SRT system consists of a pair of monorail twin tracks (one for ascent, the other for descent) which makes a full turn every 3 segments i.e. 36m. SRT stations are placed at every 3 segments, providing access to major expo pavilions and sites.

SPACE CONCEPT

600 m

12m

- 12m floor to ceiling segment height will allow up to 3 storey pavilion construction with independent quarternary circulation system. The space will then be converted into "real-estate-in-the-sky" after the 2005 expo.

Height   :600m
Organisation   :50 segments of 12m each
                                 every segment allows for the construction
                                 of 3-4 storey buildings
Function during Expo 2005   :vertical containment of programmatic
                                 requirements of the Expo
Function after Expo   :vertical real estate development
Total Site Area   :540ha
Proposed development area   :150ha
Proposed footprint @50segments:150/50 = 3ha
Area reserved for nature: 537ha

Estimated visitor population   : 2.5 million visitors /5months
                                    =500 000 visitors / month
                                    =about 16 500 visitors / day
Estimated staff population   : 20% of visitor population
                                    =3300
Estimated population in tower   : about 20 000 during Expo

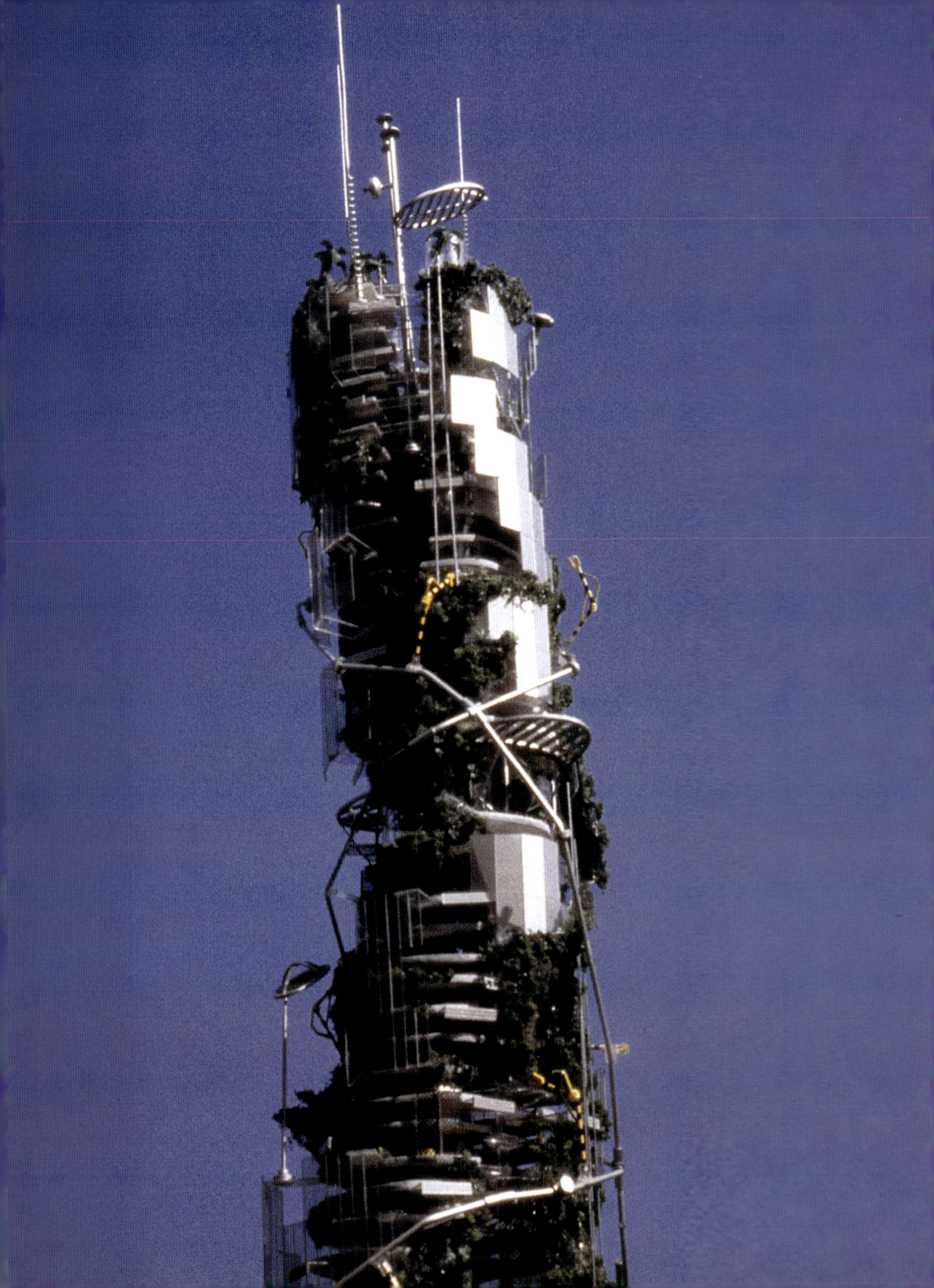

Tokyo-Nara Tower

Tokyo-Nara Tower

TYPE	:	Vertical Urbanism
LOCATION	:	Tokyo, Japan
CLIMATE ZONE	:	Temperate
VEGETATION ZONE	:	Deciduous Forest

AREAS:

GFA	:	448,536 m²
NFA	:	313,674 m²
SITE AREA	:	22,500 m²
PLOT RATIO	:	1:20
NO. OF STOREYS	:	156
STATUS	:	Prototype
DATE	:	2003

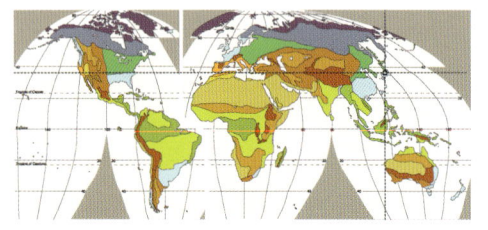

CLIMATE REGION

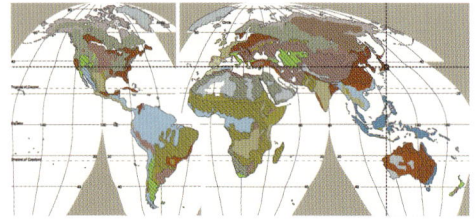

VEGETATION ZONE

Conceptual

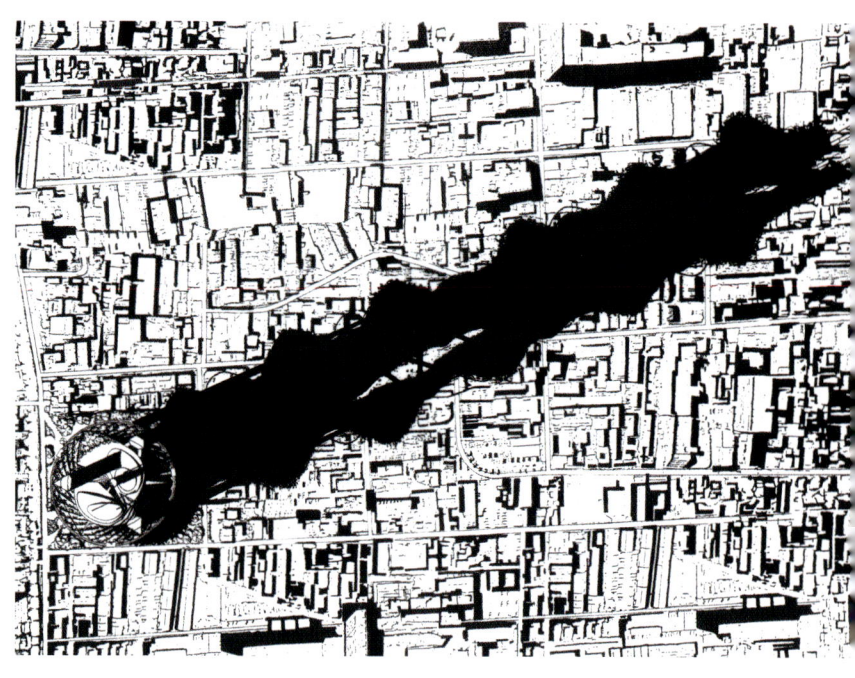

▲ Tokyo-Nara Tower; site plan and shadow study

This concept design offers perhaps Yeang's most radical interpretation of the skyscraper. The design combines Yeang's theories of bioclimatic design and vertical urbanism, placing them within a high-tech aesthetic that offers a dramatic interpretation of how green buildings could develop. Designed for an exhibition and conference curated by Kisho Kurokawa in Nara, Japan, the building's programme was influenced by the Japanese 1960s' Metabolism movement, which placed a premium on prefabrication, advanced technology and flexible modules which could be plugged into efficient service cores. Yeang's model was further exhibited in New York and London.

Yeang has described this 500 metre-high skyscraper as a "hyper tower", summing up its height, ambition, performance and notions of placemaking. It precedes his design for the 2005 Nagoya Expo Tower by some considerable margin, but many of the ideas underpinning the tower's form and performance are the same. The authors of the book *Architects Today*, who describe the tower as "the hanging gardens of Ken Yeang", draw attention to the fact that "the result is a scaly, organic skin rather than a shiny, smooth corporate sheath".

The design utilises vertical landscaping that spirals around and throughout the tower. Vegetation, and its careful positioning, is used to cool the building as well as control air movements through strategic planting. The large mass of planting is designed to work in tandem with the building's mechanical systems, supplementing their performance and reducing the energy load. Robotic devices akin to "cherry pickers" are incorporated into the architecture of the tower as landscape maintenance devices; these systems would also clean and maintain external fixtures such as glazing and cladding.

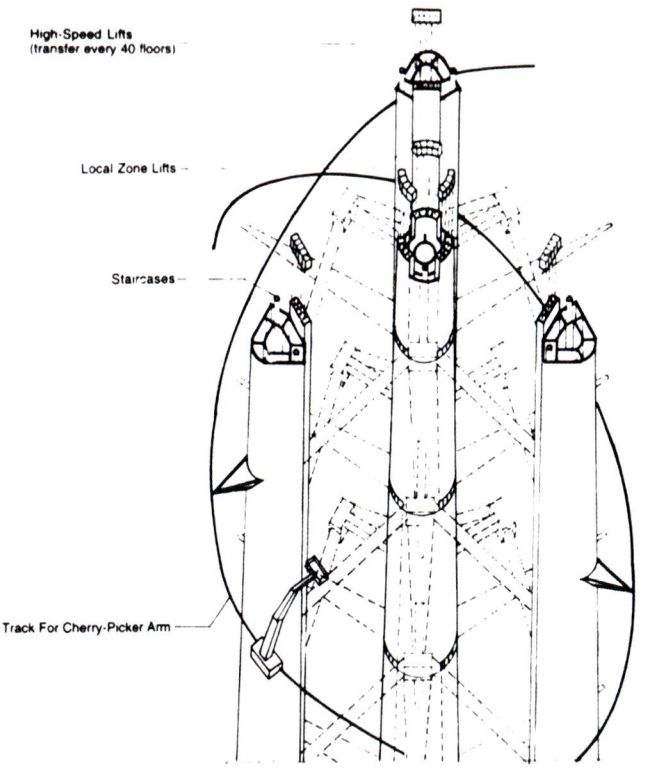

▲ Vertical circulation

The building is configured like a giant screw; the central core supports triangular-shaped floorplates which spiral up the tower, stepping up and around the core in radial fashion and leaving spaces for large atria and skycourts. This configuration enables daylight to penetrate right into the centre of what would otherwise be a very deep and dark floor plan, while controlling air movement. These open, terraced, vegetated spaces – which operate as the buildings lungs through their air filtration and supply of oxygen – are connected by bridges and stairways. Wind flues, which can be adjusted with dampers, bring fresh air deep into the building.

Lift and service cores, manufactured from in situ cast concrete and clad in perforated metal screens, are located on the east–west axis. Designed for a tropical environment, the tower's north- and south-facing façades would therefore be the cooler faces; glazed, these façades are, nonetheless, provided with sun shades to carefully manage light penetration. With its vertically spiralling green façade and rotated floor plates, the Tokyo Nara Tower provides a prototype for the EDITT Tower and an influence on the Solaris design.

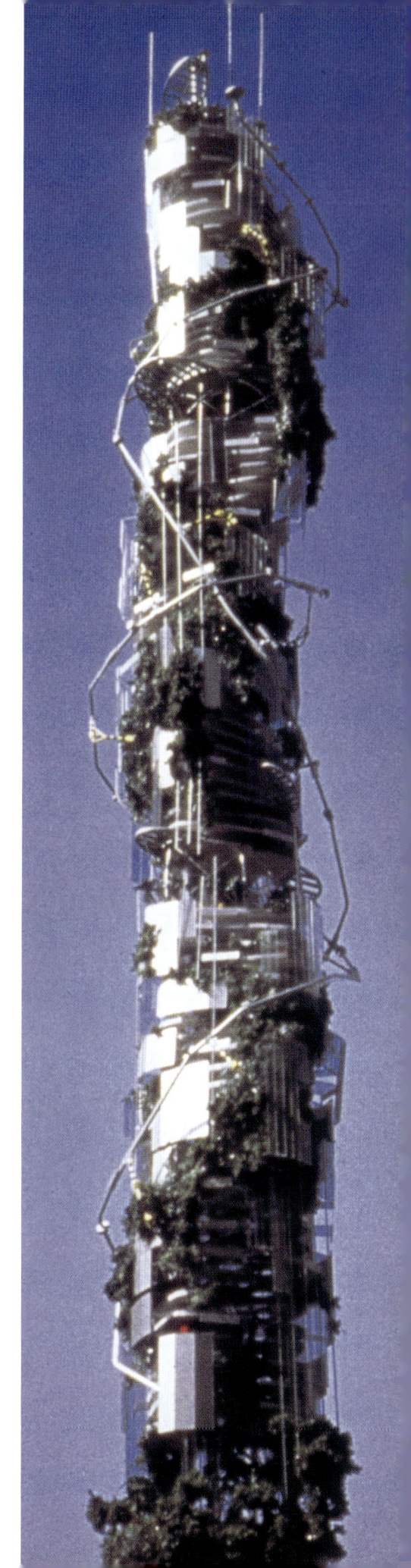

▶ Photograph of model

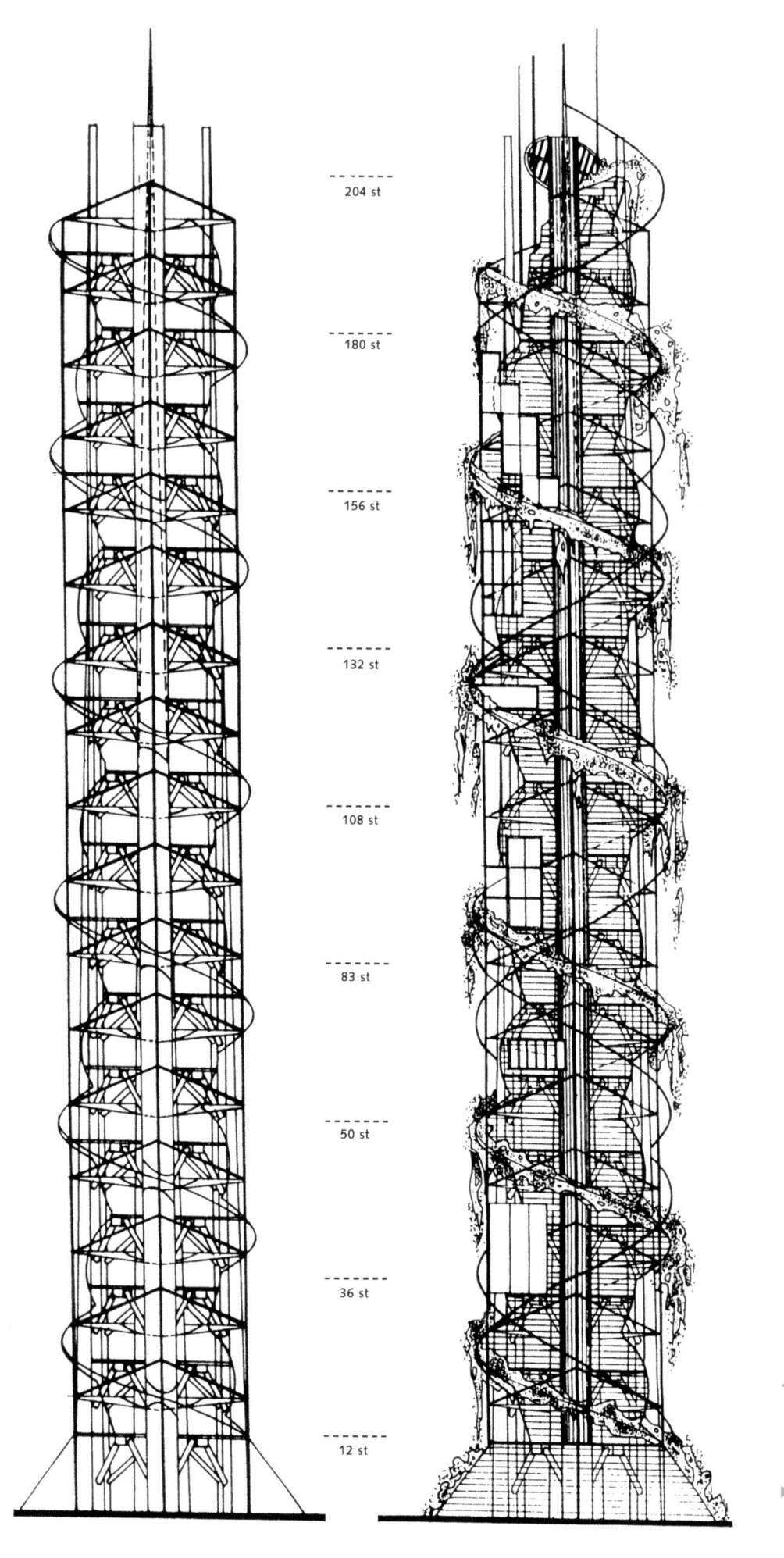

204 st
180 st
156 st
132 st
108 st
83 st
50 st
36 st
12 st

◁ Drawings of spiralling structural system (left); vertical landscaping (right)

▶ Photograph of model: upper elements

160 ECOARCHITECTURE | THE WORK OF KEN YEANG

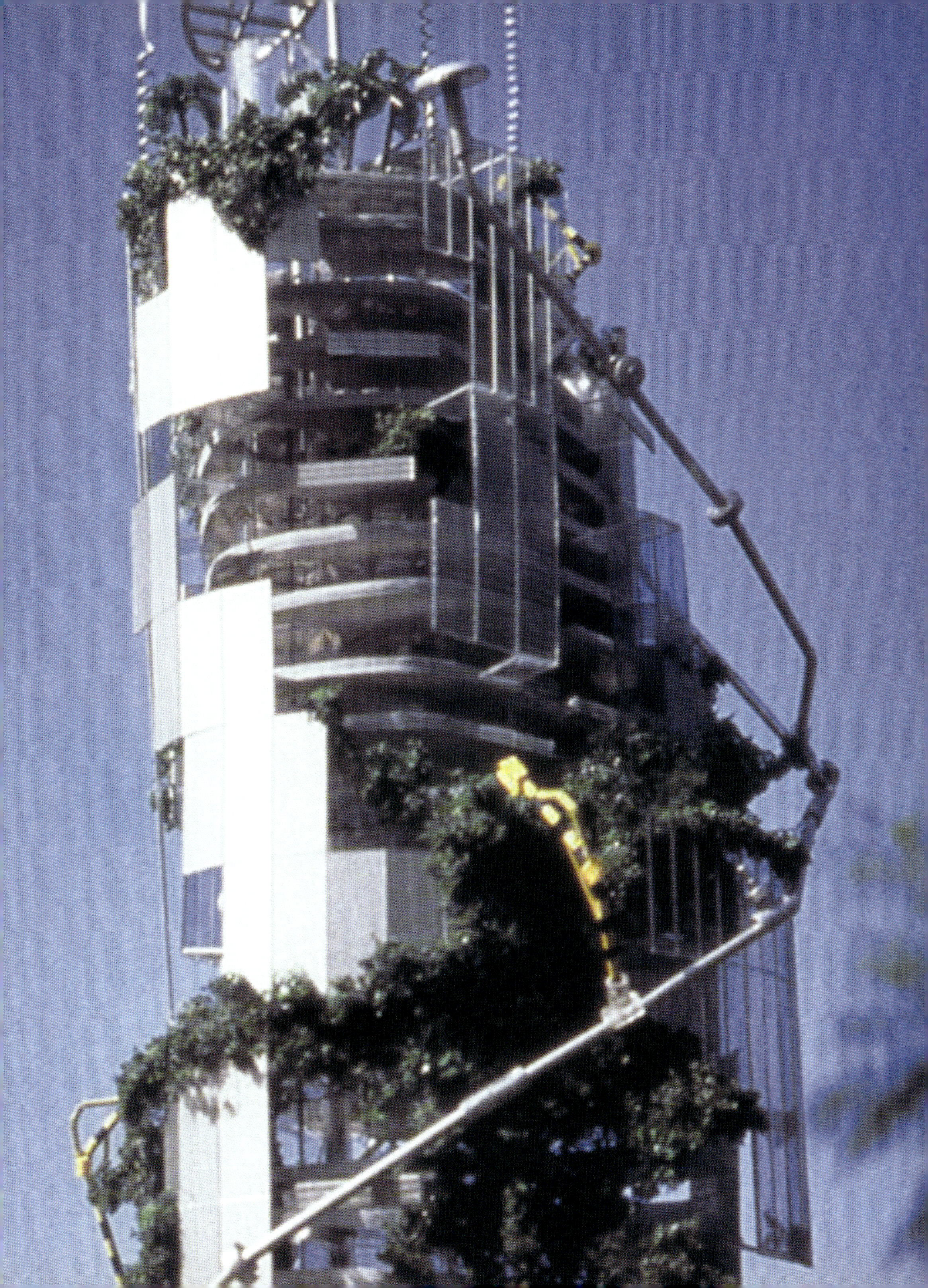

STUDY OF PRINCIPAL FEATURES

1. Seasonal Changes

2. Climate Predictability

Climate is a complex interaction of the atmospheric forces of radiation, air movement and atmospheric pressure. Near the sun's face, micro climatic forces become more influential and the global understanding become less predictable.

3. Solar Radiation

As the sun's rays passes through the atmosphere its energy is reduced. However, as it hits the cloud level it is reflected intensifying radiation towards the tower at lower levels.

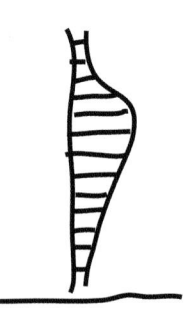

4. Rainfall

Clouds precipitate water which falls to the ground As it falls some is lifted by rising air currents and some is evaporated so that its intensity is reduced.

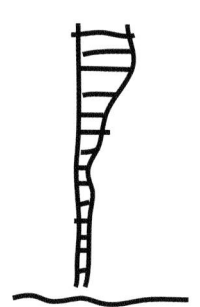

5. Speed of Climatic Change

The ground provides a source of thermal inertial moderating sudden climatic variations.

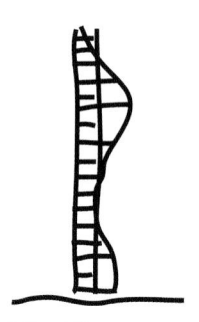

6. Humidity

Humidity varies throughout the year, however it is the greatest at ground level and within cloud cover.

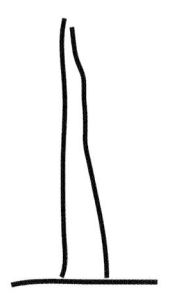

7. Air Temperature

Air temperature drops with height.

8. Air density

The density of the atmosphere reduces with height.

9. Ground Noise

Street noise for example is less noticeable beyond five storeys.

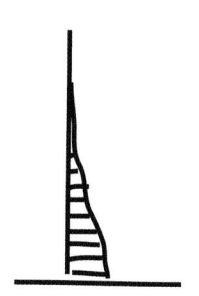

10. Concentration of Pollution

The main sources of pollutants are from vehicles and industry Vehicles deposit more pollutants at ground level wheras industry deposit it at high level.

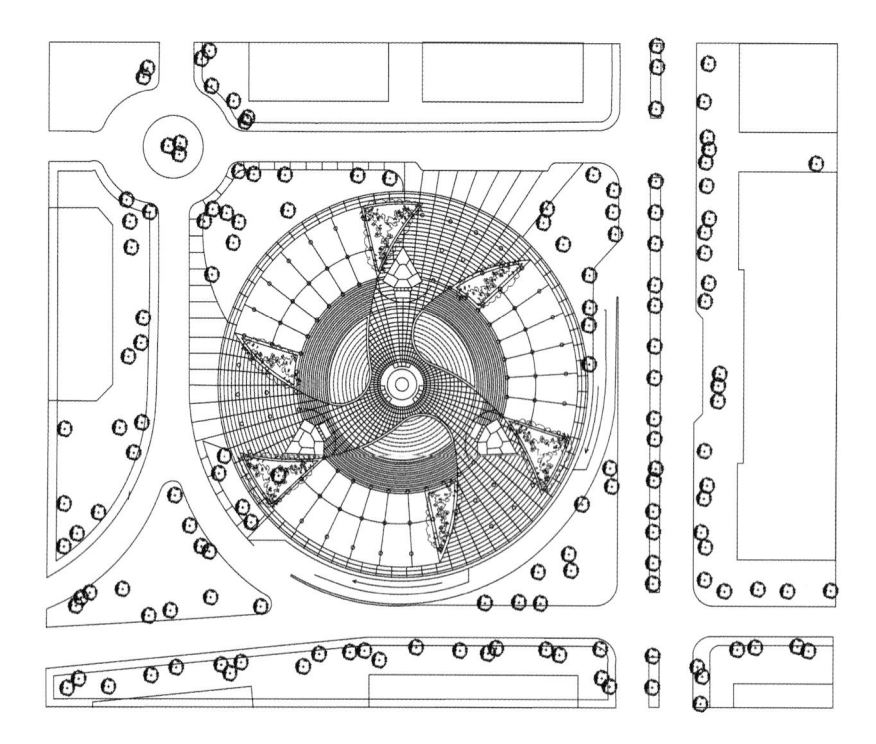

Site Plan (ground floor)

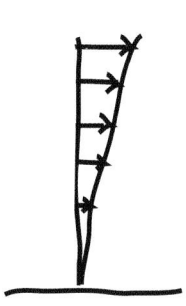

11. Wind Velocity

The friction of the earth surface and building landscape reduce airflow.

12. Air Pressure

As the density decreases with height so does its pressure.

13. Torsion and Wind Forces

Wind forces twist the tower. The torsion is greatest at the base where the tower is restrained reducing with height.

14. Bending Stresses due to horizontal wind loads

Wind forces bend the tower. The bending stresses are the greatest at the base where the tower is restrained, reducing with height.

15. Horizontal shear force due to wind load

Wind forces generate shear streses, which the tower accomodates towards its base where the shear forces are the greatest.

16. Axial Column Load

Columns collect the floor loads as they descend the tower.

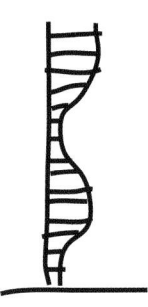

17. Views

Surrounding buildings at low level obstruct views At higher level cloud cover will also reduce visibility.

18. Vertical Movement

The movement of people increases towards the entrance at the base of the building.

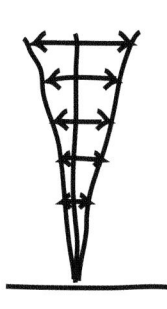

19. Horizontal Sway

As the wind passes around the tower, the pressure disbalance causes the tower to sway.

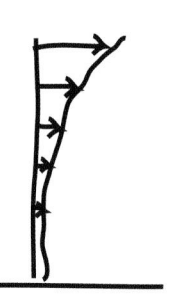

20. Horizontal Deflection

As the wind hits the tower its deflects. The greatest deflection is the furthest point from the supports at the ground.

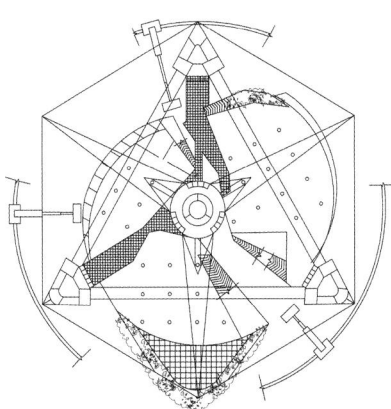

Levels 13-60

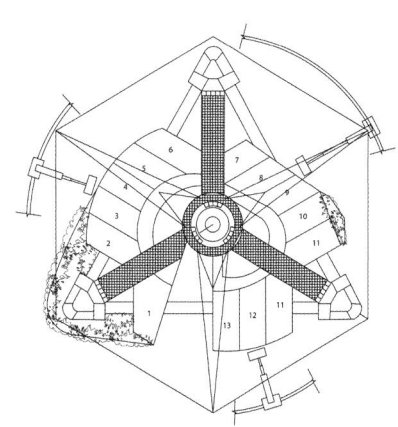

Levels 61-108

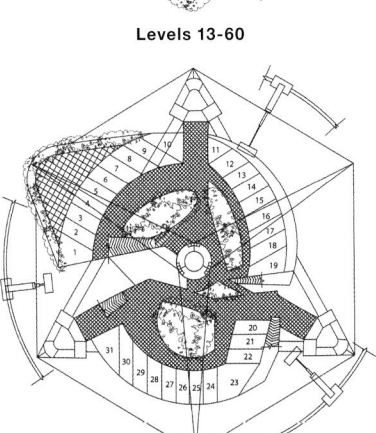

Levels 109-156

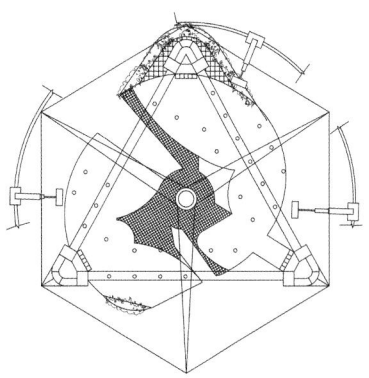

Levels 157-204

Vertical Urbanism | Tokyo-Nara Tower

CHAPTER 5 Technical Innovation

Yeang is clearly an experimenter, although he is not entirely happy with the word. Rather, he prefers to describe himself as someone who pushes boundaries, and who is attuned to new ideas and their potential, with a little lateral thinking and quiet testing, to provide breakthroughs. He is also a prolific note-taker, and he is disciplined enough to carefully file away his notes until he has amassed sufficient material for a book. This is entirely characteristic of the man: methodical, rational, inventive and bold. The following three projects, ranging in scale from the very small to the epic, are highly illustrative of the ways that Yeang's inventiveness can help make the dream of eco-mimicry a realisable goal. In particular, the following case studies feature the following design tactics:

Evaporative Cooling Systems. Introduced with the small Chartered Bank Pavilion in Kuala Lumpur, the combination of an air-curtain and a water diffuser sprays a "cool, frothy mist" at the entrance and over internal discussion tables. The devices create cool, refreshing zones in an environment where air conditioning is typically the only way to escape the heat.

Wind-Wing-Walls. Taking advantage of increased computer power and the ability of software to accurately predict atmospheric conditions and microclimates, Yeang used Computational Fluid Dynamics to help design a system in which office spaces are naturally ventilated by capturing, controlling and channelling wind. Using "wind-wing-walls", effectively large fins to direct prevailing air currents, the Menara UMNO Tower was an investigation into potential for constructing an entirely naturally ventilated skyscraper for the tropics.

The Ecocell. Designed for the West Kowloon Waterfront masterplan, an ecocell is a specially-designed void which can extend, in principle, from roof garden down to the lowest basement level. Carrying vegetation via a spiral ramp, the ecocell facilitates daylighting, natural ventilation and rainwater collection into below grade spaces.

As described elsewhere in this book, Yeang has also developed ideas for transparent tubes, located on a façade, which can direct sunlight deep into an interior; while opaque tubes can encase the transparent elements, controlling solar gain and providing shade when needed. Yeang has also investigated the use of fibre optics to transmit daylight deep into a building's interior. Furthermore, Yeang has collaborated with the Queensland University of Technology on the development of "Light-Pipes", devices which incorporate laser-cut prisms that focus and intensify light, directing daylight through internally mirrored tubes. Simulations suggest that 400 lux of lighting can be directed 12 metres into a building's interior. This work received an award from the journal *Far East Economic Review* in 2003.

Price Solutions Financial Kiosk
Credit Cards
SME OneAccount
Credit Cards

Standard Chartered Bank Kiosk

Standard Chartered Bank Kiosk

TYPE	:	Technical Innovation
LOCATION	:	Kuala Lumpur, Malaysia
CLIMATE ZONE	:	Tropical
VEGETATION ZONE	:	Rainforest

AREAS:

SITE AREA	:	120 m²
PLOT RATIO	:	Not Applicable
NO. OF STOREYS	:	1
STATUS	:	Built
DATE OF COMPLETION	:	2003

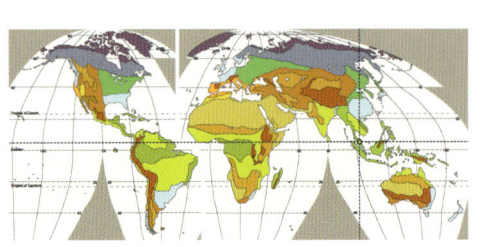

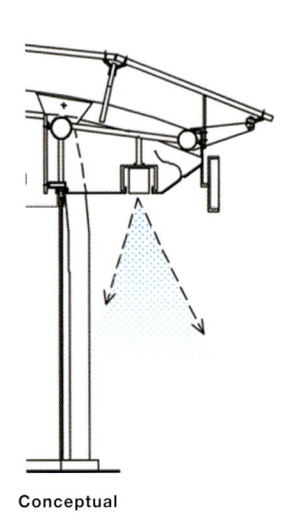

▲ The kiosk as a brand-making exercise

CLIMATE REGION

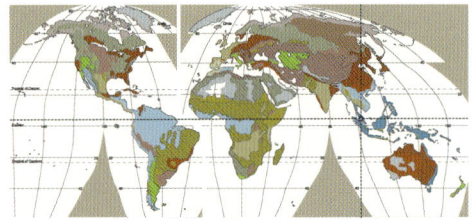

VEGETATION ZONE

Conceptual

This steel and glass kiosk in Kuala Lumpur is one of Yeang's smallest commissions, yet it embodies an interesting and important (and yet to be repeated) experiment in evaporative cooling. Designed for Standard Chartered Bank, the kiosk is situated on a prime city location, taking advantage of heavy pedestrian traffic to help the bank market new products to "upmarket" customers. (It is situated on a busy walkway in the entertainment district of the city centre surrounded by upmarket hotels and shopping malls.) This faceted object was designed to attract people's attention, and the combination of "air curtains" and "cooling demisters" does just that by creating a "frothy, cooling zone" in the hot, humid tropics.

A jet of cool air positioned at the entrance of the kiosk is paired with a system which sprays a fine mist of water. This combination forms a cool, artificial cloud which, in a tropical environment, provides welcome relief for passers-by and therefore operates as an attractive lure for the bank's marketing operation. It is here that staff are positioned to hand out brochures. A similar system is at work inside this little building, cooling the air above meeting tables in the consultation area; here, fine sprays of mist are integrated into the centre of ceiling fans, forming what Yeang refers to as "a cool and misty zone".

Built for around £50,000, the Standard Chartered kiosk offers a "bite-sized" demonstration of Yeang's drive for experiment and innovation. The budget was so small that the building's effectiveness had to be achieved cheaply, and here Yeang exploits a simple, natural phenomenon with great success. Interestingly, Yeang says that he does not consider himself to be a significant experimenter – "I really don't use the word experiment very often. I think of myself more as someone who pushes boundaries," he says. The system developed for this building has not found its way into any of Yeang's projects since. "I would use it again, but no opportunities have presented themselves yet."

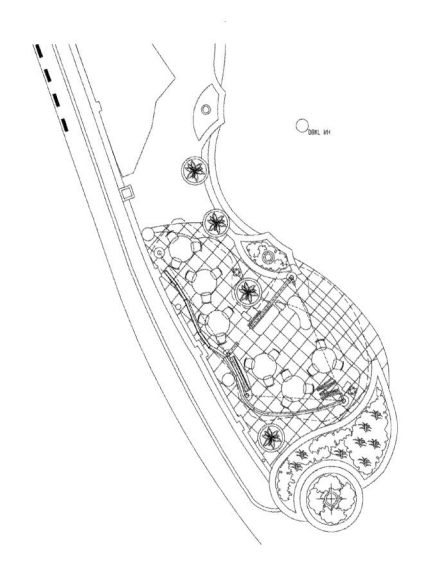

SUMMARY OF DRAWINGS

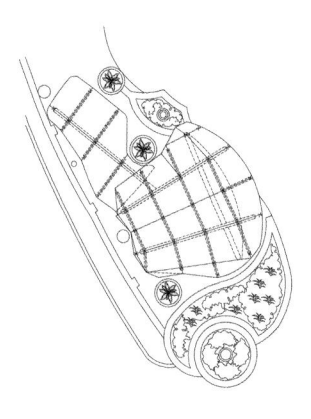

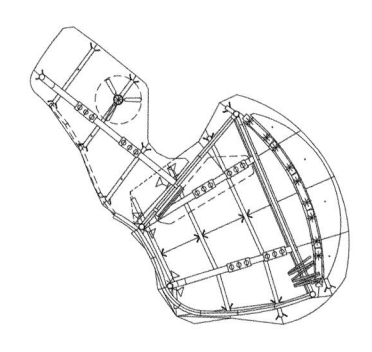

Ground Floor Plan

Roof Plan

Reflected Ceiling Plan

Yeang explains his approach to innovation in the following way: "We start by preparing a set of green design ideas that we feel deserve investigation and serious development. From this set of ideas, we would explore one or two of them within a single building project, client and budget permitting. Through this process we acrue, over time, a considerable set of ideas spanning several building or masterplanning projects. Then, at a point when we begin to feel relatively confident that some of these ideas work, we assemble a compatible set of innovations into a single building project. Once built, this becomes a bench-mark project."

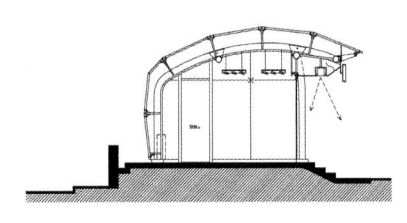

Section A-A

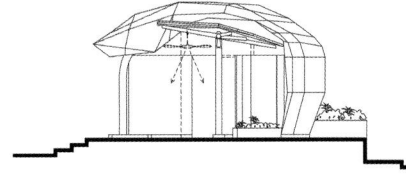

North-West Elevation

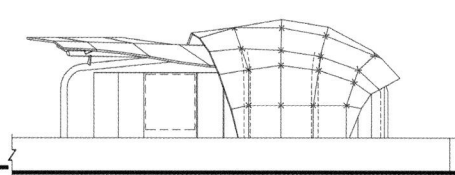

South-West Elevation

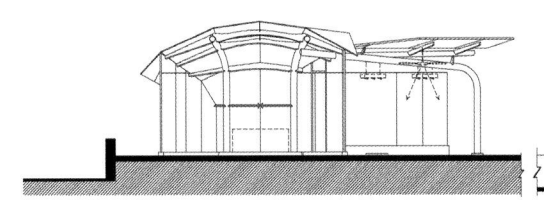

Section B-B

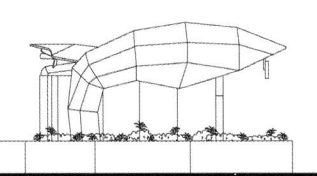

South-East Elevation

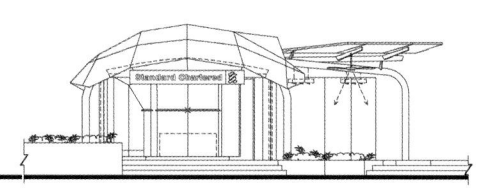

North-East Elevation

Technical Innovation | Standard Chartered Bank Kiosk

Kios Kewangan
Price Solutions Financial Kiosk
Credit Cards
Credit Cards

◀▲ The completed kiosk

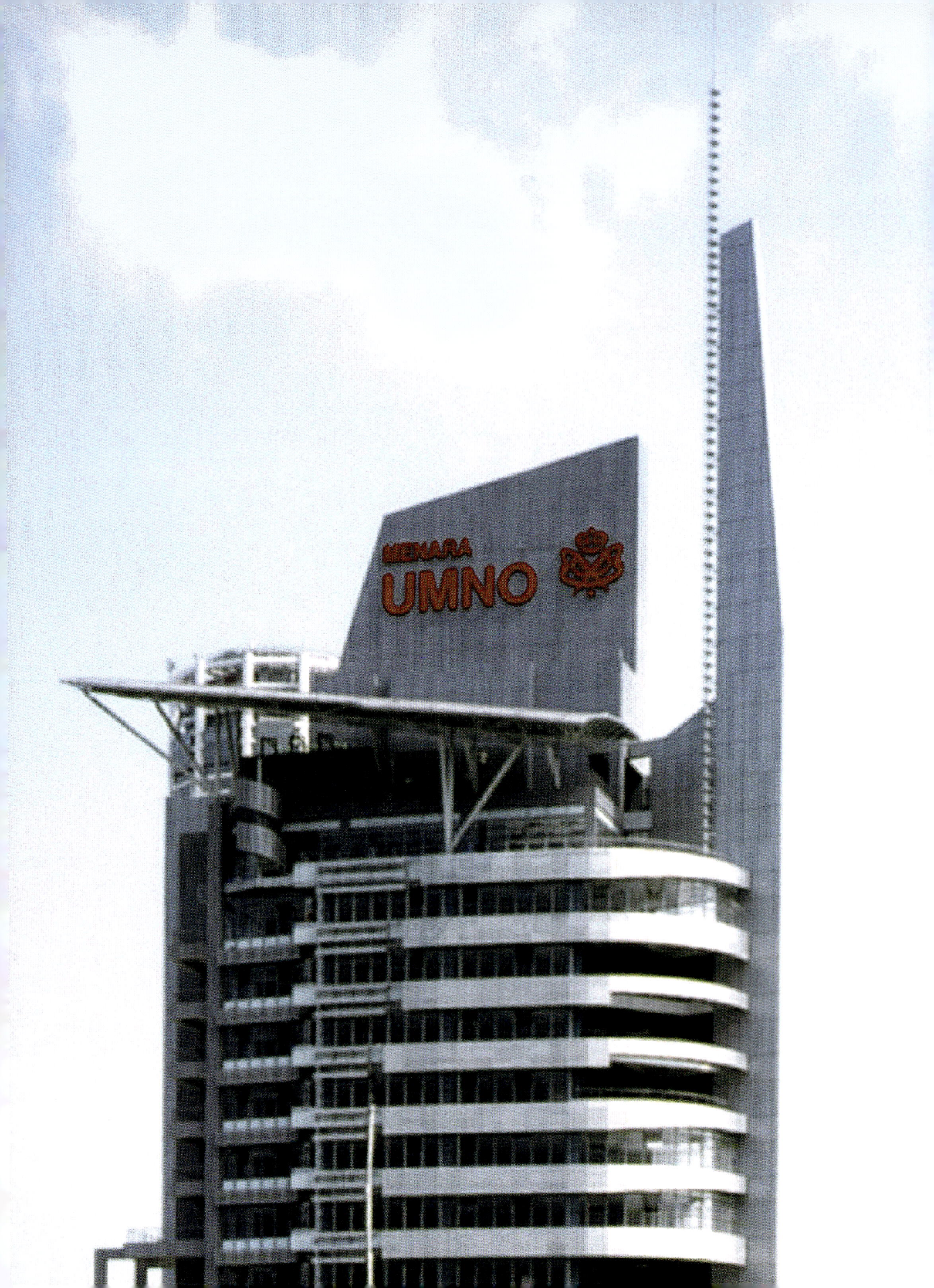
MENARA
UMNO

UMNO Tower

UMNO Tower

TYPE : Technical Innovation
LOCATION : Penang, Malaysia
CLIMATE ZONE : Tropical
VEGETATION ZONE : Rainforest

AREAS:
GFA : 10,900 m²
NFA : 8,192 m²
SITE AREA : 1,920 m²
PLOT RATIO : 1:5.5
NO. OF STOREYS : 21
STATUS : Built
DATE OF COMPLETION : 1998

▲ Photograph of the UMNO Tower, with historic neighbours

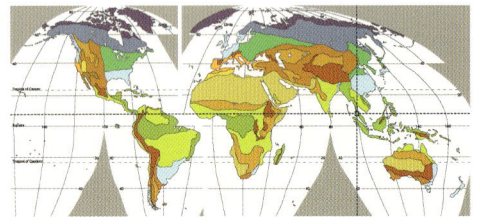

CLIMATE REGION

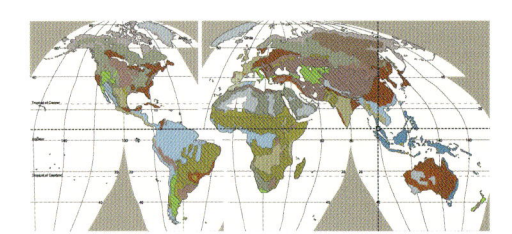

VEGETATION ZONE

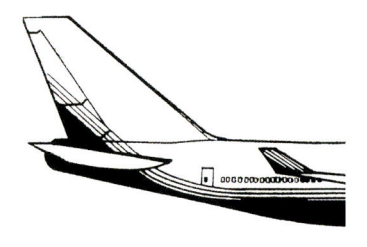

Conceptual

Yeang sought to design the UMNO Tower as one that is specifically engineered to use wind instead of conventional air conditioning to create interior comfort. The project is a further example of Yeang's inventiveness, particularly as an investigation into the possibilities of creating a naturally ventilated skyscraper. Located within the commercial district of Penang, the 21-storey tower provides banking accommodation at ground and first-floor levels; apart from an auditorium on the sixth floor, the rest of the building is given over to office space.

What makes this building especially interesting is that, early in the design phase, the client asked Yeang to consider dispensing with a central air conditioning facility – the rationale was that tenants often like to install their own "package" systems. This would, of course, make the building cheaper to construct, but ran the risk of allowing the façades to become disfigured through accumulated A/C condensor boxes. Yeang responded in two ways. Firstly, he designed an external sun-shading system which allowed A/C units to be installed within specially designed cavities, keeping them unseen. Secondly, Yeang developed his notion of "wind-wing-walls", which first saw the light of day in the Roof Roof House of 1985. As it turned out, however, the building was eventually fitted with a central air conditioning system (half way through construction, in fact), but the wind walls, which are this building's most defining characteristic, still serve to supplement the conventional M&E solution, reducing energy loads and dependency on fossil fuels. The UMNO Tower also comprises open floors in which no workstation is more than 20 feet from an openable window, allowing occupants to maintain local control over their micro-environment.

By working closely with Professor Phil Jones of Cardiff University in the UK, the design team employed computational fluid dynamics to model prevailing winds and predict how air flow could be captured and controlled by the building's wind-catching devices. The CFD analysis proved the efficacy of the idea, underpinning the design and direction of the building elements which would control the speed, behaviour and distribution of

▲ Wind walls are prominent features of the tower

the air flow. Essentially, large fins scoop up wind and channel it deep into the building via recessed vents which modulate its strength. Focusing on three wind entry points around the building's perimeter, "wind pockets" manifest themselves as small skycourts which take advantage of established boundary conditions. "This building as technical experiment demonstrated a fair potential in the use of wind-wing-walls to use natural air flow to cool and ventilate tall buildings," says Yeang. "It does, however, need considerable further development. Ideally, an automated system connected to a wind anemometer [a wind speed and strength measuring device] would control the vent system, responding to atmospheric behaviour in real time."

The 93.5m high building, iconic for its wind-wing-walls and over-sailing roof, has become a distinctive landmark in central Penang. The building received an RAIA International Award in 1998.

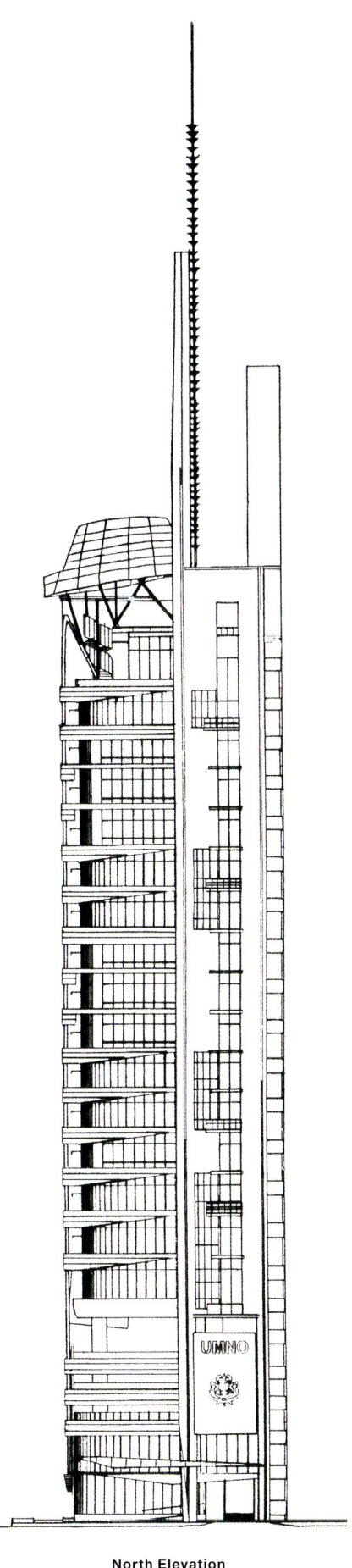

North Elevation

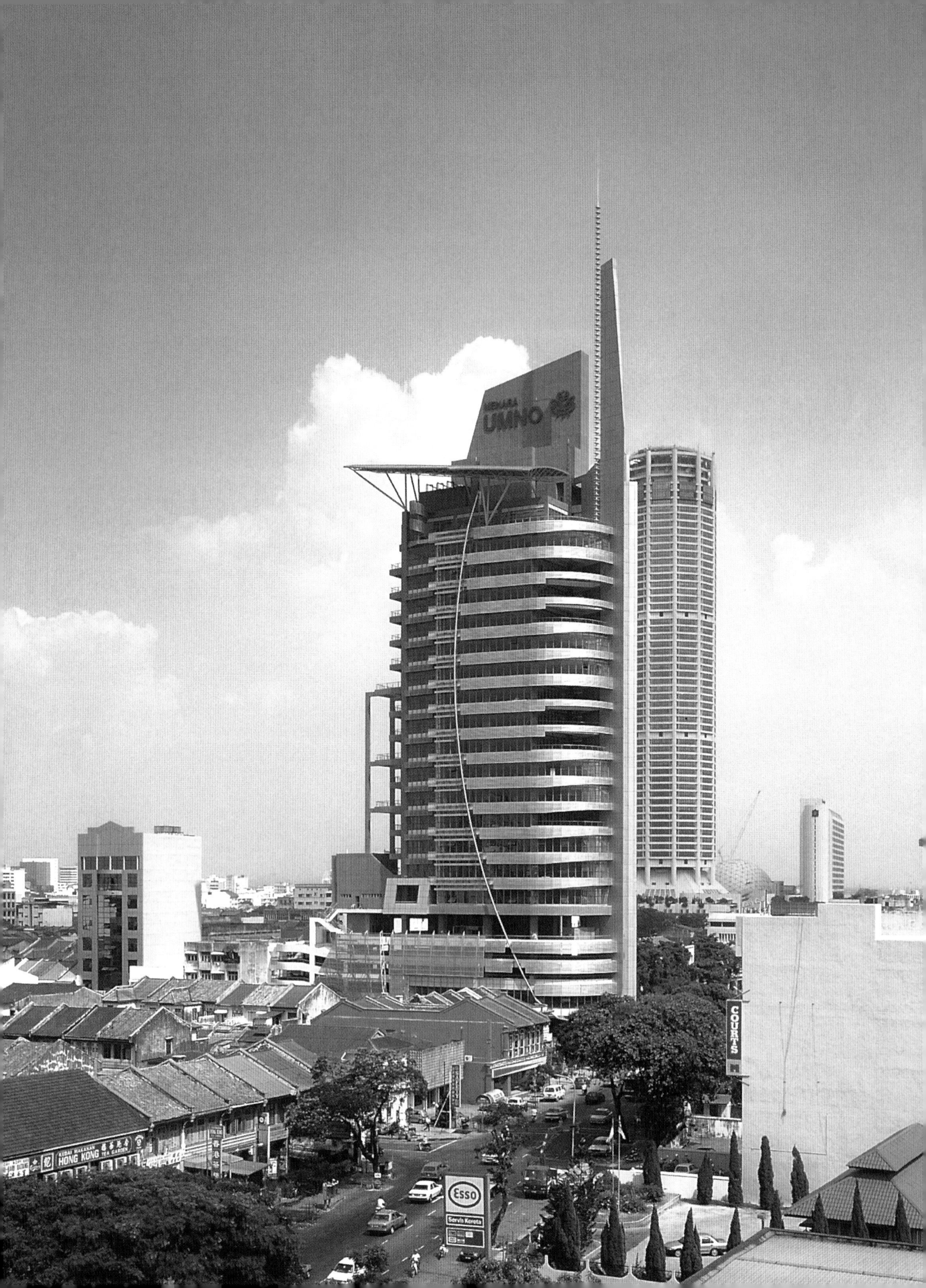
UMNO
COURTS
HONG KONG
Esso
Servis Kereta

SUMMARY OF PLANS

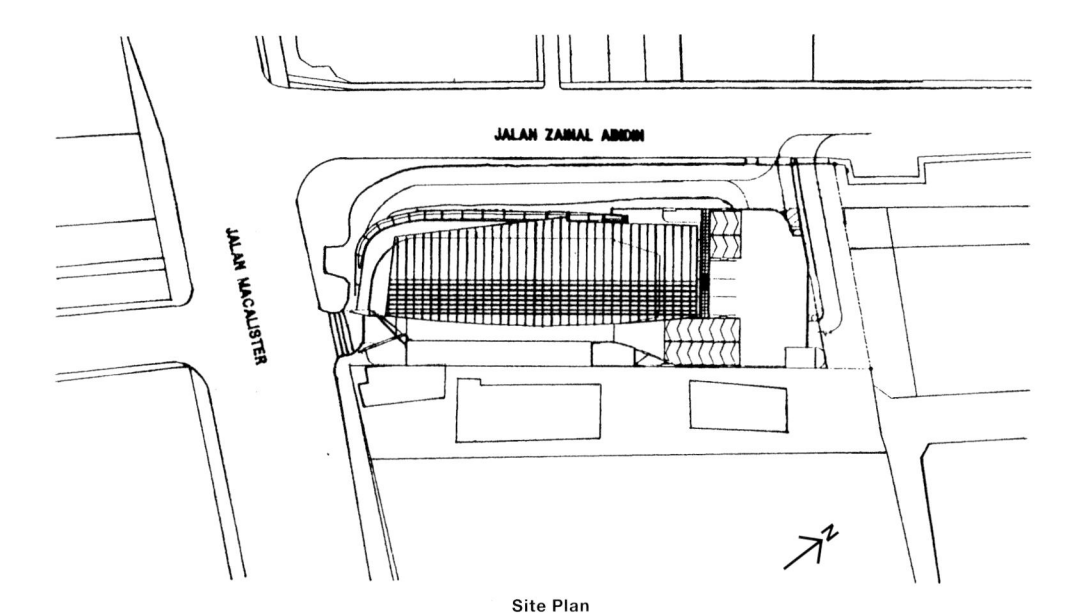

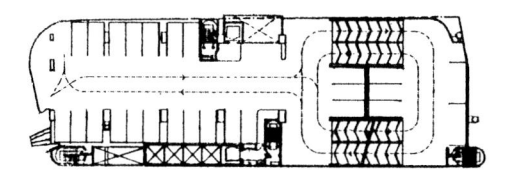

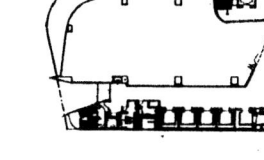

Site Plan

Levels 3 - 6

Level 7

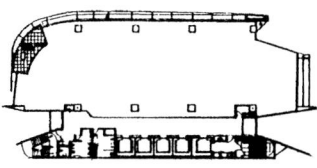

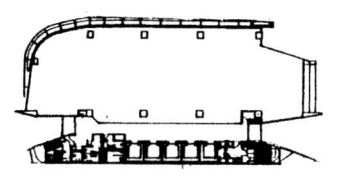

Level 8

Level 9

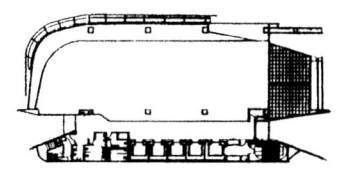

Levels 11 - 16

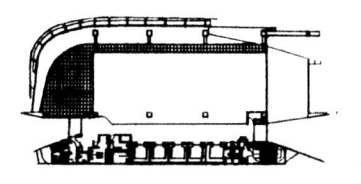

Levels 10, 17 - 21

◀ View of the tower's west façade

Technical Innovation | UMNO Tower

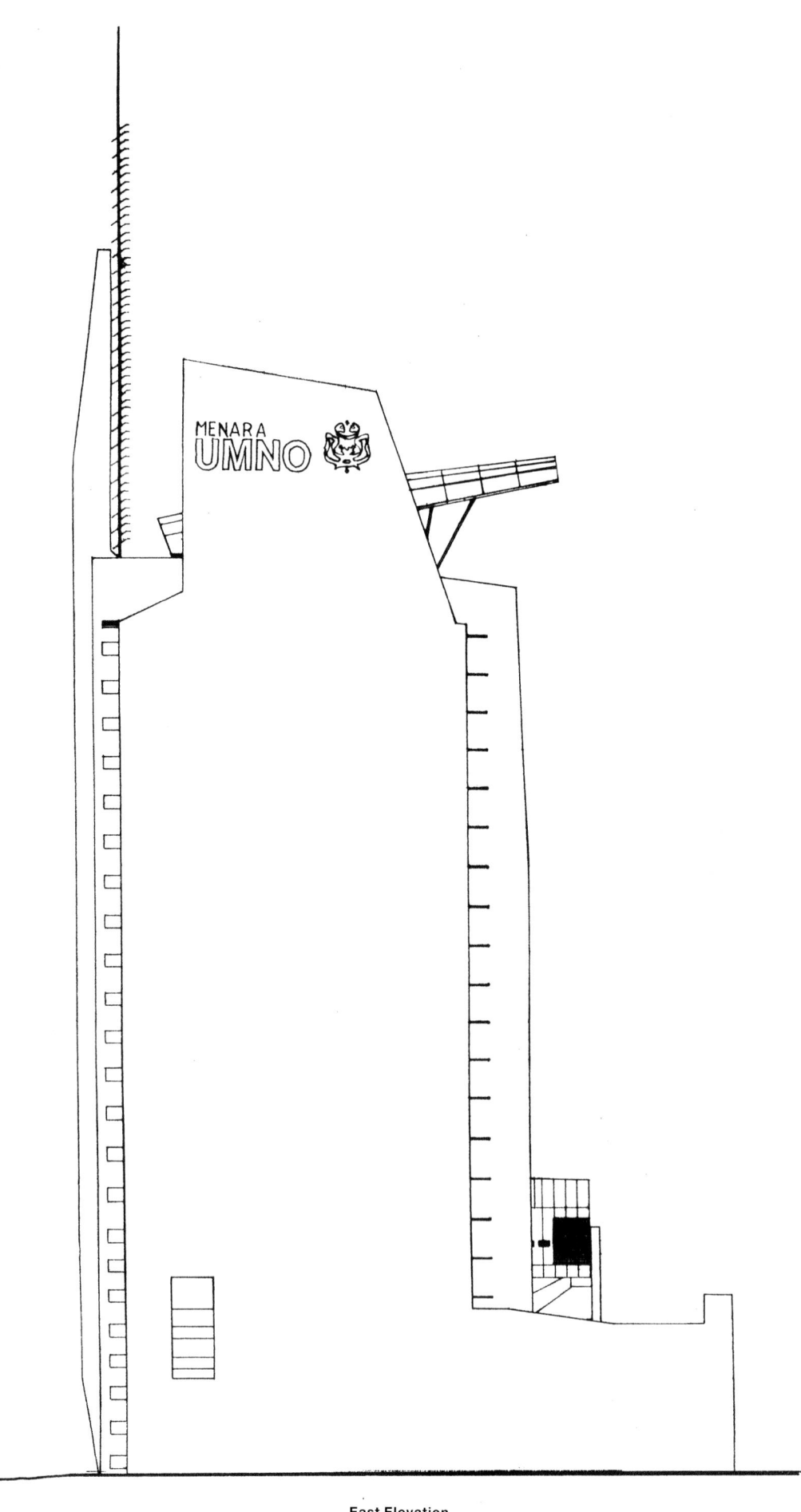

East Elevation

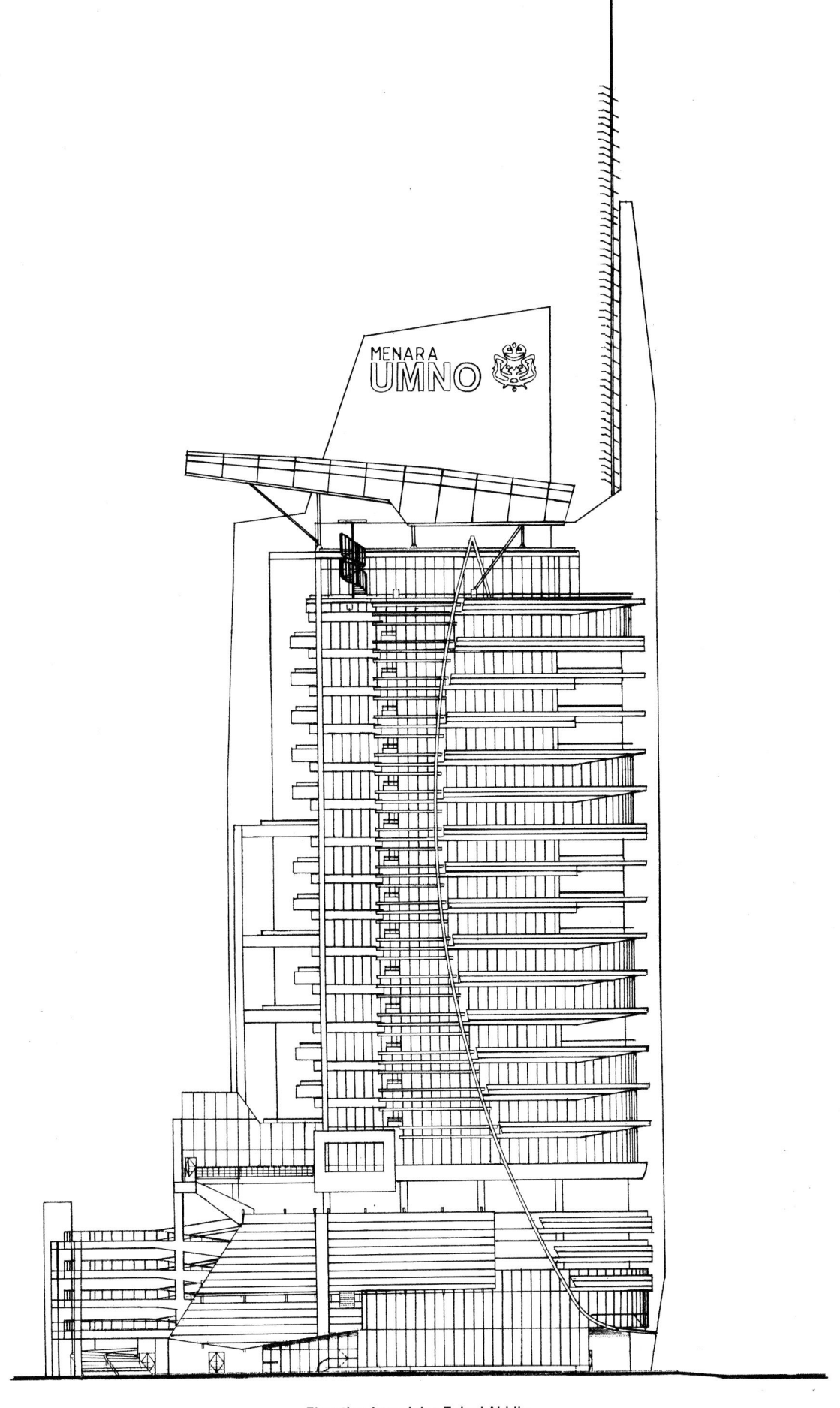

Elevation from Jalan Zainal Abidin

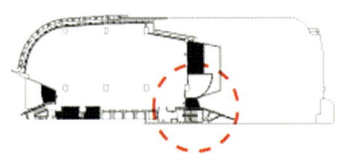

WING WALL AND WIND POCKET DETAILS

Key Plan (See Details Below)

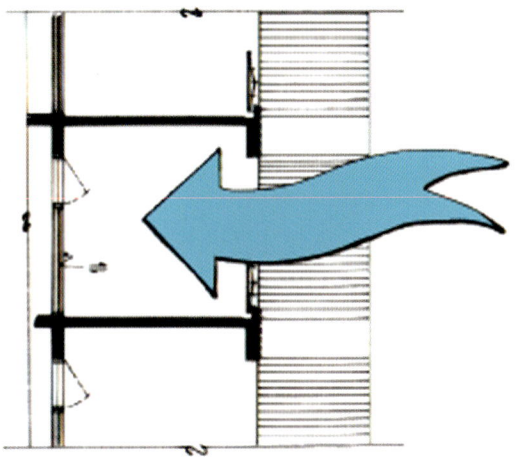

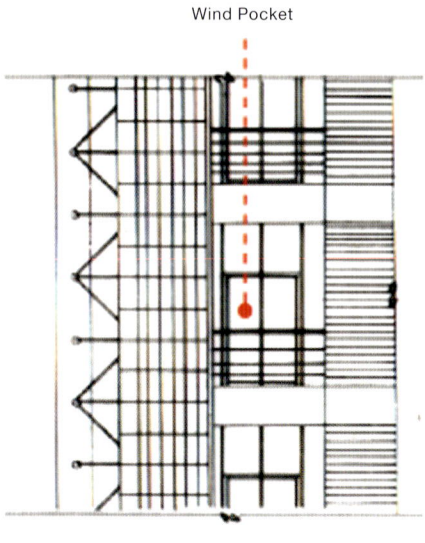

Adjustable doors and window panels to control percentage of opening for natural ventilation and create natural conditions of comfort inside the building

Wind Pocket

Adjustable glass window to naturally ventilate

Wind Pocket Section

Wind Pocket Elevation

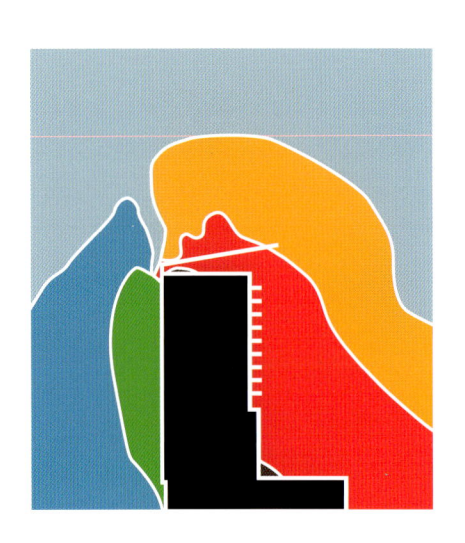

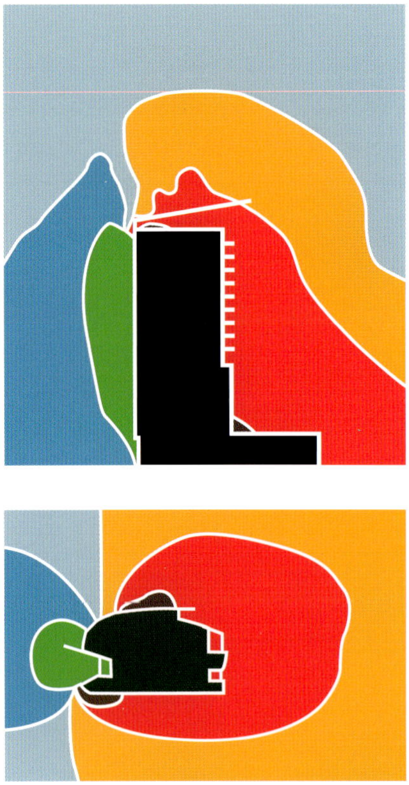

Openable Balcony Door

Wind Pocket - Balcony

Wing Wall

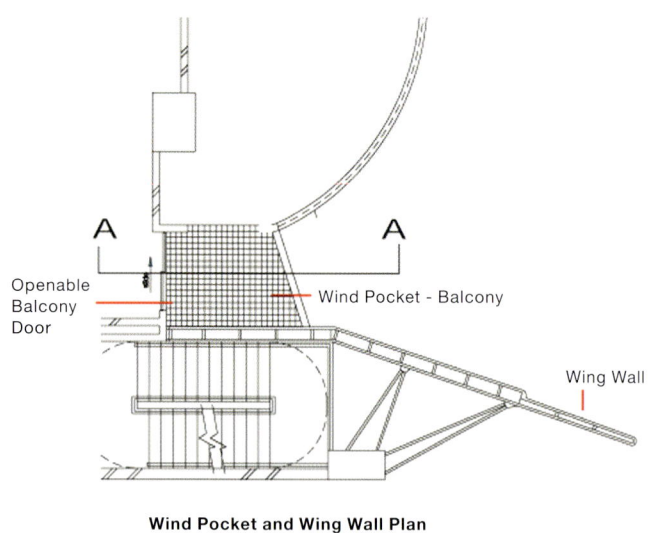

Wind Pocket and Wing Wall Plan

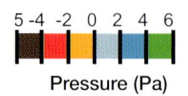

CFD Analysis Results
(Elevation above; Plan below)

-5 -4 -2 0 2 4 6
Pressure (Pa)

180 ECOARCHITECTURE | THE WORK OF KEN YEANG

SUN SHADING DETAIL

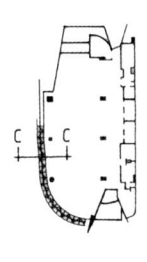

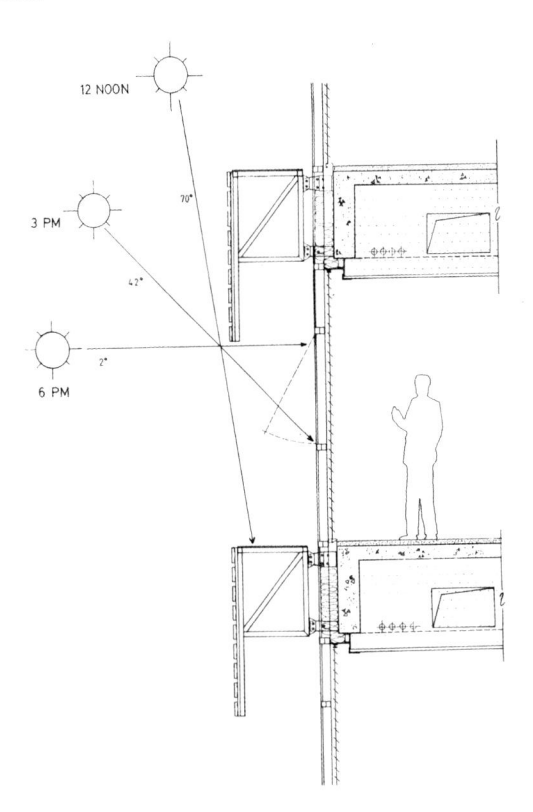

12 NOON
3 PM
6 PM

CANOPY DETAILS

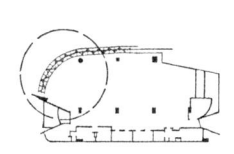

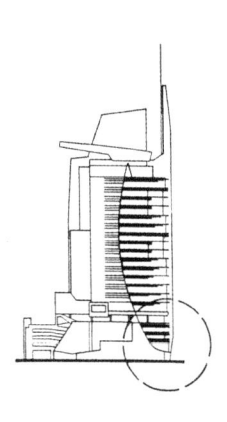

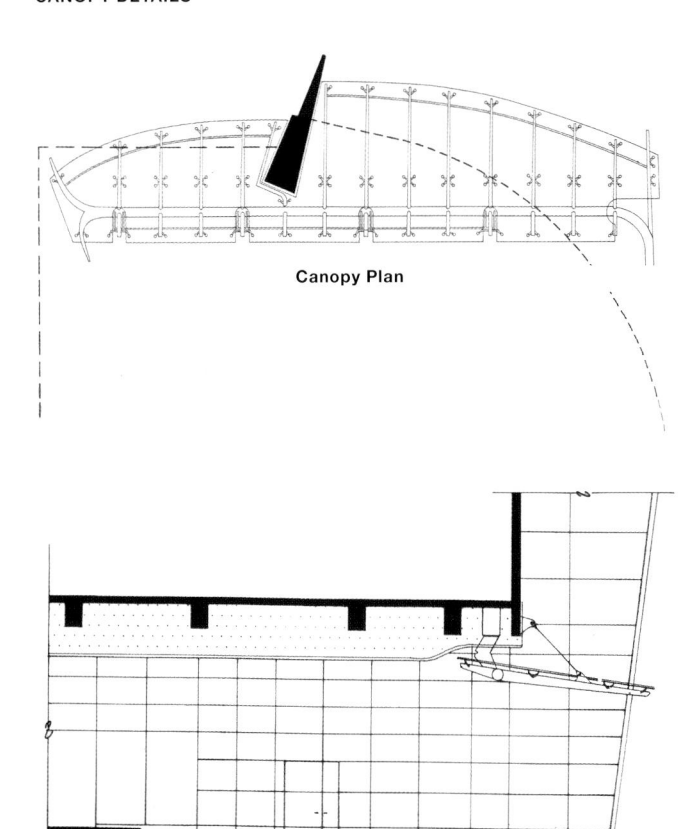

Canopy Plan

Canopy Section

Technical Innovation | UMNO Tower

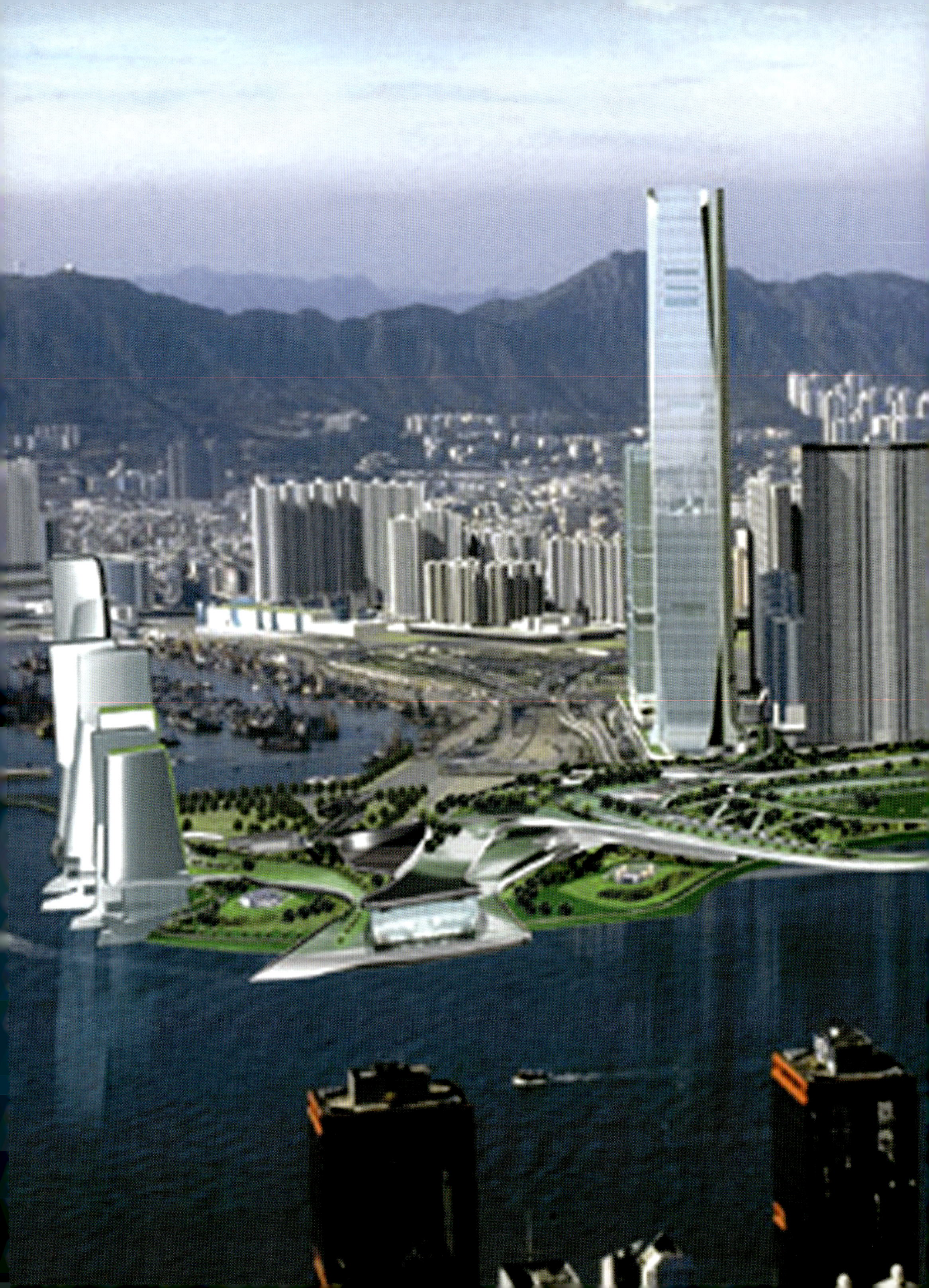

West Kowloon Waterfront

West Kowloon Waterfront

TYPE : Technical Innovation
LOCATION : Kowloon, Hong Kong
CLIMATE ZONE : Subtropical
VEGETATION ZONE : Temperate Rainforest

AREAS:
GFA : 720,000 m²
SITE AREA : 240,000 m²
PLOT RATIO : 1:3
NO. OF STOREYS : 21
STATUS : Competition
DATE : 2001

▲ View from the south

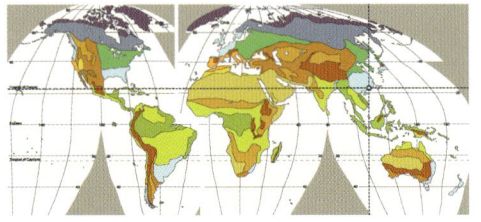

CLIMATE REGION

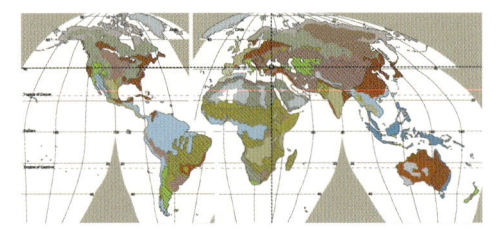

VEGETATION ZONE

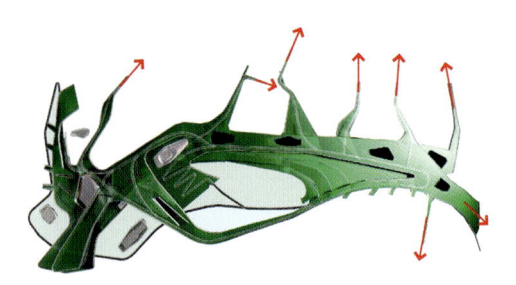

Conceptual

Yeang's competition entry for the masterplan of a 240,000-square-metre site on the West Kowloon Peninsula on the southern tip of mainland China in Hong Kong demonstrates how the architect's ideas can span large-scale urban districts, as well as individual buildings, while allowing him to present for the first time the notion of the "ecocell", a multi-layered, vertical void which provides environmental benefits from basement to rooftop. Yeang's complex solution for such a large site was underpinned by a unifying "green jacket" which links all buildings and infrastructure, above and below ground, reserving 94 per cent of the surface area for parkland. Yeang has since deployed this design strategy within the BATC and Plaza of Nations projects.

"One of my key strategic approaches to ecodesign is biointegration – integrating the synthetic with the natural, essentially integrating everything that humans make and do with the natural environment in a seamless and benign way," says Yeang. "This is an ecological design solution that seeks to provide an environmentally sustainable urban ecosystem as a major park within the intensive city of Hong Kong, while fufilling the arts, cultural and recreational programmes of the community."

Here the green jacket of a rooftop park extends across the entire site and links to the existing Kowloon Park via ecobridges, providing Hong Kong with its largest, continuous open parkland. Other features contained within the masterplan include 30, 45 and 60 storey "pier tower" apartment blocks, each of which juts out into the harbour; hotels and office towers of similar sizes, also configured as piers; an opera house and amphitheatre; a broad, stepped plaza; a marina and fishing museum; and below-ground retail and car parking facilities. Located on reclaimed land, the site lies at the tip of a densely populated peninsula close to the nearby Mass Transit Railway. Yeang describes his design as offering a new "necklace" of buildings and event spaces to this district, creating a new destination and urban hub.

The parkland provides the roof of a multi-level retail centre which bulges upwards towards the centre of the site, sloping gently downwards towards the east and west; it is at the south-eastern edge that a landscaped bridge reaches across to

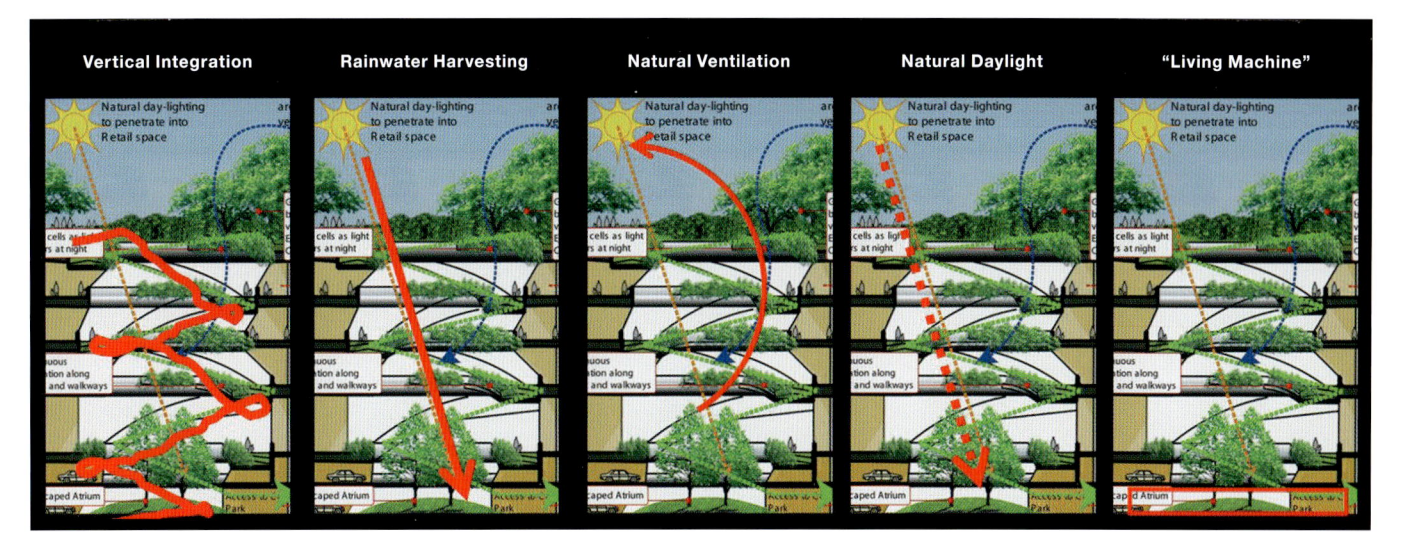

▲ Ecocell concept diagrams

Kowloon Park – like the EDITT Tower, the project seeks to colonise the city through green linkages. The new landscape created by embanking retail and parking units beneath this new ground level is, however, punctuated by "ecocells" which bring light, vegetation, fresh air and rain water right down into the lowest levels. Half a dozen of these openings populate the masterplan, extending the ecosystem down to basement level, at which point rainwater is harvested and sewage treated through algae-filled tanks and ponds. "This was an opportunity to create a living machine – a constructed wetland," says Yeang. These ecocells also function as circulation nodes, with spiral ramps and stairs linking levels and providing surfaces on which vegetation is brought deep into the site in continuous strips. They function as "vertical integrators", linking the multi-layered sandwich of the sub-ground levels. The ecocell concept developed for this project was adopted in Yeang's Singapore National Library building.

Architect, educator and critic Leon van Schaik describes Yeang's concept of the ecocell as helping to construct "a new nature". "The ecocell is a concept [Yeang has] developed as a means of integrating the inorganic mass of the built components with the organic landscaping. In essence it is a cell-like void that is cut into the building and slicing down through all floors from the uppermost to the basement... If through these designs we inhabit steep valleys and caverns, then we may be able to retreat from the country and allow it to be repaired," van Schaik wrote in the book *Ecocells* (Wiley-Academy, 2003)

Yeang says designers (in the same way as medical practitioners design prosthetic limbs) need to understand the relationship between artificial systems and their host organisms. The built environment, he says, is an artificial system that must integrate physically and systemically with the ecosystems of the biosphere. In other words, according to Yeang, the artificial and the natural must be made to work holistically – the building becomes part of the biosphere's systemic processes.

▲ Photo of a typical ecocell (from Solaris)

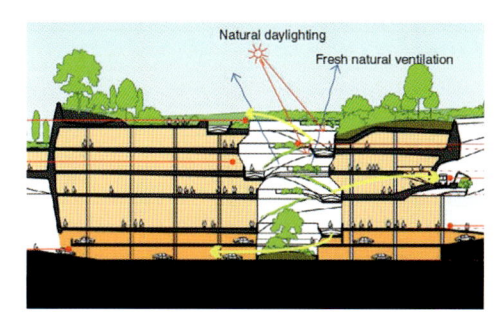

▲ Section of the commercial pier

Technical Innovation | West Kowloon Waterfront 185

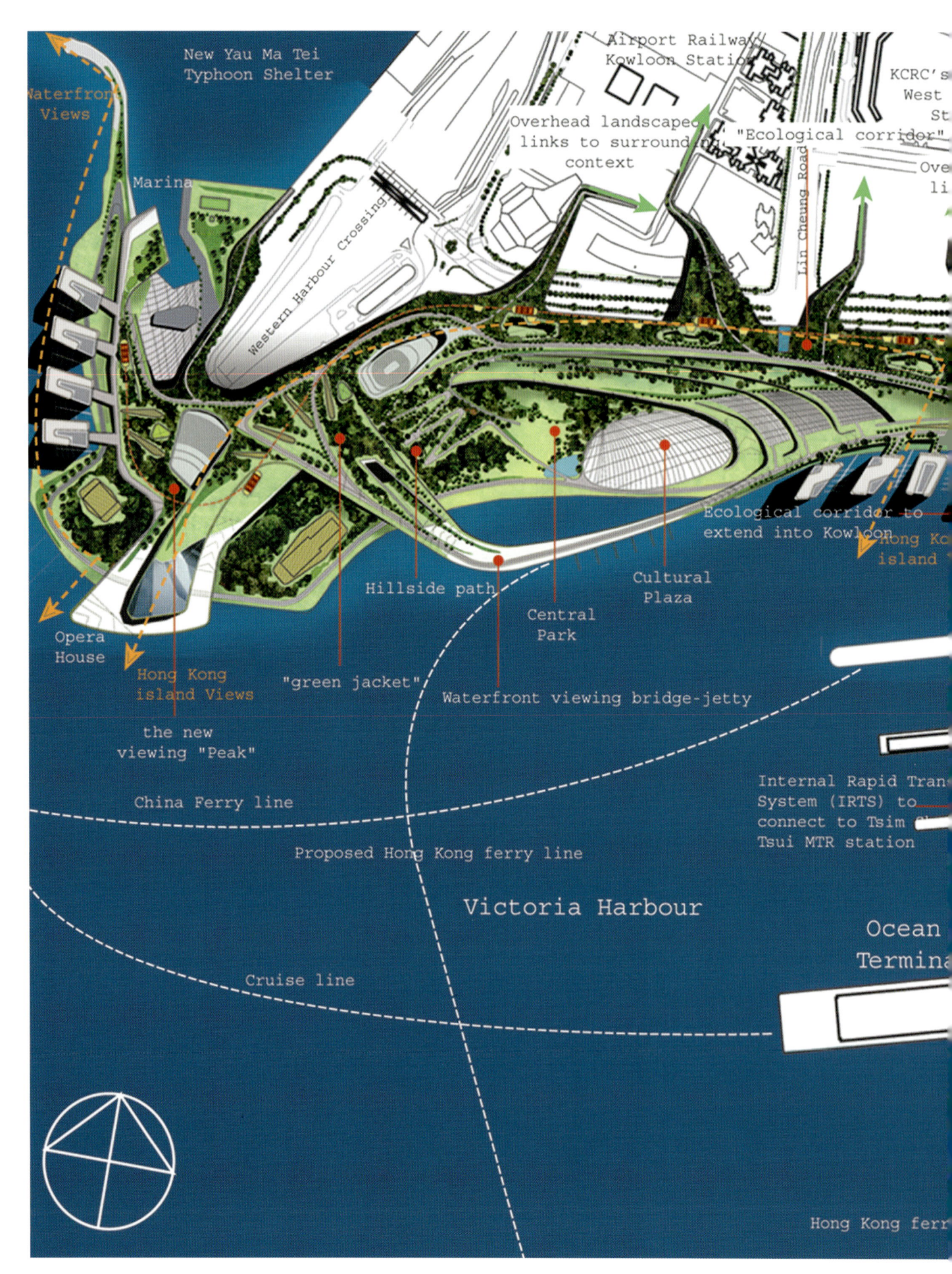

▲ Masterplan in wider context: ecocells and ecological corridors

Rail
landscaped
surrounding
ext

Link to
Kowloon Park

Technical Innovation | West Kowloon Waterfront

▶ Overhead landscaped links to surrounding context

Technical Innovation | **West Kowloon Waterfront**

CHAPTER 6 Vertical EcoInfrastructure

Yeang's new direction in terms of green design and ecoinfrastructure goes far beyond the use of endemic plant species. Around 2003 the architect began to assemble all that he had learned and set out a clear, comprehensive system embracing the creation of viable habitats within the built form, the setting of biodiversity targets, and the ways of achieving them over the life of the building. "This gave green infrastructure its own metrics, setting out a framework for similar quantitative targets to be set for the other ecoinfrastructures – the grey, the blue and the red," says Yeang. From this thinking emerged a new set of projects with a definitive green aesthetic and a more analytical approach to ecological design.

This work is best described through the projects which follow in this section, including (among others) the far-sighted EDITT and Solaris Towers, the DiGi Technical Operations Centre and the Zorlu and Gyeong-Gi masterplans. The EDITT Tower was a competition entry for an eco-tower in Singapore, which received second place. The design is often used to represent the icon of a green building – an aesthetic that is a combination of technology and greening vegetation.

The scheme was extensively covered in several dozen international publications. "In the EDITT Tower we tried to balance the inorganic mass of the tower with more organic mass, which means bringing vegetation and landscaping into the building. But we didn't want to put all the landscaping in one location. We wanted to spread it over the building, integrated with the inorganic mass and ecologically connected," says Yeang. "In many ways it feels like a human made ecosystem in a tower form."

Solaris, designed within the parameters of a Zaha Hadid masterplan, marks the start of more organic forms, as well as an engagement with certification systems. Designed for a hot, humid climate (again in Singapore) the building is a specific response to its latitude, with façade systems that are optimised for shade and daylighting. The tower is one of Yeang's exemplary projects in terms of "green ecoinfrastructure".

These ideas were pushed further in proposals for Zorlu and Gyeong-Gi, which appear to mesh the artifical realm with the natural world in astonishing ways. The DiGi Technical Operations Centre, too, shows Yeang's aptitude for greening buildings, but this is an interesting case – data centres are very energy intensive, so Yeang's job became one of mitigation. It was a project about judgement, even ethics.

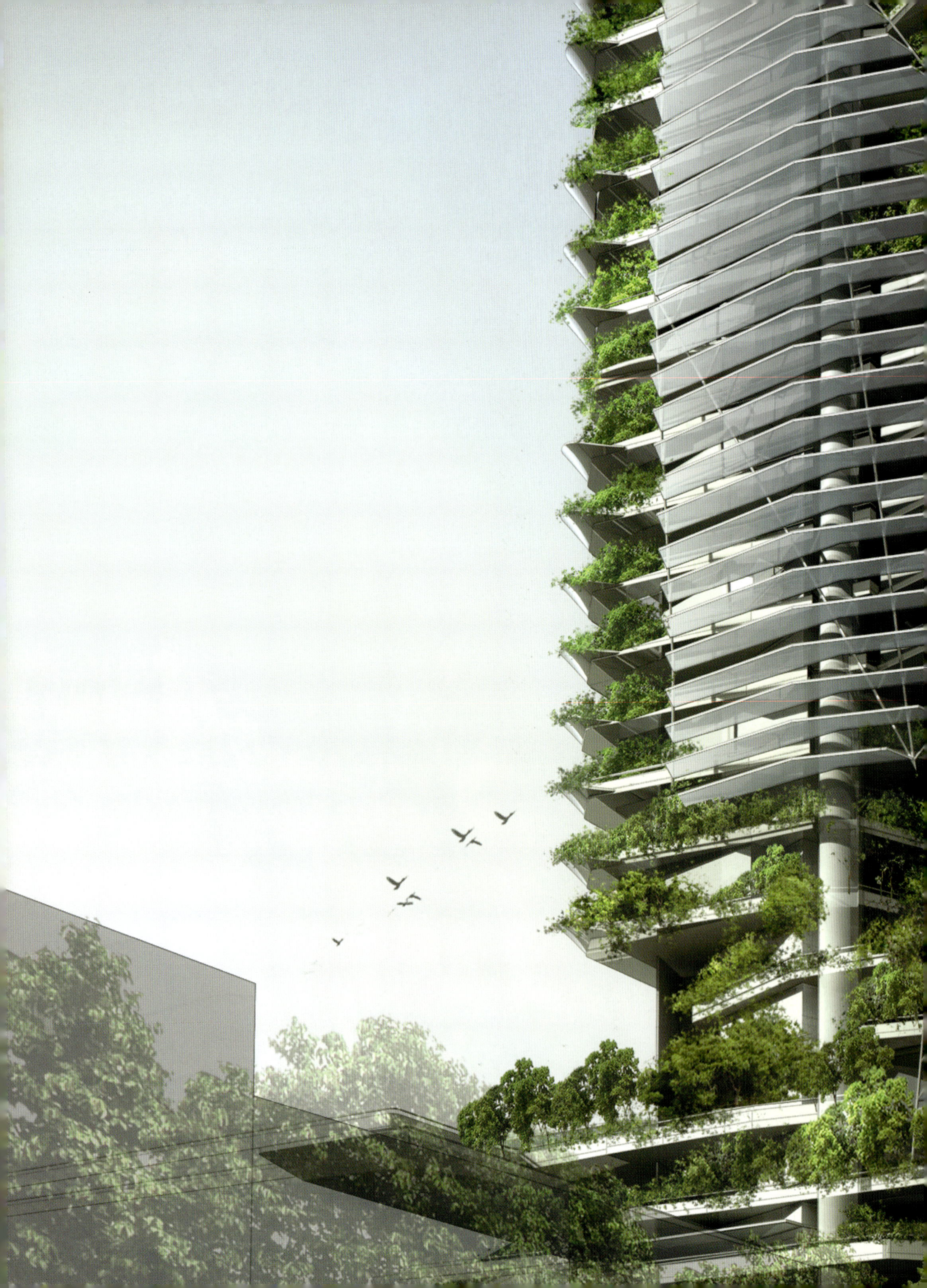

EDITT Tower

EDITT Tower

TYPE	:	Vertical EcoInfrastructure
LOCATION	:	Singapore
CLIMATE ZONE	:	Tropical
VEGETATION ZONE	:	Rainforest

AREAS:

GFA	:	3,771 m²
NFA	:	3,567 m²
SITE AREA	:	838 m²
PLOT RATIO	:	1:4:5
NO. OF STOREYS	:	26
STATUS	:	Competition
DATE	:	1998

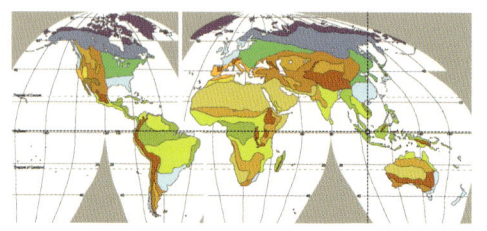

CLIMATE REGION

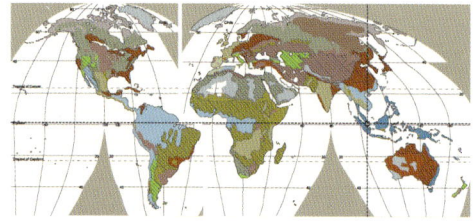

VEGETATION ZONE

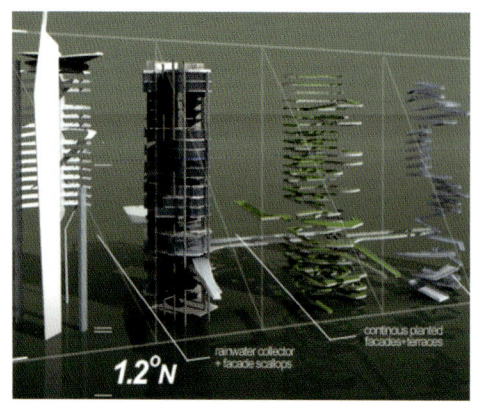

Conceptual

EDITT Tower: view of model

The EDITT Tower was designed as the entry for a competition organised by the Urban Redevelopment Authority in Singapore and the National University of Singapore for a mixed-use, multi-storey, cultural, leisure and multi-media complex in the city's entertainment district on a site near the National Library. The significance of this project is the manner in which Yeang's grey and green ecoinfrastructural systems are fused into a single built form to arrive at an aesthetic that is, he says, "self-evidently declarative of a green architecture". The project echoes, in this respect, Yeang's approach to the MAAG project in Zurich (pages 124-33).

With this tower, which won second place in the design competition, Yeang demonstrated his early approach to ecological tower design. In addition to addressing the client's programme, Yeang began the design process by studying the site's ecology and its properties, mapped against a "hierarchy of ecosystems" illustrated in his ecological taxonomy of sites (see below).

Using this taxonomy, Yeang identified the area as a "zeroculture" site, essentially a devastated ecosystem with little remaining topsoil or tertiary flora and fauna. The ideal response to such a condition would, in Yeang's terms, be to rehabilitate the site by reintroducing organic mass, enabling ecological succession – balancing the existing inorganic mass of the urban site. The design of the tower, which draws its aesthetic from Yeang's earlier work on the Tokyo Nara concept scheme, included densely planted façades and vegetated terraces, intended to replace (as far as is practicable) the biomass lost to the new building's footprint. Plant selection was to be limited to species found within a one-mile radius of the site, supplementing and stimulating the regrowth of indigenous flora to encourage the site's biodiversity. This approach would be developed in

▲ Analysis of views to surroundings

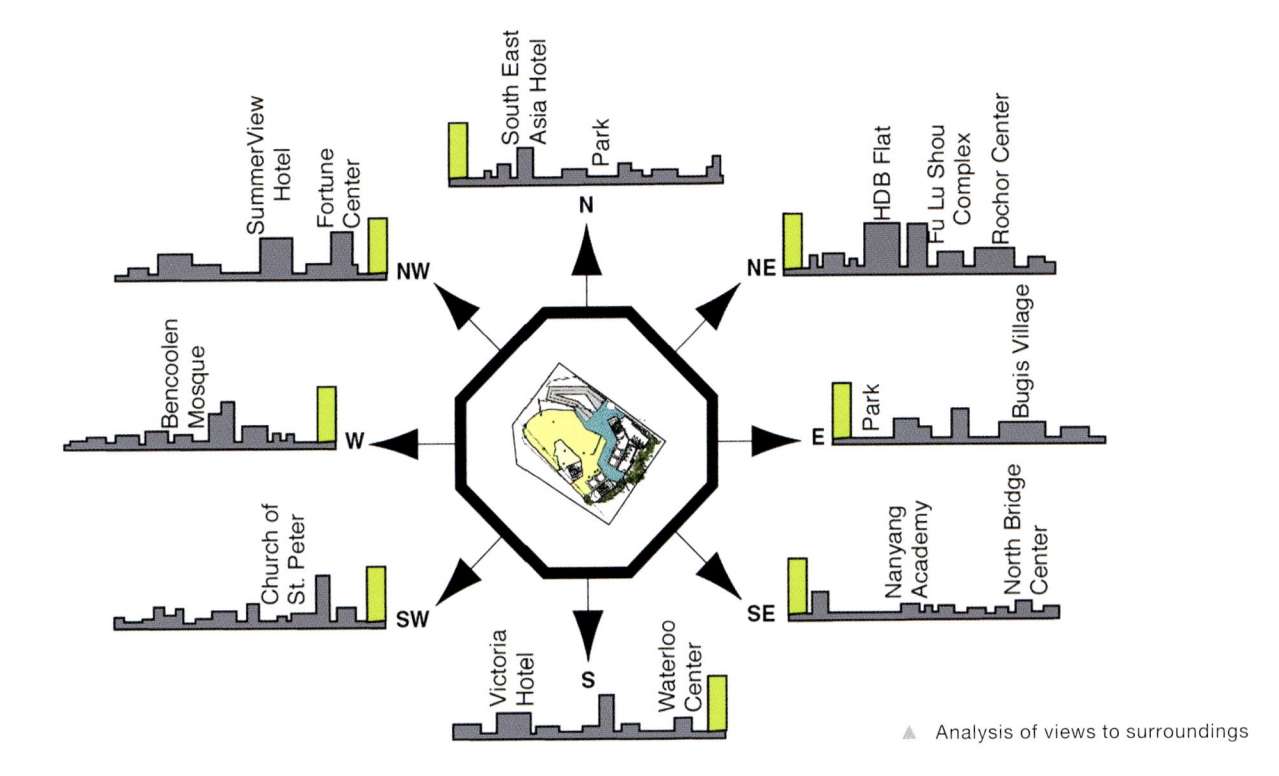

Yeang's Gyeong-Gi scheme (pages 240-57) which sought to create new viable habitats and biodiversity targets.

One of the challenges of vertical urban design is maintaining a continuity and "ecological nexus" from the ground plane to the upper floors. Placing vegetation within buildings is not new or unique – many achitects (such as Emilio Ambasz, James Wines and MVRDV) have done so. What differentiates Yeang is that his greenery is always linked both within the built form and to the ecology of the ground plane, as demonstrated in this project. On occasions, vegetation is further linked and extended down to the lowest basement level (an idea first explored at IBM Plaza, and developed with the Solaris and Kowloon Waterfront projects).

Urban design is about placemaking, and yet spatial compartmentalisation is a defining characteristic of the skyscraper typology. One of Yeang's strategies for reconciling the continuity issue is the use of wide, landscaped ramps; from ground level to the sixth floor these ramps would be lined with the sort of retail and leisure facilities ordinarily found in horizontal streetscapes. Vegetated ramps, designed to create a continuous spatial flow from the public to semi-public zones, are imagined as a "vertical extension of the street". Yeang recalls that the idea of the continuous vegetated ramp also came up in conversation with Metabolist architect Kisho Kurokawa, who pointed out that in Bruegel's painting of the Tower of Babel (circa 1563) it was depicted as a mountain-like tower with a spiralling ramp. Taking his cue from Bruegel, Yeang devised a green ramp that starts from a basement-level ecocell (see Kowloon Waterfront, pages 182-9). which climbs up the façade as a continuous stretch of planting and culminates at the roof. "As well as adding to the biomass and ecological diversity of the site, the ramps relieve the rigid stratification inherent in tall buildings," says Yeang. This strategy later came to be fully realised in the Solaris building, also located in Singapore (pages 200-9).

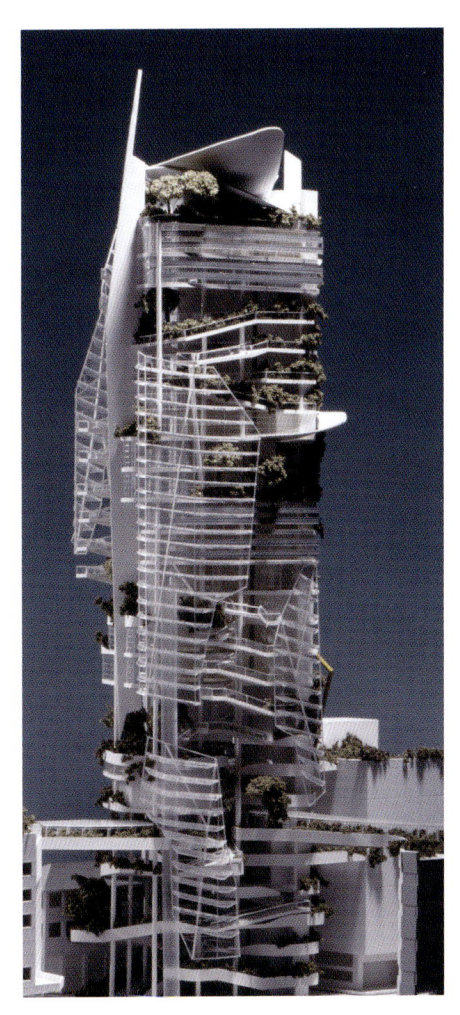

▲ Elevational view of model

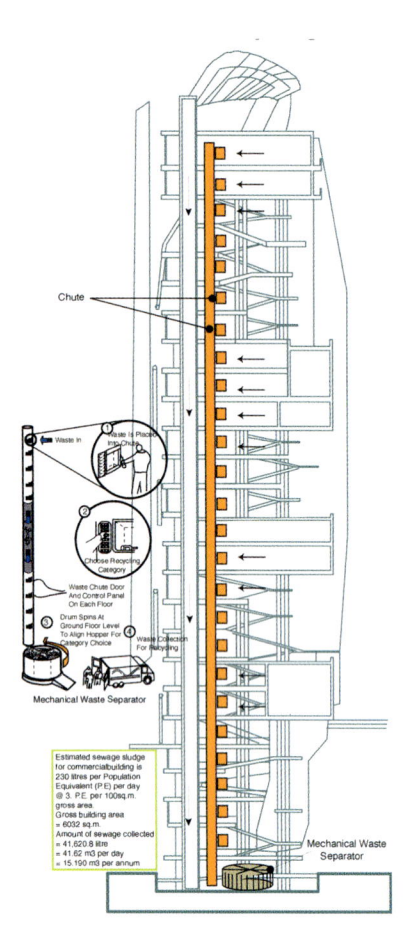

Waste Recycling Diagram

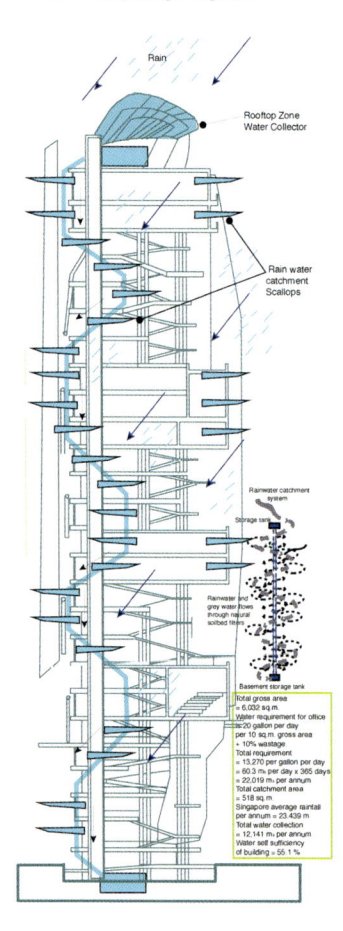

Water Purification Diagram

The building, also characterised by vegetated bridges, was also designed to adapt to future developments: numerous walls and floors could be moved or removed.

In a city famous for its torrential rain, the building is designed to collect rainwater. Yeang devised scallop-shaped sun shades as rainwater harvesting devices, compensating for the minimal roof area of a tower. These shades effectively expand the surface area of the façades, retaining rainfall and diverting it into collection tanks for watering the tower's vegetation. Sun shades also provide a useful cooling effect on the facade. When grey water recycling is factored in, it is estimated the building will supply 55 per cent of the water it needs for irrigation and WC flushing. There are also facilities that allow the tower to convert sewage into biogas and fertilizers.

Roughly half the surface of the EDITT Tower was designed to be covered in a vegetative blanket. The passive architecture also allows for good natural ventilation internally. Furthermore, photovoltaic panels supplement the electricity needs of the building. Yeang sees the EDITT Tower as a model for eco-friendly tower design in the tropics.

At the time of the competition Yeang felt that the EDITT Tower was as close as he could practically get to a coherent model of ecodesign, but already he was working on ideas which would eventually push the agenda much further.

"EDITT Tower is a project where we wanted to exemplify all our ideas in a single building," Yeang told CNN in 2007. "I should add it is a tower, and towers are the most unecological of all building types. Generally a tower uses one third more energy and materials to build and to operate than other structures. But towers, as a built form, will be with us for a while, until we find an economically viable alternative. My contention is that if we have to build these towers then we should make them as humane and as ecological as possible."

Ecosystem Hierarchy	Site Data/Requirements	Design Strategy
Ecologically Mature	Complete Ecosystem Analysis and Mapping	Preserve, Conserve, Develop Only on No-Impact Areas
Ecologically Immature	Complete Ecosystem Analysis and Mapping	Preserve, Conserve, Develop Only on No-Impact Areas
Ecologically Simplified	Complete Ecosystem Analysis and Mapping	Preserve, Conserve, Increase Biodiversity, Develop Only on No-Impact Areas
Mixed Artificial	Partial Ecosystem Analysis and Mapping	Preserve, Conserve, Increase Biodiversity, Develop Only on No-Impact Areas
Monoculture	Partial Ecosystem Analysis and Mapping	Increase Biodiversity, Develop in Areas of Non-Productive Potential, Rehabilitate Ecosystem
Zeroculture	Mapping of Remaining Ecosystem Components	Increase Biodiversity and Organic Mass, Rehabilitate Ecosystem

▲ Yeang's "ecological design model", drawn up in 1995, describes the relationships between processes, activities and environment.

Exploded Axonometric Diagrams

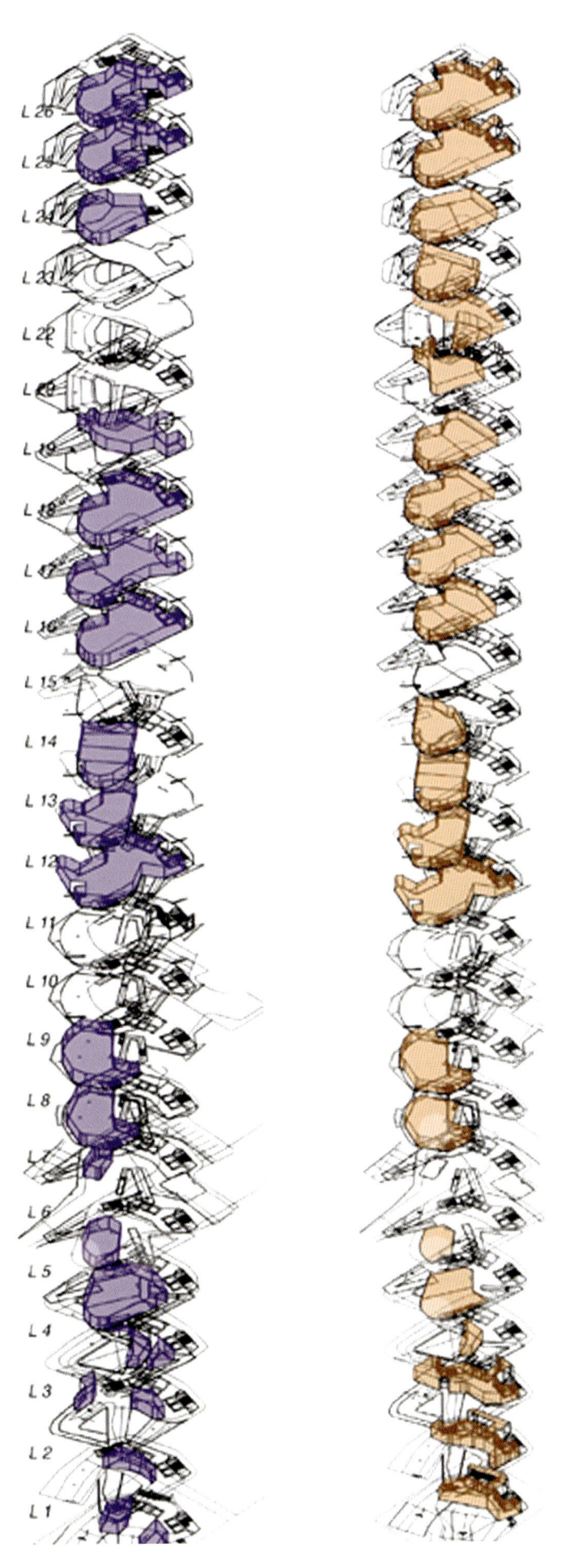

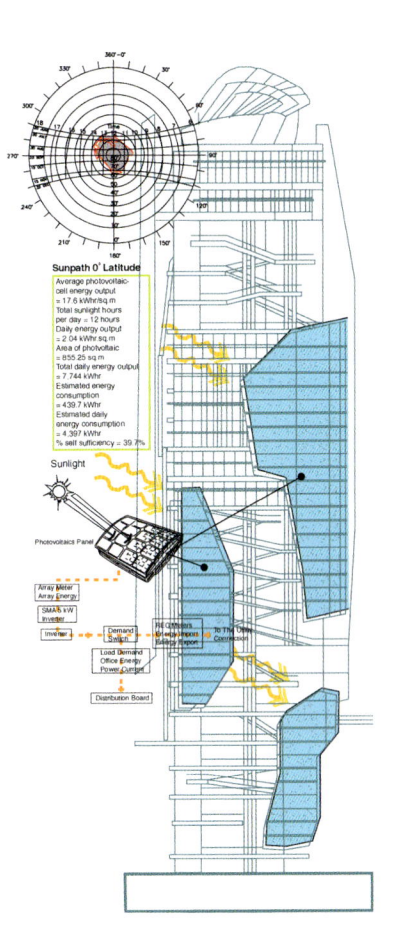

Photovoltaic Study

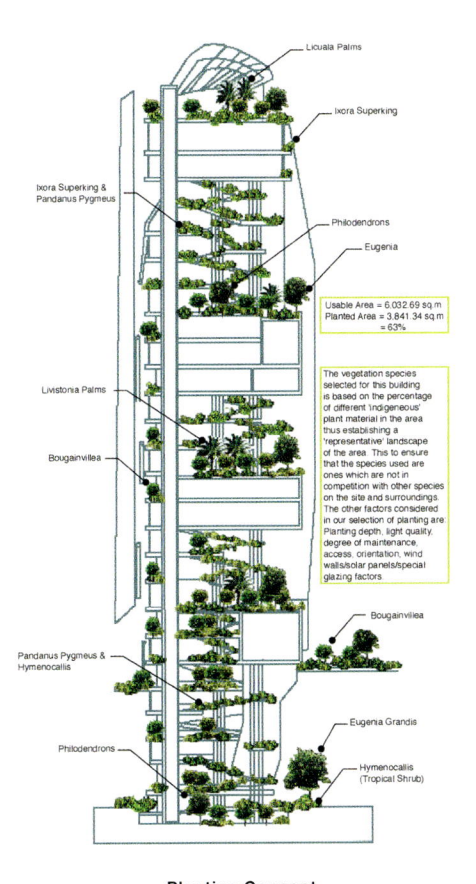

Planting Concept

Vertical EcoInfrastructure | EDITT Tower

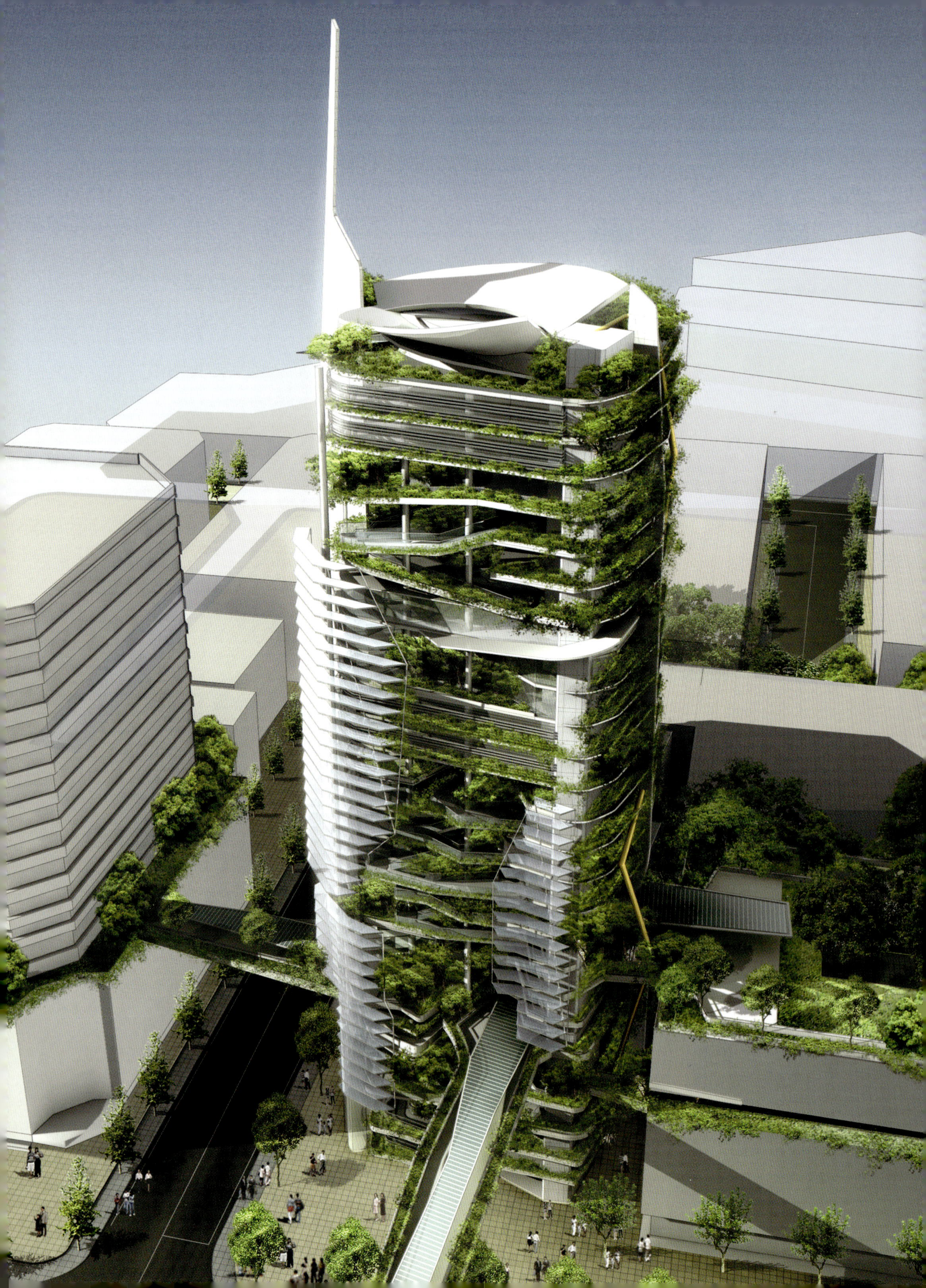

◀ Aerial view

▲ Ground level view with skycourts clearly visible

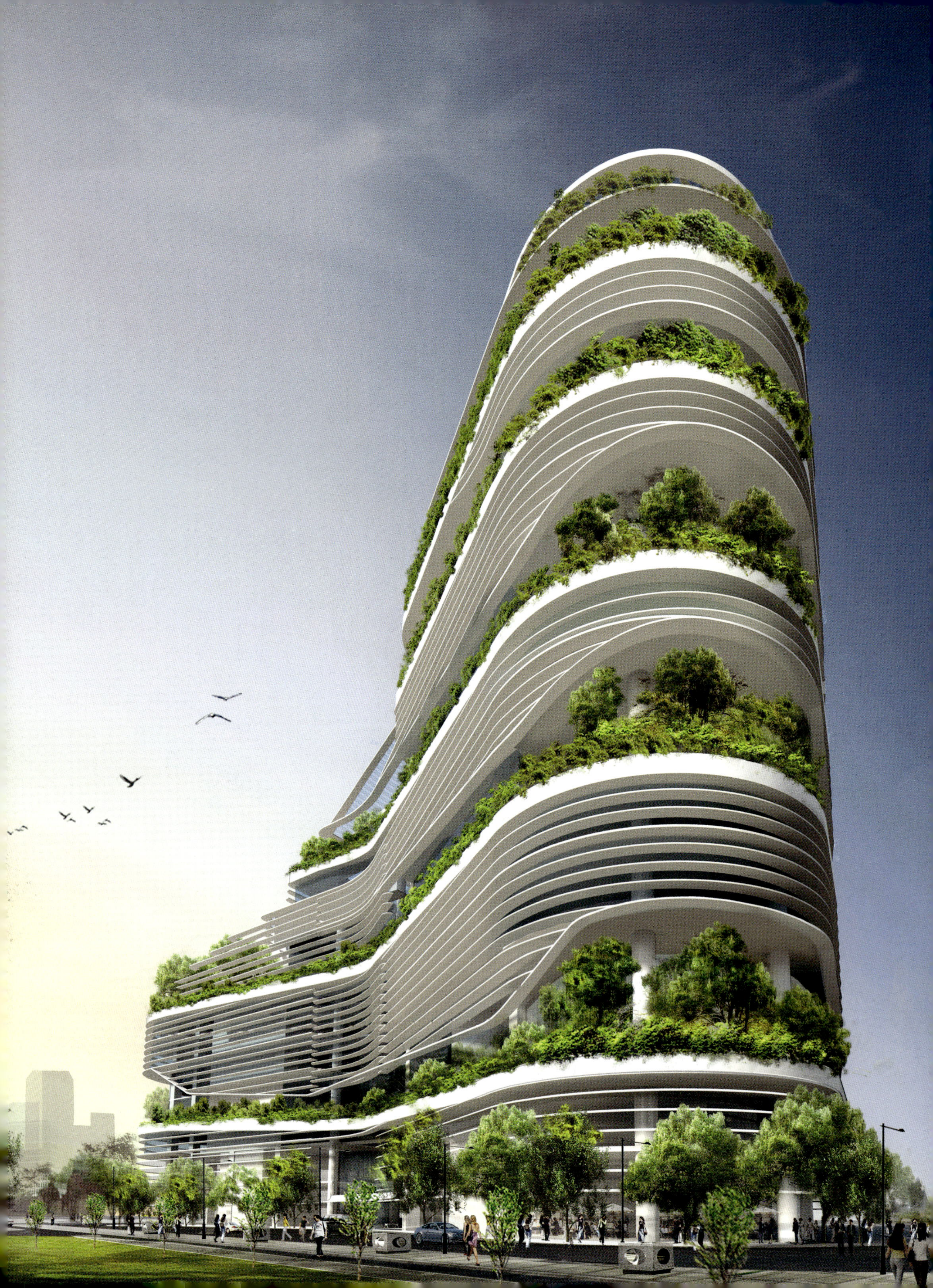

Solaris

Solaris

TYPE	:	Vertical EcoInfrastructure
LOCATION	:	Singapore
CLIMATE ZONE	:	Tropical
VEGETATION ZONE	:	Rainforest

AREAS:

GFA	:	51,282 m²
SITE AREA	:	7,734 m²
PLOT RATIO	:	1:6.5
NO. OF STOREYS	:	15
STATUS	:	Built
DATE OF COMPLETION	:	2010

▲ Aerial view of roof gardens

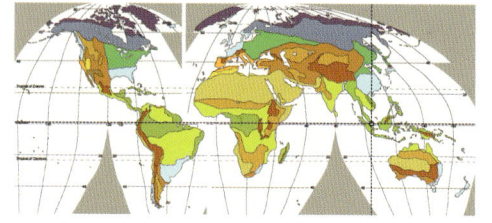

CLIMATE REGION

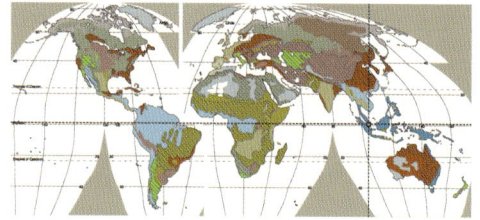

VEGETATION ZONE

Conceptual

Designed in late 2008 the Solaris building is one of Yeang's greenest buildings to date, although some unbuilt schemes (and some in design at the time of writing) promise to be greener still. What is especially significant, though, is that the client, the Assistant CEO of a landholding group, specified a very green building from the outset, reversing the conventional scenario in which the architect persuades the client to build a sustainable project. Yeang was actively sought out by the project's lead architect, CPG Consultants, to work as the "architect of design". "This was particularly gratifying," says Yeang. Singapore's regulatory and tax systems help in this regard, as achieving Green Mark Platinum accreditation led to the Client receiving an extra 2 per cent of the plot ratio. The client received this additional buildable area allowance after the project was awarded a BCA Green Mark Platinum rating.

The building lies within the 30-hectare Fusionopolis development situated to the west of Singapore's Central Business District. It is an ambitious, multi-phased showcase for research and development in interactive media, the physical sciences, engineering and technology. The six-phase project, set within London-based architect Zaha Hadid's masterplan, began with a first phase building by Japanese architect Kisho Kurokawa which opened in October 2008. Yeang's contribution to the project is part of Phase 2 – a stepped building which rises to a height of 15 storeys, serving businesses involved in R&D within the IT industry. Public spaces, flexible offices and laboratories wrap around a central, naturally ventilated atrium.

▲ The 1.5 km linear green ramp

Singapore has, in fact, very high standards for building performance, and Phase 2b of the Fusionopolis project was required to achieve a Platinum rating within the country's Green Mark standard. According to Yeang's site taxonomy (outlined in the previous chapter), this former military base can be described as a "mixed-artificial" site, consisting of partially devastated ecology with some revegetated areas. Yeang's response was to conserve what little greenery there was by building on areas which would cause the least ecological damage; such a low-impact solution would help improve the site's biodiversity simply through the positioning of the building.

The most prominent ecological feature of the Solaris building is the 1.5 km-long linear park that begins within a basement-level ecocell and rises upwards, wrapping itself around the building in a continuous fashion that makes it the world's longest vertically spiralling vegetated ramp. Here, though, unlike the ramp within the EDITT project, the landscaped planters are accompanied by a parallel path, turning the ramp into an accessible park and facilitating the servicing of the greenery. Recessed into the façade, the ramp fulfils a number of functions: it shades, cools and insulates the building while providing social amenity and enhancing biodiversity. Where the ramp meets a building corner, it opens out to become a terrace while sun shades above lift up to enable the growth of larger trees and admit extra sunlight. These vegetated spaces (ramp, terraces and roof gardens) therefore provide social spaces for inhabitants while performing very real sustainable functions.

▲ Section showing diagonal light shaft

Sky Terrace Section

Green Ramp Section

▲ Site plan

Rainwater harvesting tanks at basement level contain five days' supply for irrigating the vegetation, via a drip system, during drier weather. Among other vegetation, the Solaris Tower's linear park contains 1000 trees. In fact, the amount of greenery contained within this building is greater than the mere footprint of the building would allow; 113 per cent of the site area is planted.

"The ratio of vegetation to usable space is probably about 10 per cent or less," Yeang told *OnOffice* magazine in October 2008 . "Ideally, we should have almost equal space for vegetation and gross built-up space. Of course, this may not be commercially viable . . . At the end of the day, people make choices to do things because they believe in them."

The ground floor of the tower is naturally ventilated, a tactic that is facilitated by fitting the central atrium with overhead glass louvres that adopt an open position during fair-weather days but close during rainfall. The atrium's walls also include "rain check'" glazing which admits the wind but keeps the rain out. Energy load is further reduced through the deployment of a "light shaft", an innovative, passive energy device that brings daylight deep into the building through an angled shaft. The sunshades (up to 1 metre in width) also serve as light shelves which deflect daylight into the building's interiors. These horizontal shades, which fold upwards when the ramped park opens out into corner terraces, are a distinguishing element within the building's overall aesthetic.

Singapore has one of the strictest building regimes in the world in terms of environmental responsiveness and performance. Buildings which gain 90 points under the country's Green Mark certification system are awarded a Platinum rating. The Solaris project was awarded 97.5 points.

▶ Atrium view

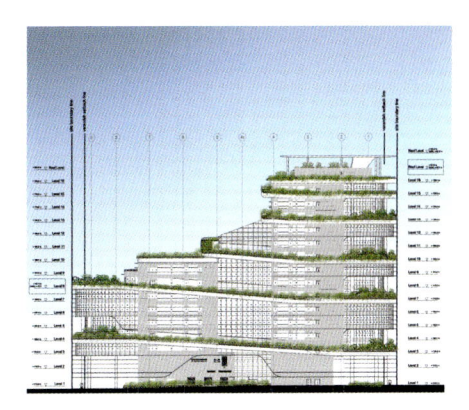

West Elevation

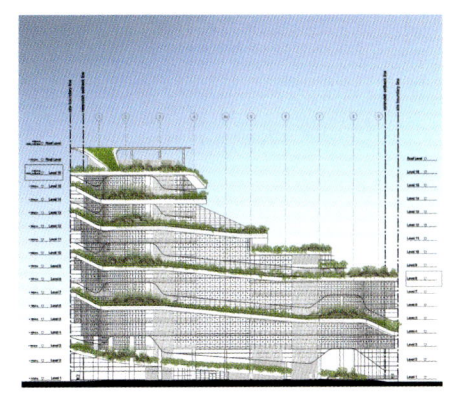

East Elevation

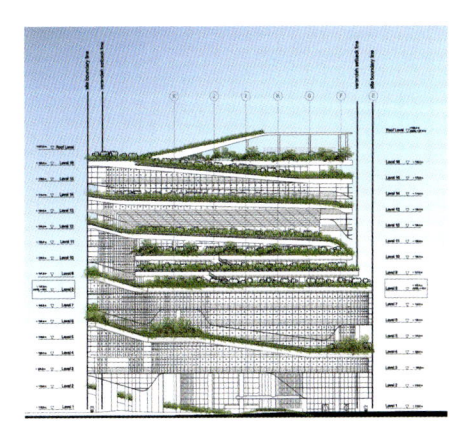

North Elevation

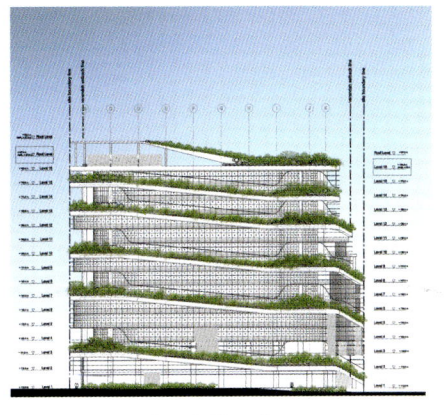

South Elevation

Vertical EcoInfrastructure | Solaris 205

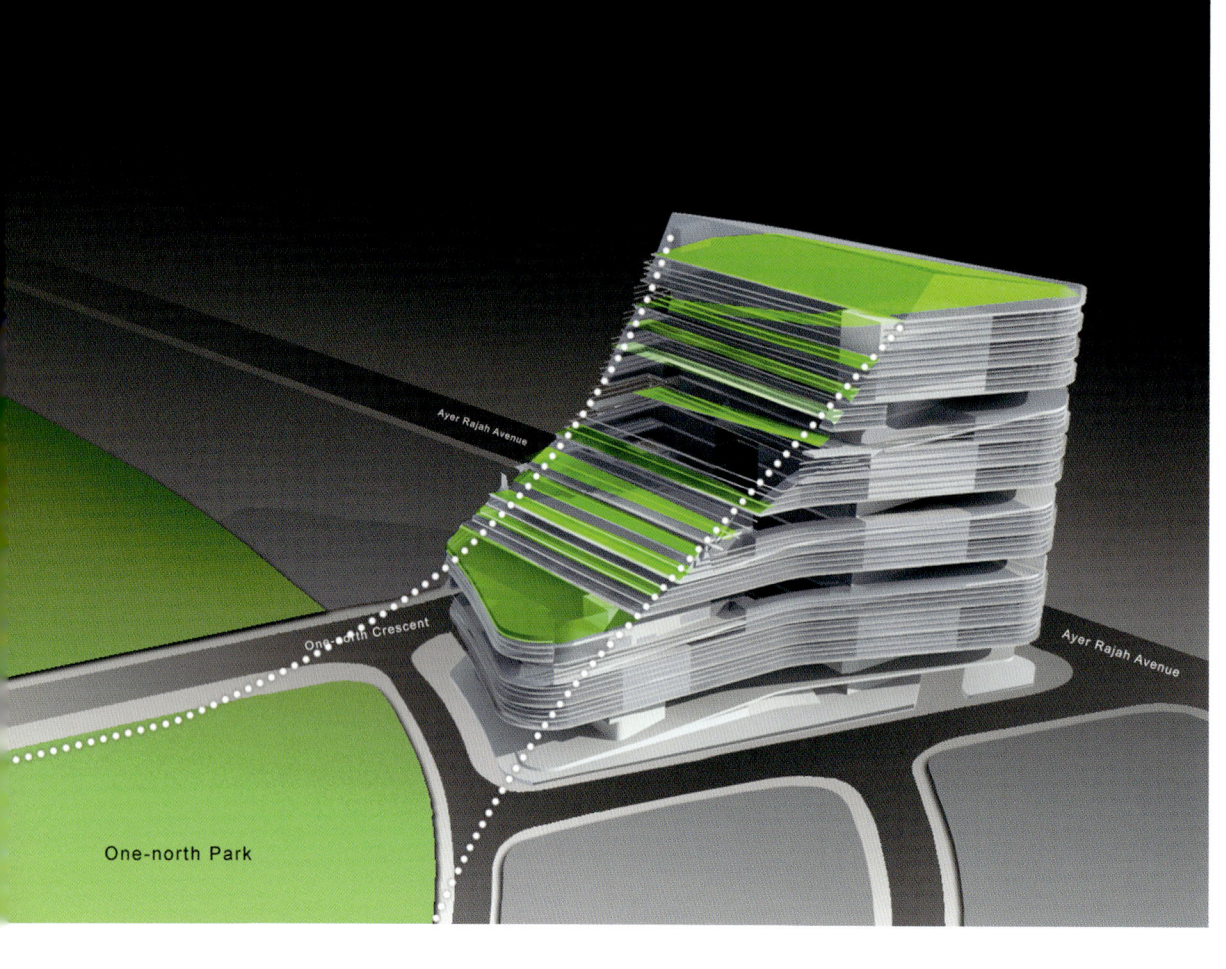

▲ Roof garden diagram showing the rising "green carpet"
▼ Continuous green ramp concept

SUMMARY OF PLANS

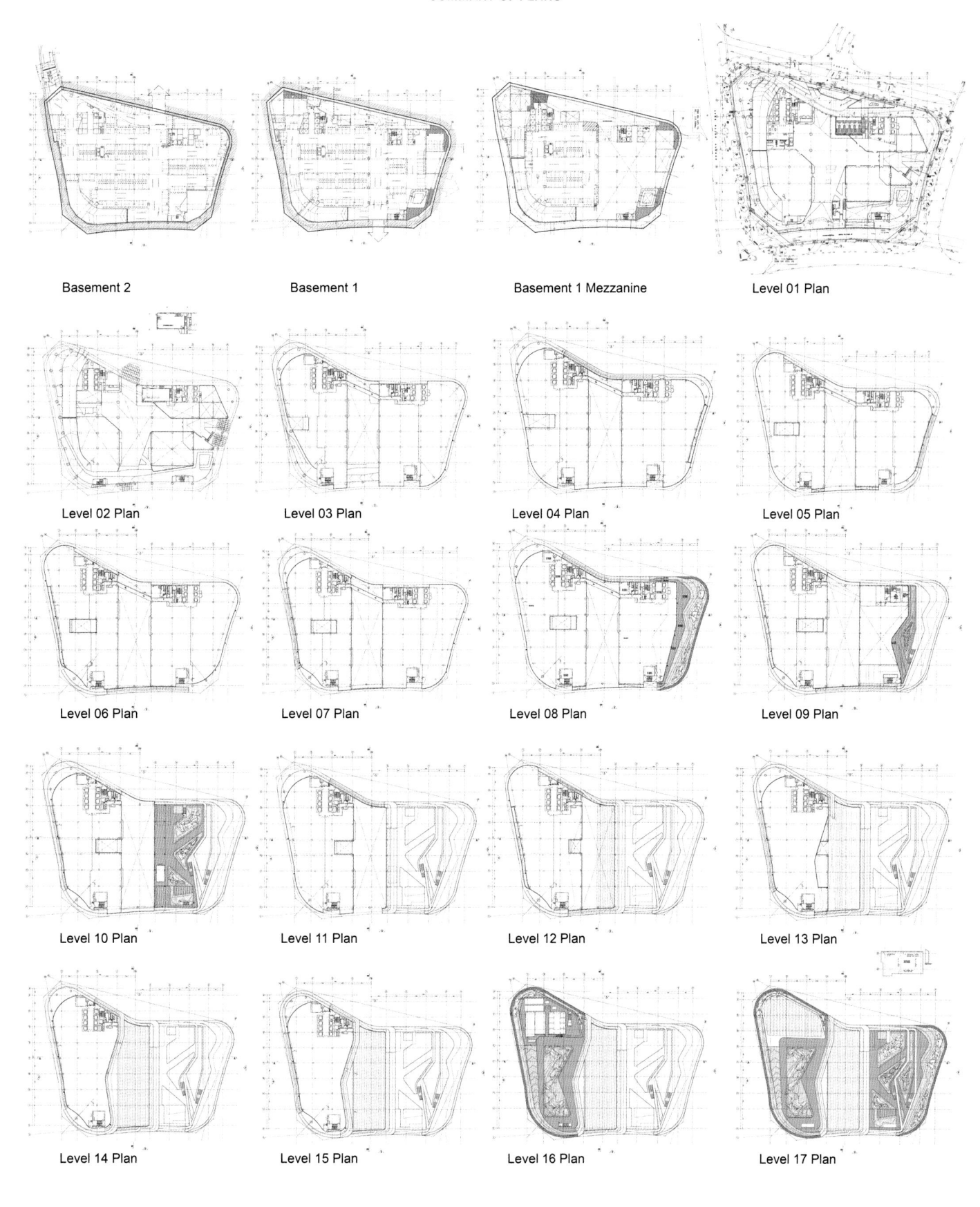

Basement 2

Basement 1

Basement 1 Mezzanine

Level 01 Plan

Level 02 Plan

Level 03 Plan

Level 04 Plan

Level 05 Plan

Level 06 Plan

Level 07 Plan

Level 08 Plan

Level 09 Plan

Level 10 Plan

Level 11 Plan

Level 12 Plan

Level 13 Plan

Level 14 Plan

Level 15 Plan

Level 16 Plan

Level 17 Plan

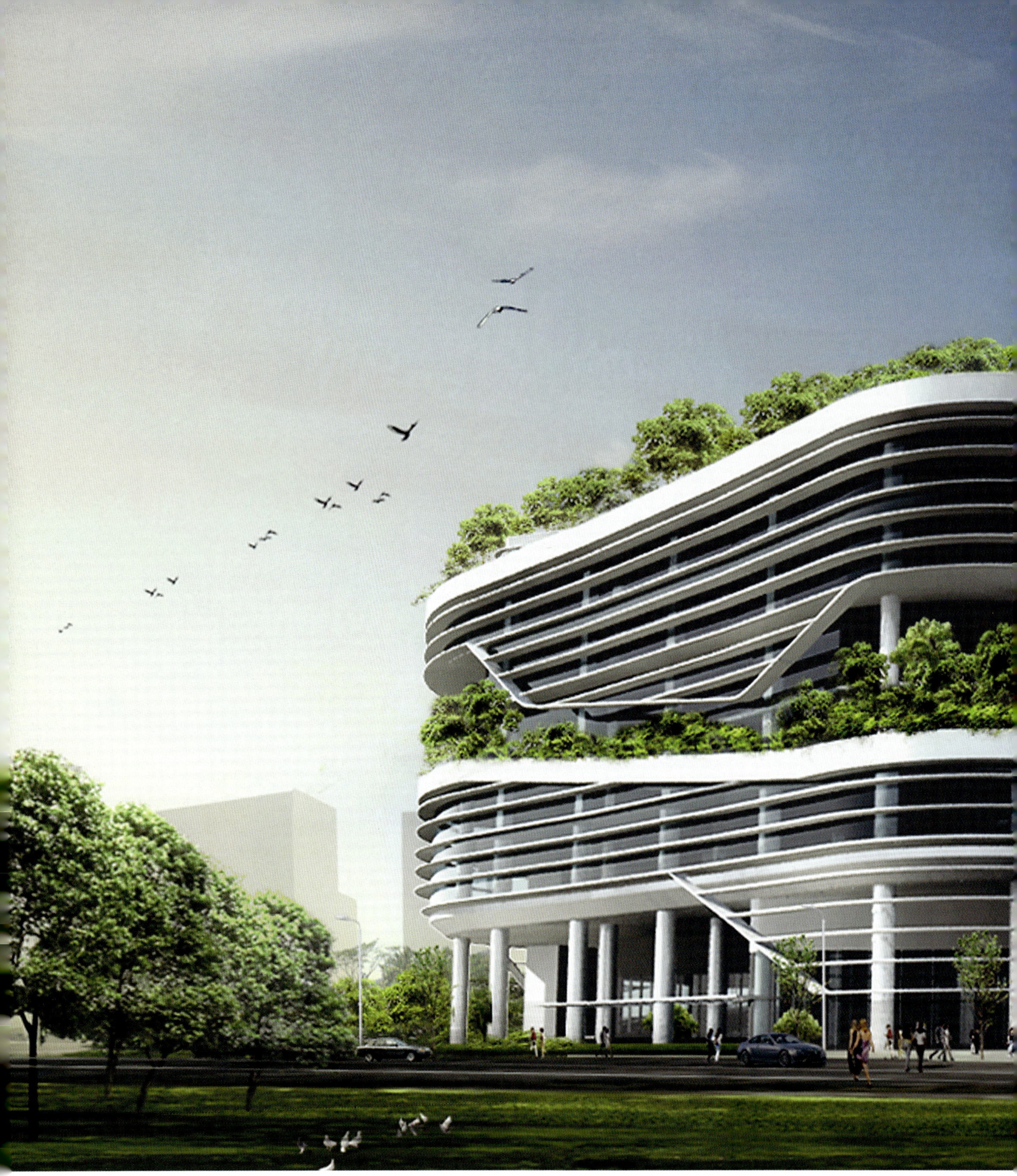

▲ View from one-north Park

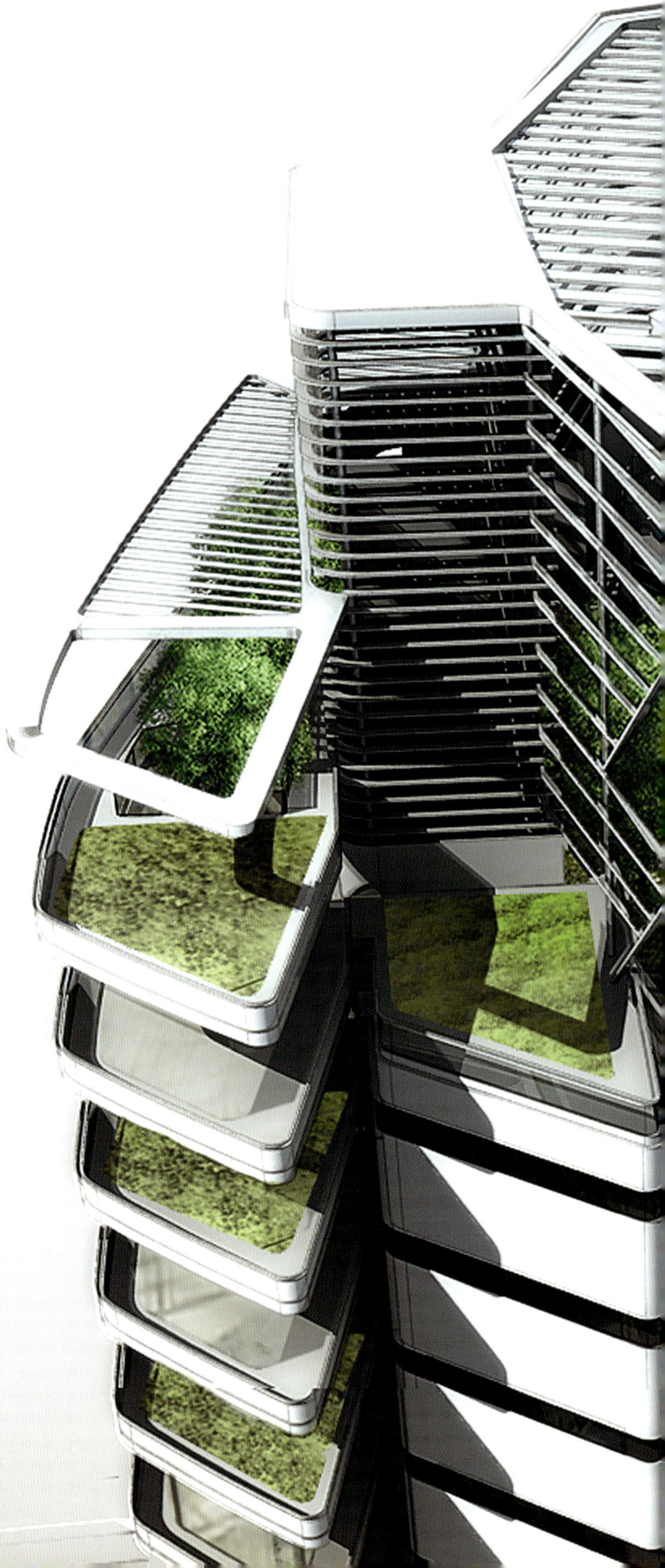

Spire Edge

Spire Edge

TYPE	:	Vertical EcoInfrastructure
LOCATION	:	New Delhi, India
CLIMATE ZONE	:	Temperate
VEGETATION ZONE	:	Forest

AREAS:

GFA	:	22,559 m²
NFA	:	17,165 m²
SITE AREA	:	4,765 m²
PLOT RATIO	:	1:4.7
NO. OF STOREYS	:	20
STATUS	:	Under Construction
DATE OF COMPLETION	:	2011

▲ Lift lobby interior

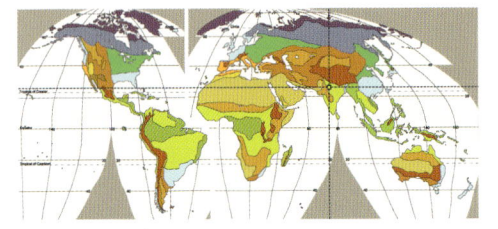

CLIMATE REGION

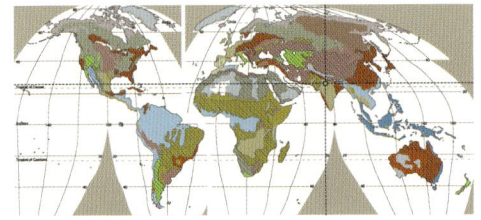

VEGETATION ZONE

Conceptual

The key design feature of this iconic tower is its green infrastructure – the continuous ramp that carries vegetation from the base and surrounding landscape to the upper levels. The design also includes provision for sky courts, and rainwater gravity filtration and collection (important for a city with very hot summers and unpredictable monsoon rains in autumn). Yeang began work on this project soon after completing the Soma masterplan and a competition entry for the BIDV Tower in Vietnam, a design which incorporated vertical green walls. Here, the site for the new business campus was simple, denuded land, scraped clean for development with none of the original ecology remaining. The site was, essentially, an eological tabula rasa. Having so recently immersed himself in the horizontal green ecoinfrastructure of Soma, Yeang took the same principles but turned them through 90 degrees, running a flat landscape vertically up the building's façade.

"The design indicates how selecting the method for designing an ecoinfrastructure – and there are many – can affect the overall architectonic aesthetics of the built form. The aesthetics further depend on how this strategy was faceted into the building," says Yeang. "For example, in Zorlu I used green ramps, walls and roofs; in the Plaza of Nations project one finds diagonal encased atriums and high level green bridges; the façades of the DiGi building are characterised by a split and splayed pattern of green walls; the Solaris and EDITT Towers are defined by a spiralling green ramp that encircles all faces of these buildings' exteriors."

The green ecoinfrastructure is placed within both the main and rear facades of the building, which links seamlessly into the surrounding campus landscape. The vegetated surface within the rear façade is aligned to a pedestrian ramp and walkway similar to that in the Solaris building, but here the ramp folds to provide spaces for special meeting rooms. The client refers to these spaces as "meeting spaces for innovation and creativity".

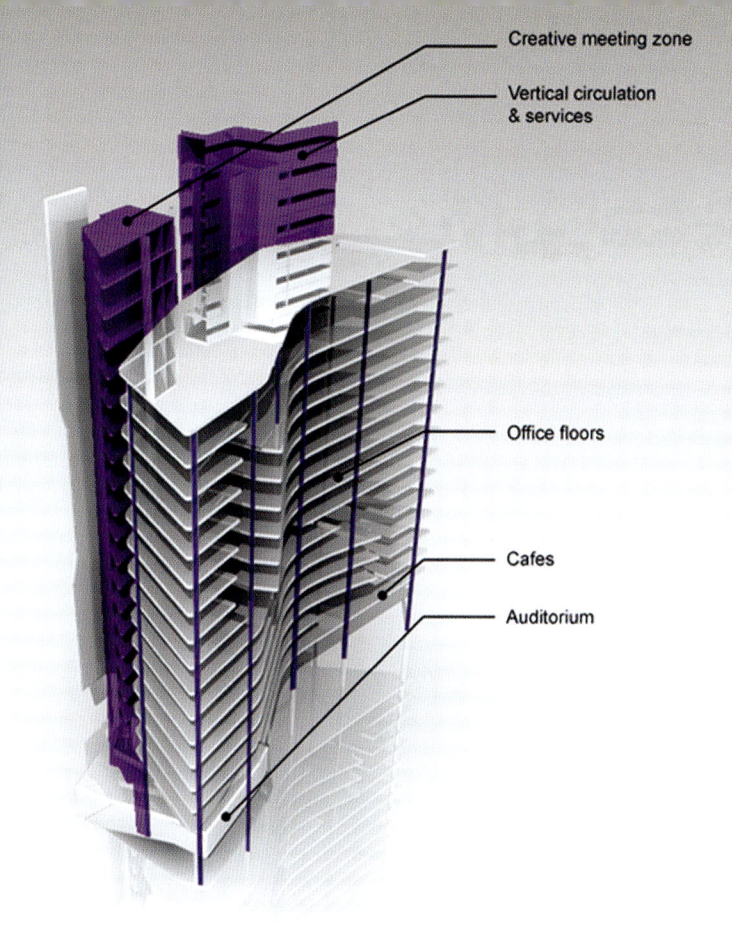

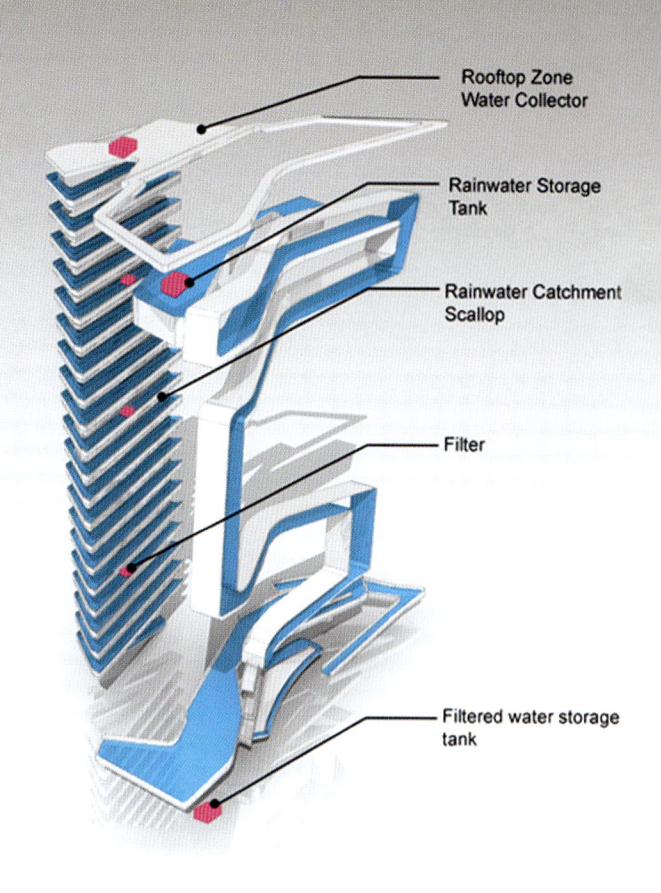

▲ Superstructure concept (left) and water management concept (right)

Other ecological features within the tower include rainwater harvesting, solar shading of the façades and the natural ventilation of the elevator cores, stairs and toilets. Yeang says that, with typical buildings, 80 per cent of their environmental impact is "pre-designed" into them through their materiality, supply chain and energy load. "Ecodesign is to seek to reduce this 80 per cent of pre-designed negative impacts on the environment. The ideal green building is ecomimetic – one which integrates seamlessly and benignly with the natural environment at three levels: physically, systemically and temporally."

Yeang adds, though, that no matter how well buildings perform, the architecture and construction professions have yet to arrive at the final ecodesign solution. "It will be some time before any of us designs the truly ecomimetic built system."

Yeang describes the client as an architect turned developer. The client's wife, from Abaxial Architects of New Dehli, is the executive architect of the project.

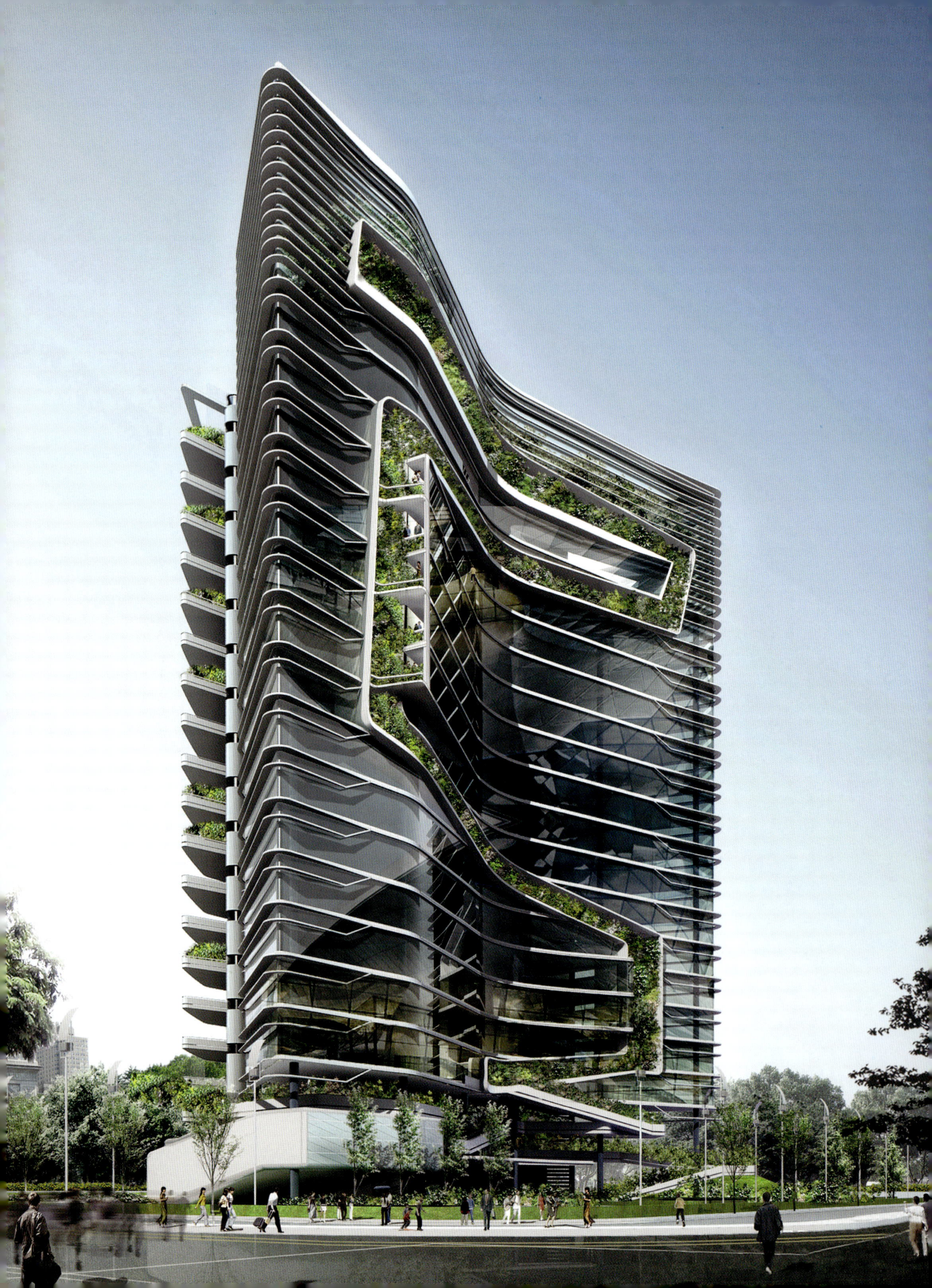

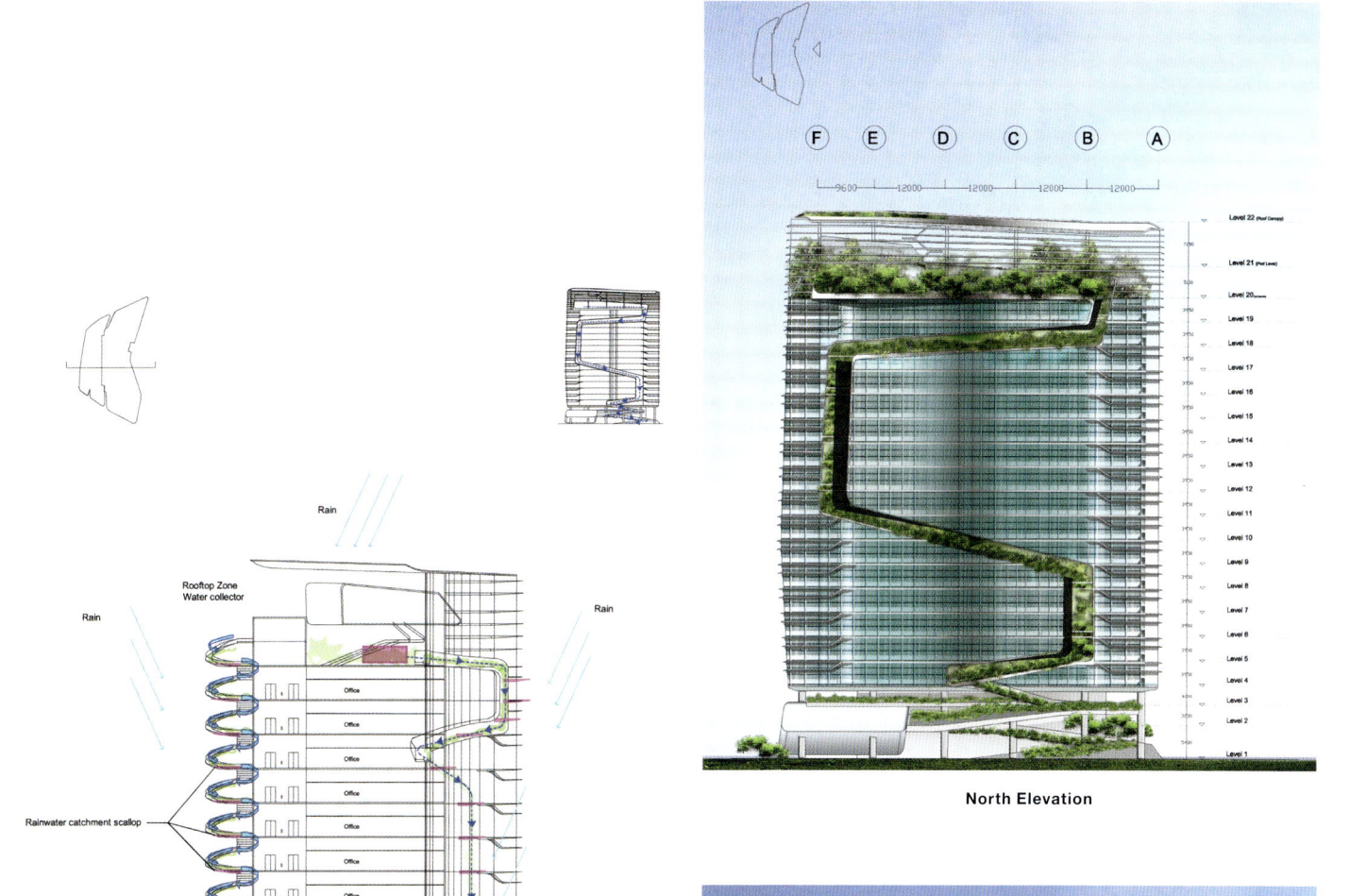

Short Section with Rainwater Harvesting System

North Elevation

South Elevation

◀ Ground level view of Spire Edge

Vertical EcoInfrastructure | Spire Edge 215

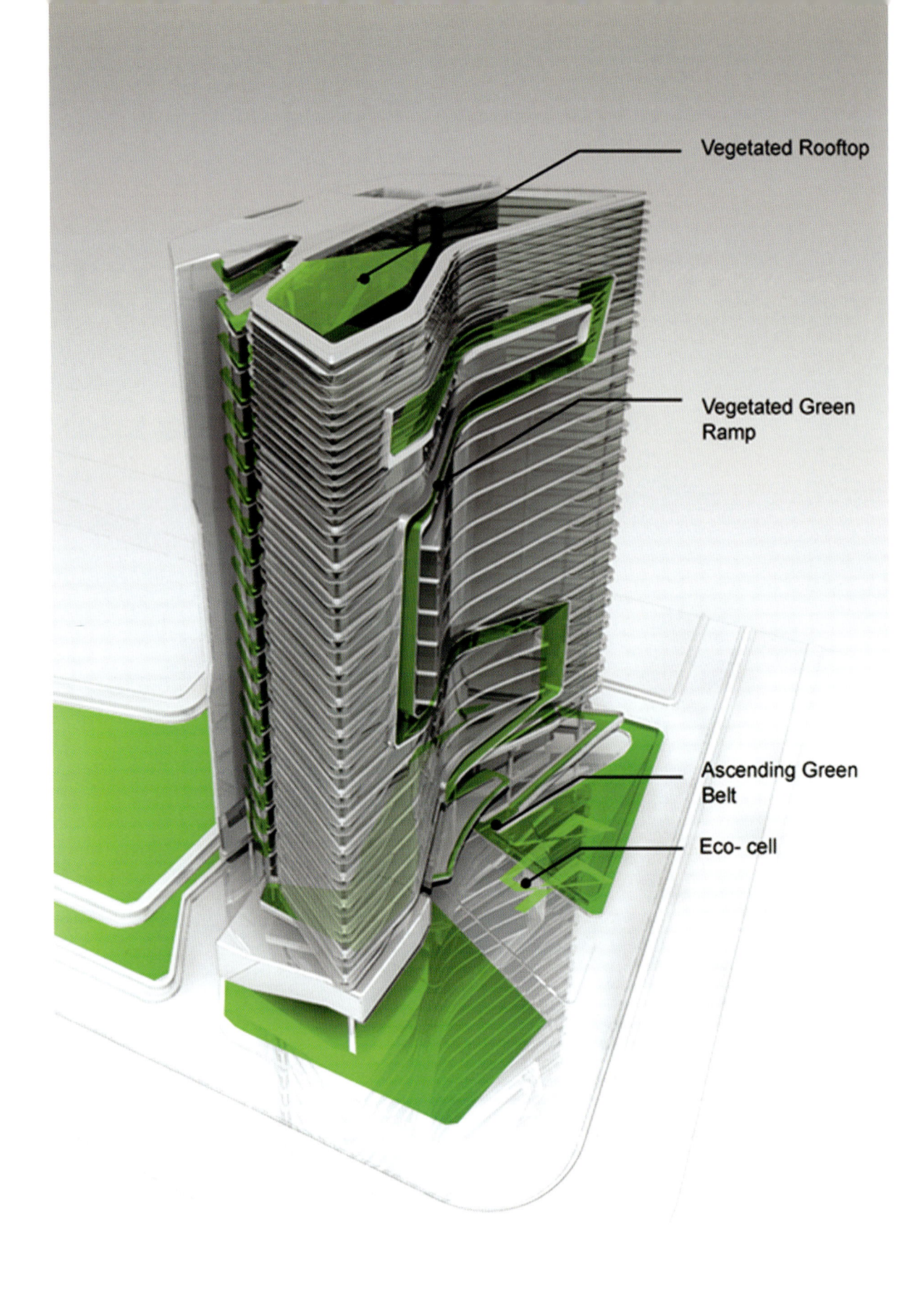

- Vegetated Rooftop
- Vegetated Green Ramp
- Ascending Green Belt
- Eco- cell

Green Link Concept

Sunshading Strategy

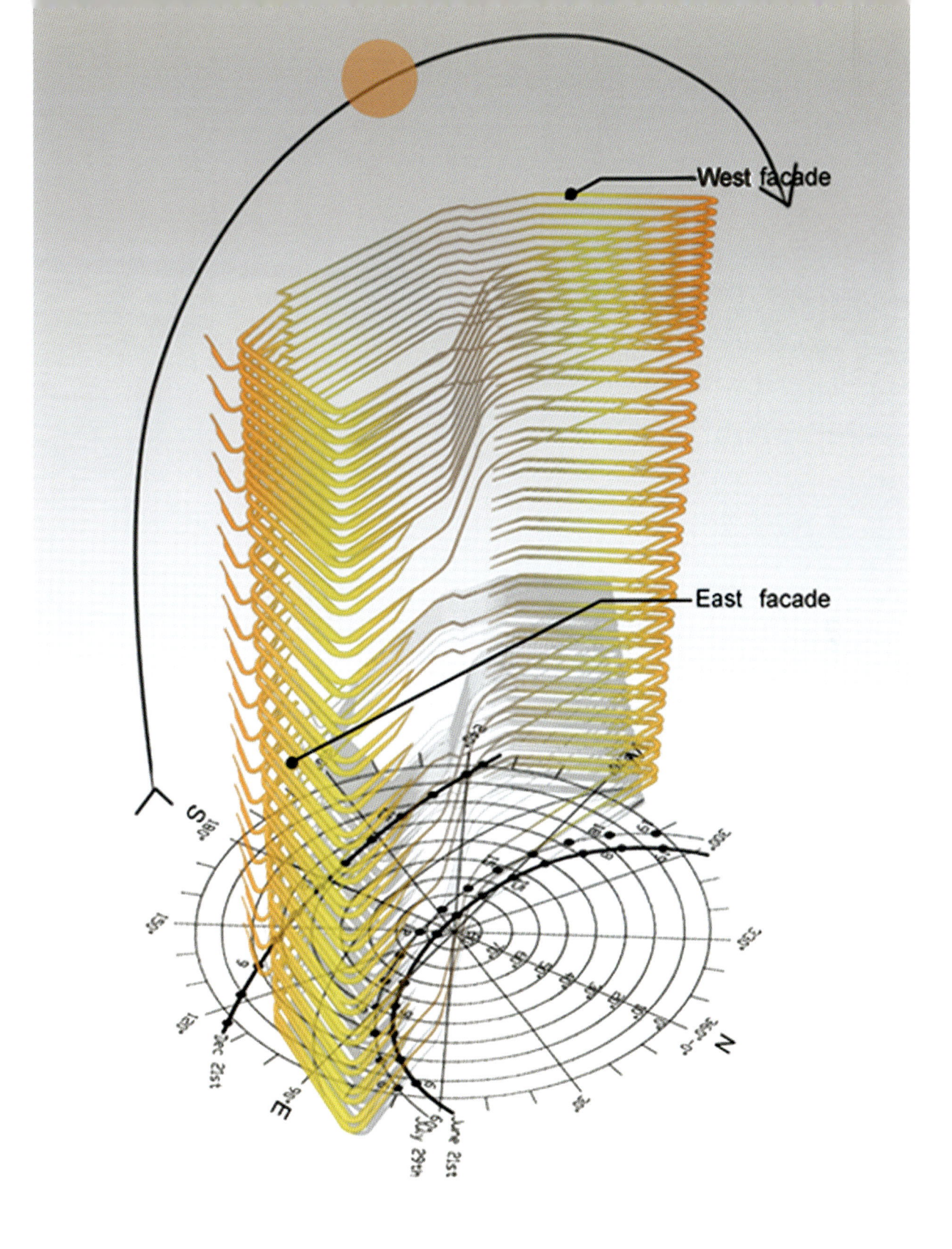

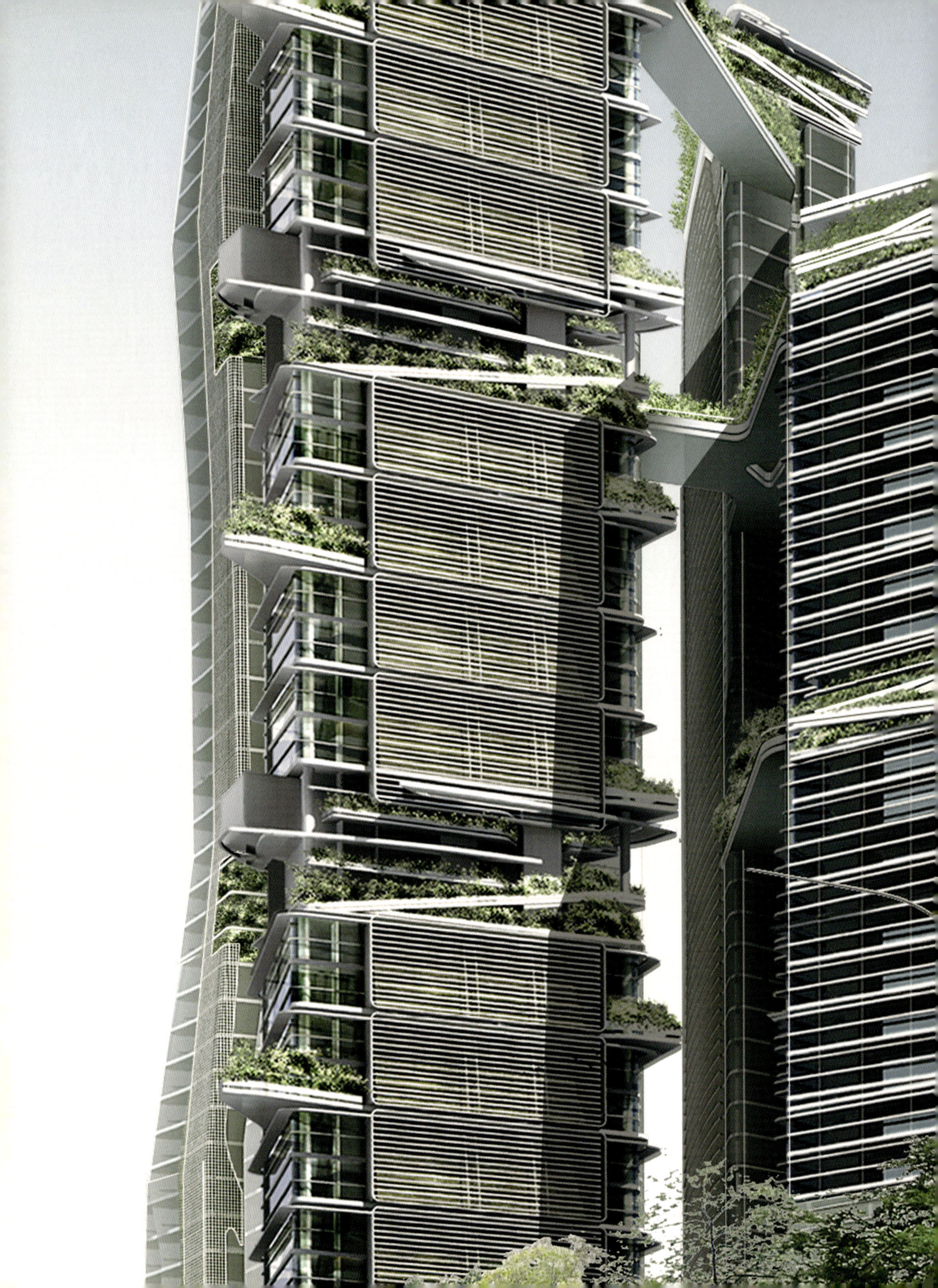

L Tower

L Tower

TYPE	:	Vertical EcoInfrastructure
LOCATION	:	Kuala Lumpur, Malaysia
CLIMATE ZONE	:	Tropical
VEGETATION ZONE	:	Rainforest

AREAS:

GFA	:	146,750 m²
SITE AREA	:	18,342 m²
PLOT RATIO	:	1:8
NO. OF STOREYS	:	46
STATUS	:	Concept design
DATE OF COMPLETION	:	2014

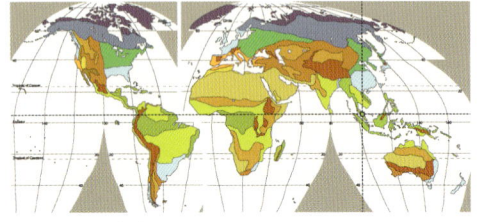

CLIMATE REGION

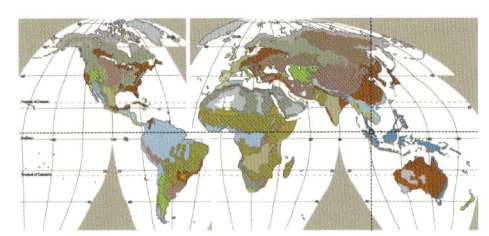

VEGETATION ZONE

Conceptual

▲ Site plan

Yeang's work, in seeking to balance the biotic and the abiotic within the built environment, has come to embrace biodiversity targets and food production. This represents a new, challenging domain for the architect, as it means that creating room for ecological recovery and growth is not enough. This is very different from giving Nature the best possible chance and hoping for the best. Furthermore, Yeang is examining the potential for urban food production.

Yeang's design for the L Tower is set on the edge of Kuala Lumpur's commercial district and comprises a podium on which sits three tall buildings containing 40-storey food production walls. Using hydroponics, a method by which crops can be grown in nutrient-filled pods without conventional soil, the building becomes something of an inner city, vertical farm. "Such is our dependence on a dwindling oil supply that major world cities like London are never more than five days from starvation. For a city to survive in a post-oil economy it is imperative that food is sourced from within a few metres, rather than from thousands of miles away. Building Integrated Food Production is being developed as a reaction to the loss of productive land to property development and the pressure to reduce food transportation, while also recognising the considerable synergies that can be realised when food production is brought within, and around, the structures where we live and work," wrote Yeang in *Architectural Design* (November/December 2008) in an article co-authored with permaculture designer Michael Guerra. "To truly sustain a city [buildings] must also provide food."

▲ Atrium

Ramps spiral around the buildings, connecting the ground plane with roof-top gardens, providing a continuous vertical "green corridor" with skycourts and screens constructed from a series of horizontally hung hydroponic tubes. "This may be the next generation of the vertical ecoinfrastructure where the greening becomes productive," says Yeang. These tubes, positioned as screens on the building façades, connected to a network of feeding pipes, are used for the growing of vegetables which can be harvested by raising or lowering the tubes via a system of pulleys. The hydroponic screens also improve the passive-mode performance of the towers themselves, controlling solar gain and providing a cooling effect.

Such a development could be part of a new wave of community-inspired, collaborative practices which enable inner city locations to be part of the solution to environmental pressures. However, Yeang is frank about the ecology of skyscrapers: "Skyscrapers are the least ecological of all building types. They use up about 30 per cent more energy and materials to create and to operate, compared with low-rise buildings. However, until we find an economic alternative, I am afraid they will continue to be built ubiquitously. This being the case, if the world's best ecodesigners ignore them, and not seek to make them as ecological and as humane as possible, then who will?"

Zoning Plan for Level 5

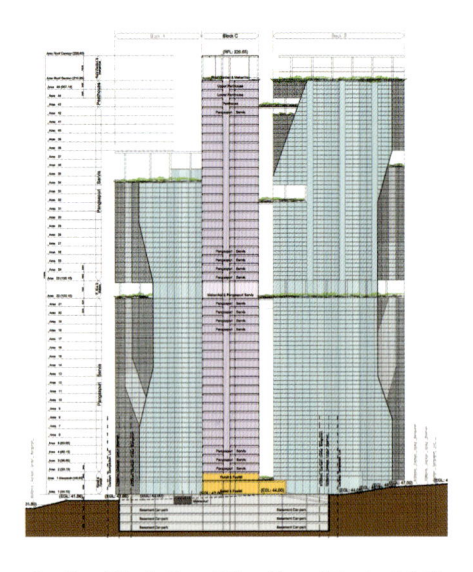

Section (Block C) and Elevations (Blocks A & B)

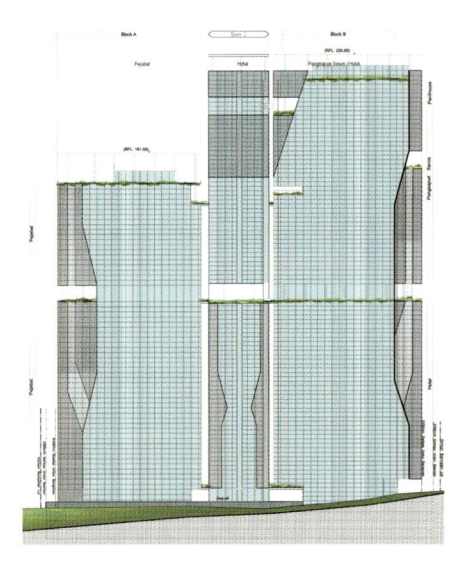

South-East Elevation

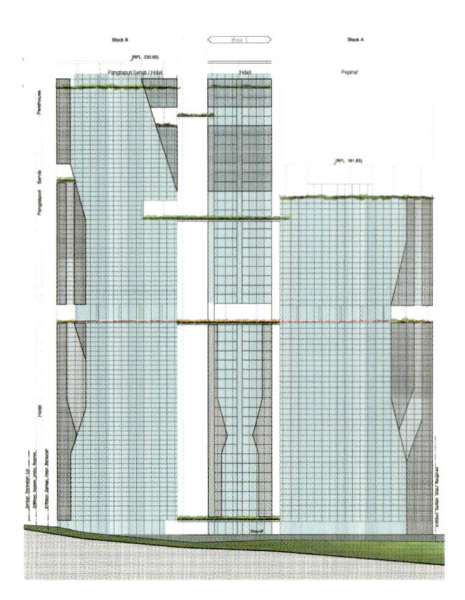

South-West Elevation

222 ECOARCHITECTURE | THE WORK OF KEN YEANG

▲ Model of L Tower

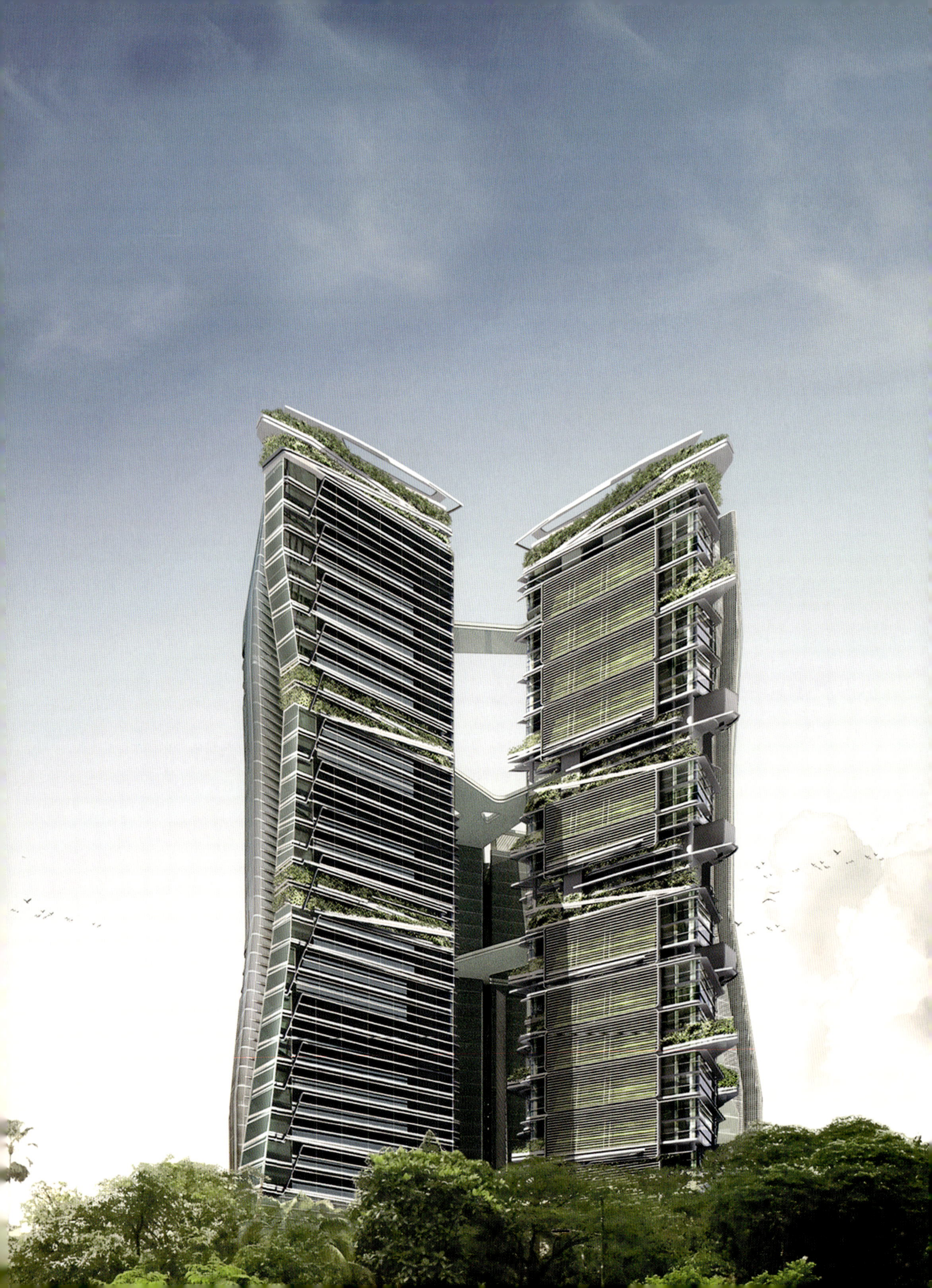

CONCEPT STUDIES

◁ Rendered computer model of L Tower

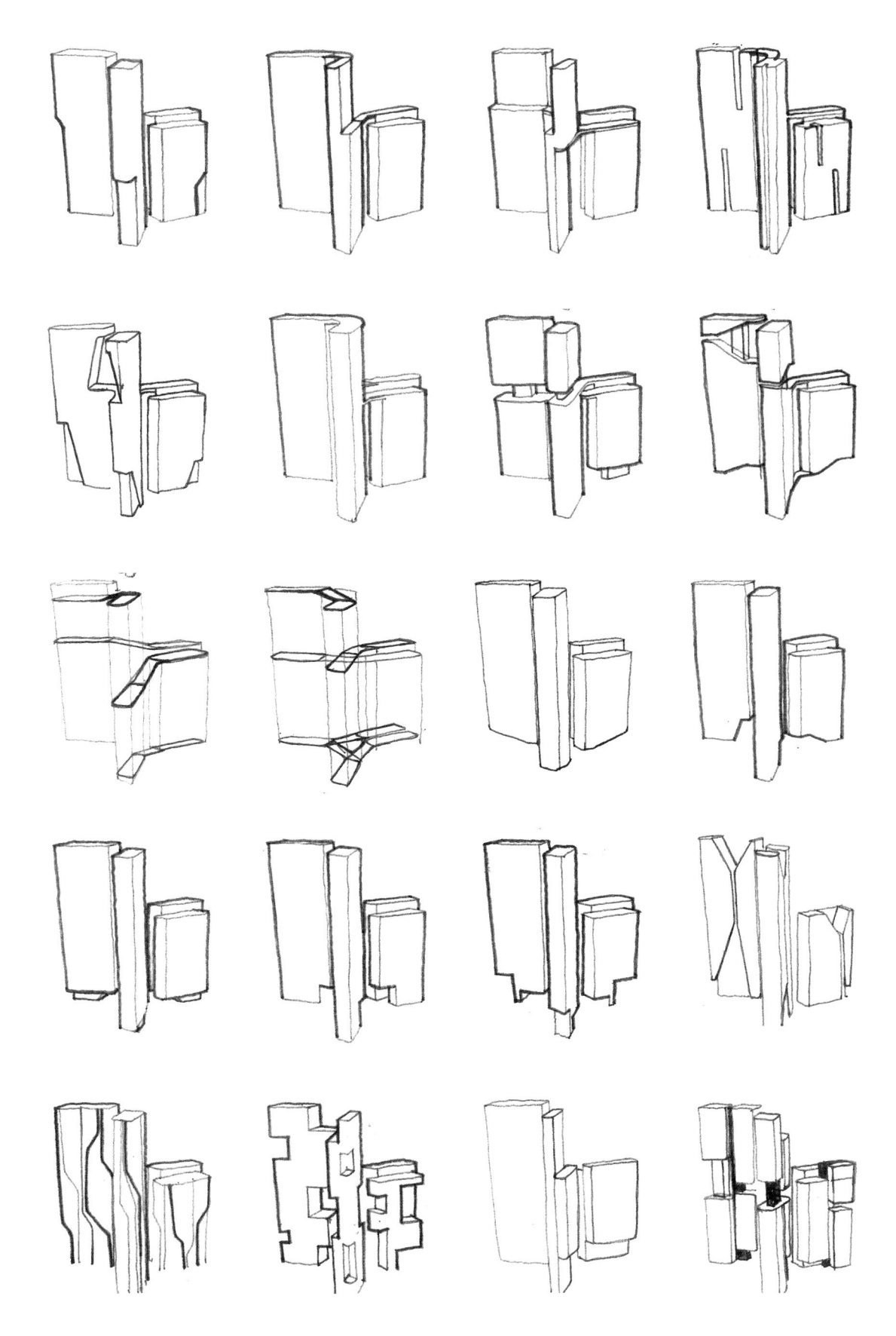

Vertical EcoInfrastructure | **L Tower**

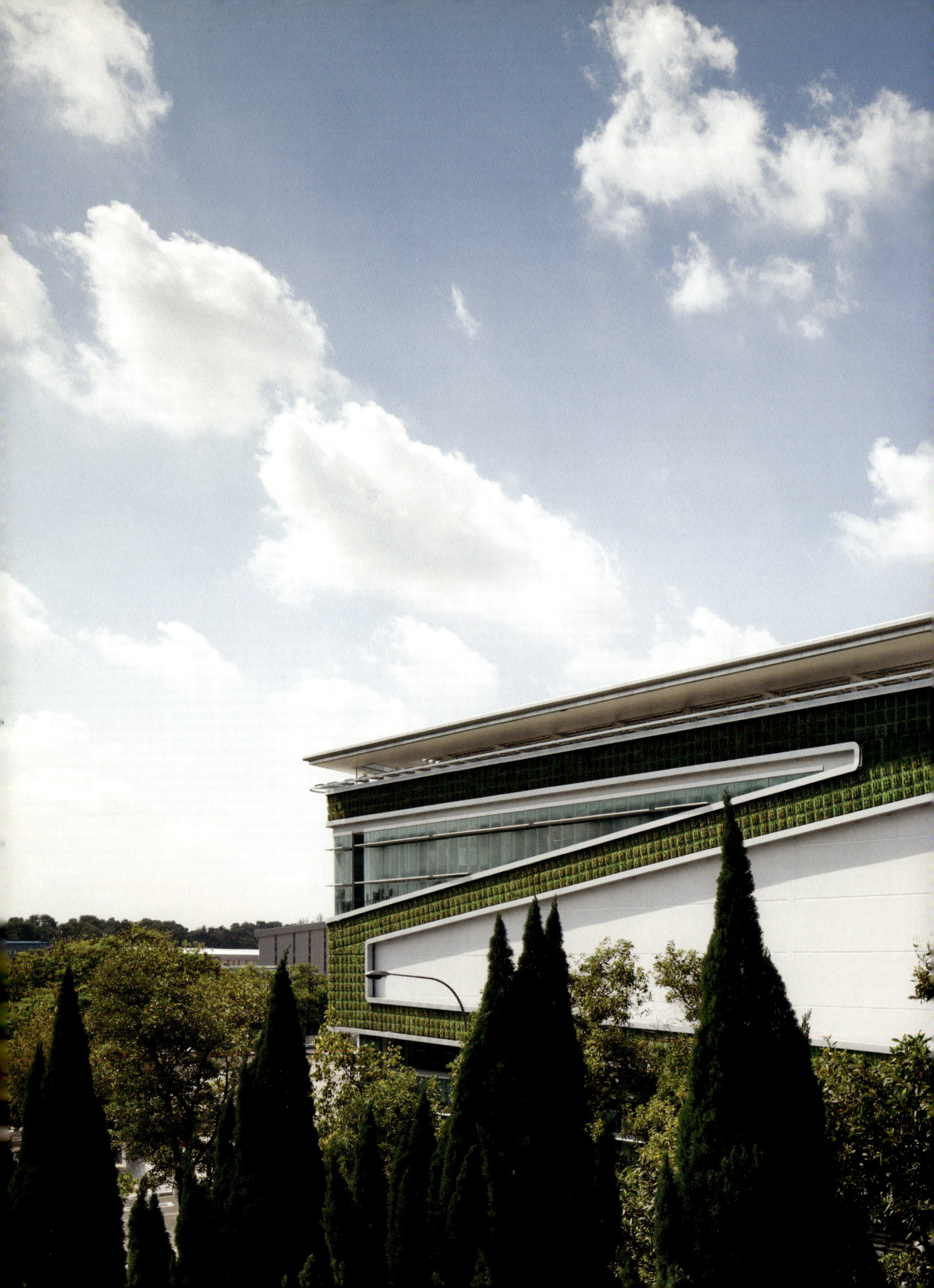

DiGi Technical Operations Centre

DiGi Technical Operations Centre

TYPE	:	Vertical EcoInfrastructure
LOCATION	:	Shah Alam, Malaysia
CLIMATE ZONE	:	Tropical
VEGETATION ZONE	:	Rainforest

AREAS:

GFA	:	12,982 m²
SITE AREA	:	8,517 m²
PLOT RATIO	:	1:1.5
NO. OF STOREYS	:	3
STATUS	:	Built
DATE OF COMPLETION	:	2010

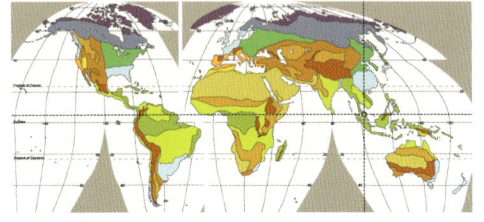

CLIMATE REGION

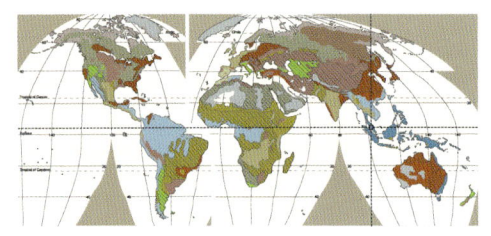

VEGETATION ZONE

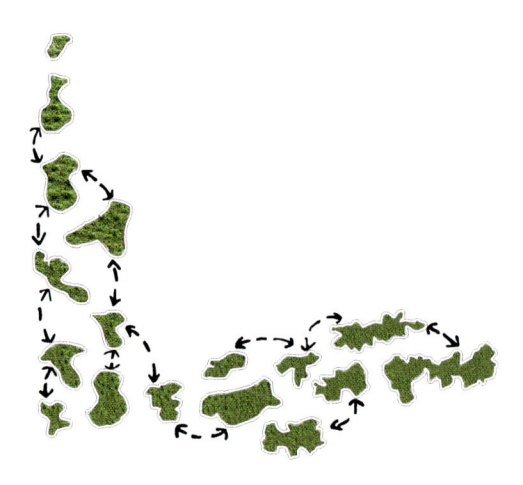

Conceptual

▲ 1,334 m² continuous green wall

This project, a relatively low-rise building for Yeang, presented the architect with an unusual brief. Commissioned by DiGi Telecommunications, a mobile phone services provider, it is for a data centre. Data centres are, by nature, energy intensive structures which no amount of eco-engineering can counter-balance – they are, effectively, 24/7 boxes filled with energy-hungry and heat-emitting computers with few window openings. Nonetheless, Yeang considers these buildings to be crucial to the operation of contemporary life, so rather than decline to participate he has sought to minimise the environmental effect of the building as best he can. "It is difficult to make a data centre green," says Yeang. The significance of this project is the bifurcating system of vegetated walls that wraps itself around the building's façade.

Located within the Shah Alam hi-tech industrial park outside Kuala Lumpur, the site contains little of its original vegetation and is, in Yeang's terms, "essentially a devastated site". Attempting to merge the building within the natural landscape was therefore pointless, but Yeang sought to green the structure to give the site an element of biodiversity. The data centre itself is a sealed box, separated from the outside environment, but the building does contain offices and amenities for staff.

Taking the green wall as a starting point, the façade contrives to enfold the building in thick, vegetated, bifurcated swathes. The façade system incorporates an extensive "vegetated skin" which is designed to "scrub and filter" the air before it enters the building's interior. The goal of this particular strategy is to decrease CO_2 levels, regulate humidity, trap dust particulates and dampen external noise.

▲ Photograph of front elevation

Furthermore, this skin will prevent excessive solar gain and harmful UV radiation while acting as a buffer against external swings in temperature. More importantly, the continuous vegetated wall around the buiding's façade increases the biodiversity of this devastated site. Photovoltaic cells are positioned on a large canopy at roof level and reduce the energy load of the building by approximately 2 per cent.

The roof also contains a tank for the harvesting of rainwater for reuse in an irrigation system, which will service the landscaped areas on the ground as well as the vegetated wall. A bioswale – a contoured landscape element which slows and purifies rainwater – has been designed to control run-off in storm and flood conditions, recharging natural aquifiers and therefore reducing the waterload of the building. Furthermore, Yeang has included the provision for green paving alternatives for the parking lot, such as modules manufactured from recycled plastic.

Yeang is deeply aware, though, that human responsiveness to the fragility of the environment is ultimately going to depend on a lot more than the skills and visions of individual architects: "Sustainable technology is only one strand in green design, but certainly not the only one. The other strands, or armatures, in ecological design include water management, closing the water loop and sustainable drainage, relating and linking with the ecology of the landscape, our human spaces, hardscapes and regulatory systems that can lead to a sustainable way of life and economy. The approach should be based on ecology and an ecomimetic design strategy, and not just on eco-engineering gadgetry. In the next 10 years, the biggest challenges will be our human systems – how can we change our ways of life, our economic systems, our social and political systems to be green?"

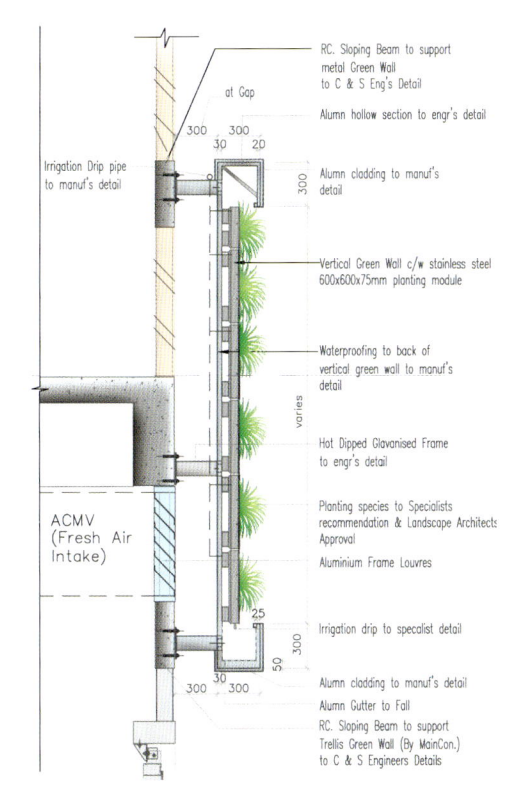

Green Wall Detail

▲ DiGi corporate logo on front façade

▲ Entrance Lobby

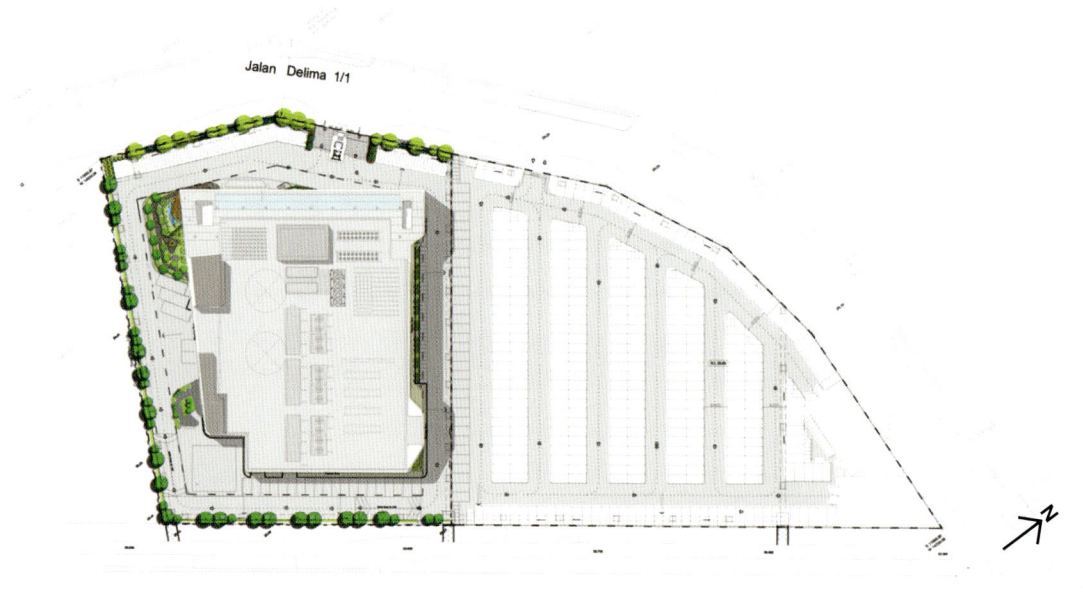

Site Plan

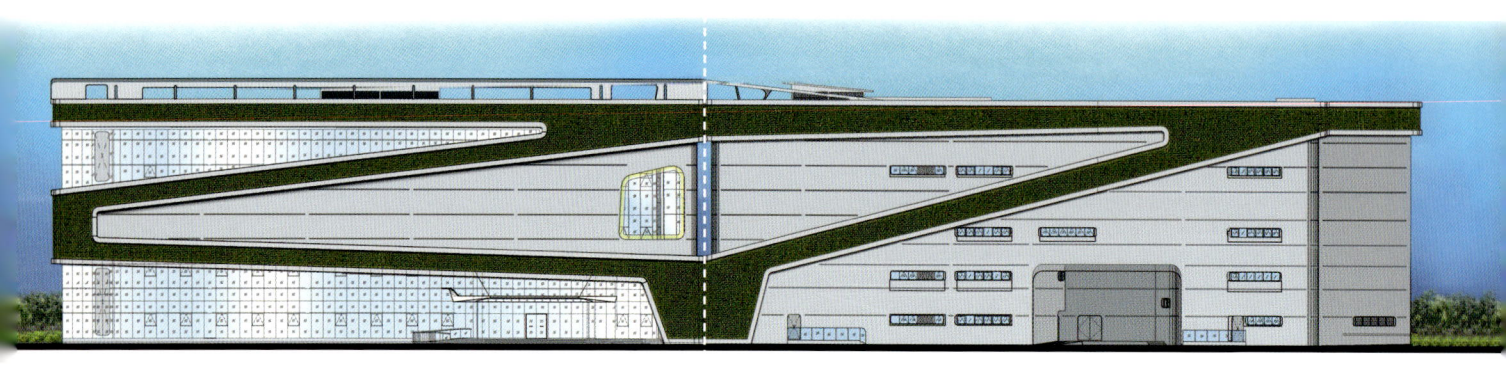

▲ North-West elevation

▲ South-West elevation

SUMMARY OF PLANS

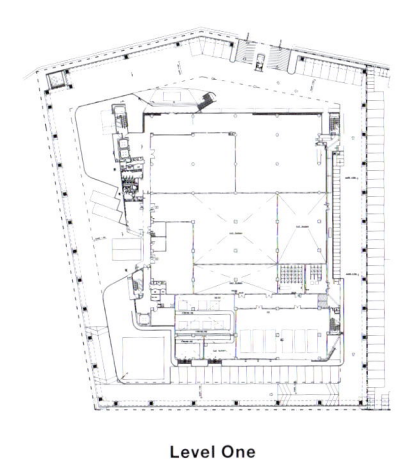

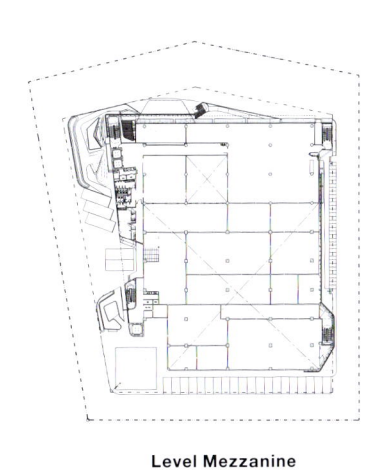

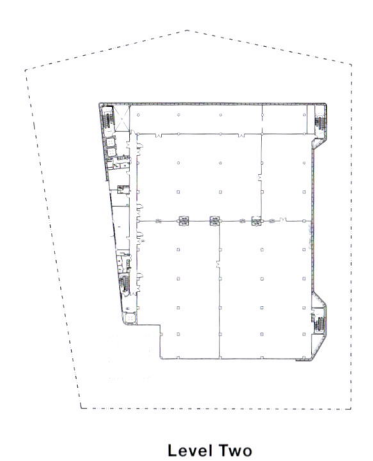

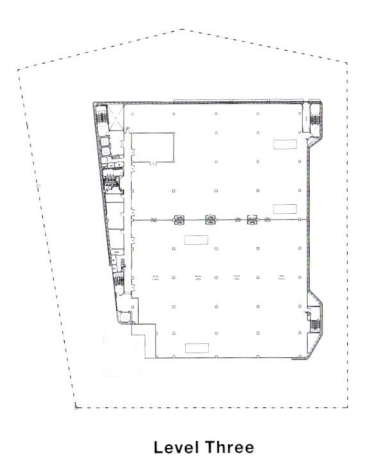

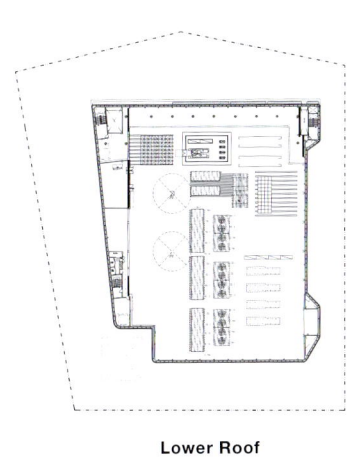

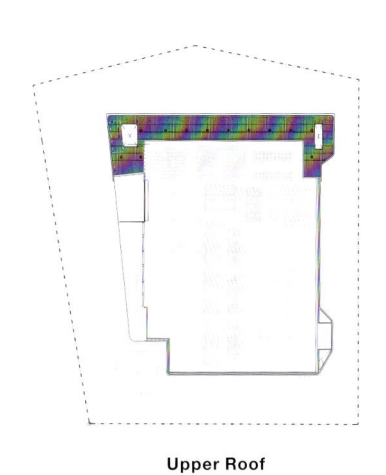

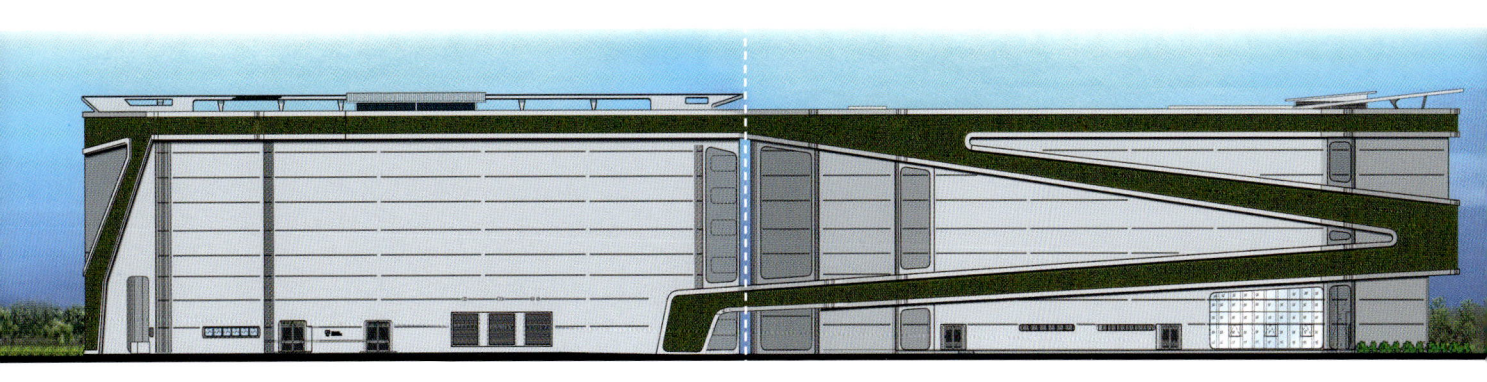

Level One

Level Mezzanine

Level Two

Level Three

Lower Roof

Upper Roof

▲ South-East elevation

▲ North-East elevation

Vertical EcoInfrastructure | DiGi Technical Operations Centre

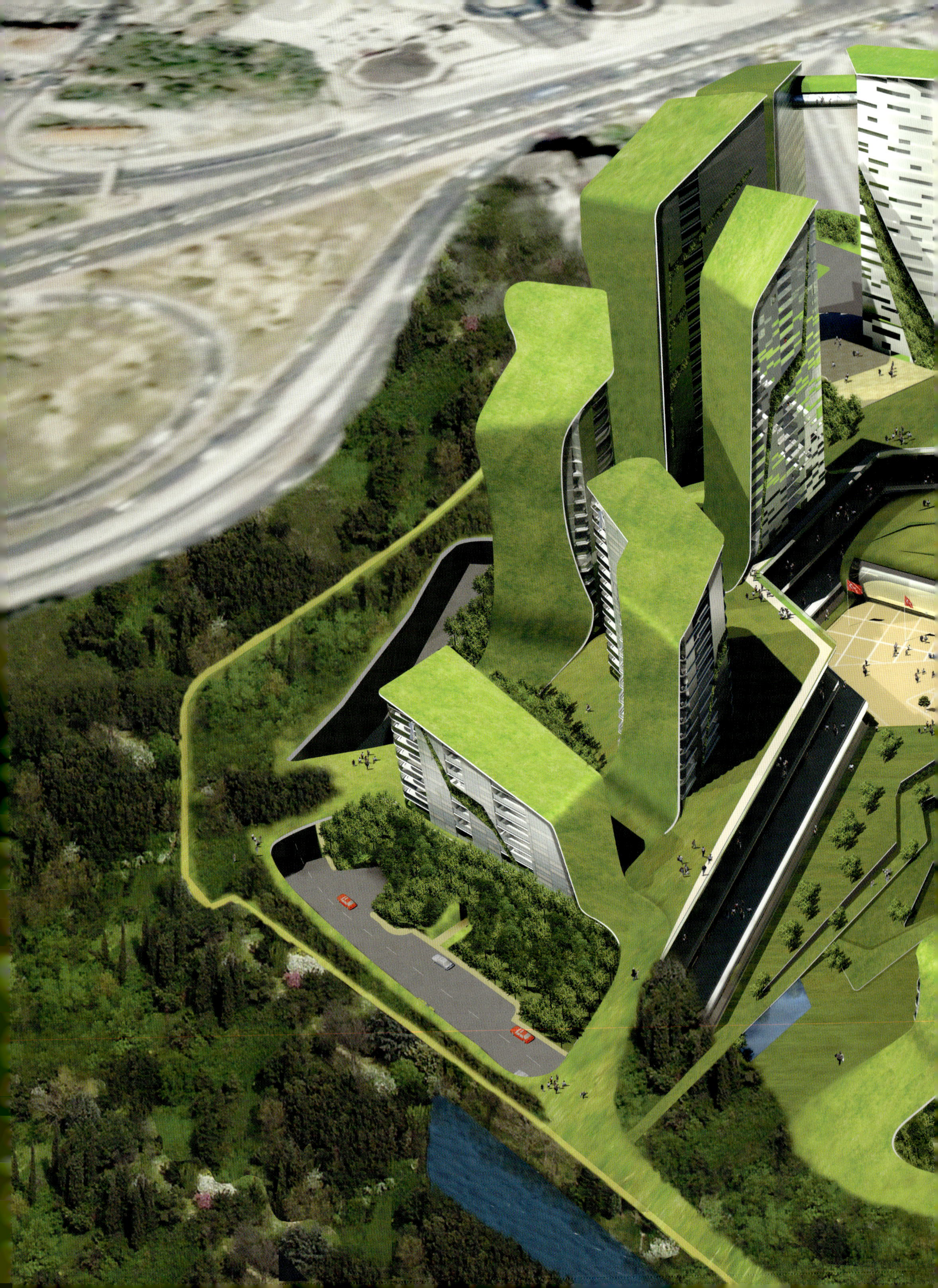

Zorlu Ecocity

Zorlu Ecocity

TYPE	:	Vertical EcoInfrastructure
LOCATION	:	Istanbul, Turkey
CLIMATE ZONE	:	Temperate
VEGETATION ZONE	:	Deciduous Forest

AREAS:

GFA	:	278,750 m²
SITE AREA	:	96,505 m²
PLOT RATIO	:	1:3.5
NO. OF STOREYS	:	20
STATUS	:	Competition
DATE	:	2007

▲ Ground level plan

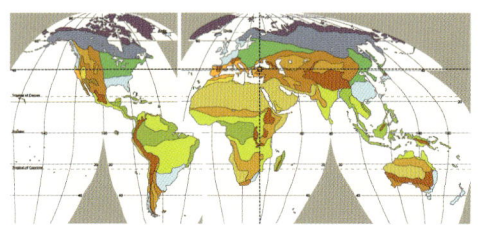

CLIMATE REGION

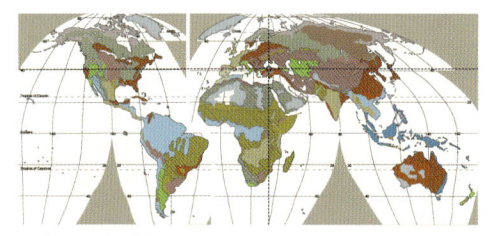

VEGETATION ZONE

Conceptual

This competition entry combines a number of Yeang's ideas and translates them into a "city within a city". Designed for a local developer in line with the city's planning strategy of creating a number of urban centres in the Marma region surrounding Istanbul, effectively alleviating the population pressure on the historic core, this high-density eco-city would have included 14 towers ranging from eight to 26 storeys in height, a new road system, underground car parking, a central ecocell, ecobridges, green façades and a sustainable drainage system. Importantly, it was conceived not as an outlying dormitory town to the dense and rapidly expanding city of more than 12 million people, but as a destination with a vibrant community of residential units, hotels, retail and office buildings, and leisure facilities. (Llewelyn Davies Yeang also further consolidated its work in Istanbul in 2006 when it won the competition, organised by the Greater Istanbul Municipality, to masterplan an area with a major transportation route at Kucukcekmece.)

At Zorlu Yeang's "urban design intention was to rehabilitate the existent ecology of a locality that had been fragmented and devastated by human activities – by agriculture, forestry, urban development and sprawl. The approach was to reconnect the ecological nexus of the site using a series of devices to give Istanbul a large, ring-shaped urban park. With a programme of social, cultural, retail and commercial activities spanning east–west across the entire park, the design recognised the need to make the venture financially viable."

Yeang's analysis of the site showed that this island site, bounded by three highways and a steep slope, contained fragments of a sensitive ecosystem; the southern boundary in particular contained greenery with considerable secondary vegetation. Yeang took this zone as his starting point – a "vegetated leading edge" from which he could

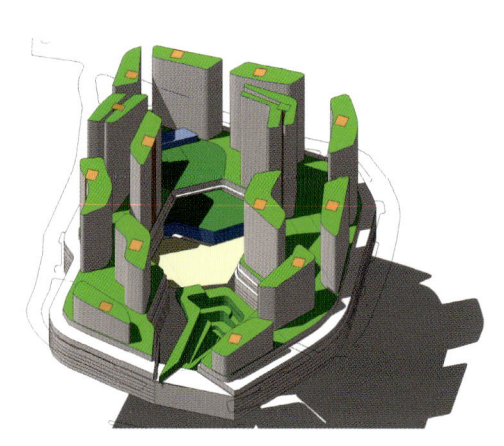

▲ North elevation

stretch the green ecoinfrastructure. This is a similar method to that used in the Soma masterplan (pages 70-83), which stretched fingers of forest edge across the development site. Ecobridges are deployed to distribute vegetation across the masterplan, spanning a 10 metre-wide perimeter road to link with the broad park/podium planted with indigenous trees and shrubs. These bridges assist in balancing what Yeang would call the abiotic and biotic content of the site. Planted ramps bring Yeang's "green ecoinfrastructure" up the façades of the towers. South-facing green walls rise to green roofs, helping create a landscaped continuum from the site's southern boundary.

This landscape also dives deep into the site, lining a large ecocell which brings light, fresh air and rainwater into the seven-storey retail and car parking podium. This continuous, planted ramp helps remove warm, polluted air (including carbon monoxide) from sub-ground levels, supplementing mechanical systems required to reduce the ambient temperature in the summer. At the base of the ecocell a large tank harvests rainwater for irrigation. Grey water is used for further irrigation. A large detention pond is also located at the south-east of the site to recharge aquifers and groundwater.

As in other projects, skycourts (interstitial zones between inside and outside) were designed to be integrated within the towers. The masterplan arranges the towers around the ecocell in an approximate spiral, granting views inwards towards the centre of the site, as well as outwards to the city and landscape beyond. "This composition, together with the green ecoinfrastructure which unifies the site, results in a uniquely green aesthetic," says Yeang. The aesthetics of the scheme sits in contrast to the more encased green ecoinfrastructure and aerial green bridges of Vancouver's Plaza of Nations project, designed for a colder climate of harsher temperature fluctuations.

▲ Aerial view showing green walls

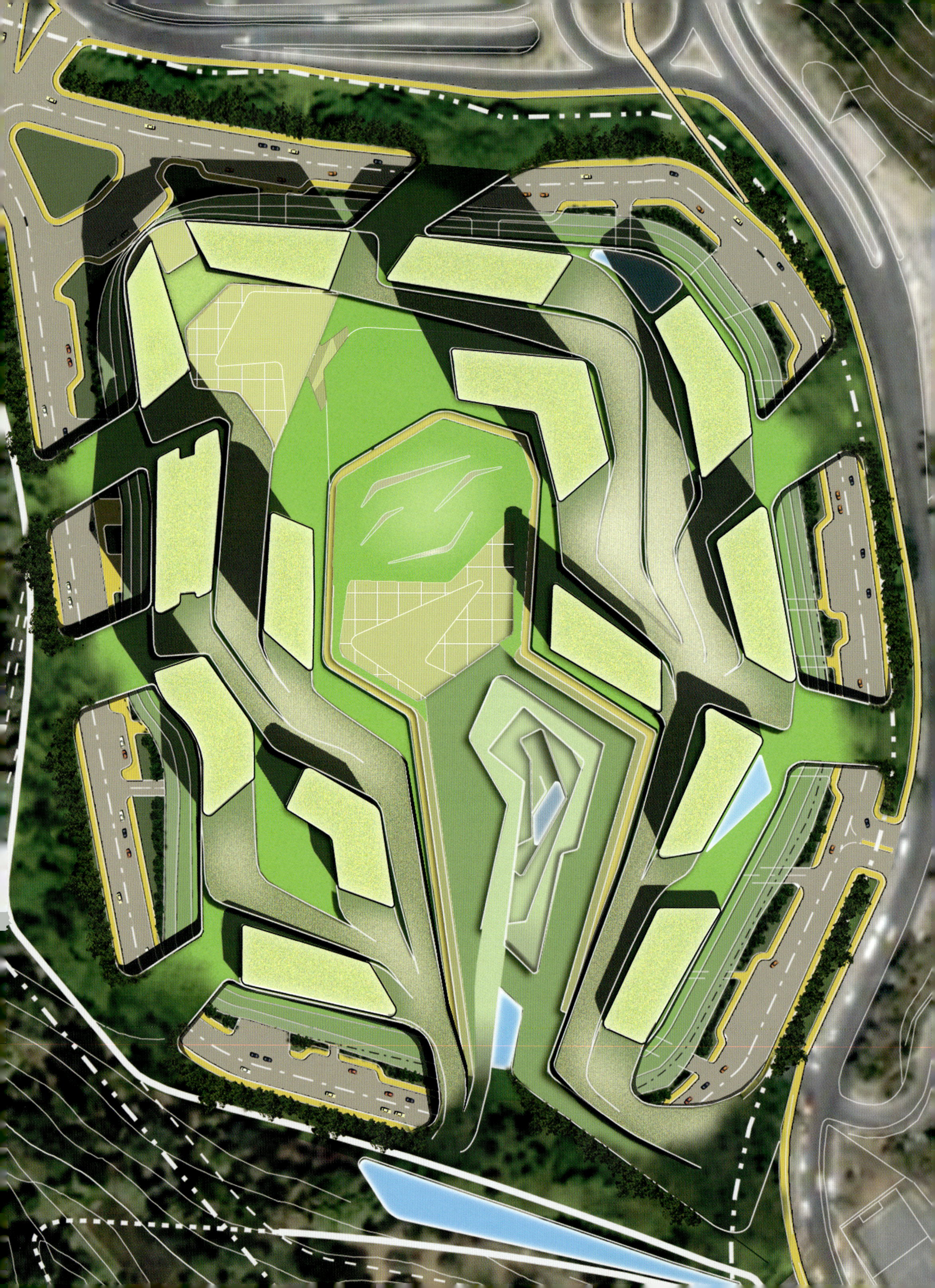

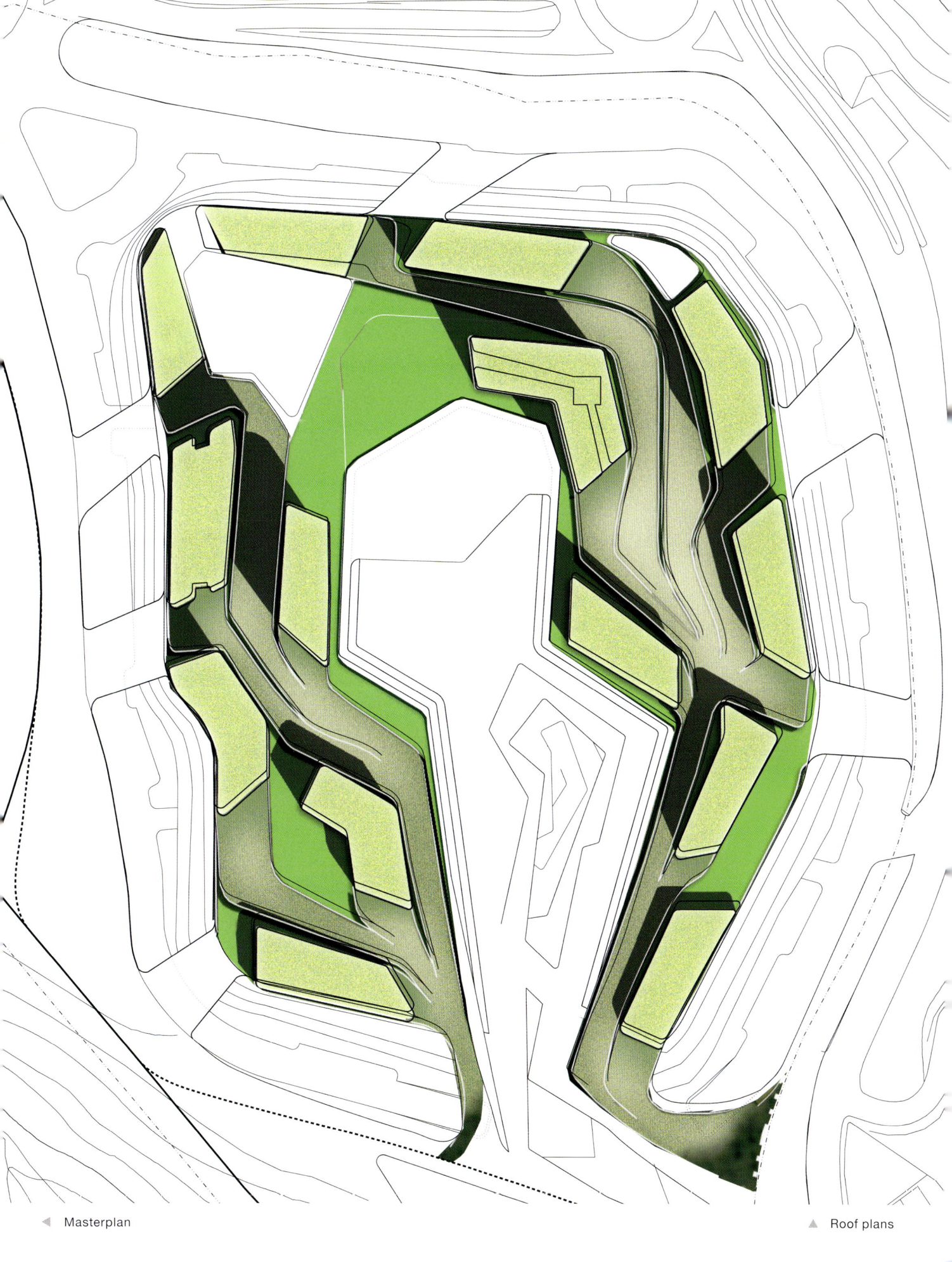

◀ Masterplan

▲ Roof plans

Vertical EcoInfrastructure | **Zorlu Ecocity** 237

▲ View of main plaza with ecocell in the centre

Vertical EcoInfrastructure | Zorlu Ecocity

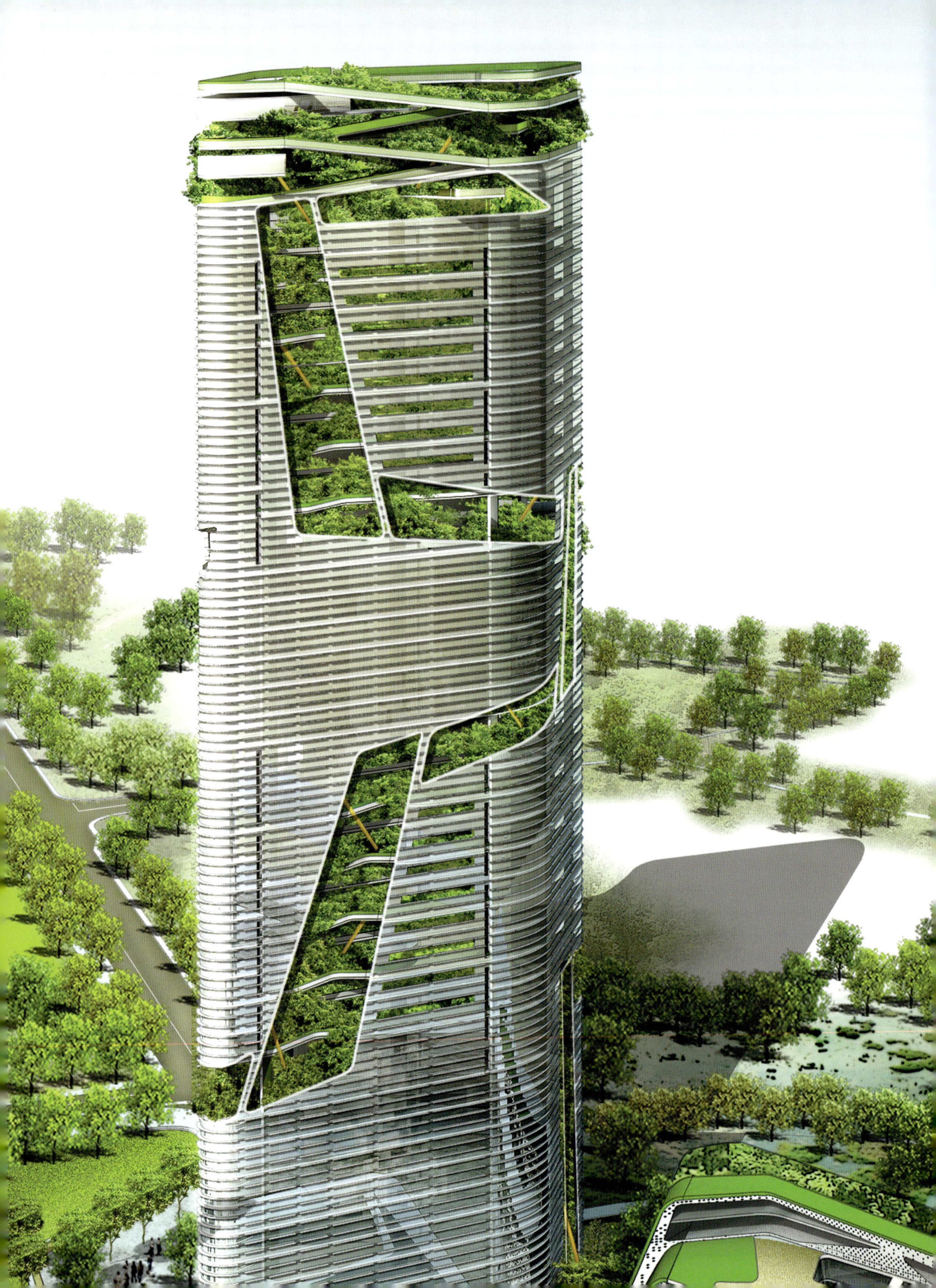

Gyeong-Gi Complex

Gyeong-Gi Complex

TYPE	:	Vertical EcoInfrastructure
LOCATION	:	Seoul, South Korea
CLIMATE ZONE	:	Temperate
VEGETATION ZONE	:	Deciduous Forest

AREAS:

GFA	:	102,416 m²
NFA	:	81,200 m²
SITE AREA	:	136,805 m²
NO. OF STOREYS	:	46
STATUS	:	Competition
DATE	:	2010

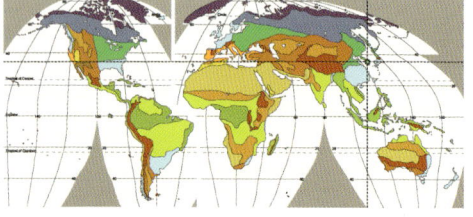

CLIMATE REGION

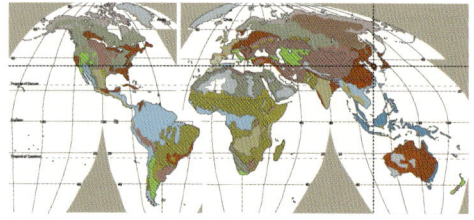

VEGETATION ZONE

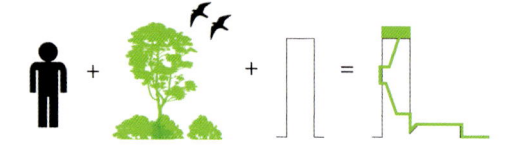

Conceptual

Yeang's competition entry for the Gyeong-Gi Complex, located outside the city of Seoul, includes the design of a masterplan and a pair of two key buildings – a 58 storey tower for central government use and an 8 storey provincial headquarters building. The Architect of Record for the project was Beyond Space Partners. Design teams were asked to draw up proposals for a site that had been cleared of all flora, fauna and top soil. "There was nothing of the earlier ecology left on the land," says Yeang, who responded by re-imagining the site as hosting a rich and diverse ecology, including a tower containing a

Masterplan

242 ECOARCHITECTURE | THE WORK OF KEN YEANG

"vertical forest". The site's ecology is recreated with a matrix of viable habitats and species, matching ecologies with the potential of green roofs, green walls, skycourts, ecobridges and a range of landscapes. The masterplan introduced forestry not only to the landscape but within the buildings themselves through the creation of extremely large skycourts embedded into the towers' form. This vegetation also sits atop the roof of the Provincial Council building and links to a park on the far side of an adjacent road via an ecobridge. Green areas within the built form comprise 47 per cent of the total site area.

The forested skycourts contain automated shutters that close over the colder months, during which these zones become heated winter gardens. These skycourts are partially opened during mid-seasons (spring and autumn) and become fully exposed in summer months – echoing the façade treatment of the Plaza of Nations complex designed for Vancouver. "This design is an advancement of my earlier vertical ecoinfrastructure concepts. Here, the design goes beyond the addition of indigenous landscaping and greenery," says Yeang. "It sets out to create a variety of new natural habitats within the development and relates these habitats to endemic species which were identified following research on the area's flora and fauna. Working with the ecological landscape firm Biodiversity by Design (UK), we have also set out biodiversity targets to be achieved over the life of the development, signifying a new level for green design."

Crucially, the design celebrates its ecological characteristics by looking green – something which has become important to Yeang who argues that lay-people should be able to read a building for what it is. It is not enough, he contends, for buildings to perform ecologically invisibly. "A green building deserves its own aesthetic. A green building should look like what the term indicates – green. It should look like a human-made ecosystem, a balance of organic and inorganic mass that works as a whole and which is aligned to the landscape. It should look, I believe, indeterminate – hairy even." But he warns that an eco-aesthetic must be beautiful. Rather than being a collection of applied gadgetry, an eco-building should perform in a sustainable manner through its very form and programme. That purity of function and intent will, almost inevitably, make the building beautiful.

"If we want ecostructures to be acceptable to the public they have to be aesthetically beautiful. I am pursuing the idea of an ecological aesthetic. This has nothing to do with Modernist or Postmodernist intentions," says Yeang. "The ecological approach to design will eventually influence the aesthetics of the built form. Of course, different architects will have different ways of designing green architecture. There is not just one way to get to a green design. I am essentially interested in how to integrate buildings with the ecology of the location, how to integrate the inorganic mass with the organic mass, and how to integrate the designed system's processes with the natural processes of its locality – otherwise, our designed system would be just another lump of inorganic mass, no matter how beautiful."

▲ Computer model of aerial view

▼ Provincial headquarters building entrance

▲ Tower entrance

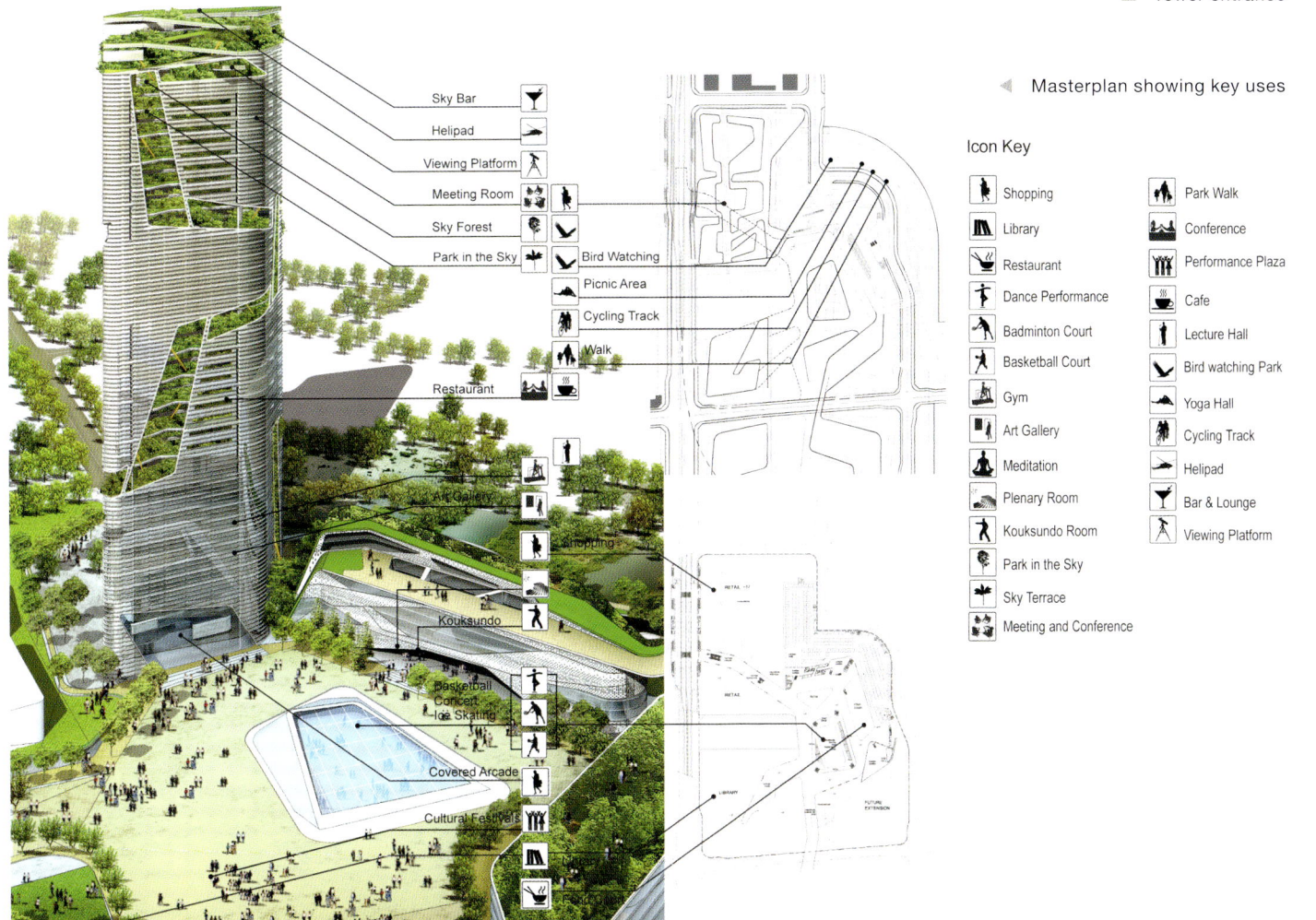

◀ Masterplan showing key uses

Icon Key

🛍️	Shopping	🚶	Park Walk
📚	Library	⛰️	Conference
🍜	Restaurant	👥	Performance Plaza
💃	Dance Performance	☕	Cafe
🏸	Badminton Court	🎤	Lecture Hall
🏀	Basketball Court	🦅	Bird watching Park
🏋️	Gym	🧘	Yoga Hall
🎨	Art Gallery	🚴	Cycling Track
🧘	Meditation	🚁	Helipad
💺	Plenary Room	🍸	Bar & Lounge
🕺	Kouksundo Room	🔭	Viewing Platform
🌸	Park in the Sky		
🌿	Sky Terrace		
🍽️	Meeting and Conference		

Tower callouts: Sky Bar, Helipad, Viewing Platform, Meeting Room, Sky Forest, Park in the Sky, Bird Watching, Picnic Area, Cycling Track, Walk, Restaurant, Art Gallery, Shopping, Kouksundo, Basketball/Concert/Ice Skating, Covered Arcade, Cultural Festivals

Vertical EcoInfrastructure | Gyeong-Gi Complex 245

SUMMARY OF PLANS (MASTERPLAN)

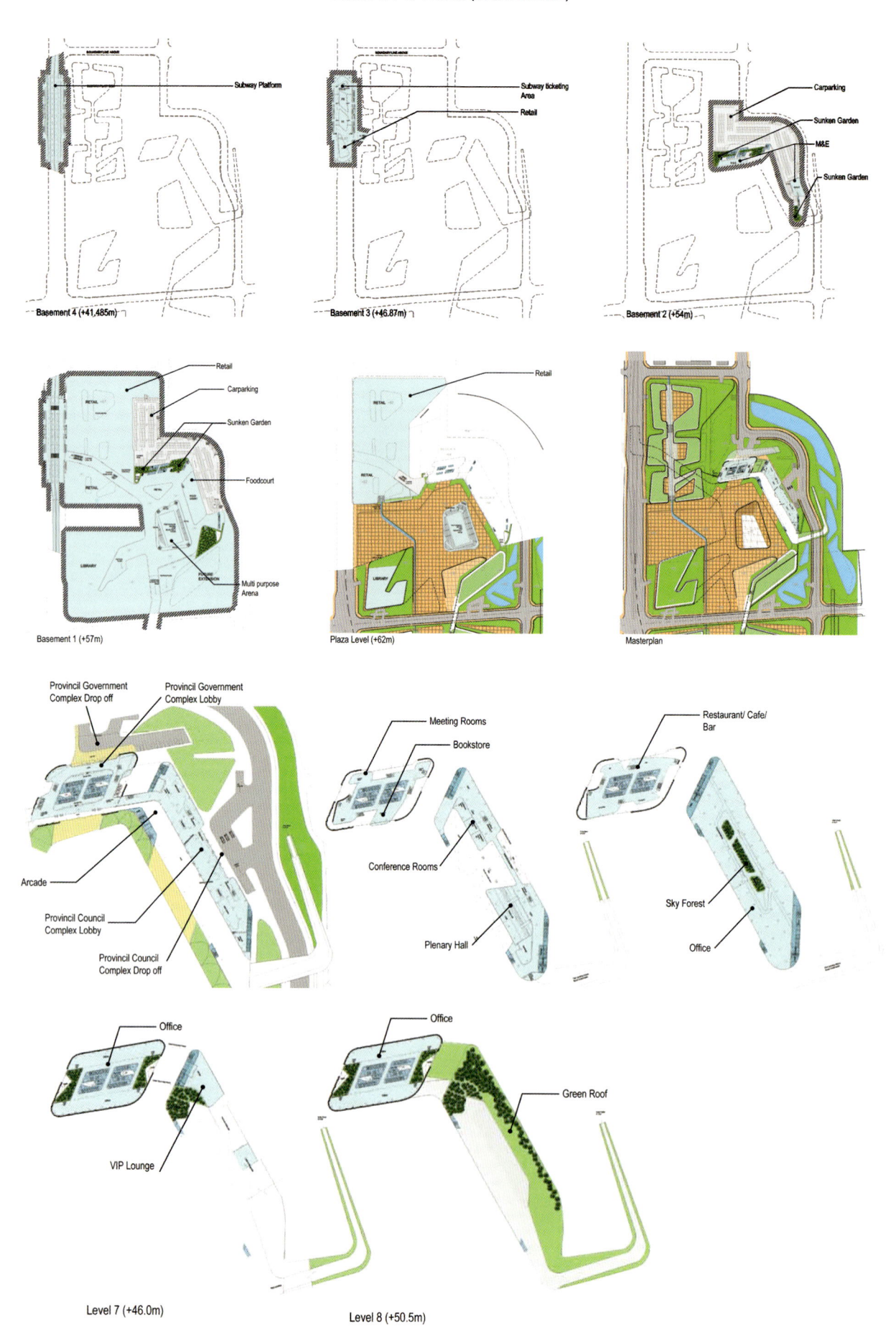

Basement 4 (+41.485m)

- Subway Platform

Basement 3 (+46.87m)

- Subway ticketing Area
- Retail

Basement 2 (+54m)

- Carparking
- Sunken Garden
- M&E
- Sunken Garden

Basement 1 (+57m)

- Retail
- Carparking
- Sunken Garden
- Foodcourt
- Multi purpose Arena

Plaza Level (+62m)

- Retail

Masterplan

- Provincil Government Complex Drop off
- Provincil Government Complex Lobby
- Arcade
- Provincil Council Complex Lobby
- Provincil Council Complex Drop off

- Meeting Rooms
- Bookstore
- Conference Rooms
- Plenary Hall

- Restaurant/ Cafe/ Bar
- Sky Forest
- Office

Level 7 (+46.0m)

- Office
- VIP Lounge

Level 8 (+50.5m)

- Office
- Green Roof

246 ECOARCHITECTURE | THE WORK OF KEN YEANG

SUMMARY OF PLANS (TOWER)

Level 9 (+55.0m)
Level 10 (+59.5m)
Level 11 (+64.0m)
Level 12 (+68.5m)
Level 13 (+73.0m)
Level 14 (+82.0m)

Level 15 (+86.5m)
Level 16 (+91.0m)
Level 17 (+95.5m)
Level 18 (+100.0m)
Level 19 (+104.5m)
Level 20 (+109.0m)

Level 21 (+113.5m)
Level 22 (+118.0m)
Level 23 (+122.5m)
Level 24 (+131.5m)
Level 25 (+136.0m)
Level 26 (+140.5m)

Level 27 (+145.0m)
Level 28 (+149.5m)
Level 29 (+154.0m)
Level 30 (+158.5m)
Level 31 (+163.0m)
Level 32 (+167.5m)

Level 33 (+172.0m)
Level 34 (+181.0m)
Level 35 (+185.5m)
Level 36 (+190.0m)
Level 37 (+194.5m)
Level 38 (+199.0m)

Level 39 (+203.5m)
Level 40 (+208.0m)
Level 41 (+212.5m)
Level 42 (+217.0m)
Level 43 (+221.5m)
Level 44 (+226.0m)

Level 43 (+221.5m)
Level 44 (+226.0m)
Level 45 (+230.5m)
Level 46 (+235.0m)

Green Infrastructure

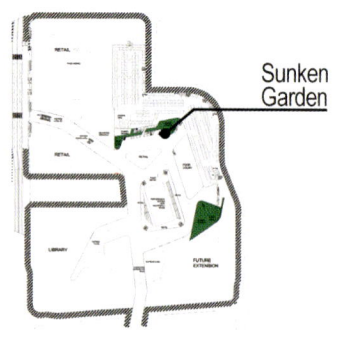

Ecocells and sunken gardens at B1 & B2 Level +57 & +54

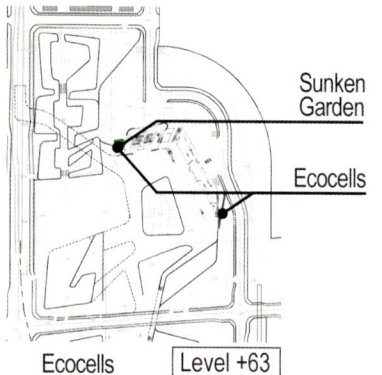

Ecocells at Ground Level Level +63

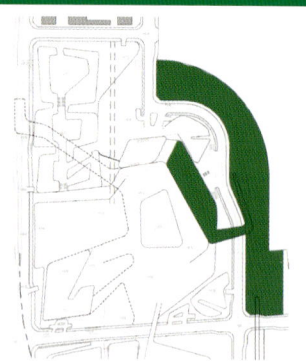

Green artery integrated into green axis on buildings

Grey Infrastructure

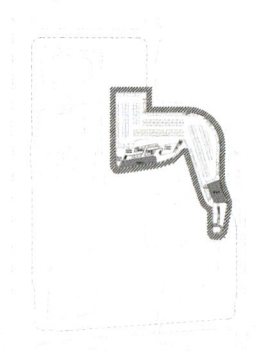

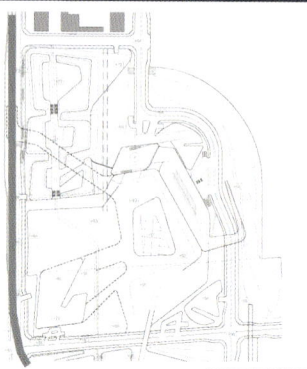

M&E Space at B1 Level +57

Subterranean Subway at underground Level +41.49

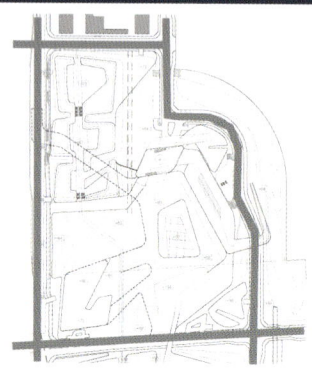

Transportation at Ground Level Level +63

Blue Infrastructure

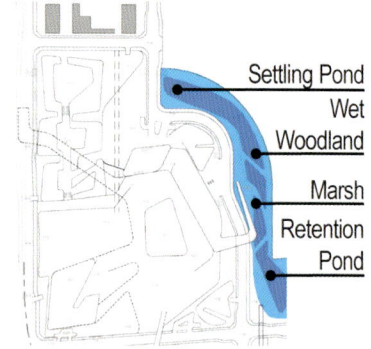

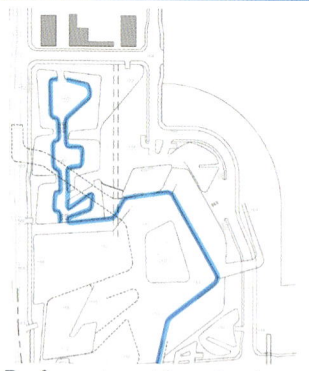

Wet Lands at Ground Level Level +64
- Settling Pond
- Wet Woodland
- Marsh
- Retention Pond

Roof as water catchment system at roof Level

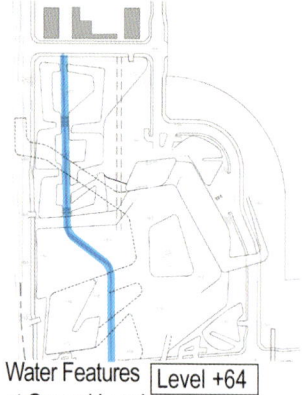

Water Features at Ground Level Level +64

Red Infrastructure

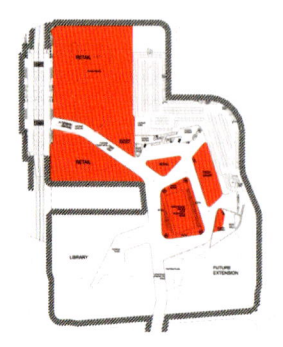

Interaction Spaces at Basement Level Level +57

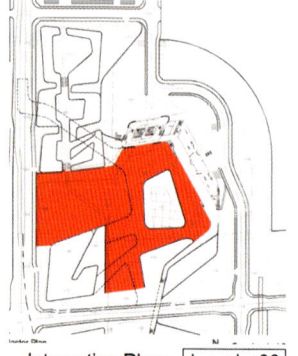

Interaction Plaza at Ground Level Level +63

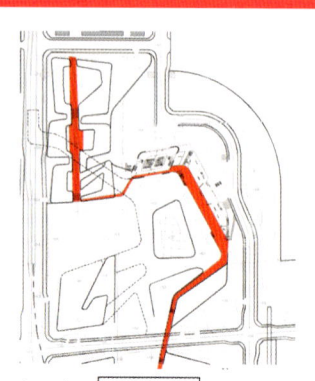

Arcade at Ground Level Level +63

GREEN, GREY, BLUE AND RED ECOINFRASTRUCTURES

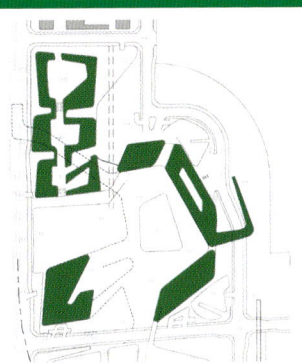

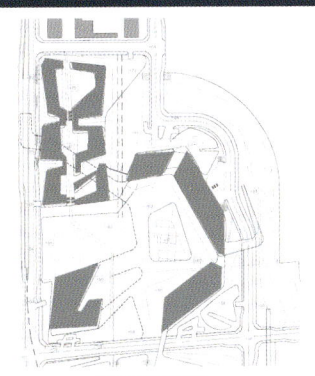

Green Roofs

Structure at Ground Level | Level +63 |

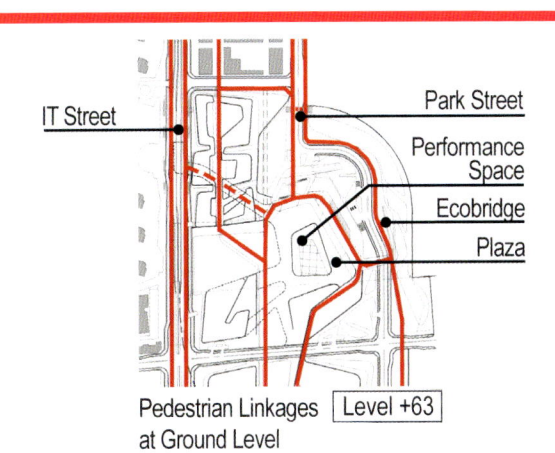

IT Street
Park Street
Performance Space
Ecobridge
Plaza

Pedestrian Linkages at Ground Level | Level +63 |

Vertical EcoInfrastructure | Gyeong-Gi Complex

SEASONAL HEATING/COOLING STRATEGIES

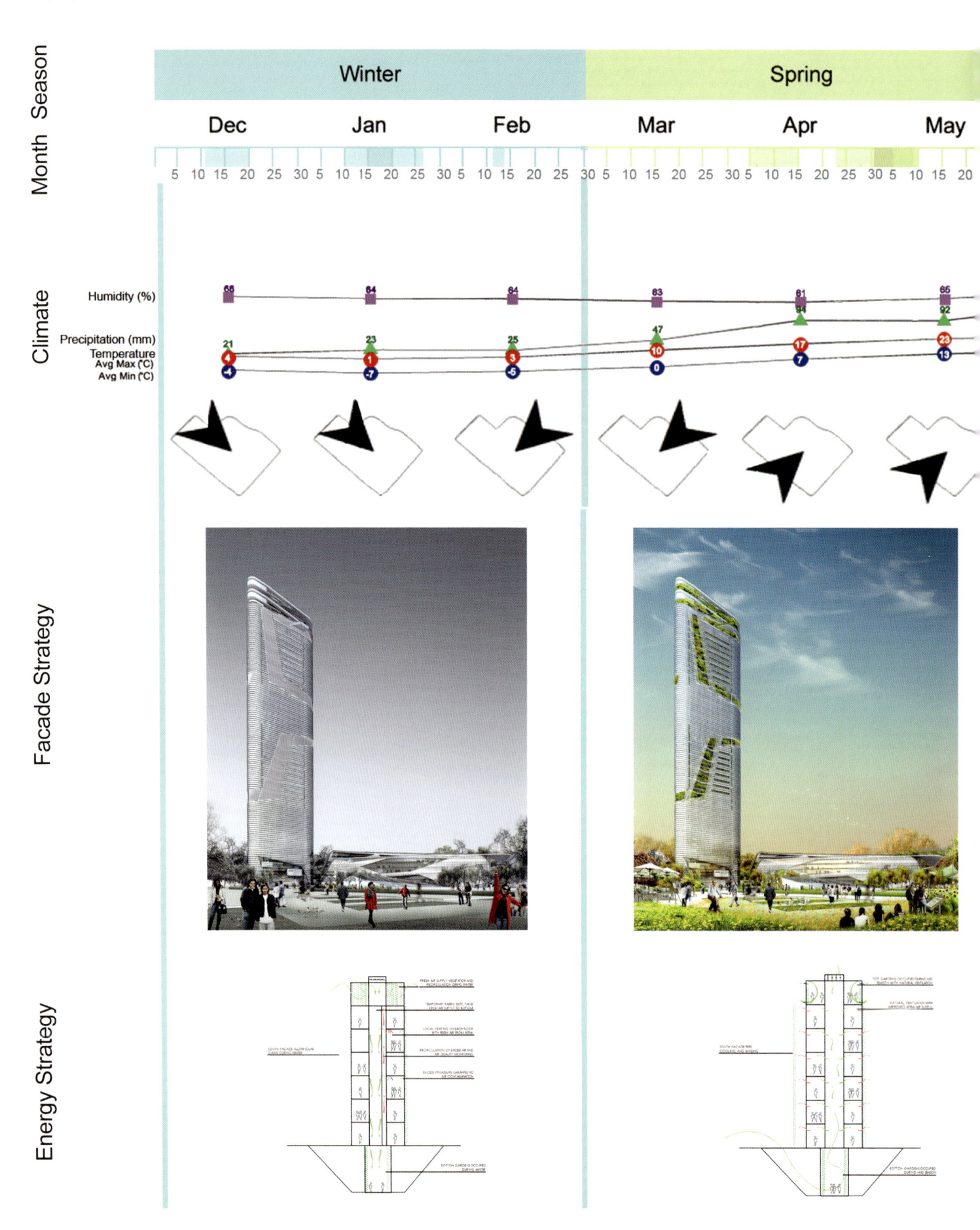

	Winter			Spring		
Month	Dec	Jan	Feb	Mar	Apr	May

Climate
- Humidity (%): 66, 64, 64, 63, 61, 65
- Precipitation (mm): 21, 23, 25, 47, 94, 92
- Temperature Avg Max (°C): 4, 1, 3, 10, 17, 23
- Avg Min (°C): -4, -7, -5, 0, 7, 13

Facade Strategy

Energy Strategy

250 ECOARCHITECTURE | THE WORK OF KEN YEANG

Summer | Autumn

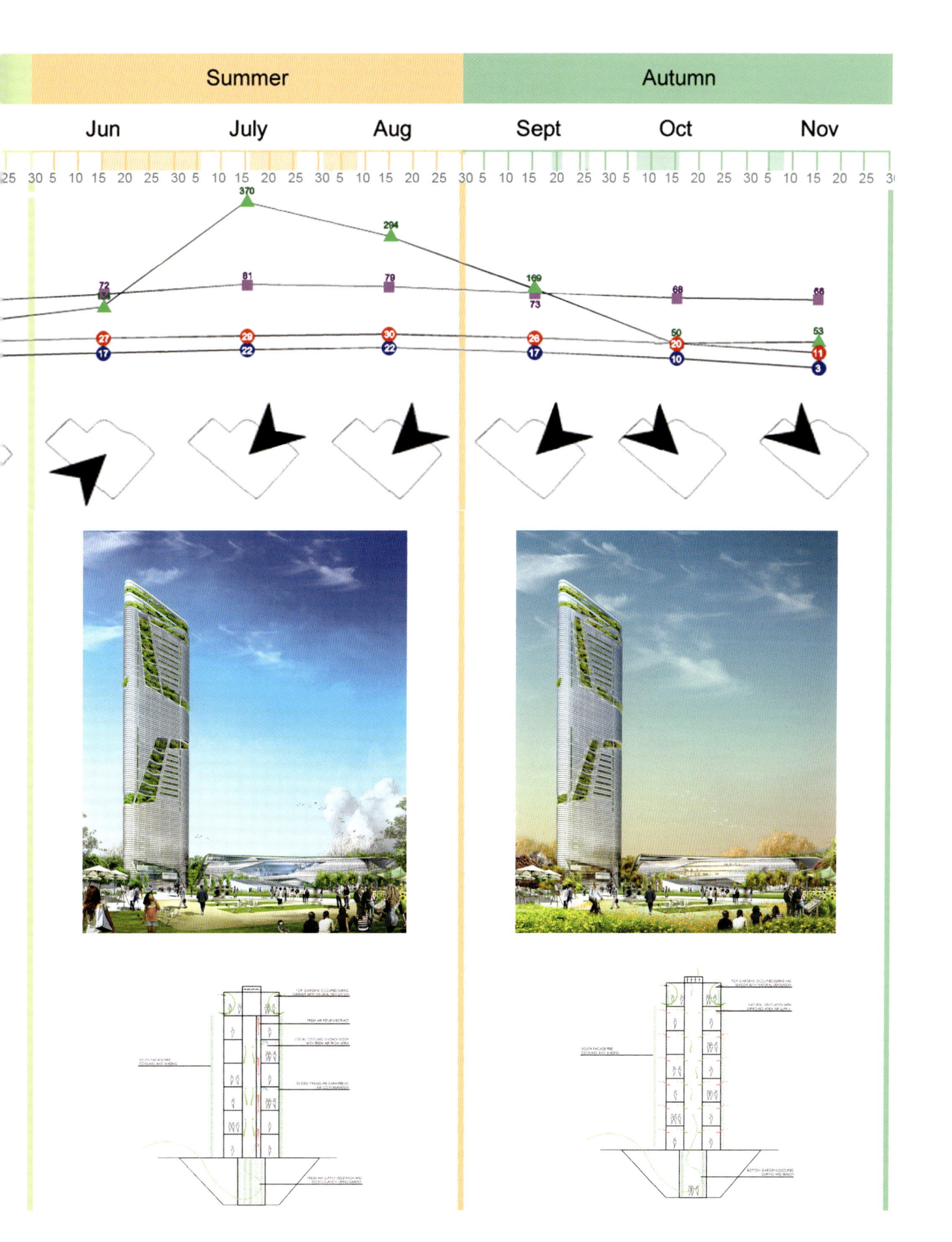

Jun | July | Aug | Sept | Oct | Nov

Vertical EcoInfrastructure | **Gyeong-Gi Complex** 251

BIODIVERSITY TARGETS

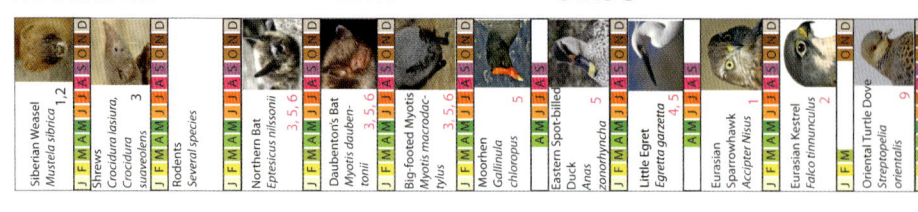

MAMMALS · BATS · BIRDS

Siberian Weasel *Mustela sibrica* 1,2	Shrews *Crocidura lasiura, Crocidura suaveolens* 3	Rodents *Several species*	Northern Bat *Eptesicus nilssonii* 3, 5, 6	Daubenton's Bat *Myotis daubentonii* 3, 5, 6	Big-footed Myotis *Myotis macrodactylus* 3, 5, 6	Moorhen *Gallinula chloropus* 5	Eastern Spot-billed Duck *Anas zonorhyncha* 5	Little Egret *Egretta garzetta* 4, 5	Eurasian Sparrowhawk *Accipter Nisus* 1	Eurasian Kestrel *Falco tinnunculus* 2	Oriental Turtle Dove *Streptopelia orientalis* 9

Habitats

Shrub Roofs — DPS, WQ, AA
— — — — F — — — — F — F

Grassland Roofs — DPS, WQ, AA
— — — F — — — — — — — F

Planted facades — DPS, WQ, AA
— — — — F — 👥 — — F — 👥

Densely wooded area — DPS *Salix pseudo-lasiogyne, Cerciphyllum japonicum, Lagerstroemia indica, Prunus glandulosa, Celtis sinensis, Iridaceae pseudoacorus* — WQ, AA
👥F 👥F 👥F/P 👥F/P F 👥 — — — 👥F F —

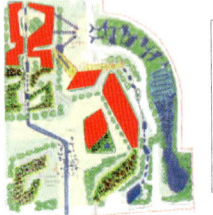

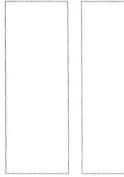

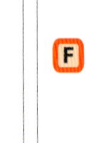

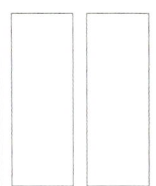

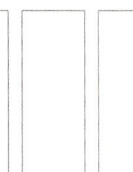

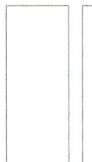

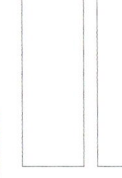

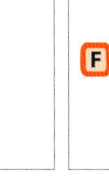

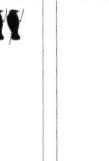

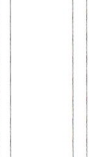

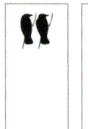

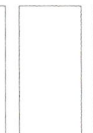

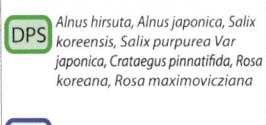

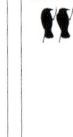

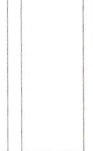

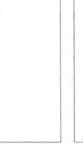

Wet Woodland — DPS *Alnus hirsuta, Alnus japonica, Salix koreensis, Salix purpurea Var japonica, Crataegus pinnatifida, Rosa koreana, Rosa maximovicziana* — WQ, AA
👥F 👥F 👥F/P 👥F/P F 👥 — — F F F —

TARGETS

1. Top of food chain for small mammals
2. Top of food chain for small birds
3. Top of food chain for invertebrates
4. Top of food chain for fish/amphibians
5. Use of artifical refuges
6. Dependent on good water quality
7. Rarity
8. Dependent on specific food plants
9. Song

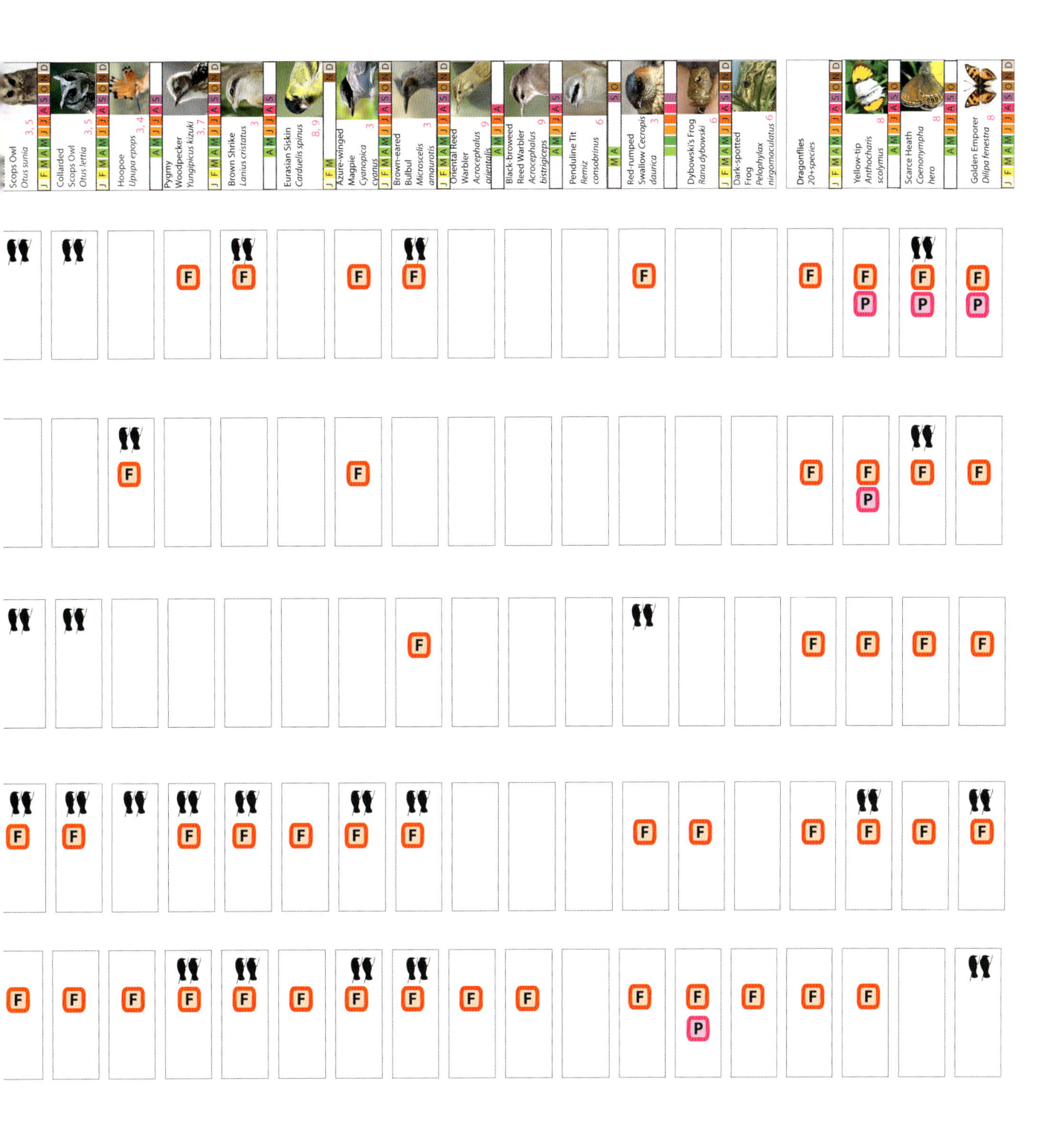

Vertical EcoInfrastructure | Gyeong-Gi Complex

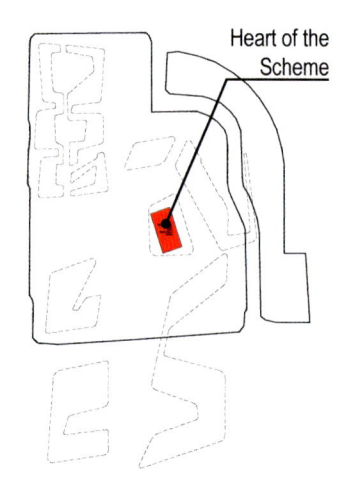

RED ECOINFRASTRUCTURE – ACTIVITY ZONES

1. Multipurpose Arena Level +57
as "Heart of the development"

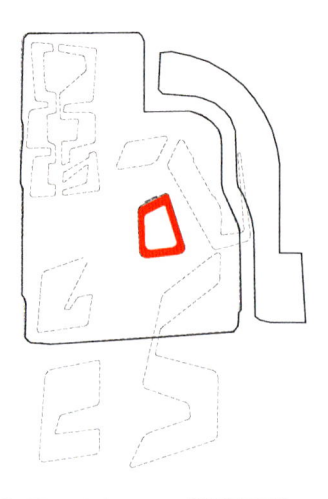

2. Tiered Seating Level +57
for Multipurpose Arena

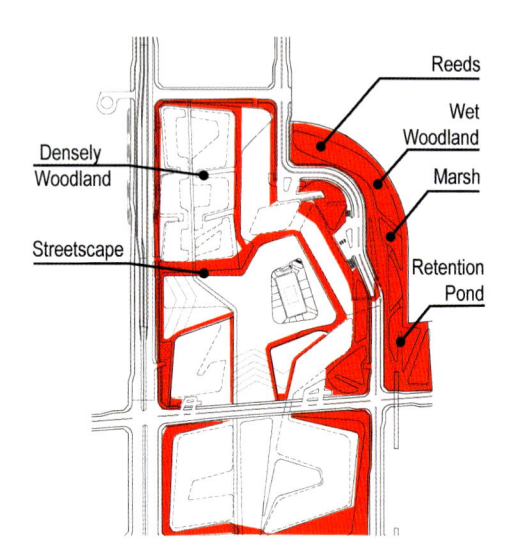

5. Landscape & Habitats Level +64
- Densely Woodland
- Streetscape
- Reeds
- Wet Woodland
- Marsh
- Retention Pond

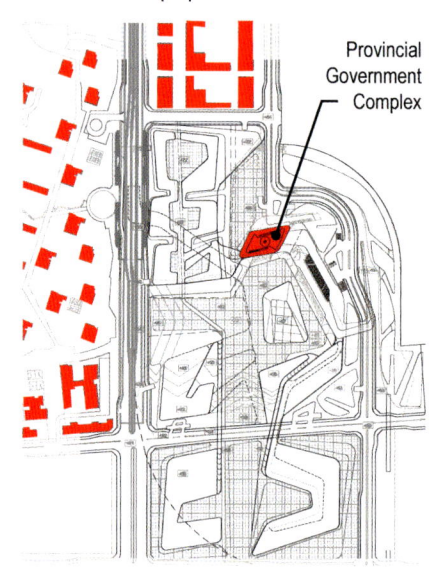

6. Provincial Government Complex Level +64

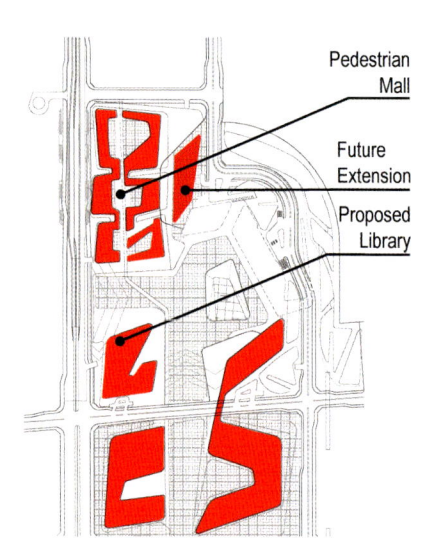

9. Surrounding Buildings Level +64
- Pedestrian Mall
- Future Extension
- Proposed Library

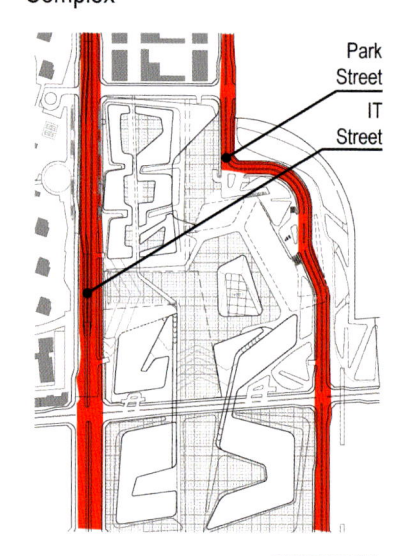

10. IT Street & Park Street Level +64
- Park Street
- IT Street

254 ECOARCHITECTURE | THE WORK OF KEN YEANG

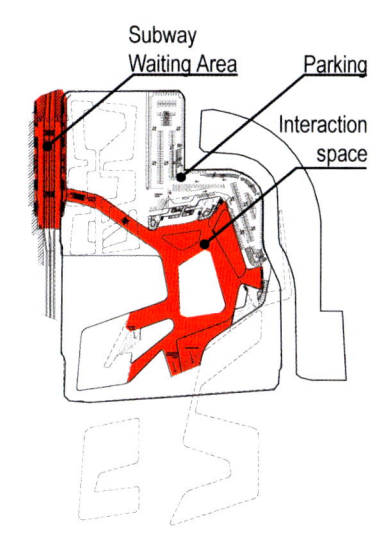

3. Concourse Level `Level +57`
From train & bus station to underground plaza

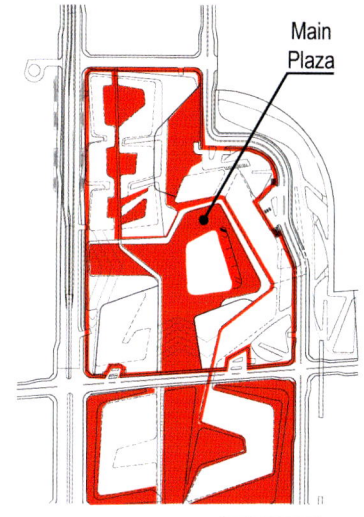

Subway Waiting Area
Parking
Interaction space

4. Public Plaza `Level +64`

Main Plaza

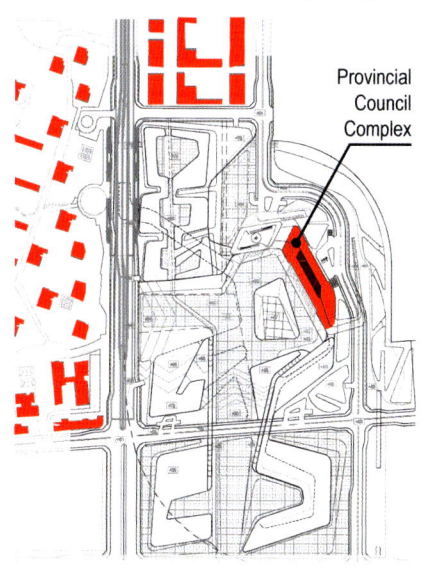

7. Provincial Council Complex `Level +64`

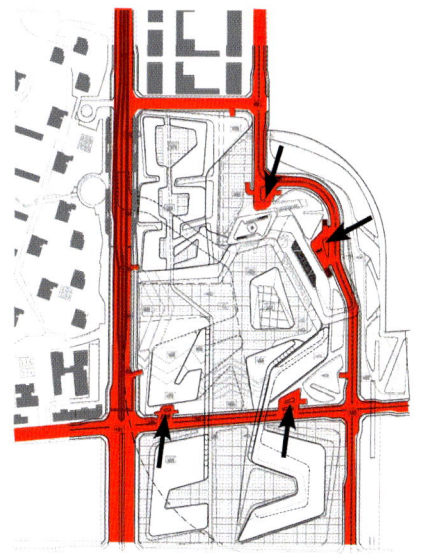

Provincial Council Complex

8. Ground Level Roads & Dropoffs `Level +64`

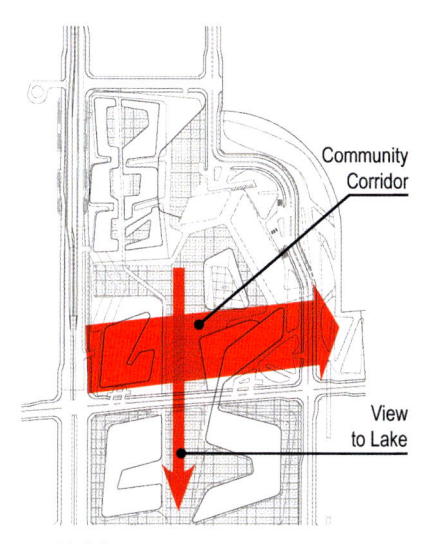

11. Views

Community Corridor
View to Lake

12. Arcade

Covered Arcade

Vertical EcoInfrastructure | Gyeong-Gi Complex 255

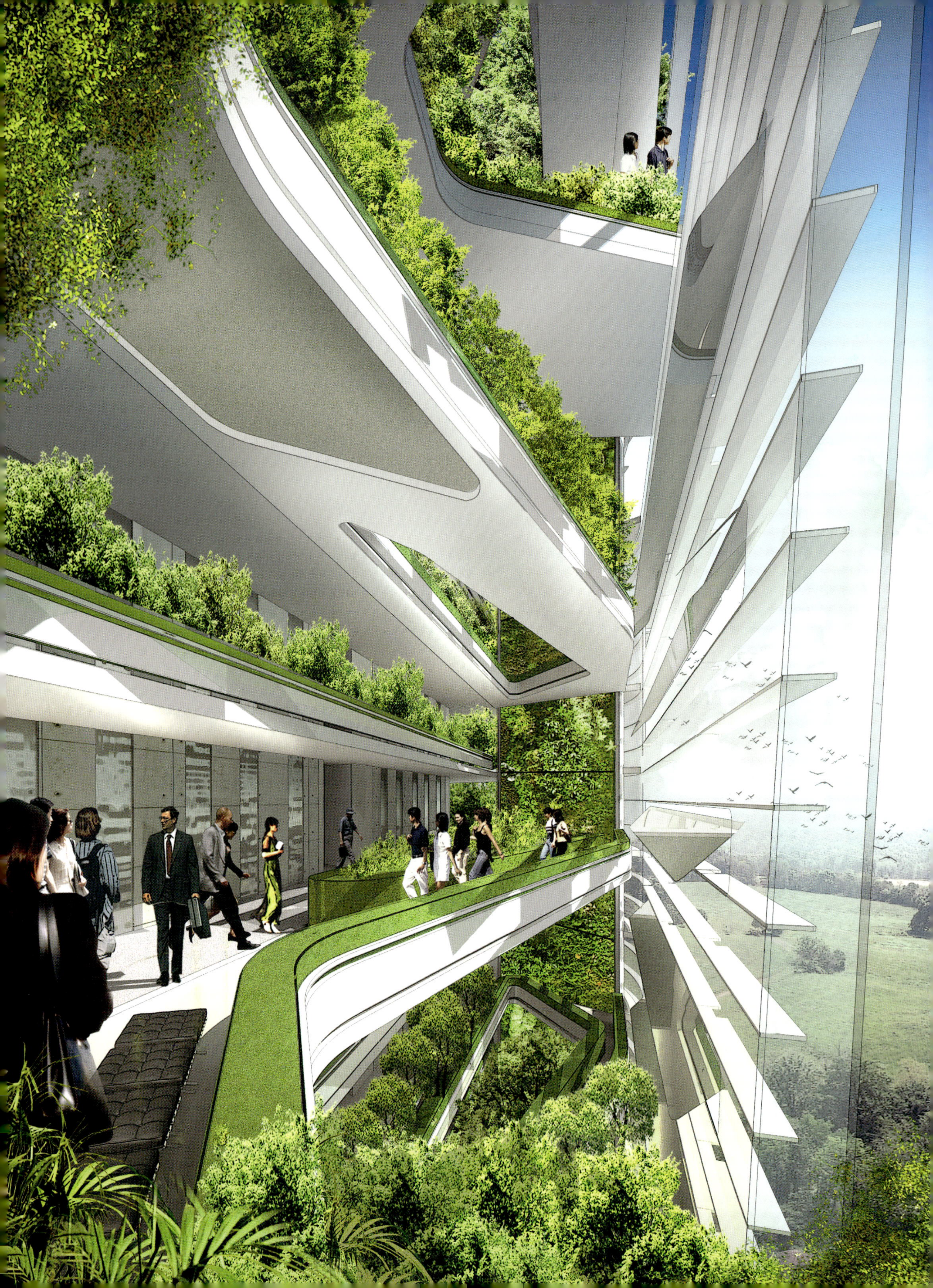

◂ Interior of a "sky forest"

▲ View of tower from the wet woodlands

Essay

We are all only too aware of the numerous pressing global social issues that need to be addressed. These include tackling abject poverty, providing clean water, adequate food, enclosures and proper sanitation. But ultimately if we do not have a clean environment – clean air, clean water and clean land – all those other pressing global issues become even more difficult and costly to resolve. Thus saving our environment has to be the most vital task facing humankind today, feeding into our fears that this millennium may be our last.

For the designer, the compelling question is: how do we design for a sustainable future? Globally, businesses and industries face similar concerns of seeking to understand the environmental consequences of their functions and processes, to envision what these might be if they were sustainable, and to take action to realise this vision with comprehensive ecologically benign strategies, with new business models, new production systems, materials and processes. More than these, our human society has to change to a sustainable way of life. We need to change how we live, behave, work, make, eat, learn, move about.

It would be a mistake to regard green design as simply about eco-engineering or cleantech. These engineering systems are indeed an important part of green design (see "grey ecoinfrastructure" below) giving us an acceptable level of comfort that is sustainable, while such technologies continue to rapidly develop and advance towards greener and cleaner engineering solutions for our built environment. However, it must be clear that eco-engineering is not the only consideration in green design.

Neither is green design just about rating systems (such as LEED, BREEAM, carbon profiling, etc.). These are certainly useful checklists and guidelines but are not comprehensive. They are valuable as a partial tick list of reminders of some of the key items to consider in green design or for comparing buildings and masterplans using a common standard. They have also been useful in proselytising green design, drawing in a wider audience. But since these systems are neither comprehensive nor ecologically holistic (an aspect crucial in ecodesign), many designers having achieved the highest level of rating (such as platinum) would ask – what next? Where do we go from here? Recent endeavours include the "Living Building Challenge" from the Cascadia Region of North America and carbon profiling.

Clearly, green design has now entered the mainstream of architecture. Ask any architect today about green design and you will get the same response – use of renewable energy systems (such as photovoltaics, wind generators, etc.), compliance with accreditation systems, carbon profiling, planning as new urbanism, etc. We need to question whether this is all there is to green design.

The contention here is that achieving effective green design is much more than the above and that green design is not as easy as it has been contended. It is complex. While still incomplete, there are a number of design strategies that can be adopted in combination to arrive as close as we can to the goal of achieving a state of stasis of our built environment with the natural environment.

I FOUR STRANDS OF ECOINFRASTRUCTURES

The first design strategy is to consider green design in terms of the weaving of four strands of ecoinfrastructures into a whole, colour coded here as follows:

- the "green" (the green ecoinfrastructure or nature's own utilities which must be linked);

```
                    → the environment (to the built system)
                        • local ecosystems,                          reintegrate
                        • biosphere & climatic processes,     ←------------
                        • global energy material resources
                        • existent building environment
                                              ↓           reuse & recycle
     →Inputs              the built system              Outputs---
       • energy,          first environmental impacts    • energy,
       • materials,       operational impacts            • materials/waste,
       • food             end impacts                    • food
       • people                                          • people
         (transport, etc)                                  (transport, etc)
                                                         • the built system
    ---Outputs ←------------                     Inputs ←
                            the biosphere
```

▲ Environmental inputs and outputs
▼ Ecological bridge; elevation

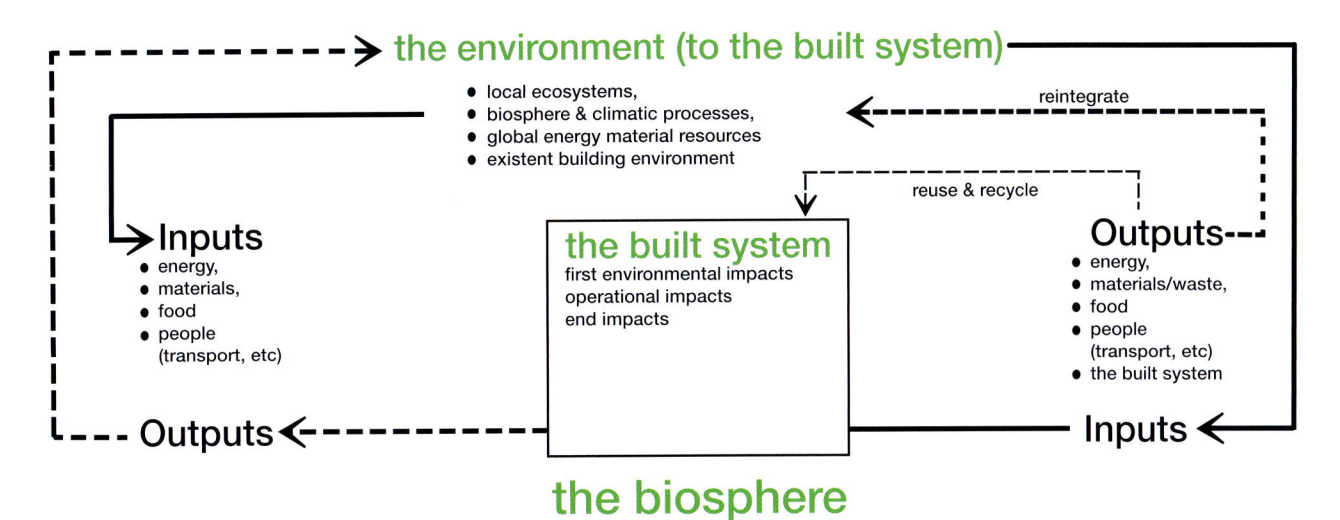

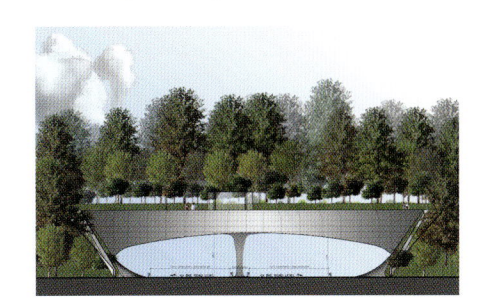

- the "blue" (water management and closing of the water cycle by design with sustainable drainage);

- the "grey" (the engineering infrastructure being the eco sustainable cleantech engineering systems and utilities); and

- the "red" (our human built systems, spaces, hardscapes, society, legislative and regulatory systems).

Green design is the seamless and benign blending of these four sets of ecoinfrastructures into a single system. This concept provides a platform for green design. Like the factors in DNA (discovered by Crick and Watson) which reduce a complex concept into four simple sets of instructions, these four sets of ecoinfrastructures and their integration provide the integrative bases for green design and planning.

The Green Ecoinfrastructure

The green ecoinfrastructure is vital to every design and masterplan. It parallels the usual grey urban infrastructure of roads, drainage systems and utilities. This green ecoinfrastructure is nature's utilities, the interconnected network of natural areas and other open green spaces within the biome that conserves natural ecosystem values and clean air and water. It also enables the area to flourish as a natural habitat for a wide range of wildlife besides delivering an extensive array of benefits to humans and the natural world alike, such as providing habitats linked across the landscape that permit fauna (such as birds and animals) to move freely. This ecoinfrastructure is nature's functioning infrastructure (equivalent to our human-made engineering infrastructures, designated here as grey, blue and red ecoinfrastuctures). In addition to providing cleaner water and enhancing water supplies, it can also generate some, if not all, of the following outcomes: cleaner air; a reduction in heat-island effect in urban areas; a moderation in the impact of climate change; increased energy efficiency; and the protection of source water.

Incorporating an ecoinfrastructure is thus vital to any ecomasterplanning endeavour. Without it, no matter how clever or advanced are the eco-engineering systems, the design or masterplan remains simply a work of engineering and can in no way be called an ecological masterplan nor, in the case of larger developments, an ecocity.

▲ Ecological bridge; eye-level view

These linear flora and fauna corridors connect existing green spaces and larger green areas within the locality to the landscape of the hinterland, and can create new larger habitats in their own right, or in the form of newly linked existing woodland belts or wetlands, or existing landscape features (such as overgrown railway lines, hedges and waterways). Clearly any new green infrastructure must also complement and enhance the natural functions of what is already present in the landscape.

The Grey Ecoinfrastructure

The grey infrastructure is the usual urban engineering infrastructure such as roads, drains, sewerage, water reticulation, telecommunications, and energy and electric power distribution systems. We need not be too prescriptive of any specific engineering system, but require only that these systems be clean technologies, of low embodied energy, be carbon neutral as much as possible and at the same time integrate with the green infrastructure rather than vice-versa.

The Blue Ecoinfrastructure

Parallel to the ecological infrastructure is the water infrastructure (the blue ecoinfrastructure) where the water cycle should be managed to close the loop, although this is not always possible in locations with low rainfall. Rainfall needs to be harvested and used water recycled. The surface water from rain needs to be retained within the site and to be returned to the land for the recharging of groundwater and aquifers by means of filtration beds, pervious roadways and built surfaces, retention ponds and bioswales. Water used within the built environment (both grey and black water) needs to be reused sustainably as much as possible.

Site planning must take into consideration the site's natural drainage patterns and provide surface-water management such that rainfall remains within the locality and is not drained away into water bodies and so lost. Combined with the green ecoinfrastructure, stormwater management bolsters the natural water processes – infiltration, evapotranspiration and the capture and use of stormwater on or near the site where it falls – generating other environmental benefits.

Waterways should not be culverted or deculverted as engineered waterways, but should be replaced with the introduction of wetlands and buffer strips of ecologically functional meadows and woodland habitats. Sealed surfaces can reduce soil moisture and leave low-lying areas susceptible to flooding from excessive run-off. Wetland greenways need to be designed as sustainable drainage systems to provide ecological services. Green buffers can be used together with linear green spaces to maximise habitat potential.

Ecodesign must create sustainable urban drainage systems that can function as wetland habitats. This is not only to alleviate flooding, but also to create buffer strips for habitat creation. While the widths of the buffers may be constrained by existing land uses, their integration through linear green spaces can allow for wider corridors. Surface-water management maximises habitat potential. Intermittent waterway tributaries can be linked up using swales.

The Red (or Human) Ecoinfrastructure
This human ecoinfrastructure consists of our human community, its built enclosures (buildings, houses etc), hardscapes and regulatory systems (laws, regulations, ethics etc). This is the social and human dimension that is often missing in the work of many green designers. It is evident that our present profligate lifestyles, our economies and industries, our modes of transport, our diet and food production, etc, need to be changed to be sustainable.

II SEAMLESS AND BENIGN BIOINTEGRATION

The second design strategy is to regard green design as biointegration – as the seamless and benign environmental integration of the synthetic and the artificial (the human made) with the natural environment. It is the failure successfully to biointegrate that is the root cause of all our environmental problems. In effect, if we are able to biointegrate all our commercial and industrial processes and functions, all our built systems and essentially everything that we do or make in our built environment (which by definition includes our buildings, facilities, infrastructure, products, refrigerators, toys, etc.) with the natural environment in a seamless and benign way, there will in principle be no environmental problems whatsoever. Successfully achieving this is of course easier said than done, but herein lies our challenge.

We can draw a comparison here between ecodesign and prosthetic design for surgery. A medical prosthesis has to integrate with its organic host, the human body. Failure to integrate successfully results in dislocation in one or in both. By analogy, this is what ecodesign should achieve: a total physical, systemic and temporal integration of our human-made built environment and our activities with our organic host, the natural environment, in a benign and positive way. Ecodesign is thus design that successfully biointegrates our artificial systems both mechanically and organically with its host system, ie with the ecosystems in the biosphere.

Designing for biointegration should ideally be on three levels: physical, systemic and temporal.

Physical and systemic integration require a discernment of the ecology of the locality. Any activity arising from our design or our business/industries must physically integrate benignly with the ecosystems. To achieve this, we must understand the locality's ecosystem before we impose any human activity or built system upon it. Every site has an ecology with a limiting capacity to withstand stresses imposed upon it: if stressed beyond

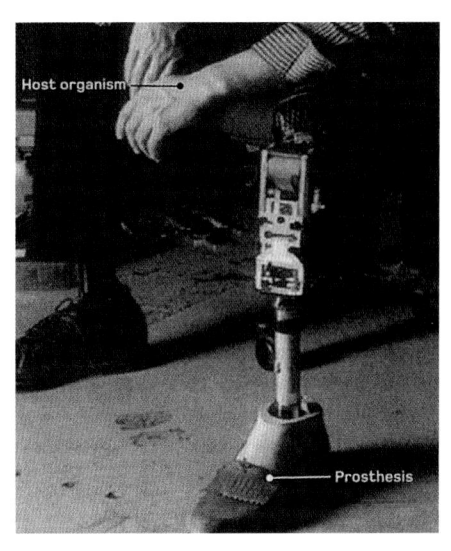

▲ Green design as seamless bio-integration: it can be compared to prosthesis design.

$$(LP) = \frac{L11 \quad L12}{L21 \quad L22}$$

Interactions	Symbol	Description
The external interdependencies of the designed system (its external relations)	L22	This refers to the totality of the ecological processes of the surrounding ecosystems, which intersect with others which interact with other ecosystems elsewhere within the biosphere, and the totality of the earth's resources. It also includes the slow biospheric processes involved in the formation of fossil fuels and other non-renewable resources. These may influence the built environment's functioning and are in turn also influenced by the built environment. It is these elements that are either altered, depleted or added to by the built environment.
The internal interdependencies of the designed system (its internal relations)	L11	This refers to the sum of the activities and actions that take place in or are related to and associated with the built environment and its users. They include the operational functions of the built environment. These will directly affect the ecosystems of the location in which they take place spatially and the ecosystem elsewhere (systemically), as well as the earth's totality of resources. These can be considered in the pattern of a life cycle of the built environment.
The external/internal exchanges of energy and matter (the system's inputs)	L21	This refers to the total inputs into the built environment. These consist of both the stock and the flow components of the built environment (or the energy and matter needed for the physical substance and form of the built environment and its attendant processes). The efforts taken to obtain these inputs from the earth's resources often result in considerable consequences to the ecosystems.
The internal/external exchanges of energy and matter (the system's outputs)	L12	This refers to the total outputs of energy and matter that are discharged from the built environment into the ecosystems and into the earth. These outputs may include the built environment's own physical substance and form, which also may need to be disposed of at the end of its useful life. These outputs, if they are not assimilated by the ecosystems, result in environmental impairment.

▲ Description of environmental interactions

this capacity, the site becomes irrevocably damaged. Consequences can range from minimal localised impact (such as the clearing of a small land area for access), to the total devastation of the entire land area (such as the clearing of all trees and vegetation, levelling the topography, diversion of existing waterways, etc).

We need to ascertain the locality's ecosystem structure, energy flow, its species diversity and other ecological properties and processes. Then we must identify which parts of the site (if any) can permit different types of structures and activities, and which parts are particularly sensitive. Finally, we must consider the likely impacts of the intended construction and use over time.

This is, of course, a major undertaking. It needs to be done day by day over the year and in some instances over several years. To reduce this lengthy effort, landscape architects developed the "sieve-mapping" technique for landscape mapping. We must be aware that this method is an abbreviated approach, generally treats the site's ecosystem statically and may ignore the dynamic forces at play between the layers and within an ecosystem. Between each of these layers are complex interactions.

Another major design issue is the systemic integration of our built forms and their operational systems and internal processes with the ecosystems in nature. This integration is crucial because if our built systems and processes do not integrate with nature's systems, then they will remain disparate, artificial items and potentially pollutive and destructive to the ecology of the locality. Their eventual integration after their manufacture and use can only be through biodegradation. Often, this requires a long-term natural process of decomposition.

Temporal integration involves the conservation of both renewable and non-renewable resources to ensure that these are sustainable for future generations. This includes designing for low-energy built systems that are less or are non-dependent on the use of non-renewable energy resources.

III ECOMIMESIS

The third design strategy is to regard green design as "ecomimesis" as imitating the attributes and properties of ecosystems – their processes, structure, features and functions. This is one of the fundamental premises behind ecodesign. Our built environment must imitate ecosystems in all respects, eg. recycling, using energy from the sun through photosynthesis, to become systems that head towards increasing energy efficiency and achieve a holistic balance of biotic and abiotic constituents.

Nature without humans exists in stasis. Can our businesses and our built environment imitate nature's processes, structure and functions, particularly its ecosystems? For instance, ecosystems have no waste. Everything is recycled within. Thus, by imitating this, our built environment will produce no waste. All emissions and products are continuously reused, recycled within and eventually reintegrated with the natural environment, in tandem with efficient uses of energy and material resources.

Ecosystems in a biosphere are definable units containing both biotic and abiotic constituents acting together as a whole. To extrapolate: our businesses/industries and built environment should be designed analogously to the ecosystem's physical content, composition and processes. For instance, besides regarding our architecture as just art objects or as engineering-serviced enclosures, we should regard it as artefacts that need to be operationally and eventually systematically integrated with nature.

As is self-evident, the material composition of our built environment is almost entirely inorganic, whereas ecosystems contain a complement of both biotic and abiotic constituents, or of inorganic and organic components.

Our myriad of construction, manufacturing and other activities are, in effect, making the biosphere more and more inorganic, artificial and increasingly biologically simplified. To continue without balancing the biotic content means simply adding to the biosphere's artificiality, thereby making it ever more inorganic and synthetic. This results in the biological simplification of the biosphere and the reduction of its complexity and diversity. We must reverse this trend and balance our built environment with greater integral levels of biomass, enhancing biodiversity and ecological connectivity in the built forms.

Ecodesign also requires the designer to use green materials and assemblies of materials, and components that facilitate reuse, recycling and reintegration for temporal integration with the ecological systems. We need to be ecomimetic in our use of materials in the built environment. In ecosystems, all living organisms feed on continual flows of matter and energy from their environment to stay alive, and all living organisms continually produce outputs. Here, an ecosystem generates no waste, one species' waste being another species' food. Thus matter cycles continually through the web of life. It is this closing of the loop in reuse and recycling that our human-made environment must imitate.

IV ECODESIGN AS A MEAN TO RESTORE IMPAIRED ENVIRONMENTS

Fourthly, ecodesign can be regarded not only as the creation of new, artificial "living" urban ecosystems or rehabilitation of existing built environments and cities, but also as a strategy for restoring existing impaired and devastated ecosystems regionally within the wider landscape to the designed system. Ecodesign must look beyond the limitations of the project site and at the larger context of the locality. Where needed we should improve the ecological linkages between our designed systems and our business processes with the surrounding landscape and hardscapes, not just horizontally but also vertically.

Achieving these linkages ensures a wider level of species connectivity, interaction, mobility and a greater sharing of resources across boundaries. Such real improvements in ecological nexus enhance biodiversity and further increase habitat resilience and species survival. Providing new ecological corridors and linkages in regional planning is imperative for making urban patterns more biologically viable.

Crucially we need to apply these concepts to retrofit our existent cites and urban developments. We must biointegrate the existent inorganic aspects of our built environment and its processes with the landscape so that they mutually become ecosystemic. We must create 'human-made ecosystems' compatible with the ecosystems in nature. By doing so, we enhance human-made ecosystems' abilities to sustain life in the biosphere.

V ECODESIGN AS A SELF-MONITORING SYSTEM

The fifth strategy for ecodesign is to regard our designed system as a series of interdependent environmental interactions, whose constant global and local monitoring (eg. through GPS and biosensors, etc) is necessary to ensure global environmental stasis, enabling an anticipatory approach to and the immediate repair and restoration of environmental devastation by humans, natural disasters and the inadvertent negative impacts of our human built environment, activities and industries. These sets of environmental interactions need to be monitored to allow for immediate appropriate corrective action to be taken to maintain global ecological stability.

VI ECODESIGN AND PLANNING

The above are strategies that can be adopted singly or in composite to approach green design. Green design goes beyond conventional rating systems such as LEED or BREEAM. While indeed being indeed useful indices for providing a common basis for comparing the greenness of building designs, they are however not totally effective design tools. They are simply not comprehensive enough in their approach to the issues of environmental design at local, regional and global levels.

Generally stated, ecological design is still very much in its infancy. The totally green building or green ecocity does not yet exist. There is still much more theoretical work, technical research and invention, environmental studies and design interpretation that need to be done and tested before we can have a truly green built environment. We all need to continue to pursue this great endeavour.

Ken Yeang

End Statement

Ecodesign applies not just to how we design, construct, use, recycle and eventually biointegrate our buildings back into the environment, but to all of our human built environment including everything that we as humans make – buildings, bridges, roads, toys, refrigerators, clothing, etc. Ecodesign concerns not just those in the design community but all whose roles in the global economy impact on the environment – resource extraction and production, manufacturing, the food industry, big business, transportation, etc. Simply stated, if we are able to biointegrate all that we make and all that we do with the natural environment in a seamless and benign way, then there will be no environmental problems whatsoever. This aspiration is, of course, easier said than done – but this is the single most vital global issue confronting us today, we being one of a multitude of species in nature. If we are not able to achieve this, this millennium may well be our last.

Ken Yeang

Books and Publications by Ken Yeang

Ken Yeang's practice as a designer has always included a considerable amount of public speaking, teaching, exhibiting and writing. "The compelling motivation for writing can be traced back to my period as a researcher at Cambridge University, where survival in academia depends greatly on the need to 'publish or perish'," he says. Japanese Metabolist architect Kisho Kurokawa also encouraged Yeang to write at a chance meeting in 1973. Kurokawa's advice was to write a book – not necessarily for publication, but for the discipline necessary in assembling and ordering a comprehensive amount of material.

Yeang's first published work, an essay on "Bionics" (concerning biomimicry, or the use of biological analogies for design), appeared in *AAQ* the journal of the Architectural Association in 1972. A further essay, "Bases for Ecosystem Design", appeared in the journal *Architectural Design* in the same year, followed by "The Energetics of the Built Environment" in 1974.

Taking his cue from Kurakawa, Yeang did eventually write a book, *The Tropical Verandah City* (Longman,1986). This work explores the idea of the tropical city as one that is linked by a continuous semi-enclosed walkway enabling inhabitants to move from one building to another, protected from sun and rain. This transitional "in-between" space also has a social function, Yeang argued, providing a zone for social intercourse and casual commerce.

A year later, Yeang wrote another book, *Tropical Urban Regionalism* (Mimar, 1987). Produced by the publishing arm of the Aga Khan organisation and commissioned by Hassan Uddin Khan, the book expanded on the tropical verandah city and used bioclimatic-based design to explore Kenneth Frampton's ideas of critical regionalist architecture.

During his tenure as President of the Malaysian Institute of Architects Yeang researched and wrote the book *The Architecture of Malaysia 1890-1990* (Pepin Press, 1992) in which he examined a number of building typologies including the courtyard house, the shop house and the Malay house.

In the meantime, Yeang began to consider publishing his doctoral dissertation, completed in 1981 - *A Theoretical Framework for the Incorporation of Ecological Considerations in the Design and Planning of the Built Environment*. An abbreviated version was eventually published in 1995 as *Designing with Nature* (McGraw-Hill), a title adapted from the book *Design with Nature* written by Ian McHarg.

By now, Yeang had built up considerable publishing momentum, and a new book has either been written by, or about, Ken Yeang every couple of years since the mid-1990s. *The Skyscraper: Bioclimatically Considered: A Design Primer* (Academy 1997) was a seminal work, summarising Yeang's work and theories on the possible future of tall buildings. The title was a tongue-in-cheek appropriation from Louis Sullivan's essay of 1896 *The Tall Office Building, Artistically Considered*. This work was followed by *Green Skyscraper: The Basis for Designing Sustainable Intensive Buildings* (Prestel, 2000) as well as the more specific *Service Cores in Buildings* (Wiley-Academy, 2000).

Yeang's subsequent research on vertical urbanism and skyscraper design led to a further book *Reinventing the Skyscraper – A Vertical Theory of Urban Design* (Wiley-Academy, 2002) which recast the skyscraper as a city in the sky.

Perhaps Yeang's seminal work is *Ecodesign: A Manual For Ecological Design* (Wiley, 2006), whose working title was the more forthright *Design for Survival*. This book builds on Yeang's very early work, including his doctoral dissertation and those papers written in the 1970s, bringing together in close detail a large body of knowledge on how designers can imitate the structure, properties and processes of ecosystems. Yeang's most recent book, *Ecomasterplanning* (Wiley, 2009) brings together his work on planning large settlements in an ecologically benign manner, demonstrating how ecomimetics can be applied to large, landscape projects as well as individual buildings.

It is also worth noting the books that have been written about the work of Ken Yeang – notably, *Groundscrapers + Subscrapers of Hamzah and Yeang*, written by Ivor Richards (Wiley, 2001); *T. R. Hamzah & Yeang (Master Architect Series)*, (Images, Australia, 1999) by Leon Van Schaik; and *Ecocells, Landscapes & Masterplans by Hamzah & Yeang*, by Leon Van Schaik (Wiley-Academy, 2003).

Acknowledgements

I am delighted to acknowledge Mitch Gelber for project managing, art editing and coordinating the delivery of this book with our designers, Sarah Sulaiman, Hafiz Shah and Eskaywoo Communication Design. I am grateful to Lord Norman Foster of Riverside for his very kind support of my ideas and work. I am also very grateful to all those who have taught me over the years and have given their incisive comments to advance the work and ideas, in particular Professor John Frazer (Queensland University of Technology), Professor Alan Balfour (Georgia Tech, Atlanta), Professor Jeffrey Kipnis (The Ohio State University), Professor Mohsen Mostafavi (Harvard Graduate School of Design), and others, too numerous to mention.

I am indebted to my Commissioning Editor, Helen Castle, at John Wiley & Sons for her unwavering support of my work over the past two decades; and to Miriam Swift for her assistance in the production of this book. My gratitude also goes to Sara Hart for authoring the book and to David Littlefield for his editorial work.

Climate and Vegetation Maps

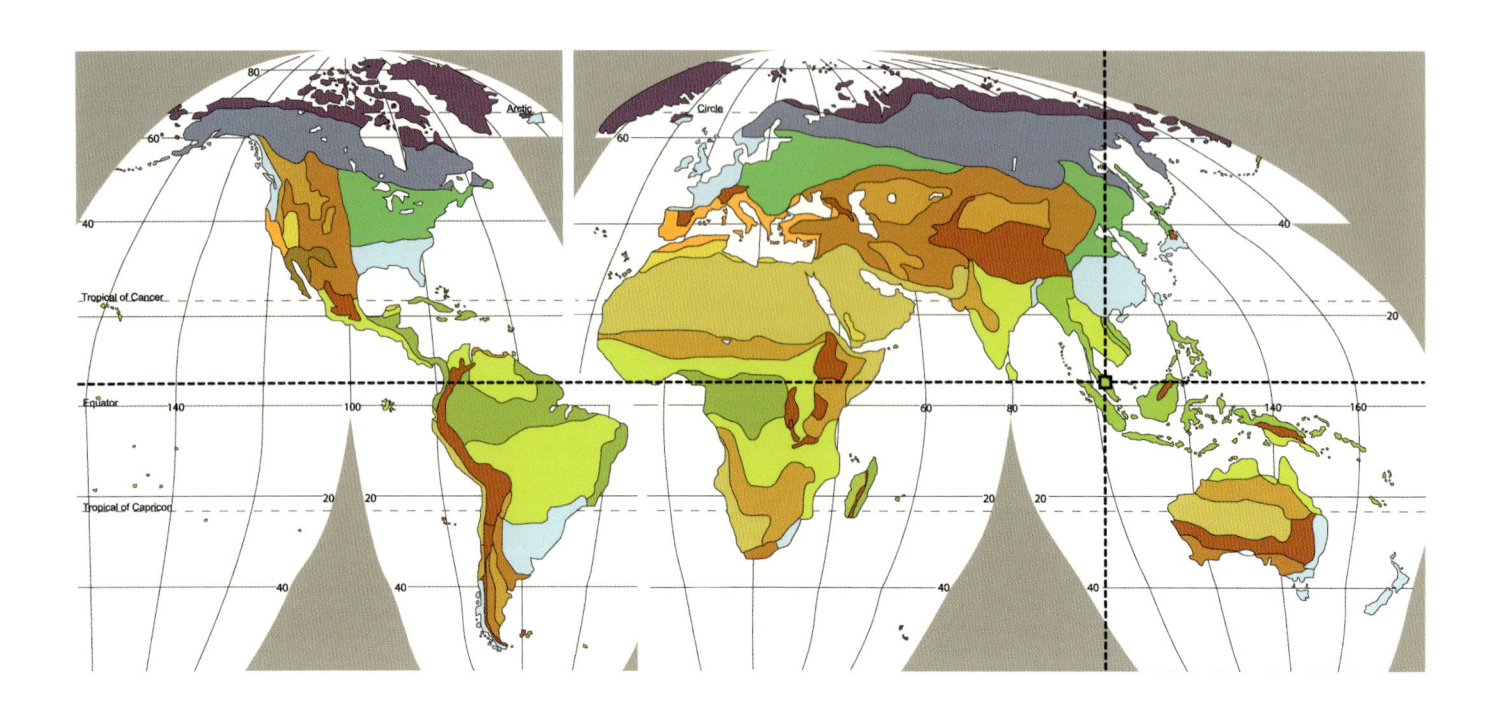

Climate Regions

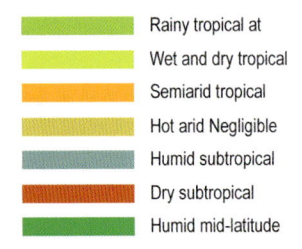

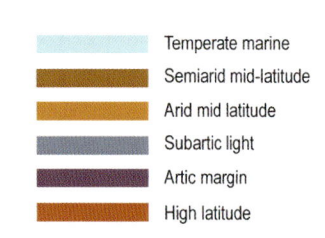

- Rainy tropical at
- Wet and dry tropical
- Semiarid tropical
- Hot arid Negligible
- Humid subtropical
- Dry subtropical
- Humid mid-latitude
- Temperate marine
- Semiarid mid-latitude
- Arid mid latitude
- Subartic light
- Artic margin
- High latitude

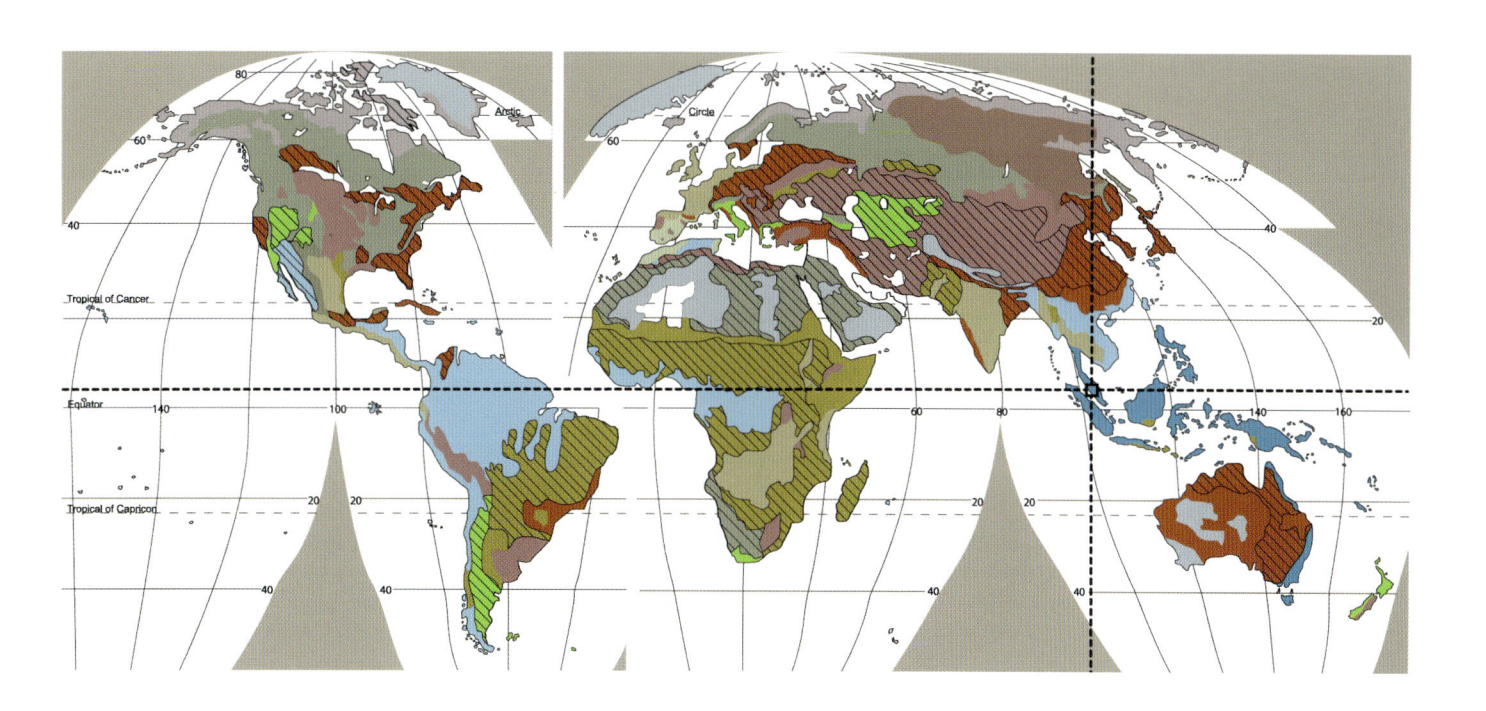

Natural Vegetation

fixed-leaved evergreen vegetation
- Broad-leved evergreen forest
- Broad-leved evergreen shrub formation
- Scattered broad-leaved evergreen shurbs
- Scattered broad-leaved evergreen dwarf shurbs

fixed-leaved deciduous vegetation
- Broad-leved deciduous forest
- Broad-leved deciduous shrub formation
- Scattered broad-leaved deciduous shurbs
- Scattered broad-leaved deciduous dwarf shurbs

Jeniferous vegetation
- Needle-leaved evergreen forest
- Scattered needle-leaved evergreen trees
- Needle-leaved deciduos forest

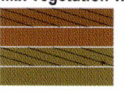

Mix vegetation with grass
- Grassland with scattered broad-leaved evergreen trees
- Grassland with broad-leaved evergreen shrubs
- Grassland with scattered broad-leaved deciduous trees
- Grassland with scattered broad-leaved deciduous shrubs

Iceland, tundra barren
- Grassland
- Patches of grass
- Lichens and grasses
- Lichens and mosses
- Barren

Climate and Vegetation Maps

Picture Credits

The author and the publisher gratefully acknowledge the people who gave their permission to reproduce material in this book. While every effort has been made to contact copyright holders for their permission to reprint material, the publishers would be grateful to hear from any copyright holder who is not acknowledged here and will undertake to rectify any errors or omissions in future editions.

Background cover image © T. R. Hamzah & Yeang Sdn. Bhd.

Back cover images (l, c, r) © T. R. Hamzah & Yeang Sdn. Bhd.

pp 5, 8 (t & b), 10, 11 (t & b),12 (t & b),13 (t & b),14, 15, 16, 17, 18, 19, 21 (r & l), 26-7, 28 (c & b), 29, 30, 31, 38-9, 40 (c & b), 41, 43, 48 (c & b), 49, 50 (t), 54, 55, 56-7, 58 (c & b), 59, 60, 61, 62, 63, 68-9, 70-1, 72-3, 74 (t r), 82, 83, 84-5, 86, 87 (t), 90-1,102-3, 106, 107 (b),108, 113 (t), 116 (c & b), 124-25, 126, 127, 128-29, 130, 131, 132, 134-35, 136-37, 138 (c & b), 139, 140, 143, 144, 145, 146-47, 148, 149, 150-51, 152, 153, 154, 155, 156-57, 158, 159, 160, 161, 162, 163, 164-65, 166-67, 168, 169, 170, 171, 172, 173, 174 (c & b), 175 (b), 176, 177, 178, 179, 180, 181, 182-83, 184, 185 (t & b), 186-87, 188-89, 190-91, 192-93, 194, 195 (t), 196, 197, 198, 199, 200-1, 202, 203, 204, 205, 206, 207, 208-9, 210-11, 212, 213, 214, 215, 216, 217, 218-19, 220, 221, 222, 223, 224, 225, 228 (c & b), 229 (b), 230 (c & b), 231, 240-41, 242, 243, 244-45, 244, 245, 246, 247, 248-49, 250-51, 252-53, 254-53, 254-55, 256, 257, 259, 260, 261, 262, 256, 257, 259, 260, 270, 271   © T. R. Hamzah & Yeang Sdn. Bhd.

p 9 © Leon van Schaik

pp 12-13, 28, 32, 33 (t, bl & br), 34, 40 (t), 41 (t), 42, 44, 45, 46-7, 48 (t), 50 (br), 50-1, 51 (bl & br), 52, 53, 58 (t), 61 (l), 64, 65, 66, 104-5, 107 (t), 109, 110, 111, 112, 113 (b), 114-15, 118, 120-21, 122-23, 138 (t), 141, 142, 174 (t), 175 (t), 195 (b) K. L. Ng Photography, © T. R. Hamzah & Yeang Sdn. Bhd.

pp 22-3 © Robert Powell 2010

pp 30-1, 31, 35, 36, 37 (bl) Courtesy of Ken Yeang © Albert Lim

pp 74 (tl, c & b), 75, 76, 77, 78, 79, 80, 81, 87 (b), 88-9 Simon Saw Planning & Landscaping, © T. R. Hamzah & Yeang Sdn. Bhd.

pp 92-3, 94-5, 96-7, 98, 99, 100-1, 232-33, 234, 235, 236, 237, 238-39 © Llwelyn Davies Yeang

pp 116 (t), 117 (t & b), 119, 185 (c) Mitch Gelber, © T. R. Hamzah & Yeang Sdn. Bhd.

pp 226-27, 228 (t), 229 (t), 230 (tl & tr) © Robert Such